DISINFORMATION

FORMER SPY CHIEF REVEALS SECRET STRATEGIES
FOR UNDERMINING FREEDOM, ATTACKING RELIGION,
AND PROMOTING TERRORISM

Lt. Gen.
ION MIHAI PACEPA
AND Prof. **RONALD J. RYCHLAK**

 WND Books

ADVANCE PRAISE

"*Disinformation* is a history of a still-hidden part of the Cold War—the part hidden as deeply as the KGB's moles in Western intelligence services—which has to be studied to truly understand how communism sought to subvert everything in its path. Like Whittaker Chambers' *Witness*, any study of the Cold War without *Disinformation* would be profoundly incomplete."

—JED BABBIN, former deputy undersecretary of defense and author of *In the Words of Our Enemies* and *Inside the Asylum: How the U.N. and Old Europe Are Worse Than You Think*

"Challenging false histories and subtle slanders, Pacepa and Rychlak take us on a journey through the Empire of Disinformation. Here we learn the theory and practice of the Big Lie deployed against Christianity—against popes and bishops. We learn how the Kremlin, even after the collapse of Communism, continues its war against the West; we learn how *dezinformatsiya* is used to inspire a deep hatred of the Jews in order to mobilize Islam as a battering ram against Israel and America—to the benefit of Russia. If you want to understand the forces at work behind the decline of Christianity and the rise of militant Islam, you must read this book."

—JEFFREY NYQUIST, author *Origins of the Fourth World War*, columnist, and radio talk show host on WIBG (Ocean City, NJ)

"As a Jew growing up in New York, I hated even hearing Pope Pius XII's name. But after seven years of investigating and 46,000 pages of pertinent documents collected, I came to the startling discovery that Pius XII was revered and praised as a hero by all Jews during, and just after, the war. If you want to know how 1 billion people were tricked into hating him, read this book by General Ion Mihai Pacepa and Professor Ron Rychlak about the Kremlin's still-secret *dezinformatsiya*. That immense machinery accomplished the worst character assassination of the twentieth century, and caused great strain between Jews and Catholics. But let me warn you: this book is scary! When you read it, you will discover how you were maneuvered like a chess piece to achieve a specific goal. You will also learn that the *dezinformatsiya* enterprise is still dividing the Judeo-Christian world with deadly international consequences."

—**GARY KRUPP**, chairman of Pave the Way Foundation, dedicated to reconciling relations among the world's religions

"Written by two foremost experts, this book is an eye-opening, demystifying work of political and historical archeology, a passionate and captivating endeavor to highlight the communist techniques of cynical deception, vicious plots, and perversely skillful concoction of propaganda legends masquerading as historical evidence. The authors display impressive erudition and unique insights into the deep secrets of the Soviet and post-Soviet disinformation machine. As a former highest-level intelligence officer within the Soviet Bloc who broke with the system for moral reasons and courageously exposed its terrorist underpinnings, Ion Mihai Pacepa is a formidable witness to and a respected analyst of the communist intrigues, schemes, and manipulations."

—**VLADIMIR TISMĂNEANU**, author of *Stalinism for All Seasons: A Political History of Romanian Communism*, director of the University of Maryland's Center for the Study of Post-Communist Societies, and president of Romania's Institute for the Investigation of Communist Crimes

DISINFORMATION

WND Books, Inc.
Washington, DC

Book designed by Mark Karis.
Cover illustration by Michael di Pietro—inspired by photograph by David Malan.

WND Books are available at special discounts for bulk purchases. WND Books, Inc.,
also publishes books in electronic formats. For more information call (541) 474-1776,
email sales@wndbooks.com, or visit www.wndbooks.com.

First Edition

Hardcover ISBN: 978-1936488605
eBook ISBN: 978-1936488988

Library of Congress information available

Printed in the United States of America
10 9 8 7 6 5 4 3 2 1

 WND Books

DEDICATION

To Mary Lou, who helped me look at my past through American eyes.
—LT. GEN. ION MIHAI PACEPA

To my daughter Lindsey and all the Lindseys in my life.
—PROFESSOR RONALD RYCHLAK

Those who cannot remember the past are condemned to repeat it.
—**GEORGE SANTAYANA**, *The Life of Reason*, vol. 1, 1905

In Russia, "duck," aside from its normal meaning, is a term for disinformation. 'When the ducks are flying' means that the press is publishing disinformation.
—**PAVEL SUDOPLATOV**, Deputy Chief of Soviet Foreign Intelligence
Special Tasks (Memoirs), 1994

AUTHOR'S NOTE

For the transliteration of Russian, we have followed the guidelines of the United States Board on Geographic Names, with the exception that *iy* and *yy* have been condensed into a simple *y* when they occur at the end of first and last names of individuals. A few familiar deviations have been retained, such as Yuri Andropov.

TABLE OF CONTENTS

INTRODUCTION

T HIS REMARKABLE BOOK will change the way you look at intelligence, foreign affairs, the press, and much else besides. Lt. Gen. Ion Mihai Pacepa is the highest-ranking defector we have ever had from a hostile intelligence service. As chief of Romanian intelligence he was for many years in the key meetings with heads of state and a participant in some of the most sensitive discussions by our enemies during the Cold War.

For starters, General Pacepa tells us that intelligence collection is rather far down the list of what Romanian, and other Soviet Bloc, intelligence services were doing all those years. Intelligence collection, he says, "has always been more or less irrelevant." I might add that whether you agree or not that this is accurate for the period of the Cold War, much intelligence collection is done today by hackers sitting at keyboards, not by case officers fine-tuning the location of dead drops.

So what were Romanian and Soviet spies spending their time on in the Cold War years? General Pacepa would say "framing," *i.e.* rewriting history and manipulating records, documents, etc., to bring that about. To what end this *dezinformatsiya*? Oh, little matters like using press leaks to destroy the reputation of a national or religious leader, engendering the spread of anti-Semitism, building up resentment against the United States or Israel in the Arab world. Soviet leader and long-time KGB head Yuri Andropov, apparently a real aficionado of *dezinformatsiya*, put it this way: "[*Dezinformatsiya* is] like cocaine. If you sniff once or twice, it may not change your life. If you use it every day though, it will make you an addict—a different man."

So, one might say, it's understandable during the Cold War, but why now? And why are many governments in the Mideast essentially doing the same thing, such as spreading the crazy stories about 9/11—that it was the CIA, or the Mossad? I would imagine it's fairly straightforward: dictators need enemies to help them have more reason to suppress their people. And we're very convenient.

Another major understanding emerges from these pages. The communists had something between no ideology and a dysfunctional one. We have one that almost all Americans would sign on to: democracy, the rule of law, and America as, in Lincoln's words, the "last, best hope of earth." For most of us we also have our religion, generally Christianity or Judaism. This brought out for the Soviet Bloc, and brings out for our current enemies, a carefully targeted attack, or framing, to destroy religion: to spread anti-Semitism, to smear the reputations of a pope and other church leaders as anti-Semites when they actually worked hard to protect Jews during the Nazi era.

General Pacepa also shows how one can undo even very carefully constructed *dezinformatsiya*, such as the 1960s play *The Deputy*, trashing the reputation of Pope Pius XII by using accompanying literature, remarkable for the doctored photographs, the deceptive editing, etc.

General Pacepa has written that there were more in the Soviet Bloc working on *dezinformatsiya* than in the armed forces and defense industry. It was, and to some extent still is, a remarkable effort.

In spite of its perfection of the art of framing, its experience, and its motive as an intelligence dictatorship who needs us as an enemy, we may see as we move into the twenty-first century that Russia is not our major problem. Its demographics are awful (low birth rate, short life span for men) and its population could conceivably be under 100 million by the middle of the century. It lives almost wholly by selling oil and gas (and uses its leverage with gas to threaten its neighbors with cutoffs). But the substantial recent discoveries of shale gas in many countries, including the United States, Poland, and many other locations, could deal Russia a heavy blow. Its gas may not earn as much income and may be less useful as a weapon, and its oil may be replaced by much cheaper natural gas-based fuels such as methanol.

None of us will feel too sorry for a shrinking group of mid-twentieth century Russians, sitting on the sidelines, desperately hoping to be noticed, with their cleverness in framing and the like increasingly irrelevant.

General Pacepa and his distinguished coauthor, Prof. Ronald Rychlak, have done something remarkable in these pages. They have not only helped us understand history and many of the current *dezinformatsiya* operations that we continue to see—especially from Russia and countries in the Mideast—but also have given us a good start in learning how to defeat them. In short, they open a world that many of us didn't know existed and almost all of those of us who did know had seriously underestimated.

—R. JAMES WOOLSEY, Chairman, Foundation for the Defense of Democracies, Former Director of Central Intelligence

FOREWORD

HERE IS A WORK that many of us have been waiting for, a book that—dare I say—*history* has been waiting for. From start to finish, it is a gem of fascinating new information, a goldmine of badly needed, long-overdue Cold War material, a light into what truly was a world of darkness. The authors are most unique: Ron Rychlak is an expert on the much-maligned Pope Pius XII specifically and on the Catholic Church generally, particularly during the Cold War. Lt. Gen Ion Mihai Pacepa, the highest-ranking intelligence official to defect from the Soviet bloc, was, remarkably, a witness to many of the events the book describes. General Pacepa remains with us still to witness to the truth and to the litany of falsehoods—despite death sentences and a $2 million bounty set upon his head by the late Romanian despot Nicolae Ceaușescu. Thus, we have a rare confluence of a scholar of religious history and an eyewitness to the dirty deeds orchestrated by communists against the religious. Here we have literal scholarship with primary sources.

The result is a book at once breathtaking and infuriating, and at times depressing. One is tempted to say that readers will not be able to put this book down, but readers may need to do just that simply to absorb the enormity of the information and to step away from this peer into the dark side. One can only look for so long before recoiling and needing a break. The sheer level of unapologetic, unmitigated, and sustained Soviet slander against religion and religious people, methodically unraveled by General Pacepa and Professor Rychlak, really is hard to endure. Yet, endure we must, because their story must be told.

Anyone who has studied or been involved in the communist movement knows that communists had a campaign for just about everything they felt could be churned into propaganda that aided and abetted their purposes. Vladimir Lenin infamously stated that the "only morality" that his Bolsheviks recognized was that which furthered their interests. This meant that lying was fully justified, that any target was legitimate, and that it was always open season on identified targets. Combine this malice and moral relativism with what Mikhail Gorbachev called the Soviet "war on religion," plus a network of servile communist parties around the world—all devoted to what George Kennan termed "the master's voice" that spoke "infallibly" from the Kremlin—and you had a literal international conspiracy to demonize the most saintly of religious figures who stood in the Soviet way. The crass art of Kremlin deceit would be a vigorous tool in this sustained effort, a hellacious effort with no moral scruples. Only now, thanks to General Pacepa and Rychlak, do we have a documented account of the effort and its insidious offshoots.

A running thread throughout this book is the case of Pope Pius XII, which makes perfect sense, given that the Pius case was at the nadir of the Soviet smear campaign, starting under Stalin and Khrushchev. The authors show that the attack against Pius was launched with a 1945 *Radio Moscow* broadcast that first echoed the extremely unfair label "Hitler's Pope." The Soviets understood that Pius XII was a mortal threat to their ideology, despising communism as much as he did Nazism. They thus embarked on an unholy crusade to destroy the pope and his reputation, to scandalize his flock, and to foment division among faiths.

General Pacepa and Rychlak have blown wide open the smear campaign against Pius XII. No one who reads this book will come away believing that Pius XII had ever favored Hitler or Nazism. And anyone who renders an opinion on the Pius controversy now must go through this book. In fact, anyone who does not cannot have his or her opinion taken seriously. With this book, the opening question posed to anyone with a negative perception of Pius as "Hitler's Pope" must now be, "Have you read the book by Pacepa and Rychlak?"

As this book crucially shows, the vicious myths created by communists to discredit Pius have, quite tragically, been unwittingly adopted by many mainstream historians and journalists. The myth, which was initially quickly rejected by a contemporary generation that lived through the real history and instantly knew better, picked up momentum among the next generations that did not live the history and did not know better. It has snowballed and has been allowed to soil the reputation of a good man who loved, helped, and even personally housed Jewish people during the Holocaust. The KGB and its accomplices perpetuated a poisonous image at complete odds with that reality. The image remains with us now. It is heartbreaking to see the rift that communists have caused between Catholics who rightly admire Pius—and even seek to canonize him—and their Jewish friends. The communists did this, and have been getting away with it—or at least until this book.

This book conclusively exposes a host of damaging lies, well beyond the Pius case. Much of the history we thought we knew, or we thought we even recently uncovered, was actually spawned as communist disinformation. As the authors note, this was a war "that broke out in 1945 and has never ended." The Soviet Union and Cold War are over, but the war on religion remains, unwittingly reinvigorated by misled scholars who have picked up "facts" that were never actually facts to begin with.

The lies have been allowed to become "history," to become "truth." But what is truth? What is history? This book has the real history. In that sense, this is a seminal work that will start the process of remedying some serious mis-education and unforgivably flawed "scholarship." And historians and scholars must carefully discern how General Pacepa and Rychlak got there: by hooking into a key concept that properly redirects historians and scholars to the truth—that is, understanding the outrageous and uniquely Soviet tactic of disinformation.

This is a crucial angle. General Pacepa and Rychlak could have simply written a standard account of Soviet persecution from a faith-based perspective. As they peeled back the layers, however, they saw the rotting marrow that was disinformation—known as *dezinformatsiya* in Russian. Of course, General Pacepa already knew this, having lived it and, regrettably, been a reluctant participant. Now, making reparation, both he and Rychlak are able to explain to the world how knowledge of Soviet disinformation explains much of what we did not know, and, even more significantly, much of what we got wrong. They have focused the spotlight at an angle that offers historians a clarity that heretofore has been lacking.

So patently dishonest was the Soviet use of disinformation that even the Soviet definition of disinformation, published in the 1952 edition of the *Great Soviet Encyclopedia*, was itself a form of disinformation. Only the surreal upside-down world of Soviet communism could produce such a litany of dishonesty. The late Vaclav Havel spoke of the "communist culture of the lie."[1] Here it is again, thrown wide open yet again. General Pacepa and Rychlak lift the scales from our eyes, and, as they do, we see a church on the cross, nailed there by merciless persecutors.

But the authors' concern is not merely the Catholic Church, or the Christian church more broadly. This groundbreaking book unravels not only the schemes against Pius XII and figures like Cardinals Stepinac and Mindszenty and Wyszynski. It shows the duplicity of groups such as the World Peace Council and World Council of Churches and Workers World Party; the bloody hands of surrogates from Vyshinsky to Romanian and Bulgarian intelligence; the Soviet role in liberation theology; the witting and unwitting roles of players like Romesh Chandra and Rolf Hochhuth and Erwin Piscator and I. F. Stone and Edward Keating and John Cornwell; the impact of paid agents, agents of influence, and dupes; the macabre black art of Soviet "necrophagy;" and much more. Most ironic, the book highlights the loathsome anti-Semitism behind the very conspirators of the original "Hitler's Pope" campaign and other disinformation efforts. The chapter on the Soviet promulgation of the insidious *Protocols of the Elders of Zion* conspiracy is an awakening. Here, the persecutors of Christ's followers resurrected an old Jew-hating standby and spread it as gospel truth to the West.

Indeed, the anti-Semitism documented in this book is shocking. The authors chronicle Yuri Andropov's anti-Zionism campaign, support of Islamic terrorism, and dual promotion of virulent anti-Semitism and anti-Americanism among Middle East Arabs. By 1978, the Soviet bloc planted some four thousand agents of influence in the Islamic world, armed with hundreds of thousands of copies of the *Protocols of the Elders of Zion*—and military weapons. The seeds they planted in the Arab world decades ago still sow hatred and destruction in the form of violence and terror. Atheistic communism sought out a handmaiden in radical Islam, with extremist Muslims exploited by Soviet manipulators who hoped to besmirch Judaism and Israel and Christianity and America and the West—and too often with tragic success. They promulgated not only acts of terrorism but egregious acts of "diplomacy" like the infamous UN Resolution 3379, declaring Zionism a form of racism.

Alas, it is no shock at all—one supposes—when one sees that the perpetrators behind these varying forms of malevolence were the same political bandits who advanced an international ideology that snuffed out the lives of more than 100 million people in the twentieth century, twice the combined death toll of the two world wars. And "bandits" is not too strong a word, or perhaps *political gangsters* would be just as fitting. For anyone who feels such language seems a little over-the-top, well . . . you had better start reading, because you are in for an ugly education. This is a sickening saga of Soviet deceit that leaves one either wanting to take a bath or—ah, yes—maybe even go to church.

Lt. Gen Ion Mihai Pacepa and Prof. Ron Rychlak have done yeoman's work. Pardon me if I say the *Lord's work*, as my better angels override my scholarly objectivity. We owe a debt of gratitude to General Pacepa and Rychlak for exposing the devils and the details behind the disinformation.

—**PAUL KENGOR**, P𝐇D, Professor of Political Science,
Grove City College

PART I

GLORIFYING THE GUILTY, FRAMING THE INNOCENT

PRELUDE

DOWN THROUGH THE AGES, everyone who has sat on the Kremlin throne—autocratic tsar, communist leader, or democratically elected president—has been preoccupied with transforming his country into a monument to himself, and with controlling all expressions of religion that might in any way impinge on his political ambitions.

Furthermore, the Russian rulers have traditionally used their political police as the means for secretly carrying out their grandiose plans. Tsarism, communism, and the Cold War may have been swallowed up by the sands of time, but the Kremlin continues these traditions.

Eventually, the Kremlin's hand reached the shores of the United States as well.

In March 1996, a sensational story jolted the American conscience. The National Council of Churches (NCC) and the Center for Democratic Renewal (CDR), two secretly Marxist organizations headquartered in the United States, held a joint press conference to announce a "huge increase" in the number of arson cases committed against black churches in the United States.

On June 8, President Bill Clinton denounced those fires in a radio address, and he proposed a new federal task force to investigate them. The president spoke with emotion about his own "vivid and painful memories of black churches being burned in my own state [of Arkansas] when I was a child." Charging that "racial hostility" was the driving force behind the fires, he pledged to place the full power of the federal government behind the investigation. On June 15, the Federal Bureau of Investigation and the Bureau of Alcohol, Tobacco, Firearms and Explosives assigned two hundred federal agents to a new task force charged to investigate black church fires.[1] By July the accounts of arson committed against black churches had snowballed, with more than twenty-two hundred articles appearing in the press to condemn what the Center for Democratic Renewal called "a well-organized white-supremacist movement."[2]

The story spread like wildfire, inflaming decent people everywhere against the perceived American racists who had caused such terrible crimes. In Geneva, Switzerland, the World Council of Churches (WCC)—the international affiliate of the National Council of Churches—flew thirty-eight pastors to Washington, DC, to provide the American government and people with more information about this unprecedented racist tragedy.[3]

On July 13, President Clinton signed into law the Church Fire Prevention Act of 1996, which made church arson a federal crime. On August 7, he also signed a spending bill that included $12 million to combat fires at churches with black congregations. A few days later, the NCC ran full-page ads in the *New York Times, Washington Post* and numerous other papers soliciting donations for its new "Burned Churches Fund." On August 9, the *Wall Street Journal* reported that the NCC had "managed to raise nearly $9 million," and that contributions were continuing to pour in "at about $100,000 a day."[4]

Then the bubble burst. It was eventually established by a private group, the National Fire Protection Association, that in recent years there had been far *fewer* church fires than usual, and law enforcement officials in the South could not confirm *any* as having been racially motivated.[5] No church burning had occurred in Arkansas during Clinton's childhood, in spite of his "vivid and painful" memories, and the National Council of Churches was accused of fabricating "a great church-fire hoax."[6]

Average Americans looked upon the NCC/CDR hoax as simply a slip of the pen, and forgot about it. No one at home or abroad asked why the whole slanderous hoax had occurred in the first place. The political damage was done, however.

The United States, which had paid with 405,399 American lives to save the world from the evils of Nazi racism and the Holocaust, now found itself slandered as a neo-Nazi, racist country. Within a few years, over 40 percent of Canadian teenagers were calling the United States "evil,"[7] and 57 percent of Greeks answered "neither" when asked which country was more democratic, the United States or Iraq.[8] In Berlin, a German cabinet minister, Herta Däubler-Gmelin, compared new president George W. Bush to Hitler.[9] Western Marxists, such as Venezuela's ruinous dictator Hugo Chavez also leapt into the fray, gleefully entertaining the United Nations in 2006 with an indirect (but clearly understood) reference to the American president by saying: "Yesterday, the devil came here. Right here. Right here. And it smells of sulfur still today."[10] By 2008, in the United States itself, some leaders of the Democratic Party even began describing their own country as a "decaying, racist, capitalist realm," unable to provide medical care for the poor or rebuild its crumbling schools.[11]

The clue to understanding the significance of the black church arson hoax lies in the documented fact that the World Council of Churches, which ignited and promoted that story, has been infiltrated and ultimately controlled by Russian intelligence since 1961. The *Mitrokhin Archive*, a voluminous collection of Soviet foreign intelligence documents smuggled out of the Soviet Union in 1992, provides the identities and Soviet intelligence code names of many Russian Orthodox priests dispatched over the years to the World Council of Churches for the specific purpose of influencing the politics and decisions of that body. In fact, in 1972 Soviet intelligence managed to have Metropolitan Nikodim (its agent "Adamant") elected WCC president. A 1989 KGB document boasts: "Now the agenda of the WCC is also our agenda."[12] Most recently, Metropolitan Kirill (agent "Mikhaylov"), who had been an influential representative to the World Council of Churches since 1971 and after 1975 a member of the WCC Central Committee, was in 2009 elected patriarch of the Russian Orthodox Church.[13]

The above slanderous attack on the United States and its churches was really nothing surprising. It reflects how the Kremlin has for centuries preferred to carry out its domestic and foreign policies by complicated deceptions. Religion frequently figures in operations of the traditionally cynical Russian leaders, who have considered themselves the only god mankind needs.

Historically, the Kremlin's manipulation of religion for its own political purposes dates back to the sixteenth century. When Ivan IV—the Terrible— had himself crowned in 1547 as Russia's first tsar, he also made himself the head of the Russian Orthodox Church, as was recognized by the patriarch in Constantinople in 1591. Muscovy had only recently been liberated by the Turks' overthrow of the Byzantine Empire, and it was from the latter that Ivan had inherited the idea of a "symphony of church and state." The difference was that, instead of having an emperor *and* a patriarch—as in Byzantium—Ivan himself wore both hats. This merger of functions persisted through all the tsars down to Nicholas II, through all the Soviet leaders from Vladimir Lenin through Boris Yeltsin, and still lives on in Vladimir Putin's Russia today.

Ivan IV was also the first head of Russia to establish his own political police, the *Oprichnina*, or separate court. Created in 1564 under Ivan's personal direction, it was mainly used to control the boyars who were threatening his reign. That tradition has also lived on, going through numerous name changes, down to the Soviet Union's threateningly familiar KGB (*Komitet Gosudarstvennoy Bezopasnosti*, or Committee of State Security) and beyond, to today's FSB (*Federalnaya Sluzhba Bezopasnosti*, or Federal Security Service). Russia's political police have always been responsible for keeping order in church and state, in accordance with commands issued by the man seated on the Kremlin throne.

Up until World War II, Russia was basically isolationist—inscrutable perhaps to foreigners—with a love of tackling problems indirectly and clandestinely rather than head-on, but not considered a threat by the rest of the world. Centuries ago, the Russian tsars were not particularly finicky about concealing their hand when conducting deceptions. Their political horizons essentially ended at the Russian borders, and they knew the Russian peasants had infinite faith in their tsar and in their Orthodox religion, which he represented. Foreign visitors were not always taken in, but that did not matter. In the nineteenth century, for example, Astolphe, Marquis de Custine, wrote extensively about his travels in Russia. He railed against the "dexterity in lying" and the "naturalness in falsehood" that he encountered in 1839, such as when the tsar tried to overwhelm the visiting Frenchman with an illumination spectacle at the imperial palace. This display was designed to conceal the fact that hundreds of spectators had drowned when a sudden squall overturned their boats. "No one will ever know the truth," he wrote in his diary, "and the papers will not even mention the disaster—that would distress the Czarina and imply blame on the Czar."[14] At the end of his trip, Custine concluded: "Everything is deception in Russia."[15]

It was during the preliminary period leading up to World War II that the Kremlin leader began seriously thinking about world domination and tinkering around with the organization and mandates of his foreign intelligence service. Elsewhere in the world, foreign intelligence services are primarily engaged in collecting information to help their heads of state conduct foreign affairs, but in Russia and later throughout the Russian sphere of influence, that task has always been more or less irrelevant. There the goal is to manipulate the future, not just to learn about the past. Specifically, the idea is to fabricate a new past for enemy targets in order to change how the world perceives them. Besides targeting Western governments—nowadays the United States in particular—the Kremlin has come to view the powerful Western religions as dangerously hostile threats.

This brings us to the title of this book. Since World War II, *disinformation* has been the Kremlin's most effective weapon in its war on the West, especially on Western religion. Iosif Stalin invented this secret "science," giving it a French-sounding name and pretending it was a dirty Western practice. As this book will show, the Kremlin has secretly, and successfully, calumniated leading Roman Catholic prelates, culminating in Pope Pius XII; it almost succeeded in assassinating Pope John Paul II; it invented liberation theology, a Marxist doctrine that turned many European and Latin American Catholics against the Vatican and the United States; it has promoted anti-Semitism and international terrorism; and it has inspired anti-American uprisings in the Islamic world.

In spite of Soviet communism's demise, *disinformation* and its undercover international apparatus are still very much alive and well today. They continue to distort the way millions of people view the United States, they still manipulate religion—every religion—and they play a substantive role in fueling today's international terrorism.

Mao Zedong would have been proud. He was famous for saying that a lie repeated a hundred times becomes the truth.

1

DRAFTED INTO THE *SECURITATE*

I WAS ONLY TWENTY-TWO YEARS OLD when I became an officer of the far-flung Soviet bloc intelligence community and its disinformation machinery, and my whole world was suddenly turned upside down.

Up until then, all I had wanted in life was to go to "America." That had been my father's lifelong dream. He spent most of his working career managing the service department at the Bucharest affiliate of General Motors, the American automobile company, and he was firmly determined that one day he would gather up his family and emigrate to Detroit, where he had relatives. Trapped by World War II and then afterwards by the Soviet occupation of Romania, he was forced to give up that dream, though not before passing his love for America along to me, his only child. The moment the United States reopened its embassy in Bucharest after the end of the war, I became one of its enthusiastic visitors and soon joined the Young Friends of the United States, an organization sponsored by the US government.

Furthermore, my best friend in those days, an older boy who was my idol, had already emigrated to the United States and was there waiting for me. The son of an engineer who had been employed by an American-owned oil company in Romania, he was my next-door neighbor and mentor until he left Romania just before the start of World War II to study in the United States. Then in October 1944, I observed a young American lieutenant stopping to stare at the rubble that had once been my family's sturdy, two-story house.

It had been flattened on April 4, 1944, during the first American bombard-ment of Bucharest. The lieutenant turned out to be my friend.

"Where is Mother?" was all he could say when he saw that his house was also gone.

"She died in the April 4 bombing," I said.

Visibly shaken, my friend, now "Lieutenant Bota," said: "I was with the squadron that dropped the bombs on Bucharest that day."

We embraced.

"You know," he told me a few days later, as he was about to leave Romania again, "I have a nice place to live over there in America. Now it's your home as much as it is mine."

Why, then, did I end up in communist Romania's political police, the Securitate, instead of in America?

Put very simply, I shot myself in the foot. When I graduated from high school, I decided to get my engineering degree before leaving for America. In that summer of 1947, when I was admitted to the Polytechnic Institute in Bucharest, the Kingdom of Romania had a coalition government in which only a few cabinet members were communists, and travel abroad was unre-stricted. A few months later, however, the communists overthrew the king, took over the entire government and closed the country's borders.

In January 1951, when the first generation of Romania's engineers and economists trained under communist rule were about to graduate, I was drafted as an officer of the massive Soviet bloc intelligence machinery. Under Soviet communism, where the government paid for your entire education, you really had no chance of choosing your employer. The government decided where you had to work, and that was that.

I was distraught. But since I did not really know what "America" meant, I was not able to assign true dimensions to my loss. At the same time, I did not really know what the *Securitate* was either. Moreover, I was just begin-ning to enjoy a certain degree of popularity among my classmates because of my *Ariciul* ("The Porcupine"), a satirical magazine I put out filled with my own cartoons. After the Nazi troops had occupied Romania and turned the Bucharest General Motors affiliate into a military unit for repairing German cars and trucks, Father had opened a car repair business of his own. It was the only place in Romania repairing American cars, and he was doing so well that he bought me a car as a reward for being admitted to the Polytechnic

Institute. That car, a small Peugeot, gave me a leg up among my colleagues, because there were only two other boys who had cars among all the roughly two thousand students at that engineering school.

The saying goes that in the country of the blind, the one-eyed man is king. That's what I was in the Securitate. That organization, established just a couple of years earlier, had at first been staffed with hastily recruited miners and other blue-collar workers. They were considered to be politically reliable, but most of them hardly knew how to hold a pen. Compared to them, I was a whiz kid. My father, who had started his life as a tinsmith in his father's shop, had been determined to see that his only child would never need to touch a hammer, so he had spent every spare penny he earned on my education. At age nine I could play Beethoven's *Kreutzer Sonata* on my violin, at twelve I was showing off Berlioz's *Idée Fixe* at the musical evenings I would organize for my fellow students, and at sixteen I was lecturing on Marcel Proust's *In Remembrance of Things Past.*

My education was, however, not the only factor that favored my intelligence career. A couple of months after I became a Securitate officer, I was called in by my boss, Capt. Fănel Lazarovici, and told to report to the chief of the *Cadre* (personnel) Directorate the first thing in the morning. The look on his face reflected my boss's commiseration. *Cadre* had already become a frightening word throughout the country, and the chief of the Securitate's Cadre Directorate was said to be a sheer terror. At least, that was what I had heard my fellow officers whisper. Just by lifting one finger, they said, he could have you promoted, demoted, or made to disappear into thin air. Of course, I was unable to close my eyes the whole night.

My shirt clung damply to my back on that April morning in 1951 when I knocked on the mahogany door with the nameplate reading *Director de Cadre.* Had "they" learned about my old visits to the American Embassy? Or about the button with the king's picture on it that I used to wear? I inconspicuously flexed the muscles in my neck to see if I was still wearing my chain. Was the cross hanging from it to blame?

Finding myself in the middle of a room the size of a tennis court, I snapped to attention and blurted out, "Long life, Comrade Colonel! Jr. Lt. Ion Mihai Pacepa reporting."

"*Chert vosmi!*" the voice behind the desk swore loudly in Russian. "By the devil, you're already a grown man!"

It took me a minute to realize that I knew that voice. That bulldog in uniform sitting behind the desk was the son of a man who had worked with my father at the General Motors dealership in Bucharest. His father was Carol Demeter—how could I ever forget him? From 1938, when Carol Demeter had been arrested for communist activity, until 1944, when he had been released by the Soviet troops, my father had personally seen to it that the prisoner's wife and son lacked for nothing.

"Do you remember that slap your father pasted on my mug?" the colonel asked. His mustache bristled at me like porcupine quills.

My flesh crawled. How could I forget? I had been with Father when he had finally located Demeter's son, who had been hanging around with a gang of loiterers and had disappeared from home a few weeks before. The imprint my father's heavy hand had left on the wayward teenager's cheek still stuck in my memory. Father had never slapped me. He had used words, not slaps, to educate me.

"Well," Colonel Demeter said when I finally managed a nod, "that slap made a man out of me." He explained that soon after that slap, he had started training to be a carpenter like his father, and then he had joined the Communist Party and found his way to the Soviet Union. "Now it's my turn to pay your father back."

My father never gave me the slightest hint that he had ever spoken to Colonel Demeter about me. Nor did Colonel Demeter actually say they had talked, although for the next ten years I would physically sense his protective hand cupped around me. Only once, in 1954, when he went out of his way to see that my father was buried with great military pomp, did he take credit for looking out for me. In his funeral oration for my father, Demeter, by then a Securitate general, rested an enormous paw on my shoulder and addressed the coffin: "Rest in peace. Your son is in good hands."

In March 1953, Stalin died ignominiously, while trying to sober up in a scorching sauna after a long drinking bout with his crony, Nikita Khrushchev. Today, few Russians like to admit that they ever worshiped Stalin. Not many Nazi admirers could be found in Germany after World War II, either. But on March 6, 1953, four million people wept in Red Square at Stalin's funeral. Sirens wailed, bells tolled, cars blew their horns, and work stopped all around the country. The whole Soviet bloc felt that an era of history had passed into oblivion with this man whose name had been synonymous with communism.

At that time, I was already a Soviet bloc intelligence officer. I was not yet, however, aware that a Soviet leader's image was so important that he would go to any lengths—even to the point of killing and imprisoning millions, rewriting history, destroying institutions, manipulating religion, and changing traditions—all in an effort to beatify himself or to demonize his competitors and enemies. Soon thereafter, however, I would be assigned to the inner circle of the despot's enormous *dezinformatsiya* machinery, which was responsible for all that image-building.

Stalin's successor, Nikita Khrushchev, began his reign by executing the whole leadership of Stalin's political police as traitors, so as to give the appearance that he condemned his predecessor's crimes. That had become a rite of succession in the Soviet Union. Only one of the first eight chiefs of the Soviet state security service who served between 1917 and 1954 is known to have died a natural death—Semen Ignatyev, who vanished into thin air in 1953, then reappeared at a provincial post and died of natural causes in 1983.[1] Feliks Dzerzhinsky, the founder of that organization, died suspiciously of a stroke in 1926, after an argument with Stalin.[2] The rest were either poisoned (Vyacheslav Menzhinsky in 1934) or executed as traitors and spies (Genrikh Yagoda in 1938, Nikolay Yezhov in 1940, Lavrenty Beriya and Vsevolod Merkulov in 1953, Viktor Abakumov in 1954).

To be on the safe side, Khrushchev executed his spy chief, Vladimir Dekanozov, as well, replacing him as spy chief with General Aleksander Sakharovsky, the chief Soviet intelligence adviser to Romania, who had been my *de facto* boss and mentor in Romania. That brought me into Khrushchev's inner circle. During the ensuing years, I would be pushed to the top of Romanian foreign intelligence and would become involved in some of Khrushchev's most important foreign political projects, from his brutal crushing of the 1956 Hungarian uprising to his construction of the Berlin Wall and provocation of the Cuban missile crisis.

Many years later I would look back on all these events and reflect on how they swept me into another world and put an end to any hope I had of working as a chemical engineer, to say nothing of becoming an American. Now, however, that I have finally been fortunate enough to settle down in this country of my father's and my own youthful dreams, I have come around to understanding that the path I was channeled into taking may have been, in at least one respect, a blessing in disguise. Eventually my intelligence career afforded me unique insights into a system of government that has changed the course of history. In fact, because Romania was a relatively small country, I believe that I, as its top intelligence officer, very possibly had a clearer picture of how the Kremlin and its *dezinformatsiya* really functioned than perhaps all but the very innermost Soviet inner circle.

2

THE TRUE MEANING OF
GLASNOST

AST-FORWARD TO JANUARY 1972. Romanian tyrant Nicolae Ceaușescu returned from the Kremlin more excited than I had ever seen him before. "You go to Moscow," he told me at the airport, extending four limp fingers in my direction. "We're pulling off a big *glasnost.*" I soon learned that Ceaușescu had spent his entire Moscow trip talking about public relations strategies with Soviet leader Leonid Brezhnev and his KGB chief Yuri Andropov. The two Soviets believed the West had reached the historic point where it was eager to encourage the least sign of thaw in a communist leader. To test this conclusion, they wanted to build Ceaușescu up and make him a big box-office success in the West, as a trial run preparatory to launching the same trick with the man in the Kremlin.

You probably think Mikhail Gorbachev invented the concept of *glasnost* to describe his effort to lead the Soviet Union "out of its totalitarian state and to democracy, to freedom, to openness," as he wrote.[1] If so, you are not alone. All of the media and most of the "experts," even in Western defense establishments, believe that too—as does the committee that awarded Gorbachev the Nobel Peace Prize. Even the venerable *Encyclopedia Britannica* defines *glasnost* as "Soviet policy of open discussion of political and social issues. It was instituted by Mikhail Gorbachev in the late 1980s and began the democratization of the Soviet Union."[2] *Merriam-Webster* agrees.[3] And the *American Heritage Dictionary* defines *glasnost* as "an official policy of the former Soviet government emphasizing candor with regard to discussion of social problems and shortcomings."[4]

But in fact, *glasnost* is an old Russian term for polishing the ruler's image. Originally it meant, literally, *publicizing, i.e.,* self-promotion. Since the sixteenth century's Ivan the Terrible, the first ruler to become Tsar of All the Russias, all of that country's leaders have used *glasnost* to promote themselves inside and outside the country.

In the mid-1930s—half a century before Gorbachev's *glasnost*—the official Soviet encyclopedia defined *glasnost* as a spin on news released to the public: "*Dostupnost obshchestvennomy obsuzhdeniyu, kontrolyu; publichnost,*" meaning, "the quality of being made available for public discussion or manipulation."[5]

Thus, back in the days when I was still a member of the KGB community, *glasnost* was regarded as a tool of the black art of *dezinformatsiya*, and it was used to sanctify the country's leader. For communists, only the leader counted. They used *glasnost* to sanctify their own leaders, and to induce hordes of Western leftists to fall for this scam.

Glasnost is one of the most secret secrets of the Kremlin, and certainly one of the main reasons for still keeping the KGB's foreign intelligence archives hermetically sealed. The Cold War is over, but the Kremlin's *glasnost* operations seem to be still en vogue. In August 1999, only days after Vladimir Putin was appointed Russia's prime minister, the KGB's *dezinformatsiya* machinery, capitalizing on the fact that he had spent many years in Germany, started portraying him as a Europeanized leader. (The fawning stories neglected to mention that he had been assigned to *East* Germany, a Soviet satellite at the time.) That same year, I went with my wife— an American writer and intelligence expert—to visit Leipzig and Dresden and tour the menacing buildings that had housed the Stasi (communist East Germany's political police) headquarters where Putin had in fact spent his "Europeanizing" years. We learned that the local Soviet-German House of Friendship—headed by Putin for six years—had been in fact a KGB front, and that the undercover KGB officers running it had simply worked out of operational offices at the Leipzig and Dresden *Stasi* headquarters. We even sat in Putin's chair, now a museum piece.

Those prison-like *Stasi* buildings had been cut off from even the normal and colorless East German life by *Stasi* guards brandishing machine guns and flanked by police dogs. Yet, even today, the Kremlin still reverentially implies that Putin's experience in Germany was similar to that of Peter the Great, allowing him to absorb the best of European culture.

At the end of the 2001 summit meeting held in Slovenia, President George W. Bush said: "I looked the man [Putin] in the eye. I found him to be very straightforward and trustworthy." Unfortunately, even President Bush was deceived by *glasnost*. Putin consolidated Russia into an intelligence dictatorship, not a democracy. By 2003, more than six thousand former officers of the KGB, who had framed millions as Zionist spies and shot them, were running Russia's federal and local governments. Nearly half of all top governmental positions were held by former officers of the KGB.[6] It was like democratizing Nazi Germany with Gestapo officers at its helm.

On February 12, 2004, Putin declared the demise of the Soviet Union a "national tragedy on an enormous scale." Nevertheless, most of the world still sees him as a modern Peter the Great. That is the secret power of *glasnost*.

"A man like me is born only once every five hundred years," Ceaușescu would proclaim, over and over again, after 1972. That was his *glasnost*, and, unfortunately, I was deeply involved in it.

For those who do not remember Ceaușescu, let me just say that he was more or less a Romanian version of the current Russian president, Vladimir Putin—an empty suit who morphed into his country's president without having held any productive job, who knew nothing about how the real world worked, and who believed that lying to the world and killing off his critics were the magic wands that would keep him in power. Like Putin, Ceaușescu had supervised his country's political police organization before becoming president. Behind the scenes, Ceaușescu, like Putin, used his intelligence machinery to override party politics as a means to power. Like Putin, he made an effort to detract attention away from his humble and colorless past by making his imperial dreams come true. And of course, they both ascended to the throne driven by the secret ambition to hang onto it for life.

After getting my marching orders from Ceaușescu in 1972, I was in Moscow a week later. KGB chairman Andropov greeted me by getting right to the point: "The only thing the West cares about is our leader." He was famous for not wasting his breath on introductory chitchat. "The more they come to love *him*, the better they will like *us*," he said. Making the imperialists believe our leaders admired *them* was the most efficacious *glasnost* tactic for now. It was as simple as that, and it worked, he said. The KGB had already achieved great success in making certain elements in the West admire—and even love—"the Comrade" (meaning first Stalin, then Khrushchev).

Andropov's dark, cavernous office breathed secrecy from every inch of its thick walls, just as his new *glasnost* did. The velvet window draperies were closed, and the only light came from the flickering flames of a fire inside the fireplace. The chairman's ascetic fingers felt cold and moist when he shook my hand. He took a seat on the side of the table facing the warmth of the fireplace, not at the head, as Soviet bureaucratic protocol required. His kidney illness had worsened and he needed to keep warm, so as to avoid having to go to the bathroom too often during a meeting.

"Let the gullible fools believe you want to perfume your communism with a dab of Western democracy, and they will clothe you in gold," Andropov declared. The creation of the image of the "new Ceauşescu" should be planted like opium seeds—patiently but tenaciously, one by one by one. We should water our seeds day after day until they bear fruit. We should promise that more openness and Westernization will be forthcoming, if only the West helps our new "moderate" Ceauşescu to defeat his "hardline" opponents at home.

Some two hours later, the KGB chairman concluded our meeting as abruptly as he had started it: "I'll lay you a million to one that the West will swallow it."

When I left the Lubyanka (KGB headquarters), I took with me a devious *glasnost* plan for image reconstruction. Ceauşescu followed it to the letter. He rebaptized the Grand National Assembly, Romania's version of the Supreme Soviet, as "Parliament," added a few religious leaders to it, and declared it the country's governing body. Of course, it remained the same rubber-stamp organization Romania had had before. Next, Ceauşescu publicly called for the Communist Party to reduce its influence on the administration and the economy of the country. That was another inspired *glasnost* trick. Then Ceauşescu staged a simulated economic decentralization, instituted dual candidates for local elections, and announced a campaign against corruption and drunkenness.

That done, Ceauşescu created the national position of "president," endowed it with broad governing powers, and awarded himself the post.

To impress the religious, Ceauşescu even marched behind a metropolitan of the church and a clutch of priests at his father's funeral. Lastly, he developed a specialty of telling anti-Soviet jokes.

It worked like a charm. Bucharest became an East European mecca, filled to the brim with Western journalists and politicians eager to get a closer look at the man who had dared to change communism for the better. A celebrity was born.

Western businessmen rushed to Bucharest, hoping to get in on the ground floor for a slice of the *new* Romania. Of course, most of them had been lured there by my undercover DIE (Romania's foreign intelligence service) operatives, who went to great lengths to pamper them during their stay. Gradually, my undercover officers became expert at "rewarding" the "friendly" visitors by setting up interviews for them with Ceauşescu, inviting them to lavish banquets held in Romania's picturesque monasteries, carousing with them at all-night parties and finding them compliant girlfriends. Or even by involving them in profitable businesses.

Today, no one remembers that Ceauşescu was once Washington's fair-haired boy. Contemporary political memory seems to be increasingly afflicted with a kind of a convenient Alzheimer's disease. But two American presidents went to Bucharest to pay Ceauşescu tribute, when none had ever gone there before. To cap it all off, my lord and master began a royal junket around the free world to sell his image—the United States, Japan, France, Italy, the Vatican, Finland, West Germany, Spain, Portugal, Egypt, Jordan, and the Philippines, to mention only a few of his hosts.

On all of these trips, Ceauşescu kept me at his right hand. He now religiously believed that *glasnost*, not Marxist ideology, was the magic wand that would make his ambitions a reality.

In 1978, I accompanied Ceauşescu on his fourth and most triumphant trip to Washington, and I was next to him when he took a historic drive throughout London with Queen Elizabeth in the British royal coach. Few now remember it, but a steady stream of front-page articles on Romania appeared in the United States, Great Britain and Western Europe at that time, extolling Ceauşescu's new "Westernized communism." The tyrant was portrayed as a new breed of communist ruler, one the West could do business with. Romania seemed a normal country—a place where people could criticize their government, visit monasteries, listen to Western symphonies, read foreign books and even point to their stylish first lady.

We were also quite successful at filling Western media airwaves with the new image of Ceauşescu. The truth is, the Western media are quite easily manipulated, for they often craft their stories from press releases and tend, on the whole, to be indiscriminate about the nature and reliability of their sources. Our information fit quite well with the general mood of Western acceptance of Ceauşescu as a Westernized communist. In the West, his position generally seemed a plausible and historic breach in the Iron Curtain, and almost no one stepped up to check the facts and contradict us.

In 1982, Yuri Andropov, the father of the modern Soviet *dezinformatsiya* era, became ruler of the Soviet Union itself, and *glasnost* became a Soviet foreign policy as well. Once settled in the Kremlin, the former KGB chairman hastened to introduce himself to the West as a "moderate" communist and a sensitive, warm, Western-oriented man who allegedly enjoyed an occasional drink of Scotch, liked to read English novels, and loved listening to Beethoven and American jazz. In reality, Andropov did not drink at all, for he was already terminally ill from a kidney disorder. The rest of the portrayal was equally false—as I well know, having been quite well acquainted with Andropov. As for "moderate," any head of the KGB necessarily had hands drenched in blood.

In the brief span left to him, the cynical Andropov focused on projecting his new image and promoting his protégé, a vigorous and callous young professional communist who was busy honing the same moderate image for himself—Mikhail Gorbachev.

Gorbachev introduced himself to the West exactly as Andropov had: a cultured sophisticate and aficionado of Western opera and jazz. The Kremlin has always known that this picture holds particular charm for the gullible West.

Gorbachev is thought to have been recruited by the KGB in the early 1950s while studying law at Moscow State University, where he spied on his foreign classmates.[7] As long as the KGB archives remain sealed, we will not be able to learn more details about those years of Gorbachev's life. But we do now know that after graduating from the university, Gorbachev interned at the Lubyanka, the state security headquarters,[8] where he came under Andropov's influence. Both had begun their careers in Stavropol. Andropov got Gorbachev appointed to the Soviet Politburo, and one Gorbachev biographer even describes him as Andropov's "crown prince."[9]

Meanwhile, the West's admiration for Ceauşescu's *glasnost* took on such a life of its own that it could not be stopped. In a letter dated January 27, 1983, written to Ceauşescu on his birthday, President Richard Nixon, whom I had already briefed about Ceauşescu's *glasnost* after I defected to the United States, gushed:

> Ever since we first met and talked in 1967, I have watched you grow in stature as a statesman. Your vigor, your single-mindedness, your acute intelligence—and especially your ability to act skillfully on both domestic and international fronts—place you in the first rank of world leaders . . . At 65 most people are ready to retire, but for many of the greatest leaders the most productive and satisfying years are still ahead. I am certain that your best moments will come in your second decade as President as you continue to follow the bold, independent course you have set for your people.[10]

The late Secretary of State Lawrence Eagleburger, for whose staunch anti-communism I have high regard, told me in 1988 that Ceauşescu "may be crazy with his own people, but believe me, General, he is the one who'll break up the Soviet bloc." A few months later, however, Ceauşescu was executed by his own people at the end of a trial in which the accusations came almost word-for-word out of my book *Red Horizons: The True Story of Nicolae & Elena Ceauşescu's Crimes, Lifestyle and Corruption.*

By that time, however, Washington and the rest of the West had shifted their affections. Now it was the man in the Kremlin, Mikhail Gorbachev, who was seen as the nascent democrat and touted as a political visionary. Once again, the Western media appeared to swallow their own hype. Gorbachev's rhetoric about combining "communist values" with "Western democracy introduced from the top" and a "centralized free-market economy" enthralled the world. Piles of Gorbachev's *Perestroika: New Thinking for Our Country and the World* took the place of Ceauşescu's memoirs in bookstore windows.

So much for institutional memory.

In December 1987, when Mikhail Gorbachev went to Washington, I had the weird *déjà vu* feeling of watching a reenactment of Ceauşescu's last official visit to the United States in April 1978. I had prepared and directed that visit, and during its actual performance I had also accompanied Ceauşescu.

To my mind, the two communist leaders were uncannily alike in both appearance and actions. Both men were short in stature—like most dictators. Both brought their foreign intelligence chiefs along with them—as most communist rulers did. Both boosted their national history and culture, reciting poems by their famous writers. Both were said to be fans of American movies. Both strode into Washington with firm step and swinging arms, wearing equally broad smiles on their faces and almost identical Italian suits of impeccable conservative cut on their stocky bodies. Both chose to wear a business suit to the black-tie dinner at the White House—Ceaușescu always said that the black tie was the ultimate symbol of capitalist decay, an opinion that caused me many a protocol headache on his visits abroad.

Both Gorbachev and Ceaușescu welcomed every photo opportunity in the United States, clearly indicating that they considered the American media the most effective way to polish their international image. Gorbachev's arrival was preceded by an NBC interview, just as Ceaușescu's had been by one with the Hearst newspapers. Both publicly used Washington to reaffirm their deep devotion to Marxism, although both had to acknowledge that their communist systems at home were in deep trouble. (Translation: send money.) And both were not shy about letting the West know their determination to stay in power for the rest of their lives.

After formal ceremonies, official document signing, and the requisite exchange of fancy dinners, Gorbachev again followed in Ceaușescu's footsteps by turning on the charm for members of Congress and high-level American businessmen. Both groups have often made themselves useful to foreign despots.

Both Gorbachev and Ceaușescu came to Washington accompanied by their wives, a diplomatic first. Both first ladies were promoted as intellectuals in their own right. In Washington, the Romanians publicized a scientific study by Elena Ceaușescu—actually ghostwritten by my DIE. Soviet advance publicity glowed over Raisa Gorbachev's university dissertation, even getting excerpts from it published in the American press. On her fourth visit to Washington, Elena Ceaușescu demanded that I get her an American academic title. It was not easy, but I managed to arrange a ceremony at Blair House making her an honorary member of the Illinois Academy of Science. Raisa Gorbachev returned to the United States in 1990 and was honored at a highly publicized Wellesley College graduation.

Toward the end of their visits, both Eastern bloc leaders received a taste of American democracy in action. Ceauşescu had to face the thousands of Romanian and Hungarian émigrés who besieged his residence at the Waldorf Astoria hotel in New York, calling him "Dracula" for his ultra-Marxist domestic policies. Gorbachev had to put up with a large demonstration asking for the right of Jews to emigrate from the Soviet Union. Those confrontations momentarily caused both communist leaders to let slip their smiling masks, allowing a glimpse of their steel teeth. In the end, however, both won the American public back over to their side by stopping their motorcades and impulsively plunging into the crowd to shake hands.

In retrospect, it is easy to see that all of this was a product of sophisticated *dezinformatsiya* experts and public relations crews, employing all their reliable, smoke-and-mirrors framing techniques.

At the time, however, both leaders were perceived as modern pragmatists who deserved to be supported. Indeed, they were believed by many in diplomatic and academic circles to really be—deep down—on America's side. It was argued that they needed US support to help them in impending tough struggles with their own domestic "hardliners."

I do not mean to imply that the mighty Gorbachev would necessarily have been trying to copy Ceauşescu word for word and step by step, but Andropov's resounding success at stage-directing Ceauşescu was certainly there for Gorbachev to consider. It seems particularly significant that Gorbachev, a couple of weeks after returning home from his 1987 trip to Washington, quietly awarded Ceauşescu the Order of Lenin, the highest decoration in the Soviet bloc, in spite of the two men's strong public differences. As far as I know, Ceauşescu was the only East European leader Gorbachev ever decorated with that high award.

I noted only one fundamental difference between Gorbachev's and Ceauşescu's strategies to butter up the West. Three months after Ceauşescu left Washington, the acting chief of his foreign intelligence service—this writer—was granted political asylum by the United States.

That event shattered the smiling mask Ceauşescu had worn in Washington and allowed the inner workings of his *glasnost* machine to lie spread out on the table for all to see. From among Gorbachev's innermost circle, no one has yet stepped forward with the truth about that last Soviet monarch's methods of governing the country and about his still-admired *glasnost*.

At the beginning of 2001, Gorbachev was still publicly asserting that his *glasnost* (for which he had been granted the Nobel Prize and named "Man of the Decade" by *Time* magazine) was "leading the country out of its totalitarian state and to democracy, to freedom, to openness."[11] In March 2002, however, British Prime Minister Margaret Thatcher, who had prominently endorsed *glasnost* in the 1980s, cast the first doubt on Gorbachev. She conceded that "the role of Mikhail Gorbachev, who failed miserably in his declared objective of saving Communism and the Soviet Union, has been absurdly misunderstood."[12]

3

DEFECTING TO AMERICA

GLASNOST REALLY MEANS LYING, and lying is the first step toward stealing and killing. On the memorable day of July 22, 1978, Romanian president Nicolae Ceaușescu whispered in my ear, "I w-want Noel k-k-killed." Ceaușescu stammered both when nervous and when excited. "You don't need to r-report back to me," he added. "I'll learn about it from the W-Western m-media when he croaks."

Noel Bernard was the director of Radio Free Europe's Romanian program, and for years he had been blackening Ceaușescu's carefully crafted cult of personality.

Ceaușescu continued: "And a few days later, blow up that whole w-wasp's n-nest." The "wasp's nest" was the Munich headquarters of Radio Free Europe. "With a briefcase of S-Semtex," Ceaușescu expertly specified, referring to an explosive that had been developed in communist Czechoslovakia for use in international terrorism. "We've g-got to f-finish with all that shit."

All through those twenty-seven years I had spent in the Soviet bloc intelligence community, I had been living with the nightmare that, sooner or later, orders to have someone killed would land on my plate. In 1951, when I became an intelligence officer in the KGB community, I swore to myself that I would avoid involvement in any operations that could lead to a loss of life. I may have done a lot of reprehensible things during all those years, but I had kept that resolution. Up until that moment I had been safe, since General Nicolae Doicaru, the longtime chief of Romania's foreign intelligence service, the DIE, had been in charge of "wet operations," as the KGB community's jargon termed the killing and kidnapping of political opponents abroad.

The previous June, however, Ceaușescu had anointed me as head of his Presidential House, a new position, and there was no way for me to avoid further involvement in political assassinations, which had grown into a main instrument of foreign policy throughout the Soviet bloc.

Head of Presidential House was a job essentially like chief of staff in the American White House. Ceaușescu had invented this post in April 1978, after his triumphant visit to Washington—where I had accompanied him—but within it he had also included the day-to-day handling of Romania's intelligence services. It was like being the White House chief of staff, national security adviser, director of the CIA and head of the Department for Homeland Security all at the same time.

Since 1972, when I had risen to enter the inner sanctum of the Soviet bloc, I had come to realize that sooner or later I would have to screw up my courage and break with that evil society, which I was sure would eventually either quietly collapse or else lead to worldwide cataclysm. The physical step, however, proved to be much harder than the mental one.

Privilege can generate cowardice, as it did in my case. Communist rulers have always been very generous with their spy chiefs—that is, until they tire of them and kill them off. It proved not easy for me to renounce my exorbitantly luxurious life at the top of Romanian society, my Bucharest villa with its swimming pool and sauna, my fleet of cars and drivers, my summer house at the Black Sea, and my hunting lodges in the Carpathian Mountains. "Defector"—that word used by the US government for a Soviet bloc official who chose freedom in the West—also acted as a chain around my ankles, for the word lay in frighteningly close proximity to the word "traitor."

The prospect of being involved in political killings was the drop that finally burst the dam of my indecision. On Sunday, July 23, 1978, I flew to Bonn, where I had to deliver a message from Ceaușescu to the West German chancellor, Helmut Schmidt. Soviet ruler Leonid Brezhnev had asked Ceaușescu for help in stealing the technology and blueprints for a VTOL (vertical take-off and landing) military airplane that had been developed by Fokker A.G., West Germany's main airplane producer. The Kremlin believed that using the "independent" Ceaușescu to build a cooperative venture with Fokker for producing a civilian airplane (Fokker-614) would afford the best access for stealing the VTOL technology. The German chancellor, however, had shown reluctance to approve the venture, rightly fearing that the secret military technologies involved might end up in Moscow.

"Just make sure you plant the conviction in his thick German skull that Moscow will never see one iota of anything," Ceaușescu instructed me, after he had finished dictating his message to the West German chancellor. "Promise him anything he wants."

That Sunday, the music suddenly went dead on my TAROM flight to Vienna, where I was to pick up an Austrian plane for the rest of my trip. A woman's voice cut in fuzzily with an announcement in Romanian and German: "Ladies and Gentlemen, our plane will land at Schwechat Airport in a few minutes. Captain Georgescu and his crew wish you a pleasant sojourn in Vienna and hope you will fly TAROM soon again."

The door of the plane had barely been cracked open when Romania's ambassador in Vienna, Dumitru Aninoiu, whose wife was an undercover DIE officer, hopped on board. "Welcome to Vienna, comrade state secretary," he greeted me loudly, using my cover title, as he reached out to grab my briefcase. "We'll have lunch together."

As we were leaving for the airport's VIP salon, I cast one final glance over my shoulder at the white BAC 1-11 plane with the Romanian flag painted on its tail. I knew I had flown TAROM for the last time.

Two days later, a black taxi dropped me off in front of the United States Embassy in Bonn. As I stepped out onto the sidewalk, I could hear my heart pounding in my ears. My mouth felt as if it had been freeze-dried, although the palms of my hands were unaccustomedly moist. With a few rapid steps, I crossed over to the entrance and went inside.

The lobby for the general public was small but crowded. A statuesque woman squeezed into a chic khaki safari suit and draped in several pounds of gold jewelry, who was casually leaning against the wall next to the door, suddenly stopped talking when I came in. She measured me up and down for a very long moment, as did her companion, a short, pudgy man in an ill-fitting suit of light gray silk. Some of the other people also turned to look at me. Even the old-fashioned bureaucrat behind the teller-like window, his coat sleeves protected by black sleevelets, raised his eyes to peer out at me. In short, the whole room seemed to be watching me.

Of course, I knew that it was normal for a waiting room crowd to give every new arrival a careful going-over. On that day, though, I could not think about what was or was not normal.

I approached the Marine officer, who stood like a statue, feet apart and arms crossed over his chest, barring the only door leading to the inside of the embassy, and said to him, dropping my voice as low as I could: "I am a Soviet bloc two-star intelligence general, and I want to defect to the United States."

I became a free man on July 27, 1978. Because of my extremely high position in the Soviet bloc, only the president of the United States could approve my request for political asylum. Thus, Pete, the CIA officer I talked to at the US embassy, scheduled another meeting for 10 p.m. three days later at the Dom-Hotel in Cologne, to give me the answer. Those were three very long days.

When I arrived at the Dom-Hotel that fateful Wednesday night, the first thing I did was look around for the men's room. As I opened the door, I saw Pete inside. My biochemistry was, evidently, not unique.

Pete seemed embarrassed for only a second. Then he took an envelope from his breast pocket and gave it to me. It contained a cable signed by Adm. Stansfield Turner, the director of Central Intelligence, stating that President Jimmy Carter was granting me political asylum, security protection, and help for starting a new life in America. It also said that a CIA airplane sent from Washington was waiting at the Rhein-Main Air Base to pick me up.

Reading that cable over and over again gave me an enormous feeling of relief. Not in my wildest dreams, though, had I ever imagined that I would become a free man in a restroom.

It was past midnight when our four-car motorcade came roaring up to the gate at the US Rhein-Main Air Base. I was pleasantly surprised to find a pile of clothes waiting for me on the plane, as all I had with me was the shirt and pants I was wearing.

Throughout all those years of torment in Romania, the only things of which I had been certain of were that I would not die under communism and that no matter how high I might have been shoved up the communist ladder, I would start my new life in America without any encumbrances from my past. That was why, when I set out from my room at the Intercontinental Hotel in Cologne to board the CIA plane, the only things I took with me were my passport; my personal notes; a camera containing a couple of snapshots of my daughter, Dana; and a wristwatch with the signature of King Hussein of Jordan on its dial, which I had just gotten from the king for—as he put it—saving his life from an assassination attempt organized by PLO leader Yasser Arafat.

After we had been served dinner, Pete called it a day. "Let's catch a few hours of sleep," he suggested, guiding me to the airplane's bedroom. Pete took a pair of pajamas and a travel kit out of his garment bag. After a couple of moments, he quietly put them back and, still dressed, scrunched up under the blanket covering his bed. Pete's weariness may have been less overwhelming than his embarrassment when he realized that I had neither pajamas nor toothbrush. A few minutes later, Pete was sawing wood.

Of course, I was also exhausted and could hardly believe everything was over. That whole Thursday, I had tried to look as if I had been indeed getting ready for a routine trip back to Bucharest, not for the voyage of a lifetime. I had spent the morning in the acoustically protected "bubble" at the Romanian Embassy, in the company of the DIE chief of station, General Stefan Constantin. At noon, I had again met Chancellery Minister Hans-Jürgen Wischnewski at the *Bundeskanzleramt* in Bonn to get Chancellor Schmidt's answer to Ceaușescu's message. From the twinkle in his eye and his warm handshake, I understood he must have known about my decision, and that cheered me up enormously—I had tremendous confidence in that bulldog of a man.

Afterward I had flown to Bremen, where I held a meeting with Fokker representatives, and in the evening I had been back in Cologne to meet with Frederick W. Smith, founder and chairman of the American shipping company Federal Express, who wanted to buy one hundred commercial Fokker-614 planes that would be produced in Romania in cooperation with Fokker. Then I had attended the official dinner given for me by the Romanian ambassador, Ion Morega, in the salons of the embassy, where I had even told a few jokes.

Now I, too, collapsed into bed. Not that I hoped to close my eyes. God knows, that night I was more worked up than words could tell. My thoughts turned back to what must soon be going on in Bucharest. I remembered what had occurred a couple of months earlier, when I had reported to Ceaușescu that General Nicolae Militaru, the commander of the Bucharest Military Garrison, was at that moment in the process of being recruited by Soviet intelligence. Hearing that, Ceaușescu ripped off his shirt. He closeted himself with his wife at their summer residence in Neptun, surrounded the place with a cordon of armored vehicles and security troops, and then vented his rage on his minister of interior and me.

My own positions in the Romanian government were infinitely higher than General Militaru's, and I suddenly felt a mischievous smile creeping onto my lips. Thank God, I thought. At least I won't be there having to cope with Ceaușescu's hysterics again.

It was a glorious, sunny day outside when the CIA plane landed at the presidential airport inside Andrews Air Force Base near Washington, DC, and that only magnified the fireworks popping off inside of me. For many, many years I had learned to hide my personal feelings, for that was the way of life in a society where the government had its informants everywhere and where microphones covered you everyplace you went. But on that unforgettable day, I had an overwhelming desire to dance around in a jig all by myself.

I was a free man! I knew it would not be easy to start my life over from scratch with only the clothes on my back, but I was eager to try my hand at it. I was a well-educated engineer and America was, after all, the land of opportunity, wasn't it?

To the right of our plane were a Boeing 707 and a 727 painted with the American flag and presidential seal, and that also contributed to my feeling of having arrived in a familiar place. Those Boeings were old friends of mine. I had been involved in the visits of Presidents Nixon and Ford to Romania, and I had traveled on an Air Force One provided by President Carter to Ceaușescu to tour the United States. "Welcome home," read a large banner behind them intended for President Carter, but it gave me the feeling that I, too, had come home.

A string of cars and a bunch of people were waiting for me. One man was standing in front of the red carpet. "Welcome to the United States, General," he said, shaking my hand. "You are a free man!"

Many years after that memorable day, I became friends with a Holocaust survivor whose eyes always misted up whenever he told about how one of the American soldiers who liberated his concentration camp had said to him: "You're a free man!" So do my eyes, whenever I remember those solemn words.

My first dinner as a free man, a candlelight feast that ended long after midnight, remains vivid in my memory, down to the last detail. I was feted as the only head of a Soviet bloc espionage service who had ever asked for political asylum. When I finally took myself upstairs, the new day was beginning to break. I was overwhelmed. The joy of finally becoming part of this magnanimous land of liberty, where nothing was impossible, was surpassed only by the joy of simply being alive. I was exactly three months short of the round age of fifty on that unforgettable day of July 28, 1978, and I more than ever regretted that I had kept postponing the fateful step for so many years.

When I finally reached my bedroom, I carefully locked the door from inside. Then I took a little stone out of my pocket and fervently kissed it. It was one I had picked up off the ground at Andrews. In 1973 I had started the habit of secretly kissing the American soil every time I set foot in the United States. I would always find an unobtrusive way to pick up a small stone from someplace around the airport and to bury it inside my pocket until I could bring it out and devoutly give it a kiss later that night, in the darkness and surety of my room.

I kissed my little stone once more, then opened a window and threw it outside, back where it belonged. Falling to my knees, I prayed out loud for the first time in more than a quarter century. It took me a while, as it was not easy for me to find the right words to express my great joy and thanks to the good Lord. Forgiveness for my past, freedom for my daughter and strength for my new life were all I asked for at the end.

It was already day when I finished writing a letter to my beloved daughter, Dana. Here is the passage in which I explained why I had left her an orphan:

> ... For twenty years I had the misfortune of being involved in stealing from the West its technological data, which, together with democracy and freedom, are its greatest source of respect and pride. I was involved in stealing, but I always maneuvered things so as not to be involved in assassinations... In 1978 I got the order to organize the killing of Noel Bernard, the director of Radio Free Europe's Romanian program who had infuriated Ceaușescu with his commentaries. It was late July when I

got this order and when I ultimately had to decide between being a good father and being a political criminal. Knowing you, Dana, I was firmly convinced that you would prefer no father to one who was an assassin.

That letter was repeatedly broadcast by Radio Free Europe and published in *Le Monde*. Unfortunately, Noel Bernard was indeed killed by Ceaușescu's political police, the *Securitate*, in 1981. During that same year, a twenty-pound plastic bomb exploded at the headquarters of Radio Free Europe in Munich. The bomb was planted by "Carlos the Jackal" (Ilich Ramírez Sánchez), who, according to *Securitate* documents recently released, had been supplied by the Romanians with four hundred pounds of plastic explosive, seven submachine guns and $1 million to assassinate me in the United States and to blow up Radio Free Europe headquarters.[1] Fortunately, Carlos was not able to find me. Eight employees at RFE headquarters in Munich were, however, badly injured by the explosion. Five Romanian diplomats assigned to West Germany were expelled for their involvement in that bloody operation.[2]

4

THE BLACK ART OF DISINFORMATION

IT HAS BEEN MANY YEARS since I escaped from that evil society known as the Soviet empire and came to the United States, the land of my youthful dreams. Millions around the world have been ready to pay any price to become citizens of this unique country. I am one of the lucky few who succeeded. Even today it is still difficult for me to find adequate words to express my gratitude to the US government for magnanimously granting me political asylum, despite my position at the top of the Soviet bloc intelligence community.

In 1981, I married a true American patriot, superb writer, and excellent linguist, who had also spent many years working against Soviet intelligence. Mary Lou helped me become a true American. She has spent the best years of her life assisting me to master English and to survive in spite of two death sentences hanging over my head and multimillion-dollar bounties on my scalp. She has also helped me, day after day, to build a new life under the new protective identity provided by the CIA, one that has nothing to do with Romania. It was not easy for Mary Lou, as the fellow inhabiting this new skin didn't have any real past to talk about, or any old friends from that past to count on. But she managed marvelously. We joined a yacht club, traveled around the world, made new friends, and outwitted several assassination teams.

Because the FBI learned that Muammar Gaddafi's espionage service had succeeded in persuading two former CIA contract employees (Frank

Terpil and Edwin Wilson, who had meanwhile escaped arrest by defecting to Libya) to provide internal CIA information about my whereabouts in exchange for $1 million, the CIA gave me a brand-new identity. Once again, we started our lives from scratch. New name, new past, new town, new home, new clubs, new friends. And we managed again.

My first book, *Red Horizons*, was Mary Lou's idea. She helped me to look at my past through American eyes, and she put my manuscript into good English. In 1987, Congressman Frank Wolf (R-VA) and the late and lamented Senator Jesse Helms (R-NC) handed the first published copy of *Red Horizons* to President Reagan, who reportedly would come to call it "my bible for dealing with dictators." A Romanian translation of the book printed in the United States was smuggled into Romania, and a Mao-style pocket edition was illegally printed in Hungary. In 1988, *Red Horizons* was serialized on Radio Free Europe.

In 1989, I was informed by Deputy Secretary of State Lawrence Eagleburger that my daughter had found a way to request political asylum in the United States. Soon after that, Congressmen Dick Cheney and Frank Wolf sent a letter to Ceaușescu, cosigned by some three hundred other members of the US Congress, asking him to allow her departure. Ceaușescu refused. To be on the safe side, his *Securitate* launched the rumor that I had been found dead in a New York subway station.

Frustrated by the *Securitate*'s disinformation and by the hermetical isolation of my daughter in Romania, Congressman Wolf flew to Bucharest together with Congressman Christopher Smith (R-NJ) to contact my daughter, who had been kept under virtual house arrest for ten years. They wanted to assure Dana that I was still alive, contrary to the disinformation launched by Ceaușescu. Both congressmen barely escaped from an attempt by a Romanian secret police car to run them down. Here is how Congressman Smith described it:

> A police car filled with four burly policemen, or *Securitate* members, was following us. And on one occasion, just as I turned around, the car's headlights were switched off. I thought, 'They're going to run us down.' And all of a sudden the car started racing toward us. I pushed Frank up against the wall, and the car went up on the sidewalk, just a few feet from us, and then roared down the street. We were all pushed up against the wall, and if we hadn't been aware, we would have been hit from behind.[1]

On March 13, 1989, a picture in *Time* magazine showed *Red Horizons* on the desk of President George Herbert Walker Bush.[2]

July 28, 1989, was the most important benchmark of my new life. On that day I became an American citizen. Also on that day, I was credited by the CIA as the only person in the Western world who had single-handedly demolished an entire enemy espionage service—the one I had managed. And I was given the following letter, signed by the CIA Director for Operations, a letter that became the most precious present I had ever received in my whole life:

> Dear Lt. Gen. Ion Pacepa,
>   You have made an important and unique contribution to the United States of which you can justly be proud. Therefore, it gives me great pleasure, on this momentous and solemn occasion, to wish you happiness and fulfillment in this country as a US citizen."[3]

On November 9, 1989, as I sat in front of the television set watching the Berlin Wall being torn down, my eyes welled up with tears. I was incredibly proud to be a citizen of the United States. The whole world was expressing its gratitude to this great country for its forty-five years of successful Cold War against Marxism and the Soviet empire.

During the night of December 21, 1989, I received a phone call from the head of the State Department's team monitoring the events in Romania. "They took your daughter, General." Dana was indeed plucked from her house in Bucharest and driven to the Bulgarian border, together with her husband and her in-laws. They were given to understand that they would be executed there, and that their bodies would be left along the border to indicate that they had been illegally trying to flee Romania. Fortunately, just before the group reached the border, they heard Radio Bucharest announcing that Ceaușescu had fled, and that his office was now in the hands of the people.

The two dozen *Securitate* officers escorting Dana dropped everything and ran off like rats deserting a sinking ship, leaving behind their cars, uniforms, and even weapons. When Dana got back to Bucharest, she found that the *Securitate* guard car that for eleven years had been stationed in front of her house had also been abandoned. Together with a diplomat at the United States Embassy in Bucharest, she searched the car and found not only more abandoned uniforms and weapons, but even operational files on her case. Included in the file were photographs of people who were under no circumstances to be allowed to enter their house—Congressman Wolf was among them.

On Christmas Day 1989, Romanian tyrant Nicolae Ceaușescu was executed at the end of a trial in which the accusations came almost word-for-word out of *Red Horizons*. (A second edition, published the following March, contains the transcript of Ceaușescu's trial, which clearly was based entirely on facts found in *Red Horizons*.) On January 1, 1990, the new Romanian newspaper *Adevărul* ("The Truth"), which on that day had replaced the communist *Scînteia* ("The Spark"), began serializing *Red Horizons*. In its lead article, *Adevărul* explained that the book's serialization by Radio Free Europe had "played an incontestable role" in overthrowing Ceaușescu. According to a program on Radio Romania International, "the streets of Romania's towns were empty" during the Radio Free Europe serialization of my book.[4]

The bullets were still flying over Bucharest when Congressman Wolf landed there again, this time to free my daughter. On January 6, 1999, the congressman landed in Washington with my daughter and her husband, who became the first Romanians to escape from Ceaușescu's hell and reach the United States. Their arrival was broadcast on forty-four US and international TV stations. A few weeks later, Dana's husband, a sculptor, finished a bust of Congressman Wolf and presented it to him. The second chapter of the congressman's latest book, *Prisoner of Conscience*, which is dedicated to *Red Horizons* and Dana's rescue from Romania, ends with the story of that statue:

> The bust now sits in my family room at home. My younger grandchildren yell, "Pop Pop" whenever they see it, and rub the nose. "It was certainly not the most faithful portrait of the congressman," General Pacepa notes, "but for Dana and her husband it was the symbol of their freedom."[5]

Red Horizons was subsequently republished in twenty-seven countries, and in 2010 the *Washington Post* recommended it be included on the list of books that should be read in schools, next to Whittaker Chambers's *Witness*.

So I kept writing.

In 2010, my book *Programmed to Kill: Lee Harvey Oswald, the Soviet KGB, and the Kennedy Assassination* was displayed at the annual meeting of the Organization of American Historians in Washington, DC, and an academic review called it a "superb new paradigmatic work on the death of President Kennedy" and a "must read" for "the most casual reader," for the "serious student preparing his or her own magnum opus," and for "everyone interested in the assassination of President Kennedy."[6]

Also during 2010, I finished another manuscript, dealing with disinformation and *glasnost*. My literary agent, who was also running for US Congress as a Republican, fell in love with it, but had problems interesting a major publisher in it.

By then I was already eighty-two and I thought it was time for me to hang up my war on disinformation and *glasnost* on a nail and spend the rest of my days just enjoying my new, marvelous life together with my beloved Mary Lou.

Alas, I couldn't.

A good friend, Kathryn Jean Lopez, at that time editor of *National Review Online*, forwarded me an e-mail from Professor Ronald Rychlak, who wanted to discuss with me the details of an article, "Moscow's Assault on the Vatican," that I had published in the *NRO*. That article dealt with a KGB disinformation operation aimed at changing Pius XII's strongly anti-Nazi past and, absurdly, alleging that he was in fact "Hitler's Pope." Professor Rychlak, one of the world's top experts on Pius XII, wanted me to help him write a chapter dealing with this KGB framing of Pius XII, for inclusion in a new edition of his book *Hitler, the War, and the Pope*, in which he had thoroughly documented that Pius XII had saved half a million Jews from the Nazis. I agreed. The new edition was successfully published.

Soon after that, Ron suggested we cowrite a whole book about the framing of Pius XII. We ended up building a book on Soviet disinformation, in which the framing of Pius is one of its major examples.

Disinformation has caused worldwide damage to the reputation of the United States, and now it is putting down roots in this country itself. To fight this invisible weapon, we must first recognize it for what it is and decode its hidden mission, since it is usually clothed in innocuous civilian dress— as were the terrorists who killed three thousand Americans on September 11, 2001. That is the purpose of this book.

5

THE "BEAUTY" OF DISINFORMATION

OST POLITICIANS, people in the academic world, and the media believe that disinformation is an obsolete Cold War phenomenon. As late as 1986, however, the word "disinformation" was not listed among the three hundred thousand entries of *Webster's New World Thesaurus*, or even in the twenty-seven volumes of the *New Encyclopedia Britannica*. It is widely—and erroneously—believed that the word is simply a foreign synonym for *misinformation*. Even the Microsoft Word 2010 software used to type the draft of this book underlined the word *disinforming* and suggested replacing it with *misinforming*.

In reality, disinformation is as different from misinformation as night is from day. *Misinformation* is an official government tool and recognizable as such. *Disinformation* (i.e., *dezinformatsiya*) is a secret intelligence tool, intended to bestow a Western, nongovernment cachet on government lies. Let us assume that the FSB (the new KGB) fabricated some documents supposedly proving that American military forces were under specific orders to target Islamic houses of worship in their bombing raids over Libya in 2011. If a report on those documents were published in an official Russian news outlet, that would be misinformation, and people in the West might rightly take it with a grain of salt and simply shrug it off as routine Moscow propaganda. If, on the other hand, that same material were made public in the Western media and attributed to some Western organization, that would be disinformation, and the story's credibility would be substantially greater.

In April 2003, the Western media were inundated with hundreds of horror stories about the looting of the National Museum in Baghdad. Television stations around the world showed the weeping deputy director of the museum blaming the Americans for allowing the destruction of "170,000 items of antiquity dating back thousands of years." That was a piece of *disinformation*. Eventually it was reliably reported that museum employees had hidden the supposedly looted treasures in a safe place long before the Iraq War started, and at the end of hostilities they were safe, in American protective custody. Museum officials later listed only twenty-five artifacts as definitely missing.[1] But the damage was done. Countless people around the world still talk about the devastating images of empty display cases repeatedly shown on their television screens, accompanied by accusations that the Americans had allowed that to happen.

In the course of history, many countries during wartime have used various techniques to deceive the enemy about their real intentions. At one extreme is the huge, hollow wooden horse constructed by the Greeks in the second millennium BC to gain entrance into the impregnable city of Troy. At the other extreme is the complicated and masterful operation put together by British intelligence in 1944 to make the Germans believe that the Allied forces would invade France around Calais rather than on the actually intended beaches of Normandy. Russia became the first major power to make deception a permanent national policy, which eventually distorted every facet of Russian tsarist and communist society.

According to the highly classified training manuals on disinformation that codified my previous existence, the "science" of *disinformation* (and it was specifically and proudly termed a *science*) was born in Russia, it was deeply rooted in the Russian soil and in that country's history, and there it would remain forever. The manuals taught that, born in eighteenth century Russia, *disinformation* was the fruit of the passionate love affair between Catherine the Great and Prince Grigory Potemkin, her principal political and military adviser. In 1787, Potemkin, by then the governor general of the New Russia (today's Ukraine), took the empress on a tour of the Crimea, which he had been instrumental in annexing from the Turks four years earlier. To impress her, Potemkin had arranged for sham villages to be erected along the route the empress would take. One of those empty-façade villages, erected at the mouth of the small river Bug, went so far as to welcome the empress with a triumphal arch inscribed: "This is the way to Constantinople."

It is not an accident that *disinformation* was born in Russia. In the eighteenth century, the French Marquis de Custine remarked that in fact "everything is deception in Russia, and the gracious hospitality of the Czar, gathering together in his palace his serfs and the serfs of his courtiers, is only one more mockery."[2] Custine also noted—in language that cannot be improved upon even today—that "Russian despotism not only counts ideas and sentiments for nothing but remakes facts; it wages war on evidence and triumphs in the battle."[3] General Walter Bedell Smith, a former United States ambassador to Moscow, who wrote an introduction to the 1951 English translation of the marquis's diary, stated that Custine's political analysis was "so penetrating and timeless that it could be called the best work so far produced about the Soviet Union."[4] This book is perhaps the most insightful analysis of all of twentieth-century Russia.

There is a proverb saying that lies have short legs; that may be true elsewhere, but in post-tsarist Russia *disinformation* became a national policy that played a far greater role in shaping that country's past and present than even Potemkin could ever have foreseen.

World War I and the new era it brought about swept away five emperors, eight kings and eighteen dynasties,[5] but no country was more changed than Russia. When the Great War ended, Russia looked like a mobile home community hit by a hurricane. The new communist rulers assassinated the tsar, his family and his aristocracy, abolished the country's governing institutions, demolished her millennial religion, seized the land owned by wealthy Russians, confiscated the country's banks and industrial enterprises and killed off most of their owners. Russia's history, traditions, social customs, ethical values, and everything else that had ever meant something before the October Revolution of 1917 were thrown upside down and inside out— even if only for the sake of change.

Nevertheless, the new communist rulers religiously preserved the "science of *disinformation*," realizing that this historic Russian tool fit their needs like a glove. Changing minds is in fact what communism is all about.

It is also a quintessence of Russia, going all the way back to the Potemkin villages erected to allege rural prosperity. No wonder communism, Russia and *disinformation* were such a good fit.

During the Cold War, more people in the Soviet bloc worked for the *disinformation* machinery than for the Soviet army and defense industry put together. The bloc's intelligence community alone had well over one million officers and several million informants around the world. All were involved in deceiving the West—and their own people—or in supporting this effort. To them should be added the vast number of people working for the international *disinformation* organizations that the KGB secretly created. These organizations were headquartered outside the Soviet Union, pretended to be independent international entities, and published their own newspapers in French or English. Some of those international "Potemkin villages" in which I was personally involved include: the World Peace Council (with branches in 112 countries); the World Federation of Trade Unions (with branches in 90 countries); the Women's International Democratic Federation (with branches in 129 countries); the International Union of Students (with branches in 152 countries); and the World Federation of Democratic Youth (with branches in 210 countries).

It is a typically Russian tactic not to attack a threat head-on, and *disinformation* proved a deliciously indirect way of confounding the Kremlin's enemies. The first international "Potemkin village" was founded in 1949 and given the respectable name of World Peace Council (WPC), so that it would not look Russian. Its main task was to claim authorship for Soviet-concocted materials "documenting" that the United States was a war-mongering, Zionist country financed by Jewish money and run by a rapacious "Council of the Elders of Zion." The goal was to create the fear that the United States would ignite a new war in order to transform the rest of the world into a Jewish fiefdom.

There was a major condition for *disinformation* to succeed, and that was that a story should always be built around a "kernel of truth" that would lend credibility. Over my twenty-seven years in the Soviet bloc intelligence community, I was privy to many Cold War *disinformation* operations that eventually lost steam but were never entirely compromised, because of that kernel of truth. The "kernel of truth" for the World Peace Council was that it was headquartered in Paris and chaired by the French Nobel Prize winner Frédéric Joliot-Curie, a leftist persuaded by Stalin to lend his name to this international Potemkin village.

To be on the safe side, Stalin decided to make disinformation look as if it also were historically French. In the early 1950s, my DIE (Romania's foreign intelligence, or espionage, service) was instructed by its Soviet counterpart to launch the rumor that the word *disinformation* was derived from the French—in other words, to represent this traditionally Russian ruse as a French capitalist tool targeted against the peace-loving peoples of the Soviet bloc. I do not recall the exact definition received from Moscow, but it was similar to the one that can be found in the 1952 edition of the *Great Soviet Encyclopedia*:

> DEZINFORMATSIYA (from *des* (q.v.) and French *information*). Dissemination (in the press, on the radio, etc.) of false reports intended to mislead public opinion. The capitalist press and radio make wide use of *dezinformatsiya*, in order to fool the people, entangle them in lies, and depict the new war being prepared by the Anglo-American imperialist bloc as a defensive weapon, but depict the peaceful politics of the USSR, countries of the people's democracy and other peace-loving countries as allegedly aggressive. A special role in disseminations of this sort of provocative reports, of every kind of falsehoods, etc., belongs to the American capitalist press, radio and various publication agencies, furnishing false information to the press and to other propaganda organizations. The leading circles of the USA, Great Britain, France and other imperialist governments often resort to *dezinformatsiya* in matters of international relations; numerous examples of this kind of *dezinformatsiya* are found in the well-known Sovinformburo document "Falsifiers of History (Historical report)" (1948). The Anglo-American imperialists make wide use of *dezinformatsiya* in order to conceal the predatory nature of the war unleashed by them in Korea in June 1950.[6]

Today most people believe that *disinformation* does indeed derive from some French word. But the official French dictionary, the *Larousse*, did not mention any such word as *desinformation* in 1952, or even in its 1978 edition.

Back in those early postwar days, the French government saw through Moscow's ruse. In 1954 it rejected any French paternity for the word *disinformation,* accused the World Peace Council of being a KGB front, and kicked it out of France. One of the Soviets' most trusted influence agents of that period, French philosopher Jean-Paul Sartre, tried to persuade the French government to rescind its decision. He publicly vilified the United States as a racist country suffering from political rabies.[7] It did not help. Moscow was forced to move the World Peace Council headquarters temporarily to Soviet-occupied Prague and later to the "neutral" Helsinki.[8]

(At the top of the KGB community it was known that Jean-Paul Sartre was used as an influence agent. The KGB archives are still sealed, but facts about Sartre's cooperation with the KGB have started coming to light. Here is one: In 1967, French terrorist Régis Debray published his first book, *Revolution in the Revolution*, a primer for communist guerrilla insurrection that praised communist terrorist Che Guevara to the skies. Debray dedicated his life to exporting Cuban-style communism to South America, but a few months after he published his book, a Bolivian Special Forces unit trained by the US captured him in Bolivia, together with the whole guerrilla band led by Che Guevara. Che was sentenced to death and executed for terrorism and mass murder. Debray was sentenced to thirty years in jail, but was released after three years following the insistent interventions of Sartre. In the 1980s, Debray served as adviser for Latin America to French president François Mitterrand. After that, Debray committed his life to spreading hatred against the United States. In February 2003, he published "The French Lesson" in the *New York Times,* which described Debray as "a former adviser to President François Mitterrand," but omitted to mention that he had spent years in jail for terrorism and that he was freed because Sartre vouched for him. Debray's article contains every imaginable anti-American cliché.[9] Here is one more attestation to Sartre's connection with the KGB: On June 15, 1972, the West German police captured one of Sartre's favorite pupils, German terrorist Ulrike Meinhof, who was financed by the KGB. Soon after that, she sent a letter to her ideological master, Sartre, asking him for moral support. Sartre complied. When he went to the Stammheim prison in West Germany to encourage her, Sartre was chauffeured by German terrorist Hans-Joachim Klein, a KGB agent and Carlos the Jackal's deputy for the 1975 OPEC terrorist attack in Vienna.[10])

It is no wonder that the World Peace Council was expelled from France. Behind its supposedly French façade, it was as purely Soviet as could be. Its daily business was conducted by a Soviet-style Secretariat, whose twenty-one members were undercover foreign intelligence officers from nine Soviet bloc countries (USSR, Poland, Bulgaria, Hungary, Romania, Czechoslovakia, East Germany, Albania, and Cuba). The World Peace Council also had twenty-three Soviet-style vice presidents, all communists, who were divided as follows: four represented communist countries (USSR, Poland, East Germany, and Romania); three represented communist governments loyal to Moscow (Cuba, North Vietnam, and Angola); two represented the Palestine Liberation Organization (PLO) and the African National Congress (ANC), both anti-American terrorist organizations sponsored by Moscow; four represented nonruling communist parties (United States, France, Italy, Argentina); and ten represented national-level WPC affiliates in the Soviet bloc and other Soviet puppet countries. Most of the WPC's permanent employees were undercover Soviet bloc intelligence officers specializing in "peace operations," whose task was to shape the new Western peace movements into "fifth columns" for the "socialist camp." The World Peace Council had Moscow-financed branches in 112 countries. It also put out two publications in French, *Nouvelles perspectives* and *Courier de la Paix*, which were managed by KGB—and DIE—undercover officers and controlled by the Soviet— and Romanian—disinformation service.

Even the money for the WPC budget came from Moscow, delivered by Soviet intelligence officers in the form of laundered American dollars to hide its Soviet origin. (In 1989, when the Soviet Union was on the verge of collapse, the WPC publicly admitted that 90 percent of its money came from the KGB.[11])

Over the years, Moscow created numerous international Potemkin villages in every imaginable element of Western Europe. Today, few Europeans are willing to admit they were ever influenced by these efforts to demonize the United States as a Zionist country and drive a wedge between Jews and Christians. By the mid 1950s, however, some 30 million people in Western Europe were voting the anti-American Communist ticket (35 percent of the population in Italy and 20-25 percent in France, Portugal, and Greece). That was a remarkable success for the Soviet bloc *disinformation*, considering that the United States had liberated Western Europe from Nazi occupation and rebuilt its war-decimated economies.

After the Soviet Union collapsed, most of the international "Potemkin villages" built by the Kremlin survived and continued carrying out the same anti-American messages as during their heyday. The World Peace Council moved from Helsinki to Athens, Greece, but it was still headed by its KGB-selected chairman Romesh Chandra, an Indian communist who in the 1970s required all WPC national branches to initiate demonstrations against the American war in Vietnam. After 1991, when the United States remained the only superpower, Chandra focused his WPC on "waging a struggle against the New World Order."[12] According to its current charter, the WPC has now "broadened into a worldwide mass movement" whose task is to support "those people and liberation movements" fighting "against imperialism."[13] That "imperialism," of course, really means the United States.

On December 14, 2002, Chandra convened a meeting of his Soviet-style Executive Committee, which thereupon strongly "condemned the extremely dangerous escalation of US aggressiveness on the global level." An international appeal in typically execrable Soviet-style language issued by the Soviet-style WPC Secretariat on the same day called upon "the people of the world" to organize "unprecedented mobilizations" against "American imperialism."

The World Federation of Trade Unions (WFTU), the second largest of KGB "Potemkin villages," also survived the collapse of the Soviet Union. It is still headquartered in Prague, and it still uses anti-American Cold War rhetoric. During its 14th Congress (New Delhi, March 25-28, 2000), for instance, it demanded "the immediate lifting [of the American] economic blockade against Cuba, Iraq, Iran and Libya."[14]

The Women's International Democratic Federation (WIDF) adopted a new charter during the United Nations' Fourth World Conference on Women in 1995 in Beijing, demanding in typical Cold War oratory that "the women of the world" fight "the globalization" of the "so-called 'market economies,'" which are "a root cause of the increasing feminization of poverty everywhere."[15] On March 8, 2000, the WIDF organized a "World March of Women" in Calcutta to celebrate the Soviet-established International Women's Day.[16]

The International Union of Students (IUOS), headquartered in Prague, now has 152 national unions of students from 114 countries. It continues to propagate hatred for the United States. An international appeal issued during the 2001 "International Students' Day" condemned the United States' "vengeful attacks on Afghanistan that have set back the struggle for stability in the Middle East and served to fuel further racism and intolerance around the world."[17]

While these groups hide their true ties to Moscow, they continually advance ideas and programs that support the Kremlin's causes. They are perfect outlets for continuing disinformation.

6

KREMLIN FRAMINGS

T HERE IS A WIDESPREAD belief that the worst damage from Soviet/
Russian intelligence operations against the West has been the theft
of highly classified secrets, such as the technology for the atom bomb.
Not so. The absolutely worst—and often irreparable—damage done to the
Free World has been caused by the Kremlin's disinformation operations
designed to change the past. The transformation of Stalin from the political
killer who slaughtered more than 20 million innocent people in the Soviet
Union alone into the political god over one-third of the world generated
not only forty years of Cold War, but also the greatest political hoax perpetrated in history: international respect for Marxism and admiration for
murderous communist leaders.

In KGB jargon, changing people's pasts was called "framing," and it was
a highly classified disinformation speciality. Because of those KGB framings,
there are few things more difficult for Russian and Western historians today
than to predict Russia's *past*.

In January 1934, the XVII Soviet Communist Party Congress was hailed
as the "Congress of the Victorious." Who would have predicted that 98 out of
the 139 members of the Central Committee of the Communist Party elected
at that Congress would later be framed as "enemies of the people" and put
to death by the same regime that had praised them? In fact, 1,108 out of the
1,966 delegates to this Congress were framed as "counter-revolutionaries,"

and 848 of them were executed.[1]

Over the following years, millions of other innocent Soviet citizens were framed as traitors and killed, and millions of other Russians took to the streets to condemn those "traitors" and to demand their scalps.[2] After World War II, the Kremlin's black art of framing was exported to the newly created communist countries in Eastern Europe.

Contrary to popular belief, the countries of Eastern Europe did not become proletarian dictatorships because of revolutions carried out by the indigenous communist parties—in 1945, Romania's Communist Party had fewer than fifteen hundred members. The Sovietization of Eastern Europe was accomplished by the Kremlin through subversive *framing* operations that were later stamped with an outwardly political cachet. The leaders of East European democratic parties were not politically purged; they were systematically shot or imprisoned after being framed as Nazi war criminals. That gave the Kremlin reason to stage "popular" demonstrations demanding those parties' abolition. The leading East European figures in industry and agriculture were framed as saboteurs and shot or jailed, so as to provide the local communists with pretexts to nationalize the economy and collectivize agriculture. It was a long and bloody framing process that lasted well over ten years.

The Kremlin's framings can be negative, for demotion, or positive, for promotion; either way, they can literally affect the course of world history. Admirable Westerners have been slandered or "framed" as criminals, and criminally unworthy characters in the Soviet/Russian sphere of influence have been portrayed or "framed" as saints.

During the Stalin era, more than 7 million "uncooperative" Soviet citizens were marked for demotion, framed as Zionist spies or Nazi collaborators, and executed or sent to gulags. The useful ones were framed positively, even glorified. All the initial leaders of the East European countries (Walter Ulbricht in Germany, Klement Gottwald in Czechoslovakia, Georgi Dimitroff in Bulgaria, Mátyás Rákosi in Hungary, and Gheorghe Gheorghiu-Dej in Romania) were absolute nobodies who swore loyalty to the Kremlin's religion, Marxism-Leninism-Stalinism, and they were framed into national heroes by the Soviet *dezinformatsiya* machinery.

Once installed on their countries' thrones, those empty suits adopted the Kremlin's framing practice as their own. On August 23, 1944, Romania's heroic King Michael led an audacious coup d'état that overthrew the pro-Nazi government, ending the country's alliance with Germany. He then had Romania join forces with the Allies against Hitler. In 1945 the king was decorated by President Harry Truman, whose decoration decree stated that King Michael had "single-handedly pulled Romania out of the war" although he "had no control over the country which was allied with the German aggressor."[3] The king's action had been so courageous and unique that he had become the only other foreigner besides the American general Dwight Eisenhower to be decorated with the Soviet Order of Victory.[4] On July 21, 1945, fifteen days after the Presidium of the Supreme Soviet had decorated the king, Soviet marshal Fedor Tolbukin presented King Michael, who was also a pilot, with two sport airplanes as a gift from Stalin and sign of his personal appreciation.[5] The leader of the Romanian Communist Party, Gheorghe Gheorghiu-Dej, just freed from Nazi jail, was shown by the media of those days kneeling before the king and kissing his hand to thank him for his outstanding act of courage. Three years later, the same Gheorghiu-Dej, now installed by Stalin as Romania's ruler, had King Michael framed as a Nazi collaborator and Western spy and expelled him from the country.[6]

Hundreds of thousands of innocent Romanians were framed after that. Romania's Danube–Black Sea Canal trial was one of the most contemptible framing operations of that era. Inspired by Stalin, who had altered the course of the Volga, Gheorghiu-Dej decided to build a navigable canal connecting the Danube with the Black Sea. Dej's plan lay far beyond Romania's engineering capabilities at that time, and several years after the first shovelful of earth had been dug, little had been accomplished. Dej saw that there was no hope of completing the project in the foreseeable future. To extricate himself, he decided to close the construction site and blame the lack of progress on Western sabotage.

On a *Securitate* report showing the difficulties faced by the management of that mastodon project, Dej penciled in his distinctive, violet lead: "The persons named here should be arrested, publicly tried as saboteurs, and executed." The show trial took place in July 1953, accompanied by street demonstrations demanding that the "saboteurs" be publicly hanged. Three people were executed and four sentenced to long terms in jail. Soon afterward, the construction site of the Danube–Black Sea Canal was closed, and for many years the public did indeed believe it had been sabotaged by Western intelligence agents.

The Kremlin's practice of framing political or religious leaders, negatively or positively, has a long history. Imre Nagy, the Hungarian prime minister whom the Kremlin believed to have generated the Hungarian uprising of 1956, was marked for demotion. He was kidnapped from Hungary by a Soviet KGB/Romanian DIE team, framed as a Zionist spy, and hanged.[7] The details I disclosed about that framing, published in 1987 in my book *Red Horizons*, aroused so much interest in communist Hungary, that a year later the book was secretly republished there in an illegal, pocket-size samizdat Hungarian edition (now a highly desired collector's item).

On the other hand, Urho Kaleva Kekkonen, Finland's long-time president and a Soviet agent, was marked for promotion. Kekkonen was built up as a successful political leader by the KGB and its predecessors (which had ghost-written his public speeches for almost twenty years). Kekkonen was manipulated by the Soviets until 1981, when he ended his twenty-five-year term as president of the then Soviet-friendly Finland.[8] Olof Palme, also marked for promotion, was molded into a Swedish prime minister and helped by the KGB to export the Soviet welfare state to Western Europe.

Herbert Wehner, who became a member of the West German cabinet in charge of "all-German affairs" (meaning relations with East Germany), was an apprentice clerk before joining the German Communist Party in 1927 and defecting to the Soviet Union. There he was molded into a Social Democratic political leader by the Soviet political police, which later fabricated a background for him showing that he had spent World War II in Sweden— not in the Soviet Union, as was the truth. In 1946, Stalin dispatched Wehner to West Germany via Sweden. Wehner's invented biography as an anti-Nazi and anticommunist militant—a Soviet fabrication—helped him become deputy chairman of the *Sozialdemokratische Partei Deutschlands* (SPD) in 1958, to chair the SPD group in the *Bundestag* (1969–1983), and to become a member of the West German government (1969–1983). Wehner remained a top West German politician until his death in 1990.

In 1974, I had my last meeting with Willy Brandt, the chairman of the SPD, who had become West Germany's chancellor and the author of its *Ostpolitik* (an opening toward the East, meaning the Soviet Union and its East German vassal). On that day, Brandt seemed distressed. This was shortly after the arrest of Günter Guillaume, an East German "illegal" officer groomed to ingratiate himself into West German political circles. He ended up becoming Brandt's most trusted friend and adviser and practically ran the country. Guillaume's arrest was shattering, and Brandt admitted to me that he felt betrayed. One month later, Brandt would write to the West German president: "I accept political responsibility for negligence in connection with the Guillaume espionage affair and declare my resignation from the office of federal chancellor."[9]

As a matter of fact, framing KGB illegal officers as Western politicians helped the Kremlin acquire a better understanding of what was going on in some Western countries than it had of affairs in the Soviet Union itself.

The Cold War is over, but the Kremlin's framing operations seem to be still en vogue—and even to be infecting the United States.

7

STALIN'S ENCOUNTER WITH CATHOLICISM

S INCE ANCIENT TIMES, the Kremlin had manipulated religion according to its own interest. Russia's tsars appointed themselves leaders of the Orthodox Church in order to instill domestic obedience. The first Soviet tsar, Vladimir Lenin, killed thousands of priests and closed most of Russia's churches so as to make Marxism-Leninism the country's sole religion.[1] Stalin, who continued that bloody rampage, transformed Lenin's new religion into Marxism-Leninism-Stalinism, and used it to portray himself as a Soviet saint in order to keep his famished, oppressed population quiet. Twenty years after the November 1917 revolution, only five hundred churches remained open in the Soviet Union.[2]

On August 23, 1939, the Kremlin started a war against non-Russian religions as well. On that day, the Soviet foreign minister, Vyacheslav Molotov, and his German equivalent, Joachim von Ribbentrop, met in the Kremlin to sign the infamous Hitler-Stalin Nonaggression Pact. German archive documents state that Stalin was euphoric that day. He told Ribbentrop: "The Soviet government takes this new pact very seriously. I can guarantee, on my word of honor, that the Soviet Union will not betray its partner."[3]

There were many reasons for Stalin's elation. Both he and Hitler believed in the historical need to expand their territorial empires. Stalin called that need "world proletarian revolution." Hitler termed it "*Lebensraum*" (living space). Both based their tyrannies on theft. Hitler stole the wealth of the Jews. Stalin stole the wealth of Russia's Orthodox Church, and of the country's bourgeoisie. Both Stalin and Hitler hated religion, and both replaced God with their own cult.

The secret protocol of the Hitler-Stalin Pact partitioned Poland between the two signatories and gave the Soviets a free hand over Estonia, Latvia, Lithuania, Finland, Bessarabia, and Northern Bukovina. Most of these new countries were Catholic, which in Stalin's mind meant subordinated to a foreign power—the Vatican. That was unacceptable for the man who had become the Soviet Union's only god—at whose order 168,300 Russian Orthodox clergy had been arrested during the purges of 1936–1938 alone, 100,000 of whom had been shot.[4] The Russian Orthodox Church, which had had more than fifty-five thousand parishes in 1914, was now reduced to five hundred.[5]

The many hundreds of Catholic churches in those Baltic States that Hitler had just bartered off to the Soviet Union posed a new threat to Stalin's image as the country's Little Father—as the tsar had been called. Those churches were beholden to another father, Pope Pius XII, and Stalin refused to even consider allowing any rival to interfere with his absolute reign.

Stalin could not dethrone the pope, who was highly praised and out of his reach. But he could wipe the Catholic churches off the face of the map in the new Baltic countries, just as he had done with the Russian Orthodox churches.

Stalin's solution was to dispatch his favorite hangman, Andrey Vyshinsky, to Sovietize the Baltic States and, in the process, to destroy their national Catholic Churches. Vyshinsky was an old NKVD (political police) hand who had worked wonders in the cover position of public prosecutor during Stalin's war against the Russian Orthodox Church and during Stalin's Great Purges of the years 1936 to 1938. Vyshinsky knew what he had to do. More than 7 million people had been sentenced to death and shot during the years he had been Stalin's main prosecutor, just to make sure his boss was Russia's only deity.

Latvia was occupied by the Red Army on June 17, 1940, and the next day Vyshinsky arrived in Riga as Stalin's special envoy. "I accompanied Comrade Vyshinsky when he went to Latvia," General Aleksandr Sakharovsky once boasted to me, "and in 1943 I became Comrade Vyshinsky's deputy for Sovietizing Romania." (In 1951, General Sakharovsky came to Bucharest as chief Soviet adviser for the newly created Securitate, Romania's equivalent of the Soviet political police, thereby becoming my *de facto* boss. In 1956

Sakharovsky went on to become chief of the entire Soviet foreign intelligence service, a position he held for most of the Cold War years. According to Sakharovsky, the Sovietization of Romania, carried out by the same Vyshinsky, was an improved version of the Latvian operation.)

A few days after Vyshinsky arrived in Riga, he forced Kārlis Ulmanis, the Latvian president, to appoint a "people's government" consisting of members who had already been approved by Moscow. In accordance with Vyshinsky's plan, only two members of the new government were communists: the minister of interior and the chief of the national police.

After he succeeded in installing his government, Vyshinsky delivered a speech from the balcony of the Soviet Embassy in Riga, assuring the population that Moscow did not have the slightest intention of including Latvia in the Soviet Union. A couple of days later, however, Vyshinsky ordered his Latvian chief of police to arrest President Ulmanis and the main leaders of Latvia. They were then deported to the Soviet Union with the help of security police Vishinsky had brought with him to Riga. He forced the new "people's government" to schedule parliamentary elections in two weeks, and he set up a "Working People's Bloc" (controlled by undercover Soviet security police officers) to run the elections—with a single list of candidates.

Vyshynsky's elections took place on July 14–15, 1940. There was no secret ballot. Only the tabulation of the votes was secret; it was conducted by the Ministry of Interior, headed by one of Vyshinsky's men. The results claimed that 97.8 percent of the votes were for the (unknown) Bloc candidates. Soon after that, the newly born Latvian Communist Party launched the slogan "Soviet Latvia." Speaking again from the balcony of the Soviet Embassy, Vyshinsky expressed his hope that the newly elected "people's parliament" would realize the wish implied in that slogan. Of course, that is exactly what happened.

On July 21, 1940, Vyshinsky's parliament proclaimed Latvia a Soviet republic, and two weeks later Moscow's Supreme Soviet incorporated it into the Soviet Union. It did not take long for Latvia's Catholic priests to be sent to Soviet gulags and for their churches to be closed.

Soon after that, Vyshinsky integrated Estonia and Lithuania into the Soviet Union in the same manner. The entire Catholic hierarchy and about a third of the Catholic population of those two small countries was either deported or shot.[6]

8

THE KREMLIN'S NEW ENEMY

WHILE VYSHINSKY WAS DEMOLISHING the Catholic churches in Latvia, Estonia, and Lithuania, Stalin learned that Hitler intended to sign a Tripartite Pact with Italy and Japan. In September 1940, Stalin sent his spy chief, Vladimir Dekanozov—a trusted fellow Georgian covered as deputy minister of foreign affairs—to Berlin. There, during a walk in the woods, he gave Ribbentrop to understand that Stalin was ready to join the Axis. On November 12, 1940, Stalin sent his closest collaborator, Prime Minister Vyacheslav Molotov, to Berlin to finalize the details of his future cooperation with the Berlin-Rome-Tokyo Axis.

Stalin believed those talks were successful, and on November 20 he appointed his spy chief as Soviet ambassador to Germany. Dekanozov presented his letters of accreditation to Hitler on December 19, 1940, without knowing that on the previous day the *Führer* had approved Operation Barbarossa for the invasion of the Soviet Union, and that he had ordered his troops to be ready by May 15, 1941.

A few weeks later, Stalin scribbled on an intelligence report predicting that Hitler would attack the Soviet Union in June 1941:

You can send your 'source' to his f*cking mother. This is a *dezinformator*.[1]

On June 22, 1941, Hitler did indeed betray his nonaggression pact with Stalin when he invaded the Soviet Union, seeking *Lebensraum* for the German people.[2] For the first few weeks, the Nazis met no organized resistance from the Red Army. The Russians paid a heavy price for Stalin's love affair with Hitler. Ten million military men and fourteen million civilians were killed. Five million more were taken prisoner by the Nazis.

On December 7, 1941, while Hitler's armies were at Moscow's gates, Japan suddenly pushed the United States into the war by attacking the American naval base at Pearl Harbor. That attack saved Stalin's skin and gave him a new lease on life. On the following day, President Roosevelt told a joint session of Congress that December 7 was "a date which will live in infamy."[3] He requested a declaration of the existence of a state of war between Japan and the United States, and Congress voted in favor of the declaration.

Soon thereafter, the United States began supplying huge quantities of military hardware to the Soviet Union to help Stalin demolish a substantial part of Hitler's military machine. It worked.

On April 20, 1945, the Red Army reached the outskirts of Berlin, and ten days later Hitler committed suicide. (The Nazi propaganda machine announced that he had died fighting with his last breath for Germany and against Bolshevism.[4]) On May 8, 1945, Nazi Germany capitulated to the Allies, which now included the Soviet Union. Once denied diplomatic relations with most of the Free World, Stalin now joined the exclusive victors' club. He was nominated for the Nobel Peace Prize[5] and was ready to take on the world.

However, there was one more enemy Stalin wanted to defeat: the Ukrainian Catholic Church, the last Vatican enclave in the Soviet Union. The very prominent archbishop of Lvov, Josyf Slipi, and most of Ukraine's bishops, including Gregory Chomysyn, Jown Layesvki, Nicolas Carnecki, and Josaphat Kocylovsky, were framed by Stalin's political police as "Nazi collaborators." All were sent to jail or slave-labor camps. Some five hundred Ukrainian Catholic priests were sent, without trial, to gulags—officially phrased as "destination unknown for political reasons."[6] Bishop Niceta Budka was sent to a Siberian gulag—where he perished in December 1945. Hundreds of other leaders of the Ukrainian Catholic Church were also framed as Nazi collaborators.[7]

Pius XII answered by issuing an encyclical (*Orientales Omnes Ecclesiae*)[8] to the faithful in Ukraine—and indirectly to those in the Baltic States— assuring them that "God will do justice," and that "in His loving kindness He will Himself calm this terrible storm and finally bring it to an end."[9]

Stalin took Pius XII's encyclical as a declaration of war, and he answered as was his wont: six Ukrainian bishops were immediately framed as Nazi collaborators and murdered.[10] Now was the moment for Stalin to open an *ad hominem* offensive against Pius XII himself.

In those days, Stalin's most effective way to slander people was to accuse them of being pro-Nazi—a treasonous offense in World War II. In 1945, Stalin created an intelligence unit that specialized in framing people as Nazi collaborators—SMERSH. Stalin himself had a hand in coining its name. It was from the Russian words meaning "death to spies" (*smert shpionam*). Stalin subordinated the unit directly to himself. Its thugs soon became adept at the mass framing of people as Nazis, forcing them to confess and removing them from the scene by arrest, trial, imprisonment, or death.

SMERSH started out by slandering as Nazi collaborators hundreds of thousands of Soviet citizens living in areas of the Soviet Union that had been occupied by the German Army, as well as almost all of the more than 2 million repatriated Soviet soldiers who had been taken prisoner by the German *Wehrmacht*.[11]

In June 1945, the US ambassador in Moscow, Averell Harriman, reported to the State Department: "The Embassy knows of only a single instance in which a repatriated prisoner has returned to his home and family in Moscow."[12] Washington would later learn that SMERSH had framed most of those repatriates as Nazi collaborators and sent them to Soviet gulags above the Arctic Circle, where many died.[13]

Stalin's SMERSH used the same strategy to discredit Bulgaria's pro-Western leaders in order to replace them with Moscow's men. Although Bulgaria never declared war against the Allies and had been one of only three European countries (along with Finland and Denmark) that had saved their entire Jewish population,[14] Andrey Vyshinsky, whom Stalin charged to Sovietize Bulgaria, nevertheless tasked SMERSH with portraying most of the country's leaders as Nazi war criminals.

Thus, on February 2, 1945, Vyshinsky and his SMERSH unit for Bulgaria executed three regents, 22 ministers, 68 members of parliament, and 8 advisers to King Boris, after framing them as Nazi war criminals. During the following months, another 2,680 members of Bulgaria's government were executed by the Soviet security forces as Nazi war criminals, and 6,870 were imprisoned, even though most of those leaders had been instrumental in bringing Bulgaria over to the Allied side. The United States, which had helped Bulgaria stay out of the war, was momentarily nonplussed, and Moscow leapt at the chance to install its own puppet regime. That was the beginning of the end for a democratic Balkan area—for a long while.

Now Stalin and his SMERSH were ready to declare war on the Vatican itself. It was a war the communist tyrant had to win. After all, Pope Pius was the single highest-profile Christian leader in the entire world, and atheistic communism's very existence and expansion required that it discredit and demonize its chief competitor—the Christian faith.

The next section of this book (Part II) unfolds one of the most consequential and dastardly disinformation campaigns of the entire Cold War era, the framing of a much-loved, anticommunist and anti-Nazi pope—one who not only opposed Hitler and defended Jews, but even personally sheltered Jews from persecution—into a supposed "Nazi collaborator." Readers should prepare themselves for an in-depth, guided tour of a sophisticated, complicated, long-term, multifaceted campaign of pure lies and smears. That is the nature of disinformation.

PART II

ANATOMY OF A DISINFORMATION CAMPAIGN:

THE CREATION OF "HITLER'S POPE"

9

THE FAILED BIRTH OF "HITLER'S POPE"

T HE WAR BETWEEN COMMUNISM and the Catholic Church is almost as old as communism itself. In 1846, two years before Karl Marx published his *Communist Manifesto*, Pope Pius IX referred to "that infamous doctrine of so-called Communism which is absolutely contrary to the Natural Law" and which "would utterly destroy the rights, property and possessions of all men." After World War II, as the Soviet Union spread its communistic doctrine into new territories, the battle became fiercer.

On June 3, 1945, Radio Moscow proclaimed that the leader of the Catholic Church, Pope Pius XII, had been "Hitler's Pope," mendaciously insinuating that he had been an ally of the Nazis during World War II.[1] This was the first salvo of a calculated SMERSH operation designed to smear the reigning pope in the eyes of the world.

Radio Moscow's insinuation fell flat as a pancake. Just the day before, on June 2, 1945, in an allocution to the Sacred College which was broadcast on Vatican Radio, Pius XII spoke of the "satanic specter of Nazism" and noted that his predecessor, Pius XI, called it what it really was: "the arrogant apostasy from Jesus Christ, the denial of His doctrine and of His work of redemption, the cult of violence, the idolatry of race and blood, the overthrow of human liberty and dignity."[2] As for his own efforts, Pius XII explained:

Continuing the work of Our Predecessor, We never ceased during the war to oppose Nazi doctrine and practice the unshakable laws of humanity and Christian faith. This was for Us the most suitable, We may even say the only effective, way of proclaiming in the sight of the world the unchanging principles of the moral law among so much error and violence, to confirm the minds and hearts of German Catholics in the higher ideals of truth and justice. Nor was it without effect. We know in fact that Our broadcasts, especially that of Christmas 1942, were in spite of every prohibition and obstacle studied by diocesan conferences and expounded to the people.[3]

Pius also noted the death of about two thousand Catholic priests at Dachau. The wartime pontiff did not vary in his approach to the Nazis, regardless of whether the victims were Catholic priests or Jewish peasants.

The June 1944 edition of a bulletin put out by the "Jewish Brigade Group" (US Eighth Army) carried a front-page editorial that completely undermined Radio Moscow's insinuation: "To the everlasting glory of the people of Rome and the Roman Catholic Church we can state that the fate of the Jews was alleviated by their truly Christian offers of assistance and shelter."[4] The Israeli Federation of Labor's daily newspaper, *Davar*, quoted a Jewish Brigade officer shortly after Rome's liberation: "When we entered Rome, the Jewish survivors told us with a voice filled with deep gratitude and respect: 'If we have been rescued, if Jews are still alive in Rome, come with us and thank the pope in the Vatican. For in the Vatican proper, in churches, monasteries and private homes, Jews were kept hidden at his personal orders.'"[5]

Another event that took place just weeks earlier made *Radio Moscow's* insinuation outright ridiculous. On February 13, 1945, the chief rabbi of Rome and his wife, Israel and Emma Zolli, converted to Catholicism during a widely popularized ceremony. Zolli adopted the Christian name Eugenio to honor the man who, according to him, had done so much to protect the Jews during the war: Pope Pius XII, born Eugenio Pacelli. In his 1945 memoir, Zolli explained:

No other hero in history has commanded such an army; an army of priests works in cities and small towns to provide bread for the persecuted and passports for the fugitives. Nuns go into canteens to give hospitality to women refugees. Superiors of convents go out into the night to meet German soldiers who look for victims .... Pius XII is followed by all with the fervor of that charity that fears no death.[6]

It may be hard for someone who was not there, at the heart of the Fascist persecution of the Jews, to understand why Rabbi Zolli took Pius XII's name. Zolli, however, had just witnessed how thousands and thousands of lives within his own Jewish congregation, people he knew and loved, had been saved by Pius XII, and Zolli decided to pay his respects in his own way. He wrote that his conversion was based on a true religious revelation, but he chose the Christian name Eugenio and had the pope act as his sponsor (or godfather) as a way of thanking him for his efforts to protect the Jews during the war.

Radio Moscow's insinuation that Pius XII was "Hitler's Pope" attracted no attention whatsoever in the West, because the pope's heroic support of the Allies and generous aid to the Jews during World War II was still fresh in people's minds. They knew this man too well, based on the word of the highest Western authorities, for the insinuation to take hold.

On August 3, 1944, President Franklin D. Roosevelt wrote to the pontiff:

> I should like ... to take this occasion to express to His Holiness my deeply-felt appreciation of the frequent actions which the Holy See has taken ... to render assistance to the victims of racial and religious persecutions.[7]

On September 6, 1944, Winston Churchill announced: "I have spoken today to the greatest man of our time."[8] Churchill admired Pius XII's "simplicity, sincerity and power."[9] Albert Einstein wrote: "Only the Church protested against the Hitlerian onslaught on liberty. Up till then I had not been interested in the Church, but today I felt a great admiration for the Church, which alone has had the courage to struggle for spiritual truth and moral liberty."[10] The secular magazine *Wisdom* editorialized: "Of all the great figures of our time, none is more universally respected by men of all faiths than Pope Pius XII.[11]

Eugenio Cardinal Pacelli had become Pope Pius XII on March 2, 1939, as the world was on the brink of war. From his first days as pontiff, he unequivocally took the Allies' side against Hitler. One day after his coronation, Pius held a series of meetings with the US ambassador to England, Joseph P. Kennedy (father of the future president). Afterwards, Kennedy wrote to his superiors at the US Department of State indicating that the new pope held a "subconscious prejudice that has arisen from his belief that Nazism and Fascism are pro-pagan, and as pro-pagan, they strike at the roots of religion." Pius was greatly disturbed by the "trend of the times." Nevertheless, Kennedy deemed it prudent for such opinions to be kept private, and he urged the pope to enter into negotiations with the Reich.[12]

During World War II, many Germans were involved in resistance work. One of the most ambitious plans came from the High Command of the German Armed Forces, which in late 1939 began plotting to overthrow Hitler. The reaction by other nations to an anti-Hitler coup was a serious concern. If they were to stage a revolt, the British and French might take military advantage of it, occupy Germany, and mete out harsh justice. The resisters therefore wanted to reach an understanding with the Allies.

There was only one neutral leader who was trusted by the resistance: Pope Pius XII. Noted Protestant minister Dietrich Bonhoeffer was already communicating with the Vatican about his resistance work.[13] The leaders of this planned coup recruited Josef Müller, a lawyer from Munich, to travel to the Vatican to ask the pope to broker a peace agreement.

Although he was concerned about how this would impact the Vatican's neutrality, Pius XII relayed messages between Müller and the British. On several occasions Müller also brought messages concerning military plans and troop movements. Pius forwarded these warnings to the threatened governments.[14] In fact, on February 28, 1940, Pius met with the American ambassador to Italy for forty-five minutes and conveyed much potentially useful military information.[15] As others have noted: "Never in all history had a pope engaged so delicately in a conspiracy to overthrow a tyrant by force."[16]

In May 1940, anti-Hitler Germans sent a message to the Vatican concerning the German plans to invade Holland, Luxembourg, and Belgium.[17] Pius forwarded these messages on to the Allies.[18] Despite the warning, the Allies were unable to capitalize on the information. On May 10, 1940, German troops moved in. On the very night of the invasions, Pius personally drafted three messages of condolence that were then sent, via telegrams, to the Queen of Holland, the King of Belgium, and the Grand Duchess of Luxembourg.[19] They were also printed on the front page of the May 12 issue of the Vatican newspaper.[20] (Most of the 180,000 copies were confiscated shortly after they were delivered to the newsstands; news carriers were savagely beaten.[21])

Mussolini took the telegrams as a serious personal affront. He called the papacy "a disease wasting away the life of Italy," and he promised to rid himself of this "turbulent priest."[22] The editor of the Fascist publication *Regime Facista* wrote in October 1942: "The Church's obstruction of the practical solution of the Jewish problem constitutes a crime against the New Europe."[23]

According to the London *Tablet* of October 24, out of disgust at the number of Jews that were released from Nazi-occupied areas owing to Vatican pressure, the Third Reich circulated 10 million copies of a pamphlet saying that Pius XII inspired a lack of confidence in the Catholic world.[24] The pamphlet argued that earlier popes had not been friendly to Jews, and this "pro-Jewish" pope was the only one who "found it necessary to make interventions on behalf of Jews."[25] Mussolini, too, vented his displeasure over the "anti-dictatorial darts" that appeared in *L'Osservatore Romano*.[26]

Invoking Pius XII's name three times, the American bishops released a profoundly pro-Jewish statement on November 14, 1942. It said:

> Since the murderous assault on Poland, utterly devoid of every semblance of humanity, there has been a premeditated and systematic extermination of the people of this nation. The same satanic technique is being applied to many other peoples. We feel a deep sense of revulsion against the cruel indignities heaped upon Jews in conquered countries and upon defenseless peoples not of our faith . . . . Deeply moved by the arrest and maltreatment of the Jews, we cannot stifle the cry of conscience. In the name of humanity and Christian principles, our voice is raised . . . We cannot too strongly condemn the inhuman treatment to which Jewish people have been subjected in many countries.[27]

Pius sent them a letter thanking them for their collaboration.[28] He also told a Spanish diplomat, "If the Germans win, it will mean the greatest period of persecution that Christians have ever suffered."[29]

In late 1942, Pius sent three letters of support to bishops in Nazi-occupied Poland. The letters were intended to be read by the bishops to the faithful. The bishops all thanked the pontiff, but said they could not publish his words or read them aloud. Bishop Stefan Sapieha of Krakow explained in a letter dated October 28: "It displeases us greatly that we cannot communicate Your Holiness' letters to our faithful, but it would furnish a pretext for further persecution and we have already had victims suspected of communicating with the Holy See."Pius would later cite this experience in a letter to Bishop Konrad von Preysing of Berlin:

> We leave it to the [local] bishops to weigh the circumstances in deciding whether or not to exercise restraint to avoid greater evil. This would be advisable if the danger of retaliatory and coercive measures would be imminent in cases of public statements by the bishop. Here lies one of the reasons We Ourselves restrict Our public statements. The experience We had in 1942 with documents which We released for distribution to the faithful gives justification, as far as We can see, for Our attitude.[30]

In his 1942 Christmas statement, broadcast over *Vatican Radio*, Pius said that the world was "plunged into the gloom of tragic error," and he spoke of the need for mankind to make "a solemn vow never to rest until valiant souls of every people and every nation of the earth arise in their legions, resolved to bring society, and to devote themselves to the services of the human person and of a divinely ennobled human society." He said that mankind owed this vow to "the hundreds of thousands who, through no fault of their own, and *solely because of their nationality or race,* have been *condemned to death or progressive extinction.*"[31] He urged all Catholics to give shelter wherever they could. In making this statement and others during the war, Pius used the Latin word *stirpe,* which means race or nationality, but which had been used for centuries as an explicit reference to Jews.[32]

British records reflect the opinion that "the Pope's condemnation of the treatment of the Jews & the Poles is quite unmistakable, and the message is perhaps more forceful in tone than any of his recent statements."[33] A Christmas Day editorial in the *New York Times* praised Pius XII for his moral leadership:

> This Christmas more than ever he is a lonely voice crying out of the silence of a continent .... In these circumstances, in any circumstances, indeed, no one would expect the Pope to speak as a political leader, or a war leader, or in any other role than that of a preacher ordained to stand above the battle, tied impartially, as he says, to all people and willing to collaborate in any new order which will bring a just peace .... Pope Pius expresses as passionately as any leader on our side the war aims of the struggle for freedom when he says that those who aim at building a new world must fight for free choice of government and religious order.[34]

The pope's Christmas message was not hard for the Axis leaders to decipher. The German ambassador to the Vatican complained that Pius had abandoned any pretense at neutrality and was "clearly speaking on behalf of the Jews."[35] One German report stated:

> In a manner never known before, the Pope has repudiated the National Socialist New European Order . . . . [H]is speech is one long attack on everything we stand for . . . God, he says, regards all people and races as worthy of the same consideration. Here he is clearly speaking on behalf of the Jews . . . he is virtually accusing the German people of injustice toward the Jews, and makes himself the mouthpiece of the Jewish war criminals.[36]

Unfortunately, recognition that their evil actions had been noticed by the pope did not cause the Nazis to change their behavior.

On May 5, 1943, the Vatican secretariat issued a memorandum regarding the horrors being faced by Polish Jews:

> The Jews. A dreadful situation. There were approximately four and a half million of them in Poland before the war; today the estimate is that not even a hundred thousand remain there, including those who have come from other countries under German occupation. In Warsaw a ghetto had been established which contained six hundred and fifty thousand of them; today there would be twenty to twenty-five thousand. Some, naturally, have avoided being placed on the list of names. But there is no doubt that most have been liquidated. The only possible explanation here is that they have died.... There are special death camps near Lublin (Treblinka) and Brest-Litovsk. It is said that by the hundreds they are shut up in chambers where they [are] gassed to death and then transported in tightly sealed cattle trucks with lime on their floors.[37]

On June 2, 1943, in an address to the cardinals that was broadcast on *Vatican Radio* and clandestinely distributed in printed form, the pope expressed in new and clear terms his compassion and affection for the Polish people and predicted the rebirth of Poland. He assured his listeners that he regarded all people with equal good will. He then provided a bit more insight into his thoughts.

[D]o not be surprised, Venerable Brothers and beloved sons, if our soul reacts with particular emotion and pressing concern to the prayers of those who turn to us with anxious pleading eyes, in travail because of their nationality or their race (*stirpe*), before greater catastrophes and ever more acute and serious sorrows, and destined sometimes, even without fault of their own, to exterminating constraints.[38]

The pope warned the cardinals to be cautious about what they said. "Every word we address to the competent authority on this subject, and all our public utterances, have to be carefully weighed and measured by us in the interests of the victims themselves, lest, contrary to our intentions, we make their situation worse and harder to bear."[39]

In June 1943, after Italy's King Victor Emmanuel III arrested Mussolini, Hitler sent his troops into Rome. They took the city after just two days of fighting. Rome's population was swollen to almost double its size by refugees drawn by what they thought was the protection of an open city. Pius had the Vatican secretary of state write to the leaders of all religious orders and ask them to help refugees in any way they could. At first, people could pass freely into Vatican City, but when the Nazis realized the pope was offering shelter to Jews and other refugees, they began checking identification. The Church countered by providing fake identification for people wanting to enter the Vatican. Later still, many people made mad dashes to safety after dark.

All available Church buildings were put to use. One hundred fifty such sanctuaries were opened in Rome alone. "Shelters were improvised everywhere, in lofts, in storage rooms under stairs, hidden behind blind doors or cupboards, subterranean galleries, ancient Roman doors used as escape routes: all this as soon as the alert sounded—according to agreed signs, such as the convent bells—that a Nazi inspection was approaching."[40] Catholic hospitals were ordered to admit as many Jewish patients as possible, even if their ailments were fictitious.[41] Castel Gandolfo, the pope's normal summer home, was used to shelter thousands of refugees. A wartime US intelligence document reported that the "bombardment of Castel Gandolfo resulted in the injury of about 1,000 people and the death of about 300 more. The highness of the figures is due to the fact that the area was crammed with refugees."[42] No one but Pope Pius XII had authority to open his summer home to outsiders. In fact, his personal bedroom was converted to a nursery and birthing area, and about forty babies were born there during the war.[43]

Father Robert Leiber, Pius XII's private secretary and personal confidant during the war said: "The Pope sided very unequivocally with the Jews at the time. He spent his entire private fortune on their behalf.... Pius spent what he inherited himself, as a Pacelli, from his family."[44] Similarly, rescuer John Patrick Carroll-Abbing wrote:

> Never, in those tragic days, could I have foreseen, even in my wildest imaginings, that the man who, more than any other, had tried to alleviate human suffering, had spent himself day by day in his unceasing efforts for peace, would twenty years later be made the scapegoat for men trying to free themselves from their own responsibilities and from the collective guilt that obviously weighs so heavily upon them.[45]

German foreign minister Joachim von Ribbentrop testified at Nuremberg that he had a "whole deskfull of protests" from Rome.[46]

The 1943–1944 *American Jewish Yearbook* reported that Pius XII "took an unequivocal stand against the oppression of Jews throughout Europe." The head of the Italian Jewish Assistance Committee, Dr. Raffael Cantoni, who subsequently became the president of the Union of all Italian Jewish communities, reported: "The Church and the papacy have saved Jews as much and in as far as they could save Christians.... Six millions of my co-religionists have been murdered by the Nazis, but there could have been many more victims, had it not been for the efficacious intervention of Pius XII."[47]

In 1945, the chief rabbi of Romania, Dr. Alexander Safran, expressed the gratitude of the Jewish community for the Vatican's help and support for prisoners in the concentration camps. Grand Rabbi Isaac Herzog of Jerusalem wrote:

> I well know that His Holiness the Pope is opposed from the depths of his noble soul to all persecution and especially to the persecution ... which the Nazis inflict unremittingly on the Jewish people ... I take this opportunity to express ... my sincere thanks as well as my deep appreciation ... of the invaluable help given by the Catholic Church to the Jewish people in its affliction.

Chief Rabbi Herzog of Palestine, who was also father to the future president of Israel, said: "The people of Israel will never forget what his Holiness and his illustrious delegates ... are doing for us unfortunate brothers and sisters in the most tragic hour of our history ... " After the war, Herzog sent "a special blessing" to the pope for "his lifesaving efforts on behalf of the Jews during the Nazi occupation of Italy."

Grand Rabbi Herzog of Jerusalem sent a message expressing thanks for actions taken by Pius XII and the Holy See on behalf of Jewish people. After six months of research at Yad Vashem, Pinchas E. Lapide, the Israeli consul in Italy, wrote:

> The Catholic Church saved more Jewish lives during the war than all other churches, religious institutions and rescue organizations put together. Its record stands in startling contrast to the achievements of the International Red Cross and the Western Democracies ... The Holy See, the nuncios, and the entire Catholic Church saved some 400,000 Jews from certain death.[48]

He eventually increased his estimate to about 860,000 Jews.

The World Jewish Congress also expressed its thanks and donated two million lire (about $20,000) to Vatican charities. The press reported that the gift was given in recognition of the work of the Holy See in rescuing Jews from Fascist and Nazi persecution.[49] Dr. Joseph Nathan, a representative of the Hebrew Commission, expressing thanks for support during the Holocaust, said: "Above all, we acknowledge the Supreme Pontiff and the religious men and women who, executing the directives of the Holy Father, recognized the persecuted as their brothers and, with great abnegation, hastened to help them, disregarding the terrible dangers to which they were exposed."[50]

The National Jewish Welfare Board wrote to Pius: "From the bottom of our hearts we send to you, Holy Father of the Church, the assurance of our unforgotten gratitude for your noble expression of religious brotherhood and love."[51]

The *New York Times* reported that Rome's population grew during Nazi occupation because "in that period under the Pope's direction the Holy See did an exemplary job of sheltering and championing the victims of the Nazi-Fascist regime. I have spoken to dozens of Italians, both Catholics and Jews, who owe their liberty and perhaps their lives to the protection of the church. In some cases anti-Fascists were actually saved from execution through the Pope's intervention."[52] The article went on to explain that "none doubt that the general feeling of the Roman Curia was anti-Fascist and very strongly anti-Nazi." The World Jewish Congress, on December 1, 1944, at its war emergency conference in Atlantic City, sent a telegram of thanks to the Holy See for the protection it gave "under difficult conditions to the persecuted Jews in German-dominated Hungary."[53]

The end of the war saw Pius XII hailed as "the inspired moral prophet of victory,"[54] and he "enjoyed near-universal acclaim for aiding European Jews through diplomatic initiatives, thinly veiled public pronouncements, and, very concretely, an unprecedented continent-wide network of sanctuary."[55] As explained by an author and correspondent who lived in postwar Italy:

> Only by the most strenuous means had Pius XII, an extraordinary being, maintained the prestige of the Church. This tall, frail man with piercing black eyes had for twenty-five years conducted an almost incredibly arduous reign. He had literally thrown open the huge bronze doors of the Vatican and invited people to come to him. No longer was the Vicar of Christ unapproachable ... He had seen to it that for the first time since the fourteenth century foreign cardinals outnumbered Italians in the Sacred College and he had severely condemned racialism, anti-Semitism and totalitarian doctrines.[56]

Stalin lost his 1945 battle against Pius XII, but he was determined to win the war. Stalin believed in Lenin's 1904 book: *One Step Forward Two Steps Back (The Crisis in Our Party).*[57] Pius XII was, evidently, much too big a fish for Stalin's SMERSH to go after at that time. Instead, Stalin decided to focus on framing some of the cardinals whom he had inherited with the new East European satellites. They would be indicted as having been pro-Nazi, of course, as that was what had worked so well before. Stalin was sure the framing of the cardinals would prove valuable later, when the climate would be more propitious for secretly framing Pius XII without revealing the Soviet hand.

It was time for Stalin to call upon Vyshinsky again.

10

CARDINAL STEPINAC

T HE *NEW YORK TIMES* of September 6, 2009, displayed a picture of what it referred to as the "controversial" Cardinal Alojzije Stepinac's new tomb in the Cathedral of the Assumption of the Blessed Virgin Mary in Zagreb, Croatia. Stepinac, however, should never have been considered "controversial." In 1946, he was *framed* as a Nazi collaborator by Stalin's framing machinery. That same year, Louis Breier, a Jewish community leader, organized a protest in New York City to defend the memory of Stepinac. Breier declared:

> This great man was tried as a collaborator of Nazism. We protest against this slander. He has always been a sincere friend of Jews, and was not hiding this even in times of cruel persecutions under the regime of Hitler and his followers. Alongside with Pope Pius XII, Archbishop Stepinac was the greatest protector of persecuted Jews in Europe.[1]

Cardinal Stepinac's framing revealed the organic connection between Nazism and communism, and it proved that Pius XII was absolutely right to fight both. Like Pope Pius XII, Stepinac was a staunch opponent of Nazism *and* communism. Also like Pius XII, he openly defied those oppressive regimes. Both men were hated by Stalin, who ordered that both be framed. The primary difference between them was that Pius XII lived in the Vatican, where Stalin could not touch him physically, while Stepinac lived in a Soviet satellite country, where Stalin could not only frame him but also put him on trial.

Stepinac was framed by Tito's state security service, the UDBA (*Uprava državne bezbednosti*), an organization created by Stalin's political police and in those days run by a Soviet intelligence veteran, Aleksander Rankovic, and his Soviet advisers. They did such a good job that even today many believe that Stepinac was engaged in persecution of the Serbs.

Before and during the trial, Yugoslavian leader Josip (Broz) Tito made a series of public speeches condemning Pope Pius XII as an enemy of "the Yugoslav government," but he did not limit his comments to Stepinac. He asked: "On whose side, however, was the Pope? He was not defending the Yugoslav cause." The official Vatican newspaper *L'Osservatore Romano* explained that, "Tito was echoing the Moscow line."[2]

Years later, I learned from my Yugoslavian counterpart Silvo Gorenc that Stepinac's show trial had been staged by Andrey Vyshinsky, the old intelligence hand who had worked undercover as the public prosecutor during Stalin's purges. Three years after that trial, Vyshinsky became the foreign minister of the Soviet Union.

At the beginning of World War II, the area now known as Croatia was part of Yugoslavia. In March 1941, Yugoslavia formally joined Hitler's Axis. Serbian nationalists seized control of Belgrade, however, and announced that they were siding with the Allies. As a result, Hitler invaded Yugoslavia and gave his support to Croat nationalists who declared an independent Croatia.[3] The new Croat government was led by Ante Pavelić and dominated by his Nazi-like party, the Ustashe.[4] The Ustashe government enacted race laws patterned after those of the Third Reich. Jews, as well as gypsies, Serbs, communists, and dissident Catholic priests were beaten, interned in concentration camps, or murdered. The brutality of the Ustashe shocked even the Nazis.

The leader of the Roman Catholic Church in Croatia was Archbishop Aloysius ("Alojzije" in Croatian) Stepinac. Historians have noted that when the brutality began, the archbishop "almost immediately . . . used his position to speak out against the treatment of Jews and Orthodox Christians."[5] Stepinac rescued hundreds of refugees through direct action, but many more "through his sermons in which he vigorously condemned the implementation of Racial Laws."[6] The French ambassador in Zagreb was convinced that Stepinac's interventions were behind the relaxation of race laws in Croatia.[7]

Stepinac's sermons against the Ustashe abuses were so strong that soon the Church was not permitted to publish them. Catholics and others who were opposed to the regime copied and circulated them in secret, however.[8] Stepinac also provided copies of his sermons, to enable the partisans to broadcast extracts over the radio.[9] On at least one occasion, Stepinac had a copy of his sermon smuggled to Chief Rabbi Freiberger of Croatia.[10] In Italy and other occupied areas, the same was done with Pius XII's radio broadcasts.

In October 1941, the Ustashe destroyed the main synagogue in Zagreb. Shortly thereafter, at the cathedral, Stepinac roared: "A House of God, of whatever religion, is a holy place. Whoever touches such a place will pay with his life. An attack on a House of God of any religion constitutes an attack on all religious communities."[11]

In February 1942, Stepinac protested to the Interior minister about the destruction of Orthodox churches.[12] The *Associated Press* reported that, "by 1942 Stepinac had become a harsh critic" of the Ustashe, condemning its "genocidal policies, which killed tens of thousands of Serbs, Jews, Gypsies and Croats."[13] One sermon from October 31, 1943, was typical of many that the archbishop gave on the dignity of all humanity. He said:

> We have always asserted the value in public life of the principles of the eternal law of God without regard to whether it applied to Croats, Serbs, Jews, Bohemians, Catholics, Mohammedans, or Orthodox . . . .The Catholic Church knows nothing of races born to rule and races doomed to slavery. The Catholic Church knows races and nations only as creatures of God... for it the Negro of Central Africa is as much a man as the European. For it the king in a royal palace is, as a man, exactly the same as the lowest pauper or gypsy in his tent . . . . We condemn all injustice; all murder of innocent people; all burning of peaceful villages; all killings, all exploitation of the poor . . . [14]

A German Nazi general in Zagreb declared at the time: "If any bishop in Germany were speaking this way, he would not descend alive from his pulpit!"[15]

Stepinac's contempt for the Nazis is reflected in an incident that took place during the German occupation. Hans Frank, the Nazi official in charge of the occupation, continually hinted that he wanted to be invited to dinner at the archbishop's residence. Presumably, this would help legitimize Frank's position. Finally the invitation came. When Frank sat down to dine with the archbishop, he was served a meager meal of black bread (made in part from acorns), beet jelly, and ersatz coffee. Stepinac calmly explained that this was the only food he could obtain with the ration coupons provided by the Nazis, and he certainly could not risk the arrest of himself or one of his household servants by trading on the black market.[16]

In February 1944, the Chief Rabbi of the Holy Land, Isaac Herzog, sent a letter thanking the apostolic legate in Istanbul, Roncalli, for "all you have done" to save the Jews.[17] He also wrote to Abbot Marcone, the Vatican's representative in Zagreb,[18] to "express how deeply I appreciate all you have done for our unfortunate brothers and sisters," noting that he was following the good example of Pope Pius XII.[19]

In 1944–45, communist partisans under Tito occupied Zagreb. The new Socialist Federation of Yugoslavia became a Soviet satellite. Its Moscow-controlled government nationalized the economy and undertook Soviet-style persecution of the Catholic Church by confiscating property,[20] closing seminaries and schools,[21] banning Masses, and persecuting clergy.

Before coming to power, the communists "used Cardinal Stepinac's speeches in their propaganda, as the cardinal always spoke against the Nazi occupation and against the violation of human rights committed by Pavelić."[22] Now, however, the cardinal was a threat.[23] It "bothered the new regime that the Catholic Church was the only organization outside of its control."[24]

On May 15, 1945, Stepinac's car was confiscated.[25] Two days later, the UDBA arrested him. The archbishop was held for seventeen days. On the day after his release, Tito summoned Stepinac for a face-to-face meeting.[26] The communist leader wanted the Croatian Church to sever its ties with Rome. Tito argued that the Vatican had not treated Slovak nations very well. Stepinac not only corrected Tito on historical facts, he threw down the gauntlet: "I insist upon freedom for all the people. You have given no sign that you intend to respect the Constitution. I am going to resist you on every move in which you disregard the Constitution and the people."[27]

In March 1946, Tito asked the Holy See to recall Stepinac and replace him with another archbishop. When—in accordance with Stepinac's wishes—

Pius XII refused the request, the stage was set for the archbishop's rearrest.

At the beginning of September 1946, Stalin sent Vyshinsky to Zagreb. On September 18, Tito's UDBA arrested Stepinac and charged him with six criminal counts, including: helping to organize Nazi crimes; collaboration with the Nazi puppet Pavelić and his Ustashe; and responsibility for crimes committed by chaplains in the Ustashe army.[28]

Tito used his "justice" system as a "tool for solving political problems."[29] "[T]rials were quick and merciless, without any objectivity."[30] The Evangelical bishop, Zagreb's Mufti, the head of the Croatian Orthodox Church, and others were tried and executed.[31] Even priests who had no connections to the Ustashe were executed.[32]

Stepinac's trial started on September 30, 1946. That day, *Time* magazine reported on the archbishop's defiance:

> Archbishop Stepinac lashed out at the Nazi "master race" idea and condemned the execution of hostages as "inhuman and anti-Christian." He was just as fearless in condemning Communist outrages. In 1945, the Archbishop wrote in a pastoral letter: "The enemies of the Catholic Church ... the followers of the materialistic communism ... have in our Croatia exterminated with fire and sword priests and the more eminent of the faithful .... The number of dead priests is 243; 169 are in prison."[33]

The American press recognized the trial as a fraud.[34] The prosecution had fifteen months of open access to government and church documents in which to prepare its case. Stepinac's lawyers were restricted to a one-hour visit to their client and one week in which to collect evidence for the defense.[35] American Archbishop Joseph Hurley was present as the representative of Pope Pius XII. Stepinac was not, however, permitted to consult with him during the proceedings.[36] Many defense witnesses were not permitted to testify, and much of the defendant's evidence was disallowed. Key prosecution evidence was manufactured. As one author put it:

> The trial was a farce. The testimony of witnesses was falsified in court reports. Witnesses were threatened. Judges delivered long monologues, and provided the "appropriate" answers to their own questions. The courtroom was packed with Communist agitators, whose vocal demonstrations were heavily covered by the government-controlled media; only five Church representatives were allowed to be present.[37]

One hundred fifty priests from Zagreb risked arrest by issuing a statement in support of their archbishop,[38] and Pope Pius XII said: "We have the right and the duty to reject such false accusations." He called it "a very sad trial."[39]

On the fourth day of the proceedings, Stepinac gave a thirty-eight-minute speech. *Time* magazine reported that the archbishop "temporarily lost his equanimity." He "shook an angry finger at the court, and cried: 'Not only does the church in Yugoslavia have no freedom, but in a short while the church will be annihilated.'"[40] He continued:

> For seventeen months a campaign has been waged against me, publicly and in the press; and for twelve months I suffered actual house arrest in the Archbishop's palace . . . . During the war the Church had to find its way through countless difficulties. There was a desire to aid, as much as it was at all possible, the Serbian people . . . . I was *persona non grata* to either the Germans or the Ustashe; I was not an Ustasha, nor did I take their oath as did some of the officials of this court whom I see here. The Croatian nation unanimously declared itself for the Croatian State and I would have been remiss had I not recognized and acknowledged this desire of the Croatian people enslaved by the former Yugoslavia.[41]

Stepinac accused his communist prosecutors of behaving like the Gestapo. He said his conscience was clear. He also said that he was being prosecuted in order for the state to attack the Church. He denied having conducted any religious conversions in bad faith.[42]

Publication of the archbishop's statement or the arguments made by his defense attorneys was prohibited during the entire rule of the communists in the former Yugoslavia. Those who made copies and clandestinely distributed them faced criminal prosecution.[43] A government-sponsored film that appeared in theaters throughout the nation shortly after the trial falsely made it appear that Stepinac offered no defense at all to the charges.[44]

During his trial, the prosecution produced a report allegedly sent by the archbishop to the pope, dated May 18, 1943. It bitterly condemned the Serbs and the Orthodox Church. It also showed Stepinac to have been working for the Ustashe and calling on the pope to arrange for foreign intervention in Yugoslavia.[45]

Stepinac denied having written or sent this report.[46] It was not written on diocesan paper, and it did not have his address or signature. It was in

Italian, instead of the formalized Latin style normally used by the archbishop. It referred to Stepinac as *Metropoleta de Croatiae et Slovoniae*, but Stepinac never referred to himself that way. It contained detailed information about Bosnia that Stepinac was unlikely to know, as Bosnia was not part of his diocese.[47] Although the communists claimed the letter was found in the Croatian Foreign Ministry offices, Stepinac never sent his reports there. The prosecutor, Jakov Blažević, claimed to have a copy signed by Stepinac, but he did not produce it at the trial. Neither does it appear in the record of court documents.[48]

In 1950, a group of American senators sought to allow American aid to Yugoslavia only on the condition of Archbishop Stepinac's release. Realizing the need for better relations with the West after the split with the Soviet Union, and also concerned about the archbishop's declining health, Tito expressed a willingness to release Stepinac from prison if he would leave Yugoslavia.[49] As *Time* magazine explained:

> Marshal Tito, busy mending fences, made a direct offer to the Vatican last month to release imprisoned Archbishop Stepinac. Tito's condition: that Stepinac leave Yugoslavia the moment he is released. Last week the Vatican reported Tito's offer—and its own reply: no bargain. "The Holy See would be pleased if Monsignor Stepinac were freed," said the answer to Tito. "The Holy See is informed, however, that that Most Excellent Prelate, being convinced of his innocence, prefers to remain near his faithful." That seemed to hand Tito's awkward dilemma right back to Tito.[50]

Stepinac explained: "They will never make me leave unless they put me on a plane by force and take me over the frontier. It is my duty in these difficult times to stay with the people."[51]

In December 1951, Tito ordered Stepinac to be released from his cell and sent to house arrest in his native village of Krašić.[52] The Vatican still wanted Tito's regime to acknowledge Stepinac's innocence and to resolve other outstanding issues. Quoting the Vatican newspaper, *Time* magazine reported: "Another bishop, His Excellency Monsignor Peter Cule of Mostar, is still unjustly held . . . Fully two hundred priests and religious are in prison. Seminaries are still held requisitioned, and monasteries and convents are still confiscated . . . Freedom of worship . . . is suffocated."[53]

Immediately after Stepinac's transfer, Pope Pius XII announced that he would be elevated to the cardinalate. In response, Tito's government severed diplomatic relations with the Vatican.[54] Stepinac did not go to Rome to be invested as a Prince of the Church, because he knew that the Yugoslavian government would not permit him to return home. He explained: "To leave Yugoslavia in these times would mean to abandon my post and to abandon my people . . . I shall stay here, if need be, until my death."[55]

Stepinac lived in two rooms in a small house next to a beautiful little church in Krašić. He was able to say Mass and administer the sacraments. He also wrote many letters to priests and others, encouraging them in the faith, though the communists monitored all of his writings and they were subject to confiscation.[56] When a visiting journalist asked him how he felt, the cardinal replied, "Here, the same as in Lepoglava . . . I am doing my duty." When asked what that was, he said: "to suffer and work for the Church."[57]

In 1953, Stepinac refused to go abroad for treatment of a blood-clotting problem. Two American physicians were, however, permitted to come to Yugoslavia to treat him. The disease, polycythemia (sometimes called 'reverse leukemia'), involves an excess of red blood cells.[58] It prompted Stepinac to joke: "I am suffering from an excess of reds."[59]

Stepinac's health grew worse. He developed congested lungs, and he died of a pulmonary embolism on February 10, 1960. Years later, testing conducted by Vatican officials indicated that he had been slowly poisoned.

Time magazine reported that he had "never worn his cardinal's red robe. But no living prince of the Roman Catholic Church had a better right to it than Alojzije Cardinal Stepinac . . . For years, he was a silent but unforgotten symbol of the war between Communism and Christianity."[60]

Pope John XXIII honored Stepinac with a Solemn Requiem Mass in St. Peter's—a ceremony usually reserved for cardinals who have died in Rome. On the basis that Stepinac had been stripped of his archbishopric by the state, Tito decreed that the funeral could take place only in the little church at Krašić.[61] With mounting international pressure, however, he eventually gave permission for a funeral with full honors in Zagreb Cathedral.[62]

In 1985, Stepinac's prosecutor, Jakov Blazevic, acknowledged that Stepinac had been framed and that he was tried only because he refused to sever ties between Croatians and the Roman Catholic Church.[63] Blazevic said that if Stepinac had agreed to head an independent Catholic Church, he would not have been brought to court.[64]

Nearly forty years after the trial, one of Tito's senior legal officials by the name of Hrncevic, who had put together the original case against Stepinac and arranged the trial, stated: "The indictments were designed rather more for publicity than for legality."[65] Yugoslavian political dissident Milovan Djilas, who had once been close to Tito, said that the problem with "Stepinac was not his policy towards Ustashe, but towards the Communists."[66]

In October 1998, after Croatia came out from under communism's thumb, the Church beatified Stepinac.

In framing Stepinac, Stalin and his Yugoslavian viceroys unintentionally created a record that today exposes the methodology of Soviet framing. A study of that record also shows how fabricated evidence designed to frame Stepinac as a pro-Nazi has tainted the investigation of Pope Pius XII's record.

In the 1960s, Italian writer Carlo Falconi wrote *The Silence of Pius XII*, a book entirely based on documents provided to him by the communist government of Croatia—including those used to frame Archbishop Stepinac.[67] In fact, the title of each and every chapter in Falconi's book is related to Croatia.[68]

In his foreword, Falconi explained that the "central core of the Croatian documents" that had been provided to him by the Croatian (communist) government "brought to light an entirely new and unsuspected harvest of revelations on the men and the mysterious world" of high Vatican officials. Falconi's book impressed researchers because it was highly footnoted and relied on documents that had been used in litigation. *The Silence of Pius XII* shaped much of the early scholarship "documenting" that Pius XII was "Hitler's Pope."

We now know that Falconi was not looking at legitimate documents, but at communist fabrications.[69] In 1985, Jakov Blažević, who prosecuted Stepinac, confessed that the documents on which the archbishop was tried were false.[70] In 1992, one of the first acts of Parliament in the newly independent Croatia was to issue a declaration condemning the framing and "the political trial and sentence passed on Cardinal Stepinac in 1946."[71]

Though modern writers should know better, *The Silence of Pius XII*, based on false documents created by Croatian communist government, remains much cited to this day. John Cornwell's *Hitler's Pope*, published in 1999, made much use of it. In fact, Cornwell praised Falconi's "painstaking" research.[72]

Falconi and the works built upon his book have tainted the entire investigation into Pope Pius XII. As Croatian scholar Jure Krišto has explained: "The documents which both men [Falconi and Cornwell] used had, of course, been assembled by the Yugoslav secret police, then led by the Serbian Communist [head of the UDBA] Aleksandar Ranković, and fed to Falconi in order to compromise Pope Pius XII as 'Hitler's Pope.'"[73] These documents have confounded scholars of Pope Pius XII for decades.[74]

In October 2008, on the tenth anniversary of Cardinal Stepinac's beatification, thousands of people gathered to pay their respects to him.[75] For them, the cardinal was a courageous leader, a hero, and a saint. A courageous leader because he went alone to war against Nazism and communism. A hero because he won. And a saint because he sacrificed his life for the religious freedom of his followers.

In the annals of history, Cardinal Stepinac will also go down as a key witness in any future trial seeking to identify the true culprit in the vicious war against Pius XII and the Judeo-Christian world. It is a war that broke out in 1945 and has never ended.

11

CARDINAL MINDSZENTY

ESS THAN TWO YEARS after Croatian Catholic Cardinal Stepinac was framed, Stalin focused on Jószef Cardinal Mindszenty, the Roman Catholic archbishop and primate of Hungary. In the highly classified manual of *dezinformatsiya* that codified my life within the Soviet intelligence community, it was proclaimed on the first page, all in upper case letters: "IF YOU ARE GOOD AT DISINFORMATION, YOU CAN GET AWAY WITH ANYTHING." The KGB manual began with an example illustrating how framing could "neutralize even a saint." The "saint" in question was Mindszenty, called a "saintly hero" by the Vatican because of his epic resistance during his imprisonment by the Nazis (1944–45).

The KGB manual summed up the "Mindszenty case"—with customary Soviet self-importance—as one of "our most stupendous, monumental *dezinformatsiya* operations."[1] The KGB considered framing its enemies an honorable task, and it was proud to boast about a successful operation. Soviet leaders and their political police organizations lived indeed in a world of their own, and they did not fear disclosure of their ways. In reality, it was—for those days—a quite sophisticated attempt to malign the Catholic Church.

On December 26, 1948, Mindszenty was arrested by the AVO (*Allamvedelmi Osztaly*), the Hungarian subsidiary of the Soviet security police. At AVO headquarters in Budapest, Mindszenty was subjected to brutal nightly beatings and urged to sign confessions, which he refused to do. At his trial, held February 3–5, 1949, he was framed with fabricated documents and sentenced to life imprisonment. It was Stepinac revisited.

Two fortuitous circumstances make Mindszenty's case a real eye-opener into how Stalin and his security police went after Pius XII's archbishops and cardinals. The first is that Mindszenty was blessed with being able to survive with a clear head and write a detailed account of everything that had happened to him. His book, *Memoirs*, was published in New York in 1974 and provided devastating insight into the way the AVO slandered him as conspiring to overthrow the communist government and as having made illegal currency transactions. The second and unique event was that László and Hanna Sulner, a Hungarian couple who worked with the AVO to fabricate the documents used in Mindszenty's framing, managed to escape to the West immediately after the trial started and published several accounts of exactly what they had done. Theirs is a fascinating story and sheds new light on how the Kremlin went about framing Pope Pius XII himself, many years later.

Cardinal Mindszenty was born Jószef Pehm in Mindszent, a village in the Austro-Hungarian Empire, on March 29, 1892.[2] His ancestors had all been Hungarians, traceable back for many generations, and his family members were all devout Roman Catholics, as were many Hungarians. He was ordained a priest in 1915 and patriotically adopted the name Mindszenty in 1941 when the Nazis were threatening all of Eastern Europe. In 1944, Pope Pius XII made him a bishop, and on September 16, 1945, the same pope appointed him archbishop of Esztergom and primate of Hungary.

Throughout his life, Mindszenty was an outspoken and politically active defender of humanitarian principles, causing him to be arrested by various dictatorships in the up-and-down of twentieth-century Hungarian politics. His first imprisonment was from February 19 to May 15, 1919, after he publicly attacked Michael Karolyi's revolutionary government, becoming a leader in the newly founded Christian Party and editing a paper critical of the regime.[3] Karolyi's government gave way to Bela Kun's short-lived "Hungarian Soviet Republic" in 1919. The communists continued to see Mindszenty as an opponent, and he was arrested again. After several harrowing days, during which his life hung in the balance, Mindszenty was sent back to live with his parents in his home village.[4]

During most of World War II, Hungary sided with Nazi Germany but remained unoccupied, therefore becoming a refuge for European Jews.

In the spring of 1944, however, the Germans invaded Hungary under the pretext of safeguarding communications. They set up a puppet government in Budapest and immediately issued anti-Jewish laws, insisting that the Jews be confined in ghettos. The Vatican protested vigorously and regularly against the inhumane treatment of the Jews in Hungary, as did all the Hungarian bishops, including Mindszenty.[5]

Catholic churches in Hungary offered conversion to thousands of Jews to save them from persecution and deportation, just as Swedish diplomat Raoul Wallenberg saved many by giving them Swedish passports—until the Nazis caught on and began going after the converts.[6]

From November 1919 (when the Romanian army, with the consent of the Allied powers, ended Bela Kun's "Hungarian Soviet Republic") to October 1944, Hungary was headed by Adm. Nicholas Horthy. With the Nazis in control of Hungary, they began deporting Jews. This led to complaints from Catholic leaders. Horthy complained to the Germans that he was being bombarded with telegrams from the Vatican and others, and that the nuncio was calling on him several times each day.[7] In the face of these protests, Horthy withdrew his support from the deportation process, making it impossible for the Germans to continue. In a cable to Pope Pius XII, Horthy wrote: "It is with comprehension and profound gratitude that I receive your cable and request you to be convinced that I shall do all within my power to make prevail the demands of Christian humanitarian principles."[8]

Horthy agreed to work against the deportations and even signed a peace agreement with the Allies. More than 170,000 Hungarian Jews were saved from deportation on the very eve of their intended departure.[9] The Germans, however, would not be dissuaded.

The Germans arrested Horthy in October, put Hungary under the control of a group of Hungarian Nazis known as the Arrow Cross, and the deportations resumed. On October 31, 1944, the Hungarian bishops, including Mindszenty, protested. That same month, Pius joined in an effort to raise money to support Hungarian refugees, urging all the faithful to redouble their efforts on behalf of all victims of the war, regardless of their race.[10] Almost every Catholic Church in Hungary provided refuge to persecuted Jews during the autumn and winter of 1944.[11]

On November 26, 1944, Mindszenty was again arrested. This time it was for his opposition to the pro-Nazi Arrow Cross government, and he was charged with treason. Fortunately, he avoided trial and was freed when the German troops left on April 4, 1945. The country then came under Soviet occupation.

Remarkably, Mindszenty was able to leave the country on November 30, 1945, and travel to Rome, where on February 21, 1946, he received the cardinal's hat from Pope Pius XII. When he came back to Hungary, Soviet troops were still in the country, and religious and political conditions were as bad as ever. That fall, the local state security service arrested a group of "conspirators" against the communist government. They were tried the following March. The leaders were condemned to death, the others to long prison terms. On October 24, 1947, Mindszenty protested vigorously to the premier.

In May 1948, the communist authorities had no trouble subduing the Hungarian Reformed Church, by the simple expedient of removing the heads of the Church and replacing them with others who were willing to go along with the new regime. The Catholic bishops could not so easily be replaced, since they were appointed by the pope.

Mindszenty continued to protest, as Church schools were closed and religious orders banned by the communist government. Schoolchildren and factory workers were ordered into the streets to demonstrate against him, proclaiming: "We will annihilate Mindszentyism! The well-being of the Hungarian people and peace between Church and state depend on it."[12]

On the morning of November 19, 1948, the police arrested Mindszenty's secretary, Dr. András Zakar, as he was about to enter the archiepiscopal palace in Esztergom and carted him off to the notorious No. 60 Andrássy Street, state security headquarters in Budapest. Mindszenty realized that he himself would soon be arrested. On December 16, he convened a final conference of bishops at the palace. As the bishops left, the police blocked the road, searched each car, and had each passenger identify himself—evidently in the suspicion that the primate would try to escape with the bishops.

Stalin undoubtedly wanted Mindszenty arrested, framed, and "neutralized"—not necessarily killed, because that would make international waves, but removed from the scene for life, perhaps so physically mistreated and mentally addled that he would never again be able to challenge the communist rulers. Since the war, the Soviets' tried-and-true method had been wherever possible to slander their enemies as having been pro-Nazi. The Hungarian primate, however, was widely known as having used his Church to protect Jews, as having publicly denounced the Nazis over and over again, and as having been imprisoned by the Nazis' Hungarian allies, the Arrow Cross. Some other plausible peg would have to be found for the framing.

When the Soviet state security officers and their surrogates in the satellite countries of Eastern Europe were ordered to frame someone—that is, to change his past and the way the public perceived him—the first thing they did was to collect as much information as possible on the target: where he had traveled, who his contacts were, what kind of letters and documents he had written, especially those providing samples of his handwriting and signature.[13] Accordingly, on December 23, 1948, squads of policemen forced their way into Mindszenty's archiepiscopal palace and meticulously rummaged through every room, especially the archives, alleging the search was in connection with the case of Dr. Zakar, the secretary being held under arrest. During the search, Mindszenty, his visiting mother, and three local priests were locked in a small dining room. When the police were finished, they asked him to sign a record of the search. He refused, but took the occasion to protest the arrest of two priests of the archdiocese.

After the search, the chief of the secretariat, Dr. Gyula Mátrai, told Mindszenty that his secretary, Dr. Zakar, had come to the palace with the police and had shown them around. According to Mátrai, Zakar had acted oddly, running down the halls, laughing constantly, and with a strange look on his face and in his eyes. The primate could only suppose that he must have been beaten and drugged into submission and cooperation. Mátrai also reported that in the archives the police had shown particular interest in a collection of metal cylinders. These were of various lengths and diameters and were used to safeguard valuable archdiocesan papers, such as property deeds and blueprints, and to protect them from dust and decay. The police took one empty cylinder with them. Later, at the trial, they would allege that Zakar had revealed its special hiding place to them, and they would produce its supposedly incriminating contents.

On the night of December 26, 1948, a large police squadron noisily drove up to the palace. Colonel Décsi of the security police, followed by eight or ten of his men, burst into Mindszenty's apartment, found him kneeling in prayer, and ordered him to come with them. When he asked to see a warrant for his arrest, one policeman scoffed that they did not need one, bragging that they could find traitors, spies, and currency smugglers even when they wore a cardinal's robes.

For the next thirty-nine days, Mindszenty was imprisoned and interrogated at 60 Andrassy Street. There the guards—laughing loudly, telling dirty jokes, and smoking in his unventilated room—stripped him of his clothing and gave him only what he called a harlequin "clown suit" to wear. Every day the colonel interrogated him and insisted he sign "confessions," which he refused to do. Every night, a major would beat his naked body with a rubber truncheon until he collapsed, but the guards prodded him so that he could not even sleep. They also urged him to eat, claiming they would order whatever he wanted from a restaurant. Knowing that prisoners were usually drugged, he at first refused all food, but then in his starved state he succumbed to consuming a little bread or clear broth. A team of three silent doctors examined him before every meal and left pills for him to take. He tried to crush the pills into the uneaten food, or make them stick to the roof of his mouth and later hide the crumbs in his shoe. After two weeks, he grew weaker (and, as he later realized, probably did get blurry-minded from drugs present even in the clear broth), and he agreed to sign the minutes of his previous interrogations, although he was later sure he had never signed any "confession of guilt in the sense of an indictment."

From the beginning, Colonel Décsi told the archbishop exactly what confessions were required from him. The charges boiled down to Mindszenty's allegedly treasonous contacts with the American Embassy in Budapest and with Otto von Hapsburg, in connection with a plot to stir up a Third World War. Supposedly Mindszenty had orchestrated the theft of Hungary's crown jewels, and he planned to overthrow the communist government, draw up a cabinet for the future kingdom of Hungary, and then bring the ancient Crown of Saint Stephen to Budapest in order to crown Otto von Hapsburg as king.

This may sound like the plot for an overblown historical novel, but it is what the Hungarian security police came up with after digging through all those files they had collected from the palace archives—not to forget that metal cylinder, which would become a tangible exhibit at Mindszenty's trial.

The Soviet disinformation experts always said a good framing operation had to be built up around a "kernel of truth," and here it was. The security police knew that Mindszenty had met with Otto von Hapsburg in the United States in the summer of 1947. In fact, the cardinal had attended a Marian Congress in Ottawa that year, and he agreed to meet afterwards with the

Hapsburg heir, at the latter's request, in Chicago. Mindszenty asked him for help in obtaining and transporting charitable gifts from Americans to the Hungarian Church. In that same connection he had also been in touch with Cardinal Spellman, the archbishop of New York, and with the American Embassy in Budapest. Mindszenty had also written many letters—obviously now in the hands of the police—expressing his wish that the Holy Crown be returned for safekeeping to Rome and entrusted to the care of Pius XII, during the current "difficult period of tribulations and vicissitudes."

On the evening of February 2, 1949, Mindszenty was dressed in a new black suit and escorted to the building of the Budapest People's Court by a large detachment of police, headed by Colonel Décsi and Lt. Gen. Gábor Péter, an undercover Soviet security police officer who was the chief of Hungary's AVO. The next morning a barber came to make the cardinal presentable. He put on his black suit again and set out for the courtroom, accompanied by six other "conspirators." Later, four were treated as irrelevant, and only three were allegedly in on the conspiracy: the cardinal-primate, his secretary, and "a monk whose health had been shattered."

The show trial was conducted from February 3–8, 1949. Mindszenty reportedly confessed to the crimes he was accused of, agreeing that he had written the letters supposedly found in the cylinder that discussed plotting to overthrow the government. In his book, he wrote that he was so physically and mentally exhausted that he scarcely knew what he was saying. All the defendants were found guilty. He was sentenced to life imprisonment.

On February 12, 1949, Pope Pius XII condemned the jailing of the cardinal and excommunicated everyone involved in his trial and conviction.

On February 6, before the trial was even over, handwriting experts Lázlo and Hanna Sulner escaped to Austria and began telling their story to the press. They denounced the trial as a farce, displaying microfilms of the *fabricated* documents they had produced for the Hungarian security police in order to frame Mindszenty.[14] They attested that several months before the search of the archiepiscopal palace, they had been given copies of the documents allegedly found in the metal cylinder produced at the trial, with instructions to "edit" them. These actually were copies of letters and memoranda that the cardinal had ordered to be destroyed so as not to involve others after his anticipated arrest; a typist in the cardinal's secretariat had been intimidated into providing the materials to the police.[15]

Even more interesting is the Sulners' description of how they operated. Hanna's father had been a pioneer in handwriting analysis and an authority on questionable documents. Hanna studied criminology and took over her father's business after his death, later to be joined by Lázlo, who became her husband. Hanna's father had invented a device that took words and phrases from manuscripts and put them together as desired to form a new manuscript, and Lázlo developed this technique to such perfection that even experts could not detect the forgery.[16]

The Sulners and their device came to the attention of the Hungarian secret police in September 1948, when they showed Lázlo a list of cabinet members Mindszenty was allegedly going to appoint after the overthrow of the government. Lázlo immediately dubbed it a forgery and produced a better list, which was later amended and used as evidence at the trial.

On January 4, 1949, Lázlo was asked to produce a confession by Mindszenty in accordance with the typewritten draft the police provided. The Sulners were also asked to forge other documents, signatures, and marginal notations for the case. When they did not work quickly enough for the police, they and their entire apparatus were moved to police headquarters. A steady flow of documents resulted, some of which were produced by ignorant, inexperienced police officers and resulted in what Mindszenty described as "outlandish form and spelling, such as my confession."[17] The Soviet security police would have immediately learned from their Hungarian counterpart about the Sulners' virtually foolproof technique for fabricating documents. As a result, it is clear why disinformation and framing experts in any of the Soviet bloc intelligence services were insatiable in their efforts to collect as many original documents as possible on a target.

At the time that I was involved in the Soviet operation against Pius XII that will be discussed later in this book, I could not understand why the Soviets kept asking him for more and more essentially uninteresting documents from Vatican files. It is now apparent that they were looking for a little "kernel of truth" of the Otto von Hapsburg kind, or they may have been seeking words and signatures that could be perfectly duplicated by the Sulner technique to produce an entirely different "original."

During the Hungarian uprising of 1956, Cardinal Mindszenty was set free, but his freedom lasted for only a short while. Soon the communists regained control of the government, and he sought asylum in the US

Embassy in Budapest, where he lived for the next fifteen years. On September 23, 1971, under Vatican pressure, the government of Hungary allowed Mindszenty to leave the country. He moved to Vienna, but continued his primacy of the Hungarian Catholic Church until December 1973, when, at the age of eighty-two, he was replaced. He died in Vienna on May 6, 1975. In 1991, as soon as Hungarian communism collapsed, in accordance with his wishes, his remains were expatriated to Esztergom by the democratically elected government in Budapest.

Mindszenty's life and his battle against the Kremlin's framing were the subject of the 1950 film *Guilty of Treason,* which author and historian Steve O'Brien called "an extraordinary time capsule from the start of the Cold War," that "illustrated how the Communists were out to besmirch the Vatican's high churchmen."[18] In 1955, a slightly fictionalized version of the Mindszenty case was the subject of another movie, *The Prisoner,* starring Alec Guinness. That film opened with the cardinal's arrest and with his *real* statement that any reported confession would be "a lie or the result of human weaknesses."[19]

The Mindszenty Museum in Esztergom, which opened after communism collapsed, is another monument to Mindszenty's life and to the Kremlin's criminal framing of him,[20] as is the Mindszenty Foundation in St. Louis, Missouri.

12

MORE FRAMINGS

ARDINALS MINDSZENTY AND STEPINAC were not Stalin's only high-ranking Catholic victims outside of the inscrutable Soviet Union. Several other cardinals in Eastern Europe also suffered. Josef Cardinal Beran of Czechoslovakia was one of them. Arrested by the Gestapo on June 6, 1940, Beran, at that time a bishop, was imprisoned in Pankrác, Theresienstadt, and at the Dachau concentration camp. After the war, he was appointed archbishop of Prague and primate of the Church in Czechoslovakia. When the communists took over in 1948, Beran prohibited his clergy from taking an oath of loyalty to the new regime, calling it "treason to the Christian faith." He also protested the new regime's seizure of Church property and the infringement of religious liberty.

In June 1949, the newly created Czechoslovakian political police arrested Beran and convicted him in a show trial. He was reimprisoned from 1949 to 1963. Even upon his release, Beran was impeded from exercising his episcopal ministry. He repeatedly offered his resignation to the pope, but it was always refused. In 1965, Beran moved to Rome in exchange for governmental concessions to the Church. Pope Paul VI made him a cardinal that same month.[1]

Stefan Cardinal Wyszyński of Poland was another of the Kremlin's victims.[2] When the Second World War broke out in 1939, Wyszyński served as chaplain of a unit of the *Armia Krajowa,* a Polish anti-Nazi underground resistance organization. This caused him frequently to be a target for the

Germans. After the war, Pius XII appointed him Bishop of Lublin. After the death of Cardinal Hlond in October 1948, Wyszyński was named metropolitan archbishop of Gniezno and Warsaw.

The new communist government in Poland was hard on the Catholic Church. The conflict increased following Pope Pius XII's 1950–1955 decrees against communism (discussed further in the next chapter). The Kremlin and its Polish viceroys unleashed a new round of persecution against the Polish clergy. Numerous priests were arrested and accused of collaborating with "reactionary underground movements."[3]

Wyszyński tried to reach a working agreement with the regime in 1950, but it did not hold. Pope Pius XII appointed him cardinal and primate of Poland on January 12, 1953,[4] but his persecution continued. Wyszyński was arrested on September 25, 1953. He was quickly imprisoned (eventually moving to house arrest).[5] At the beginning of 1954, there were nine Catholic bishops and several hundred priests in Polish prisons.[6]

Wyszyński was incarcerated for a little over three years. In 1956, when the short-lived Hungarian Revolution was ignited, Poles organized street demonstrations demanding religious freedom and Wyszyński's release.[7] The Catholic clergy joined in the call for his freedom. On October 28, 1956, Wyszyński was set free, and he returned to his post. Within two years, however, the communist propaganda machine again went after him with enough personal attacks that his cause drew the attention of the Western media.[8]

In 1966, Wyszyński oversaw the celebration of Poland's Millennium of Christianity, the one thousandth anniversary of the baptism of Poland's Prince Mieszko I. The communist authorities refused to allow Pope Paul VI to visit Poland. They also prevented Wyszyński from attending overseas celebrations. In the 1970s, however, Wyszyński gave his support to the growing Solidarity movement. Pope John Paul II was elected in 1978, and the communist officials could not prevent *his* papal trip. That 1979 visit sparked a revolution that led to the eventual downfall of the Soviet bloc.

Cardinal Wyszyński died on May 28, 1981, at age seventy-nine. To commemorate the twentieth anniversary of his death, the postcommunist Polish government celebrated 2001 as the Year of Stefan Cardinal Wyszyński, who also became known as the Primate of the Millennium.

The Ukrainian Greek Catholic Church (UGCC), which had been in communion with the Holy See since the Union of Brest in 1595–96, was in tension with the Russian Orthodox Church, especially after the communists took power. The conflict was largely overlooked during the Second World War, because the churches had the same negative opinion of the Nazis. Unfortunately, the conflict reemerged when the war came to an end.

On April 11, 1945, the Ukrainian Catholic bishops were arrested, including Archbishop Josyf Slipyj. From 1920 to 1922, Slipyj had studied at the Pontifical Oriental Institute in Rome and the Pontifical Gregorian University. In 1939, with the blessing of Pope Pius XII, Slipyj was ordained as the archbishop of Lviv. He became the head of the UGCC in 1944. Now, along with the other bishops, he was accused of collaboration with the Nazis and sentenced to forced labor in the Siberian Gulag.

In response, Pius XII issued his encyclical *Orientales Omnes* of December 23, 1945. In it, the pope not only condemned communism; he openly and specifically attacked Moscow Patriarch Alexis. The situation got worse March 8–10, 1946, when Soviet authorities forcibly convened an assembly of 216 priests, and the so-called Synod of Lviv was held at which the Ukrainian Greek Catholic Church was forcibly "rejoined" to the Russian Orthodox Church and forced to revoke its union with Rome. The UGCC first became a "Church of Silence," then a "Church of Martyrs," as many Ukrainian Catholics who were interned by the communists were tortured and/or murdered.

Archbishop Slipyj was the heart and soul of the underground Ukrainian Catholic Church, even though he was imprisoned in the Siberian Gulag. News of his courageous witness spread, especially after some of his prison writings were released into circulation. In 1957, Pius XII sent him a congratulatory letter on the fortieth anniversary of his ordination to the priesthood, which of course the communist authorities confiscated. In light of it and of Slipyj's own writings, they cracked down even harder and added seven years to his sentence.

Stalin's death in 1953 did not make it easier on Slipyj or the UGCC. Soviet Premier Nikita Khrushchev was just as hard on religion as his predecessor had been. A fortunate combination of events, however, led to Slipyj's release.

In October 1962, Pope John XXIII opened the Second Vatican Council, and with it a new approach toward the world ("aggiornamento"). This included searching new avenues to ease the suffering of Christians under communist rule, while at the same time being sure not to withdraw any of the Church's warnings about Marxist-Leninist ideology. The new approach was described by Msgr. Igino Cardinale, chief of protocol at the Secretariat of the Holy See, as being "ready to engage in relations with any state," as long as there was a reliable assurance that "freedom for the church and the sanctity of the moral and spiritual interests of its citizens" were respected.

Just a few days after Vatican II opened, the Cuban Missile Crisis broke out. President Kennedy, a Catholic himself, sought help from the Vatican. He contacted the author Norman Cousins, who in turn contacted the Holy See. On October 24, 1962, John XXIII issued a dramatic appeal to the relevant leaders not to remain deaf to "the cry of humanity." On October 28, Khrushchev told President Kennedy that the missiles would be withdrawn. Many historians believe Pope John's public appeal provided Khrushchev with a face-saving way to change course, depicting himself as a savior of world peace, rather than an outfoxed aggressor who blinked. Kennedy thanked John XXIII for his help.

Shortly after this, Cousins met with Khrushchev as an intermediary for the Holy See, to discuss world peace, religious freedom, and Archbishop Slipyj. By early 1963, the Soviets agreed to release Slipyj on the condition that he would remain in exile, and that his freedom would not be exploited by the Church for "anti-Soviet" purposes. The release was to be regarded as an amnesty, and Slipyj was still officially considered an enemy of the Soviet government. The Holy See agreed not to exploit the matter, but made no promises about restricting its admonitions against communism.

On January 23, 1963, Slipyj was set free. He arrived in Rome in time to participate in the Second Vatican Council, but his freedom was complicated by the fact that Russian Orthodox observers had been invited to attend the council. Their presence deeply shocked the Ukrainian bishops who thought that the Holy See was conceding far too much to these accessories to the Soviet suppression of the Ukrainian Greek Catholic Church. The Holy See, however, believed that this approach accomplished ecumenical and political goals without compromising genuine principles.

Slipyj had been secretly (*in pectore*) named a cardinal by Pope Pius XII in 1949, but in 1965 Pope Paul VI named him publicly. At that time he was the fourth cardinal in UGCC history. In 1969 Pope Paul VI created the new office of major archbishop, appointing Slipyj as its first incumbent. He died in Rome on September 7, 1984. In 1992, after the fall of the Soviet Union, his relics were returned to St. George's Cathedral in Lviv.

13

GLOBAL WAR ON RELIGION

J ANUARY 1951, three years after Cardinal Mindszenty was arrested, Stalin was riding high. Since the end of World War II he had dramatically expanded his empire through the skillful application of, alternately, the naked sword and the veiled hoax. He now had dominion over twenty-one countries—fifteen union republics and six European satellites. The borders of his real estate extended from the North Pole to the 35th parallel and enclosed twelve seas belonging to three oceans (Arctic, Atlantic and Pacific), 27,000 lakes and 150,000 rivers with a total length of 2 million miles. Counting the communist revolution in China that had been initiated and organized by Soviet advisers and was now about to succeed, the ruler in the Kremlin would oversee more than a third of the world's population.

Stalin believed the time was ripe to gather all of Germany under the communist umbrella. Germany was the cradle of Marxism—Karl Marx's birthplace—and it was a matter of personal pride for Stalin to see it communist. In June 1948, he sealed off West Berlin, hoping to compel the Western Allies to surrender the entire city to the Soviet occupation forces. West Berlin was a tiny oasis in the Soviet-occupied part of Germany, and the Soviet ruler was sure that the small Allied military force controlling the Western sectors was no match for the surrounding armored units of the Red Army. Stalin miscalculated. Never in his wildest nightmares could he have anticipated that the United States would set up the Berlin Airlift in order to keep West

Berlin alive. Nor could he have dreamed that his blockade would cause the birth of the North Atlantic Treaty Organization (NATO) in April 1949, and one month later propel the three Western occupation forces to unite their zones into a new West German nation—thereby setting the stage for the eventual collapse of all German communism. On May 12, 1949, Stalin admitted defeat and ended the Berlin blockade. Five months later he also relinquished his dream of bringing the whole of Germany into "our camp," when he established an East German nation in that portion of the country occupied by the Red Army.

Stalin was not a good loser. By mid-1949 he was faced with a Western Europe firmly bonded to the United States, and he knew that the Soviet Union did not have the military strength to break up that unity by force. Realizing that his strong-arm methods would no longer work, Stalin turned his thoughts to an old Russian weapon of the emotions that had so successfully been wielded by him and all the tsars before him: anti-Semitism. He was convinced that the hatred for Jews had deep roots in Europe, and he wanted to turn that hatred against his new enemy. Thus, Stalin decided to portray the United States as a Zionist realm owned by Jewish money and run by a greedy "Council of the Elders of Zion" (Stalin's derisive epithet for the US Congress), whose militaristic sharks wanted to transform the rest of the world into a Jewish fiefdom. At that time, Western Europe was grateful to the United States for restoring its freedom and economic prosperity. Stalin, however, was convinced that could be changed by exploiting Europe's historical anti-Semitism and fear of a new war.

Having thus set the strategy, Stalin started the action. He appointed, as the Soviet Union's minister of foreign affairs, an expert in manipulating religion: Andrey Vyshinsky, the undercover intelligence officer who had long managed Stalin's war against the Catholic Church. Next, Stalin sent, as Soviet ambassador to Washington, another undercover intelligence officer who specialized in manipulating religion: Aleksandr Panyushkin. (In 1953, Panyushkin would become chief of the entire Soviet foreign intelligence service, the PGU—*Pervoye Glavnoye Upravleniye*, First Chief Directorate of the KGB—a position he would hold until 1956.)

Vyshinsky's main task was to unify the Soviet Union's diplomatic and intelligence machineries, and to use them for creating a strong West European aversion for American Zionism and its militaristic sharks, so as to eventually force the American "occupation" troops out of the Old World continent. Once that was accomplished, Vyshinsky would use the same intelligence and diplomatic apparatus to help Western Europe "decide its own fate." Italy and France, which had the largest communist parties in Western Europe, would become "people's republics" by parliamentary means.[1] Greece, the only noncommunist country in the Balkans by then, needed only a "spark" to explode.[2] Twice, in 1944 and 1947, the Greek communists had succeeded in setting up their own governments in Greece, and without any American troops in Europe they would be able to do it again. Spain might also change soon, as the "hated dictator," Francisco Franco, who had crushed the Soviet-sponsored Spanish Civil War, seemed to be losing his grip on that nation. The hope was that *La Pasionaria* (Dolores Ibarruri, the honorary chairperson of the Spanish Communist Party), who had been living in Moscow since the end of the Civil War, would set that country on fire again. A "free" Spain would then help "liberate" Portugal as well.

Panyushkin's main task was to persuade America's leftists to create peace movements in the United States. Demonstrating for peace to promote war was nothing new. Before World War II there had been scores of peace demonstrations in the United States that were fueled by Nazi sympathizers— they did not want to stop Hitler from conquering Europe, they wanted to stop Washington from going to war against Hitler.

The Cold War was born. Stalin called it World War III, as I learned in January 1951 when I joined that war as a young officer of the far-flung Soviet bloc intelligence machinery. General Aleksandr Sakharovsky, who in 1949 created Romania's political police, the Securitate, and was now its chief Soviet adviser and its *de facto* boss, explained to his Romanian subordinates that World War III was not directed against the American people. It was directed against America's "Zionist bourgeoisie" and its militaristic sharks, who wanted to ignite a new world war in order to sell their weapons. The socialist camp would eventually seize all the American arms factories from the hands of the Zionist bourgeoisie so America's proletariat could build cars to supply the rest of the world.

That was heady stuff. Most Romanians had never heard of Zionism, but they all dreamed about owning a car. I also had no idea what Zionism meant, but I could feel the monkey being dropped onto my back. I was a young engineer being told that I had an important job to do for my country, and of course I was ready to serve. At the time, the Securitate work schedule was between 7:30 in the morning and 10:00 in the evening, but young officers seldom left for home before midnight—and that was seven days a week. They really had no time to think for themselves, nor were they supposed to. Young officers just went along with the tide, and that is what I did—for a while.

According to Sakharovsky, World War III was conceived to be a war without weapons—a war the Soviet bloc would win without firing a single bullet. It was a war of ideas. It was an intelligence war, waged with a powerful new weapon called *dezinformatsiya*. Its task was to spread credible derogatory information in such a way that the slander would convince others that the targets were truly evil. To ensure the credibility of the lies, two things were required. First, the fabrications had to appear to come from respected and reputable *Western* sources; and second, there had to be what Sakharovsky called "a kernel of truth" behind the allegations, so that at least some part of the story could be definitively verified—and to ensure that the calumny would never be put to rest. In addition, the originator had to do his best to ensure that the story got plenty of publicity, if necessary, by having agents or leftist sympathizers in the West publish articles putting the desired spin on the alleged information.

The Securitate's first major *dezinformatsiya* task in the new World War III was to help Moscow reignite anti-Semitism in Western Europe by spreading thousands of copies of an old Russian forgery, *The Protocols of the Elders of Zion,* in that part of the world. It had to be done secretly, so no one would know that the publications came from the Soviet bloc.

The *Protocols,* which claimed that the Jews were plotting to take over the world, was a Russian forgery, compiled by a disinformation expert, Petr Ivanovich Rachovsky, who worked for the Okhrana (Department for Protecting the Public Security and Order) in the days of the tsar. Rachovsky was assigned to France at the time of the 1897 Zionist Congress, and he had been inspired by the enormous wave of anti-Semitism whipped up by the Dreyfus Affair.[3]

Rachovsky lifted most of his text directly from an obscure, 1864 French satire called *Dialogue aux Enfers entre Machiavel et Montesquieu* ("Dialogue in Hell Between Machiavelli and Montesquieu") written by Maurice Joly and accusing Emperor Napoleon III of plotting to seize all the powers of French society. The *Okhrana* officer essentially substituted the words *the world* for *France* and *the Jews* for *Napoleon III.* During the Russian Revolution of 1905, the *Okhrana* republished its forgery in Paris under the name of a mystic Russian priest, Sergius Nilus, as part of an antirevolutionary propaganda campaign.

"Here is the future of the world," Sakharovsky told the management of the *Securitate* in 1951, when he brought a copy of the Nilus edition to Bucharest and ordered it to be translated, multiplied and surreptitiously disseminated around Western Europe. In 1978, when I broke with communism, the Securitate was spreading the *Protocols* around in the Middle East as well.

In 1957, when I was chief of the DIE station in West Germany, the same Sakharovsky, now head of the whole Soviet foreign intelligence service, launched another *dezinformatsiya* operation focused on reigniting anti-Semitism in West Germany, which at that time was the European epicenter of NATO. "Zarathustra" was the KGB code name for this operation, to symbolize that German anti-Semitism was as immortal as Friedrich Nietzsche's aphoristic book *Also Sprach Zarathustra* ("Thus Spake Zarathustra").

Operation "Zarathustra" was designed to portray Germany as the breeding ground for a new wave of anti-Semitism that was spreading throughout Western Europe. One of the main players in the "Zarathustra" operation was the foreign component of the East German *Stasi* (*Stasi* was the popular nickname for the *Ministerium für Staatssicherheit*, Ministry for State Security, including for its foreign intelligence arm, the *Hauptverwaltung Aufklärung*, HVA, or Main Intelligence Directorate). My DIE was also assigned to this task, because Romania had a large ethnic German minority that could be pressed into service. Around Christmas 1959, numerous synagogues and Jewish memorials were simultaneously desecrated in West Germany. This alleged recrudescence of anti-Semitism was created by Soviet bloc illegal officers, most of whom had been supplied by the East German HVA and the Romanian DIE.

Former KGB Colonel Oleg Gordievsky, who collaborated with the British intelligence service for many years before defecting to Great Britain, revealed that the KGB had first tested this operation in the Soviet Union. In the second half of 1959, the KGB dispatched illegal officers to a village near Moscow, where they vandalized a Jewish cemetery and successfully shifted the blame. Soon after that, the KGB repeated this operation in West Germany,[4] and a couple of months later in France, which had Europe's largest Jewish community.[5]

The new anti-Semitism revived by the "Zarathustra" operation appears not only to have been spread throughout Western Europe, as the Kremlin intended, but also kept alive over the years. This streak of European anti-Semitism intensified after March 29, 2002, when Israel began its military campaign against Palestinian terrorists, and it reached a peak a month later, when various Nazi and neo-Nazi factions celebrated the 113th anniversary of Adolf Hitler's birthday on April 20. A synagogue in Marseilles, France was doused in gasoline and burned to the ground, and one in Lyon was damaged in a car attack; a third was firebombed in Germany, and another was desecrated in Belgium. In Kiev, Ukraine, fifty youths chanting, "Kill the Jews" attacked a synagogue and then beat up a rabbi. In Britain, which takes pride in having a "multicultural" society, police logged at least fifteen anti-Jewish episodes in the month of April 2002 alone, prompting Jonathan Sacks, Britain's chief rabbi, to say that anti-Semitism was on the rise in Europe as a whole.[6]

Totalitarianism always requires a tangible enemy. The Jews, who for centuries had not been protected by the power of a state, proved a convenient enemy for both Nazism and communism. Nowadays the general perception is that Nazi Germany was the cradle of anti-Semitism—and it is not easy to change that perception. Nevertheless, before the words *Nazi Holocaust* were on everyone's tongue, we had the Russian word *pogrom*, meaning massacre.[7] To the ancient Greeks, a holocaust was simply a burnt sacrifice. It was not until the 1930s that the German Nazis invented the Jewish Holocaust. Long before that, however, the Russian tsars had their Jewish pogroms. The 1939 edition of an authoritative Russian dictionary defines pogrom:

> The government-organized mass slaughter of some element of the population as a group, such as the Jewish pogroms in tsarist Russia.[8]

Russia's first major pogrom against the Jews took place on April 15, 1881, in the Ukrainian town of Yelisavetgrad. Russia's administration and army were experiencing gross corruption with associated difficulties, and emissaries from St. Petersburg called for the people's wrath to be vented on the Jews. The impoverished peasants obliged.

A month later, Tsar Alexander II was assassinated by a band of nihilists. His successor, Alexander III, decided to save Russia from anarchical disorder by transforming it into a nation containing only one nationality, one language, one religion, and one form of administration. The new tsar began his policy by instigating more pogroms. A wave of killings, rapes, and the pillaging of Jews spread quickly to hundreds of other towns, reached Warsaw, and moved on to the rest of the Russian empire.

Tsarist authorities held the victims responsible for the violence. In an 1881 memorandum to Tsar Alexander III, the chief of his political police, Count Nikolay Ignatyev, blamed the pogroms on "the Jews' injurious activities" directed against the peasantry. A tsarist investigative commission concluded: "The passion for acquisition and money-grabbing is inherent in the Jew from the day of his birth; it is characteristic of the Semitic race, manifest from almost the first page of the Bible."[9]

These anti-Semitic ideas were soon embodied in the previously mentioned *Protocols of the Elders of Zion,* forged by Tsar Alexander III's political police, the *Okhrana.*[10] This forgery has proved to be the most resilient piece of *disinformation* in history.[11] In 1921, the *Times* of London published a devastating exposure of the forgery by printing extracts from the *Protocols* side by side with the passages from the Joly book that had been plagiarized.[12] That did not stop the *Protocols* from becoming the basis for much of Hitler's anti-Semitic philosophy as expressed in *Mein Kampf.* In fact, Nazi Germany later translated the *Protocols* into many languages and flooded the world with them, to allege that there was an old "Jewish conspiracy" aimed at world domination, and to demonstrate that the persecution of Jews was a necessary self-defense for Germany. In the early years of the twenty-first century, the *Protocols* was filmed and broadcast on various Islamic television networks. Electronic versions can still be found on the Internet.

In April 1903, another major pogrom took place in Kishinev, then the capital of the Bessarabia province of the Russian empire. The pogrom started after a boy, Mikhail Rybachenko, was found murdered in the town of Dubossary, about twenty-five miles north of Kishinev. Although it was clear that the boy had been murdered by a relative (who was later found), the Russian media insinuated that he was murdered by the Jews. The pogrom spanned three days. The *New York Times* described it as follows:

The anti-Jewish riots in Kishinev, Bessarabia, are worse than the censor will permit to publish. There was a well laid-out plan for the general massacre of Jews on the day following the Russian Easter. The mob was led by priests, and the general cry, "Kill the Jews," was taken up all over the city. The Jews were taken wholly unaware and were slaughtered like sheep. The dead number 120 and the injured about 500. The scenes of horror attending this massacre are beyond description. Babes were literally torn to pieces by the frenzied and bloodthirsty mob. The local police made no attempt to check the reign of terror. At sunset the streets were piled with corpses and wounded. Those who could make their escape fled in terror, and the city is now practically deserted of Jews.[13]

A second Kishinev pogrom took place on October 19–20, 1905. By the time it was over, nineteen Jews had been killed and fifty-six injured. A large proportion of Jewish families who have found security, prosperity, and happiness in the United States came here as a result of these early pogroms.

The Soviet dictators, like the tsars before them, needed a tangible enemy. Vladimir Lenin, the leader of the Bolshevik revolution, who surrounded himself with Marxist Jews, dropped the Kremlin's traditional anti-Semitism and unleashed his wrath against the country's aristocracy and wealthy landowners. In 1918, a periodical of Lenin's *Cheka* called *Krasnyy Terror* (*Red Terror*) ran an article by Martyn Ianovich Latsis, one of Dzerzhinsky's deputies. He explained:

We are not waging war against individuals. We are exterminating the bourgeoisie as a class . . . . During investigation, do not look for evidence that the accused acted in word or deed against Soviet power. The first questions that you ought to put are: To what class does he belong? What is his origin? What is his education and profession? And it is these questions that ought to determine the fate of the accused. In this lies the significance of the Red Terror.[14]

Stalin, who grew up in the far reaches of Georgia, where the Jews had been serfs (until 1871, when serfdom was abolished there), transformed his Georgian anti-Semitism into a national and international policy. Fearing the competing communists who had fought for Lenin's revolution, Stalin framed a few of them as agents of Zionist espionage and made the others look guilty by association.

When Stalin wanted to get rid of his main rival, Leon Trotsky (né Lev Davidovich Bronstein), his political police framed Trotsky as a Jewish spy of American Zionism and had him expelled from the country. That insinuation later allowed Stalin to have Trotsky barbarically killed with an ice axe in Mexico City by a Soviet illegal officer (Ramón Mercader) without causing most of Russia even to blink. Once again, the Jews were the country's enemies.

The first chairman of the Comintern,[15] Grigory Zinovyev, who was also born into a bourgeois Jewish family, was framed as head of a "Terrorist Center for the Assassination of the Leaders of the Soviet Government and CPSU [Communist Party of the Soviet Union]," which was supposedly financed by America's Zionism.[16] He was shot on August 21, 1936. The man named by Lenin in his testament as the most capable of the younger generation, Georgy Pyatakov, was also framed as having been involved in an invented Zionist conspiracy and was shot.

Out of the seven members of Lenin's Politburo at the time of the October Revolution, only Stalin was still alive when the massacre was over. The rest were framed as Zionist spies and executed. Stalin hated competition.

After the state of Israel was constituted in 1948, the Soviet Union became one of the first countries to recognize it. As told to me by Generals Sakharovsky and Panteleymon Bondarenko (aka Pantyusha), Stalin did that because he hoped to fill Israel with Russian Jews recruited as Soviet spies and tasked to transform that country into a springboard from which to launch a Soviet expansion into the Middle East.

In 1948, however, Golda Meir was appointed Israel's minister plenipotentiary to the Soviet Union. There she was enthusiastically greeted by tens of thousands of Russian Jews. Therefore, Stalin's political police, at that time called the MGB (*Ministerstvo Gosudarstvennoy Bezopasnosti,* or Ministry of State Security), organized a two-month total mail intercept throughout Russia. The results were presented to Stalin in December 1948, in the form of a report showing that an impressive number of Russian Jews had started promoting the idea of emigration to the newly created state of Israel.

Fearing that such mass requests would tarnish the image of the "workers' paradise" he was trying to project, Stalin quickly reacted. He dissolved the Jewish Anti-Fascist Committee created during the war; closed the Jewish schools, theaters, and synagogues; and arrested the most prominent Russian

Jewish intellectuals.

Even the wife of Vyacheslav Molotov, Stalin's strongest political supporter and his prime minister since 1930, was exiled to Siberia for the sole
reason that she was a Jew. Once that was done, Stalin unleashed a violent
public campaign calling for the execution of "Jewish speculators." When
Israel started developing strong ties with the United States, Stalin moved
his anti-Semitism abroad. He labeled Zionism as the main tool used by
the United States to undermine the "socialist camp," and he committed
unlimited Soviet political, military, and financial support to Israel's historical
enemies, its neighboring Arab states.

The following year, to maintain his position as boss over the new Communist Party stars beginning to shine in Eastern Europe, Stalin framed a
few of them as tools of Zionist espionage services. In 1949, he framed the
communist leaders of Hungary, László Rajk and György Palfy, as Zionist
spies and had them hanged. After that, Stalin's political police organized a
monstrous show trial in Prague, at which the head of the Communist Party,
Rudolf Slánský, and ten other Czech leaders, most of them Jews, were framed
as Zionist spies and hanged. Then Stalin asserted that those countries were
on the verge of falling into Zionist clutches, so he had a few million people,
mostly Jews, expelled from their communist parties, allegedly to preserve
the "purity of Eastern European Socialism."

14

THE VATICAN'S NEW CRUSADE

I N MARCH 1946, Winston Churchill, speaking at Westminster College in Fulton, Missouri, said: "From Stettin in the Baltic to Trieste in the Adriatic, an Iron Curtain has descended across the Continent."[1] Shortly thereafter, President Harry Truman elevated the US delegation to the Vatican to the rank of embassy, named Myron Taylor as ambassador, and asked Pope Pius XII for help to stop the Soviet expansion.

Truman reasoned that communism was the mortal enemy of religion— *of all religions*—and he believed its expansion could be stopped only "through a concerted religious effort" that would place the superiority and strength of what he called "truth and freedom" before the peoples of the world.[2] Truman also believed that the Roman Catholic Church would be his strongest ally in this moral battle.

As he had cooperated with the United States in opposing the Nazis, Pius obliged.

In his book *The Lonely Cold War of Pope Pius XII*,[3] Peter C. Kent, a professor of history at the University of New Brunswick, documents how Pius XII openly engaged the Vatican on the side of the United States. In July 1949, the Holy Office issued a decree stating that "the faithful who profess the materialistic and anti-Christian doctrine of the Communists, and particularly those who defend or propagate this doctrine, contract *ipso facto* excommunication."[4] This was so because:

Communism is materialistic and anti-Christian: although the Communist leaders sometimes declare in words that they do not attack religion, in fact they show that they do by their doctrine and by their acts, which are hostile to God, to the true religion and to the Church of Christ. Therefore it is forbidden to register as a member of a Communist party or favor it in any way.[5]

Pius XII's *Sanctum Officium* made it clear that the Vatican was indeed at war with communism, and he issued a series of decrees condemning the Kremlin's crusade against the Catholic Church, including: Decree on usurpation of Church functions by the state, on June 29, 1950; Decree on illegitimate state-ordered ordinations of bishops, on April 9, 1951;[6] and Decree on publications favoring totalitarianism and communism, on June 26 and July 22, 1955.[7]

The Kremlin labeled Pius "the Cold-War pope."[8] Thus, Soviet leaders instructed M. M. Scheinmann, a researcher at the Historical Institute of the Soviet Academy of Sciences in Moscow, to produce a report alleging a Vatican-Nazi conspiracy against the Soviet Union.[9] Scheinmann's report contained invented details about an alleged "Secret Pact" the Vatican had signed with Hitler.[10] Republished in 1954 in German as *Der Vatican im Zweiten Weltkrieg*, that phony report became a *dezinformatsiya* tool, but it attracted little attention from a generation that had seen with its own eyes how vigorously Pius XII had fought Nazism.

In 1950, President Truman approved one of the most important US government documents of that time: National Council Report 68, or NSC 68. This was a fifty-eight page top-secret report of the US National Security Council (declassified in 1975), which set forth the strategy of containment and became a significant weapon in the Cold War. By 1950, the Soviet Union had detonated an atomic bomb, installed a communist government in China, and expanded its reign over a third of the world. The NSC report described the challenges facing the United States in cataclysmic terms. "The issues that face us are momentous," the document stated, "involving the fulfillment or destruction not only of this Republic but of civilization itself."[11]

NSC 68/1950, which was signed by President Truman on September 30, 1950, contained a two-pronged political strategy aimed at taking the moral high-ground in the new East-West conflict. A few weeks after it was signed, Truman launched his "Campaign of Truth," which he defined as "a struggle, above all else, for the minds of men." Truman argued that the propaganda used by the "forces of imperialistic communism" could be overcome only by the "plain, simple, unvarnished truth."[12] The Voice of America, Radio Free Europe, and Radio Liberation (soon to become Radio Liberty) became part of Truman's containment offensive.[13] He asked the Vatican to enroll in this effort to stop the communists and what he viewed as their elemental godlessness.

Pius XII again obliged. At his request, the Holy See acquired a 988-acre area at Santa Maria di Galeria, some eleven miles north of Rome, for a new broadcasting center. In 1952 the Italian government granted the site extraterritorial status, and in 1957 the new radio center was put into operation. Soon after that, Vatican Radio was broadcasting in forty-seven languages. This tool, which had been used during World War II to help the resistance oppose the Nazis,[14] now became a powerful anticommunist weapon. (Today it has more than two hundred journalists in sixty-one countries, and it produces some forty-two thousand hours of simultaneous broadcasting a day.)[15]

The Vatican's role as strong enemy of Nazism and a deadly enemy of communism is one of Pope Pius XII's most important legacies. Vatican Radio was part of those efforts. Both Nazism and communism wanted to ensure that the people of the world had no other gods but those approved by the government. Pius XII's endeavor to keep the faith in the one true God was an inspiration to his successors and played a significant role in helping the West win the Cold War.

Unfortunately, those efforts put Pius XII and the Vatican at the top of the Kremlin's enemies list.

15

LIBERATION THEOLOGY

KHRUSHCHEV WANTED TO GO DOWN in history as the Soviet leader who exported communism to the American continent. In 1959 he was able to install the Castro brothers in Havana, and soon my foreign intelligence service became involved in helping Cuba's new communist rulers to export revolution throughout South America. It did not work. Unlike Europe, the Latin America of those years had not yet been bitten by the Marxist bug. (In 1967, Castro's pawn Che Guevara was executed in Bolivia, after failing to ignite a guerrilla war in that country.)

In the 1950s and 1960s, most Latin Americans were poor, religious peasants who had accepted the status quo, and Khrushchev was confident they could be converted to communism through the judicious manipulation of religion. In 1968, the KGB was able to maneuver a group of leftist South American bishops into holding a conference in Medellín, Colombia. At the KGB's request, my DIE provided logistical assistance to the organizers. The official task of the conference was to help eliminate poverty in Latin America. Its undeclared goal was to legitimize a KGB-created religious movement dubbed "liberation theology," the secret task of which was to incite Latin America's poor to rebel against the "institutionalized violence of poverty" generated by the United States.[1]

The KGB had a penchant for "liberation" movements. The Palestine *Liberation* Organization (PLO), the National *Liberation* Army of Columbia

(FARC), and the National *Liberation* Army of Bolivia were just a few of the "liberation" movements born at the KGB. The Medellin Conference did indeed endorse liberation theology, and the delegates recommended it to the World Council of Churches (WCC) for official approval. The WCC, headquartered in Geneva and representing the Russian Orthodox Church and other smaller denominations throughout more than 120 countries, had already come under the control of Soviet foreign intelligence. It remains politically under the control of today's Kremlin, through the many Orthodox priests who are prominent in the WCC and are at the same time Russian intelligence agents. Dissident Russian priest Gleb Yakunin, who was a member of the Russian *Duma* from 1990 to 1995, and was briefly given official access to KGB archives, released a great deal of information in *samizdat* reports identifying the Orthodox priests who were agents and describing their influence on WCC matters.[2] For example, in 1983 the KGB dispatched forty-seven agents to attend the WCC General Assembly in Vancouver, and the following year the KGB took credit for using its agents on the WCC selection committee to arrange for the right man to be elected WCC general secretary.[3]

World Council of Churches general secretary, Eugene Carson Blake— a former president of the National Council of Churches in the United States—endorsed liberation theology and made it part of the WCC agenda. In March 1970 and July 1971, the first South American Catholic congresses devoted to liberation theology took place in Bogotá.

Pope John Paul II, who had experienced communist treachery first-hand, denounced liberation theology at the January 1979 Conference of the Roman Catholic Bishops of South America (CELAM), held in Pueblo, Mexico: "This conception of Christ as a political figure, a revolutionary, as the subversive of Nazareth, does not tally with the Church's catechism."[4] Within four hours, a twenty-page rebuttal of the pope's speech carpeted the floor of the Conference. Cardinal López Trujillo, the Conference's organizer, explained that the rebuttal was the product of "some 80 Marxist liberationists from outside the Bishops' Conference."[5] I recall that the Romanian DIE had earlier been congratulated by the KGB for having provided logistical support to such liberationists.

In 1985, the KGB-managed World Council of Churches elected its first general secretary who was an avowed Marxist: Emilio Castro. He had been exiled from Uruguay because of his political extremism, but he managed the WCC until 1992. Castro strongly promoted the KGB-created liberation theology, which is today putting down strong roots in Venezuela, Bolivia, Honduras, and Nicaragua. In those countries, the peasants have supported the efforts of Marxist dictators Hugo Chávez, Evo Morales, Manuel Zelaya (now exiled to Costa Rica), and Daniel Ortega to transform their countries into KGB-style police dictatorships. In September 2008, Venezuela and Bolivia booted out the US ambassadors during the same week and called for Russian military protection.

Russian military ships and bombers are back in Cuba—for the first time since the Cuban missile crisis of 1962—and also in Venezuela. Brazil, the world's tenth largest economy, also moved into the Kremlin's fold under its Marxist ruler, Lula da Silva. In 2011, da Silva was succeeded by a former Marxist guerrilla, Dilma Rousseff. During that same year, the newly elected president of Peru, Ollanta Humala, rushed to Buenos Aires to seek inspiration from Brazil's Marxist guerrilla president. With the addition of Argentina, whose current president, Cristina Fernández de Kirchner, is also moving the country into the Marxist fold, the map of Latin America now looks mostly red.

A few years ago a black version of liberation theology began growing in a few radical-leftist black churches in the United States. Black liberation theologians James Cone, Cornel West, and Dwight Hopkins have explicitly stated their preference for Marxism because Marxist thought is predicated on a system of oppressor class (whites) versus victim class (blacks), and it sees just one solution: the destruction of the enemy. James Cone explained:

> Black theology will accept only the love of God which participates in the destruction of the white enemy. What we need is the divine love as expressed in Black Power, which is the power of black people to destroy their oppressors here and now by any means at their disposal. Unless God is participating in this holy activity, we must reject his love.[6]

The predominantly black Trinity United Church of Christ in Chicago is part of this new movement. Its pastor, Reverend Jeremiah Wright, who in 2008 became religious adviser to the presidential campaign of Senator Barack Obama, became famous for screaming out "not God bless America, but d damn America!" Senator Obama's presidential campaign apologized Reverend Wright's slip of the tongue. By June 2011, however, the same

Reverend Wright was touring the United States to preach, in packed-full black churches, that "the state of Israel is an illegal, genocidal ... place," and that "to equate Judaism with the state of Israel is to equate Christianity with [rapper] Flavor Flav."[7]

Obama, of course, was by then in the White House.

In the 1960s, Che Guevara became a kind of icon for the liberation theology movement. At that time, the Kremlin's popularity stood at an all-time low. The Soviets' brutal suppression of the 1956 Hungarian uprising and their instigation of the 1962 Cuban missile crisis disgusted the world, and every Soviet bloc ruler tried to save face in his own way. Khrushchev replaced the "immutable" Marxist-Leninist theory of the world proletarian revolution with a policy of peaceful coexistence, while pretending to be an advocate for peace. Alexander Dubček gambled on a "socialism with a human face,"and Gomulka on "let Poland be Poland." Ceaușescu announced his "independence" from Moscow and portrayed himself as a "maverick" among communist leaders.

Cuba's Castro brothers, who feared any liberalization, decided it would be simpler just to plaster a romantic revolutionary façade over their communism. They chose Che as their poster boy because he had already been executed in Bolivia—a US ally; after having unsuccessfully tried to ignite a guerrilla war, he could be portrayed as a martyr of American imperialism. The KGB immediately offered support. The Romanian DIE, which in those days enjoyed close relations with its Cuban counterpart, the DGI, was also ordered to lend a hand, and that placed me squarely in the picture.[8]

"Operation Che" was launched with the book *Revolution in the Revolution*, a primer for communist guerrilla insurrection, which praised Che to the skies. The author, French terrorist Régis Debray, was a highly regarded KGB agent.[9] In 1970, the Castro brothers shifted Che's sanctification into high gear. Alberto Korda, a Cuban intelligence officer working undercover as a photographer with the Cuban newspaper *Revolución*, produced a romanticized picture of Che. That now-famous Che, with long, curly locks of hair, wearing a revolutionary beret with a star on it and looking straight into the viewer's eyes, has since inundated the world.[10]

Che's picture became the logo for Steven Soderbergh's Spanish-language, four-hour epic movie *Che* launched in 2009, which portrays a sadistic killer who dedicated his life to bringing Latin America into the Kremlin's fold as a "true revolutionary through the stations of his martyrdom."[11]

Even the playwright given credit for writing the play that slandered Pope Pius XII, *The Deputy,* was enlisted for the effort to promote Che. *Time* magazine reported in October 1970: "At present, Che appears each evening in a new play, *The Guerrillas,* by German Playwright Rolf Hochhuth." In the play, "a young New York Senator who is also leader of a Che-style US underground movement pleads with Guevara to abandon his Bolivian battle. Che refuses. 'My death here—in a calculated sense—is the only possible victory,' he says. 'I must leave a sign.'"[12] Further advancing the KGB's interests, the play also charged the United States with racial and political murder.

The KGB was also instrumental in embellishing a diary Che kept during his student years and in transforming it into a propaganda book, *Das Kapital Meets Easy Rider,* later renamed *The Motorcycle Diary.* Today, Che is an icon of the liberation theology movement, and of black liberation theology.

During the 2008 presidential election season, Fox's Houston TV station aired video of volunteers in an Obama '08 campaign office in that city, the walls of which were adorned with a large picture of Che superimposed over a Cuban flag.[13] Obama had attended Reverend Wright's black liberation theology church in Chicago for some twenty years.

As Raúl Castro once bragged to me, "Che is our greatest public success."

16

KHRUSHCHEV'S WAR ON
THE VATICAN

NIKITA KHRUSHCHEV WAS AN EXPERT at changing people's pasts in order to realize his own future. In fact, he rose to the Kremlin by changing the past of Lavrenty Beriya, his main rival for the Soviet throne. Khrushchev was enormously proud of that accomplishment. According to his own memoir, the framing of Beriya began during the June 26, 1953, meeting of the Presidium of the Communist Party. Khrushchev came to that meeting with a gun in his pocket, and he played the starring role in the drama from beginning to end: "I prodded [Premier Georgy] Malenkov with my foot and whispered: 'Open the session, give me the floor.' Malenkov went white; I saw he was incapable of opening his mouth. So I jumped up and said: 'There is one item on the agenda: the anti-Party, divisive activity of imperialist agent Beriya.'"[1] After Khrushchev had proposed that Beriya be released from all his party and government positions, "Malenkov was still in a state of panic. As I recall, he didn't even put my motion to a vote. He pressed a secret button, which gave the signal to the generals who were waiting in the next room." The generals immediately arrested Beriya and took him away.[2]

With Beriya securely locked up in a cell, Khrushchev easily managed to wrest the top governmental job away from his closest ally, Malenkov.

My first personal encounter with Khrushchev's practice of rewriting people's pasts occurred on October 26, 1959. On that day, Khrushchev landed in Bucharest for what would become known as his six-day vacation. Khrushchev had never before taken such a long vacation abroad, but his stay in Bucharest was not a vacation either. He was brought there by his new spy chief, General Aleksandr Sakharovsky, who until recently had been the chief intelligence adviser for the Securitate, Romania's equivalent of the Soviet security police. Sakharovsky wanted to introduce Khrushchev to the Romanian ruler, Gheorghe Gheorghiu-Dej, and get his help in a couple of German matters—Romania had the second-largest ethnic German minority group in the Soviet bloc.

One of Sakharovsky's projects was to seek Romanian cooperation in the smearing of Pius XII. The pope had died a few months earlier, and thus could no longer defend himself. Sakharovsky and Khrushchev wanted to pull off a kind of Beriya operation. They intended to change Pius's past image from Jew-defender to Jew-hater so as to compromise the Vatican—the same way they had changed Beriya's past from ferocious anti-imperialist to imperialist agent. Khrushchev and Sakharovsky naturally realized that they could not put the Vatican out of business, but they did hope that by representing its head as a Jew-hater they could ignite a war between the Catholics and the Jews that would distract both groups from making any serious attempt to condemn Khrushchev's next planned move: a military blockade of West Berlin.

I had just been recalled from my assignment in West Germany and appointed head of Romanian industrial espionage (the collection of scientific and technological intelligence), and was still considered Romania's "German expert." As such, I attended most of the discussions with Khrushchev and Sakharovsky. "Religion is the opiate of the people," I heard Khrushchev say, quoting Marx's famous dictum, "so let's give them opium."

Changing the widely admired anti-Nazi Pius XII into a pro-Nazi pope would indeed be a monumental task, but Khrushchev and Sakharovsky had thought it through carefully. At that very moment, the KGB was creating the Christian Peace Conference (CPC), a new international religious organization headquartered in the Soviet-occupied city of Prague, whose secret task was to discredit both the Vatican and the world's leading Jewish organizations. The Romanian foreign intelligence service, the DIE, would contribute to the CPC staff a small army of undercover intelligence officers and co-optees. The CPC would be subordinate to the World Peace Council (WPC), another Kremlin creation, also headquartered in Prague. The KGB was already funding the WPC, and my DIE also contributed to it.

Khrushchev's plans for taking over West Berlin never materialized. Overnight on August 13, 1961, he sealed off East Berlin with a barbed wire fence, which later became the infamous Berlin Wall, and he loudly proclaimed victory. His Christian Peace Conference, built upon an organization originally founded in Prague by the Czech political police, the StB (*Státní bezpečnost*), and headed by an StB agent (Prof. Joseph Hromadka), became an influential KGB front. The Kremlin's *dezinformatsiya* machinery introduced the CPC to the world as a global ecumenical organization concerned with the problems of peace. In reality, the Christian Peace Conference was tasked to help the KGB discredit the Vatican and its main political supporter, the United States, throughout the Christian world.

The KGB appointed Metropolitan Nikodim of Leningrad (who worked for the KGB under the code name "Adamant") as vice president and shadow manager of the CPC,[3] and gave him an advance of $210,000 to start spreading the word around the Christian community that Pius XII had been a Jew-hater.[4]

Soon after Khrushchev left Bucharest, the chief of the KGB disinformation department, General Ivan Agayants, informed the management of the DIE that all employees of the Soviet patriarchate's External Affairs Department and all religious servants involved in *foreign* religious work were now secretly either KGB civilian employees or agents.[5] The Romanian *Securitate* and my DIE were tasked to ensure that those organizations had equal representation in the country's religious affairs.

In 1960, Khrushchev's KGB ordered its sister services in Eastern Europe to create a special desk tasked to counteract the Vatican's "poison." Another desk charged with producing intelligence officers able to act "under foreign flag" inside the Vatican was formed within the supersecret illegals department of the Romanian DIE—which I later supervised—and in other bloc foreign intelligence services.[6]

The intelligence structure needed to make the Vatican toothless by changing Pius's past was already in place. The first thing to do was to have as many intelligence assets as possible start spreading the word all around the world that Pius had indeed been "Hitler's Pope"—that simple, catchy epithet launched by Radio Moscow in 1945.

The Soviet story line would be that before becoming pope, Pius XII had served as nuncio in Germany, where he caught the anti-Semitic virus and became a Nazi sympathizer. The truth was the exact opposite. In fact, while he was serving as nuncio in Germany, the future pope had frequently condemned racism, anti-Semitism, and excessive nationalism. As early as 1921, a newspaper article quoted him warning about a new and dangerous political movement that was a different perspective from the communists. In 1923, he reported to Rome that a militant group ("followers of Hitler and Ludendorff") were persecuting Catholics and Jews.[7] He referred to this group (not yet known as Nazis) as "right-wing radicals." The following year, on May 1, in a handwritten draft report to Secretary of State Gasparri, the nuncio wrote: "Nazism is probably the most dangerous heresy of our time."[8] In another handwritten report dated three days later, he wrote: "The heresy of Nazism puts state and race above everything, above true religion, above the truth and above the justice."[9]

It was not Pius XII's attitude toward the Nazis or the Jews that made him a target of this Soviet disinformation campaign. It was his attitude toward the Kremlin and its political police. Pius was the first pope to excommunicate communists, but John XXIII was proving just as obstinate. On April 13, 1959, he issued a decree reaffirming and strengthening the one released under Pius XII.[10] John forbade Catholics from voting for communists or sanctioning them in any way.

Khrushchev decided to retaliate against the Church by "excommunicating" a pope in his own way: by completely changing Pope Pius XII's past. The saint would become a sinner.

17

PREPARATIONS FOR FRAMING
PIUS XII

I N FEBRUARY 1960, Khrushchev formally approved a joint Communist Party/KGB operational plan for destroying the Vatican's moral
authority in Western Europe. Since 1945, the Kremlin had fought the
Vatican indirectly by framing many of its priests and top clergymen in the
Soviet Union and in its new territorial acquisitions "liberated" at the end of
the war, slandering them either as Nazi war criminals or as enemies of peace.
Now the Kremlin wanted the KGB to frame the Vatican on its home turf,
using its own priests.[1] Concocted by KGB chairman Aleksandr Shelepin
and by Alexei Kirichenko, the Soviet Politburo member responsible for
international policy, the new plan was constructed around Stalin's 1945
idea of portraying Pius XII as "Hitler's Pope."

The framing of Cardinals Mindszenty and Stepinac had fizzled out,
in the end giving the Kremlin and its political police thugs a black eye. Both
churchmen were framed by identifiably Soviet bloc intelligence tricks and
propaganda, eventually damaging the Kremlin more than the Vatican.
Moscow could no longer afford to apply such heavy-handed and obvious
framing procedures.

Therefore, Shelepin and Kirichenko decided that the framing of Pius
XII should be based on a fictionalized scenario, supported by genuine,
slightly modified Vatican documents (whether or not specifically related
to Pius XII), the originals of which would never be released to the public.

At that time there was an unflinching KGB rule for handling modified and counterfeited documents: they should be made available only in the form of retyped documents or in specially prepared photocopies, as even the most perfect counterfeit by today's standards might become vulnerable to future detection techniques.[2]

The KGB knew what it had to do. It just needed a few Vatican documents to give the operation an aura of authenticity—a "kernel of truth." Romania had a fairly large Roman Catholic community, so her people and foreign intelligence service, the DIE, were asked to help.

General Sakharovsky, who until shortly before that had been the chief KGB adviser to the Romanian DIE and had just been appointed to head the Soviets' entire foreign intelligence service (the PGU, or first chief directorate of the KGB),[3] knew I was in an excellent position to contact the Vatican regarding approval to search its archives. The year before, as deputy chief of the Romanian Trade Mission in West Germany, I had negotiated a "spy swap" with the Holy See, involving four prominent Catholics who had been sentenced to long terms in prison on spurious charges of espionage at the end of a 1951 trial against the Vatican nunciature in Bucharest.[4] The four had been exchanged for two DIE officers (Col. Constantin Horobet and Maj. Nicolae Ciuciulin) caught spying in West Germany.[5]

"Seat 12" was the code name for the Romanian side of the KGB's operation against Pius XII. The name was an allusion to the pope as occupant of the seat of Saint Peter, and to Pius XII himself.[6]

In carrying out this mission against Pope Pius XII, I was introduced to an influential member of the Vatican's diplomatic corps. His name was Agostino Casaroli. In fact, Casaroli was commonly called the Vatican's "secret agent" in communist Europe, and he was known for dressing in civilian clothes to meet with communist officials.[7] Pope John Paul II later named him cardinal and secretary of state for the Vatican.

Romania's relations with the Vatican had been severed in 1951, when Moscow staged a show trial framing the Vatican's nunciature in Romania as being an undercover CIA front and closed its offices.[8] The nunciature buildings in Bucharest had been turned over to the DIE, and they now housed a foreign language school.

I had arranged a spy exchange the year before, but now the Soviet bloc needed a new cover story. It was decided that if Romania were to seek a loan from the Vatican, that would provide a possible explanation for why that nation was changing its position vis-à-vis the Holy See.[9] I was instructed to tell Casaroli that Romania was ready to restore diplomatic relations with the Holy See in exchange for access to its archives and a $1 billion-dollar, interest-free loan.[10] I was also instructed to tell the Vatican that Romania needed access to the archives in order to find historical roots that would help the Romanian government publicly justify its change of heart toward the Holy See. Of course, this was simply a ploy. Ceaușescu had no intention of restoring diplomatic relations with the Holy See.

The loan would, of course, have been welcome, but it was never a true aim. Moscow just wanted to open Vatican doors for a few DIE agents. Suggesting that Romania needed money provided a "cover" motivation for the proposal. The Vatican did agree to discuss the loan—although it was never made—and also agreed to what seemed a simple request: to allow three Romanian priests to do some research in Vatican archives. With that agreement, I had accomplished my part of the plan.

As John Koehler explained in his book *Spies in the Vatican: The Soviet Union's Cold War against the Catholic Church,* the Vatican was not exempt from the Kremlin's efforts to infiltrate foreign governments. David Alvarez made the same point in his similarly titled book, *Spies in the Vatican: Espionage & Intrigue from Napoleon to the Holocaust.* Among the more notorious infiltrations, in 1952 Father Aligheri Tondi, a professor at the Gregorian Academy, was identified as a KGB agent.[11] In 1963, Polish intelligence placed a cooperative bishop in the Vatican.[12]

For the Seat 12 assignment to Rome, the DIE chose three priests who were also co-opted agents. There they were given access to certain Vatican archives. It is worth noting at this point that the term "Vatican Secret Archives" is somewhat of a misnomer. It refers to the central repository for all of the acts promulgated by the Holy See. These archives contain the state papers, correspondence, papal account books, and many other documents that the church has accumulated over the centuries. The word "secret" in the title does not have the modern meaning; it simply indicates that the archives are the pope's own, not those of a department of the Roman Curia. Since 1881 they have been open to outside researchers. Thus, the concession from the Vatican—permitting Romanian priests to enter these archives—was not really significant. It did, however, provide an air of authenticity, as British author John Cornwell would demonstrate decades later when he falsely claimed to have had special access to them.[13]

The DIE agents secretly photographed some unimportant documents, and the DIE sent the films to the KGB via special courier.[14] The documents were not incriminating; they were mainly things like press reports and transcripts of unclassified meetings and speeches, couched in the routine kind of diplomatic language one would expect to find in such material. Nevertheless, the KGB kept asking for more. Even if these documents did not actually provide any compromising information on Pius XII, the insinuation that his new image was based on "original Vatican documents" would dramatically improve the credibility of the whole framing operation. Of course, the KGB also hoped it might stumble across some obscure "kernel of truth" that could be used for *dezinformatsiya* purposes.

At that time, I was managing Romania's industrial espionage, and I had no reason or opportunity to know the true identity of the DIE agents sent to the Vatican to search its archives.[15] Those agents were handled by the DIE's Vatican desk. At the DIE, the identity of all intelligence agents used abroad was extremely well protected, known only to their handlers and to a handful of their superiors. Any indiscretion could indeed cause diplomatic nightmares.

After my account of this operation was first published in 2007, historians and volunteer researchers started looking into the recently opened *Securitate* archives in Romania. So far, researchers have been able to identify by name only one of the three DIE agents: Fr. Francisc Iosif Pal, SJ.[16]

Pal had been recruited as a *Securitate* agent in 1950, when he was detained in the infamous Romanian prison of Gherla. His task was to inform on other Catholic priests who were also detained there. Among those he reported on were Fr. Godo Mihai, SJ, Fr. Chira, SJ, and Bishop Emil Riti (1926–2006).[17] Pal's cooperation with the *Securitate* in organizing the 1951 trial against the Vatican nunciature in Bucharest was revealed in a 2008 book published by William Totok, a Romanian-born German researcher.[18] Pal's involvement with the Vatican archives was first disclosed by Aurel Sergiu Marinescu in a study on the history of Romanian exiles.[19] It was confirmed by Romanian researcher Remus Mircea Birtz.[20] It is still unknown whether Pal was sent to the Vatican using his own identity, or on a false passport— a practice frequently used by both the Securitate and the DIE.

Nothing that Pal or the other DIE agents found in Vatican archives could be used as a basis for fabricating believable evidence that made Pius seem sympathetic to Hitler's regime or unconcerned about the Jews.[21] Moscow expected that. The KGB just wanted to be able to claim that it had on hand original Vatican documents, so as to give the impression that its allegation that Pius XII was "Hitler's Pope" was based on rock-solid evidence.

18

THE DEPUTY

ON FEBRUARY 20, 1963, a play entitled *Der Stellvertreter. Ein christliches Trauerspiel* (*The Deputy. A Christian Tragedy*) premiered at the *Theater am Kurfürstendamm* in West Berlin, under the direction of Erwin Piscator of the *Freie Volksbühne* (Free People's Theatre). The play focused on the allegation that Pope Pius XII had failed to take action, or even to speak out, against Hitler's Holocaust.[1]

The play's author, Rolf Hochhuth, only thirty-one at the time, was an entirely unknown West German. Virtually everyone else involved with that play, however, had dedicated his or her life to serving Moscow, in one way or another. Even the *Freie Volksbühne*, which sponsored the play's première, was created to be a communist outlet in West Berlin. The most prominent tie to Moscow was provided by Erwin Piscator himself, the play's director. Then sixty-nine years old, he had been a member of the Communist Party since its earliest days, and he had spent his entire life producing plays that reflected the Soviet communist line, including celebrating the imminent demise of capitalist society and of capitalism's supposed clerical offshoot, the Catholic Church."[2]

In the late 1920s, Piscator worked in collaboration with the great German (and communist) playwright Bertolt Brecht at the *Theater am Nollendorfplatz*. Together, they created "electrically charged productions of, among others, *Hoppla, Wir Leben* and *Die Abenteuer Des Braven Soldaten Schwejk*."[3]

In 1929, Piscator made his first visit to the Soviet Union, where he worked briefly with the International Association of Workers' Theatres (IATB). As reported in his biography, "Communist artists came increasingly to take their cultural directives from Moscow.... it became natural for leftist German artists not merely to visit Russia but to take jobs there."[4] Accordingly, in 1931 Piscator moved to the USSR, where his initial desire was to make short propaganda films, an emerging art form in that nation. Lobbying to get started, he managed to obtain a two-hour meeting with Stalin's brother-in-law.[5] Soon Piscator was elected president of the Moscow-headquartered IATB, which then changed its name to the International Association of Revolutionary Theatres.[6]

When Romania was taken over by the Soviets after World War II, advisers from the Soviet security police and intelligence service established equivalent organizations in Bucharest. General Panteleymon Bondarenko, Romanianized as Gheorghe Pintilie but known as "Pantyusha," was the Soviet intelligence officer assigned by Moscow as the first chief of the new Romanian Securitate. Over the years, since I eventually became his boss, I learned a great deal about Soviet intelligence operations from the garrulous and often tipsy Pantyusha. Several times Pantyusha reminisced about Piscator, telling me that before becoming president of the IATB (a Soviet intelligence front), Piscator had been recruited as an influence agent by the Soviet foreign intelligence service, the INO.[7]

The foul-mouthed Pantyusha explained: "Stalin did not give a f-cking damn *kopek* for any foreign communist in Moscow who tried to get out of working with us." Pantyusha had reason to know, as he had worked undercover in the Comintern, which was sponsoring the IATB.

Piscator was born in Ulm, Germany, on December 17, 1893. He was drafted into the German army in 1915 and was sent into battle during World War I.[8] While in service in 1917 and 1918, he worked as a director and as an actor at a front theater in Kortrijk, Belgium. He joined the German Communist Party (KPD) in 1919, when it was created.[9]

The following year he moved back to Germany, where he got his start as a volunteer at the *Hof Theater* in Munich, but before long he became an actor, then a director at the *Proletarisches Theater*, a Marxist creation. Piscator wrote that one "task of the Proletarian Theatre is to spread its educational influence, through propaganda, among those of the masses who are still politically wavering and indifferent."[10]

In 1925, the KPD (the largest communist party outside of the Soviet Union at that time) asked Piscator to produce a political review.[11] He put together a team including himself, a composer nominated by the party, and a writer/lyricist/producer. They came up with "about a dozen sketches, introduced by a potpourri of communist songs" that culminated in a "Victory of the Proletariat" scene.[12] It was enough of a success that the KPD soon demanded that he stage a show for their first party conference. Piscator used the same team and produced a show with an "overwhelmingly documentary approach ... virtually every character being historical (and in many cases still alive)."[13]

The Communist Party was not completely happy with the production. Some officials thought it was too factual, which—of course—lessened the propaganda value of the production. "That may be what's wrong, comrade director ... Don't stick so slavishly to 'that's the way it happened,'" one official wrote.[14]

Piscator took the advice well and learned to fictionalize history. He soon found himself working with the leading communist playwrights in Germany.[15] He also trained young actors, though it was said that they mainly received "courses by KPD officials; 'one's party card became a certificate of competence.'"[16]

In at least one case, Piscator's company refused to produce a play because the author declined membership in the Communist Party.[17] In another case, Piscator invited "representatives of the Soviet embassy and trade delegation and of the KPD and its paper" to one of the final rehearsals of a play, only to be told that he had to rewrite it. He complied, though it meant that opening night had to be delayed by two days.[18] In the program to a production from April 1930, Piscator wrote:

> Never was it more essential than now to take sides: the side of the proletariat. More than ever the theatre must nail its flag fanatically to the mast of politics: the politics of the proletariat. More and more insistent grows the demand: theatre is action, the action of the proletariat. The stage and the masses, a creative unity, not in the "Zeittheater" but in the militant theatre of the proletariat.[19]

In the postscript to a 1934 edition to one play produced by Piscator, he wrote that his theater "was always political, that is to say political in the sense approved by the Communist Party."[20] In 1941, he set forth his theory of theater:

[I]t will be possible to make practically every bourgeois play, whether it expresses the decay of bourgeois society or whether it clearly shows the capitalist principle, into an instrument to strengthen the concept of the class struggle, to deepen revolutionary insight into historical necessities. It will be useful if such plays are introduced by a talk, so as to prevent misunderstandings and wrong effects. In certain circumstances changes can be made in plays (concern for the feelings of the author, is a conservative affair) through cuts, through amplifying certain passages, even by adding a prologue and epilogue in order to make the meaning of the whole more clear. In this way a large portion of world literature can be made to serve the cause of the revolutionary proletariat, just as the whole of world literature can be used for the political purpose of propagating the concept of class struggle.[21]

This was a recipe that he would use to perfection with *The Deputy* some two decades later.

Despite Piscator's dedication to the party, questions were raised in high communist circles about the direction of Piscator's work. The scale of his productions seemed too grand for the working class. They asked whether he was a "militant comrade or [just] a parlour communist."[22] (His relationship with Nazi Germany's propaganda minister Joseph Goebbels, who once submitted a play to Piscator and with whom Piscator considered doing a radio broadcast, may also have puzzled the ossified communist hierarchy.[23]) Ultimately, however, Piscator's "record as a supporter of the October Revolution and the Soviet regime was a good one; from the days of the Proletarian Theatre onwards, he had been caught up in the wave of pro-Soviet feeling."[24] His biographer wrote: "The overriding fact remained that he was a communist and subject to party orders."[25]

Piscator defended his ideas in his 1929 book *Das Politische Theater* ("The Political Theater"). He wrote: "any artistic intention must be subordinated to the revolutionary purpose of the whole: the conscious emphasis and propagation of the concept of the class struggle." Continuing:

We, as revolutionary Marxists, cannot consider our task complete if we produce an uncritical copy of reality, conceiving the theatre as a mirror of the times .... The business of revolutionary theatre is to take reality as its point of departure and to magnify the social discrepancy, making it an element of our indictment, our revolt, our new order.[26]

Despite the minor difficulties that came up between Piscator and Communist Party officials, he had made a significant mark on the communist-oriented theater. Along with other dramatists, he "stirred up a revolutionary whirlwind in the theater. This stir followed directly in the wake of a successful Communist revolution in Russia."[27]

In 1938, Piscator was sent to Paris by the INO on a temporary assignment with the International Revolutionary Theater Group. There, Piscator claimed, Wilhelm Pieck—head of the German KPD in the Soviet Union (whom I know to have been an undercover INO colonel)—sent word to him not to return to Moscow because of the wave of arrests then taking place there.[28] This story is usually accepted by biographers of Piscator, but it may have been disinformation. The INO may have planned all along to send Piscator to the United States, the ultimate target for Soviet intelligence.

Piscator did indeed take a boat for the United States, arriving in New York on January 2, 1939. There he opened the Dramatic Workshop at The New School for Social Research in New York City. This workshop launched the careers of many notable students, including Tennessee Williams, Marlon Brando, Walter Matthau, Rod Steiger, Shelley Winters, Harry Belafonte, Elaine Stritch, Ben Gazzara, and Tony Curtis.[29]

Neither the Soviet pogroms nor the move to the United States diminished Piscator's desire to use the stage to advance his communist agenda. Of him, in 1940 *Time* magazine wrote:

> He produced great plays frankly as propaganda, stressed all possible class-war angles, and emphasized mass effects rather than individual actors. Determined to get his audiences "into" the plays, he abolished the curtain, had actors play in the aisles, loudspeakers sound from all parts of the house. His theatre became a versatile expressive "machine," blending plays, films, radio.[30]

Of course, as the United States entered the Cold War, Piscator was more circumspect about his communist ties. As a biographer explained: "One of the difficulties in judging Piscator's American achievements is that so much of what has been written about the Dramatic Workshop has been like an exercise in public relations."[31] The Communist Party, however, still had faith in him.[32]

In 1951, following extensive FBI investigations connected with a deportation case against Piscator, he received a summons from the House Committee on Un-American Activities. Under the pressure of aggressive press reports, which called the Drama Workshop of the New School for Social Research a communist organization of "fellow travelers," and pressure from the committee's summons, Piscator abruptly went back to Germany.[33] There, he was at first treated as "'The Grand Old Man' who had outlived himself."[34]

Piscator spent nine years floating from one theater to another, but around 1960 he got back in touch with Bernhard Reich, a playwright and theater director. Piscator had worked with Reich in the Soviet Union in the 1930s. (Reich claimed it was he who had warned Piscator in 1937 not to return to the Soviet Union from France, prompting Piscator's eventual move to the United States.) Reich had been unable to escape from the USSR in the 1930s. He returned to Germany only in the mid-1950s as a "rehabilitated" Soviet critic.[35] He may have played a role in having Piscator appointed manager and director of the *Freie Volksbühne* in West Berlin in 1962.

The *Freie Volksbühne* was openly communist, along the lines of theaters Piscator had worked with in the 1920s. The idea of a Berlin theater "of the people," which underlies the *Freie Volksbühne*, can be traced back to a *Volksbühne* that was founded in 1892. (The word *Freie* was added to indicate that it was located in the free, or Western, sector of Berlin, just as the new university in the Western sector was called the *Freie Universität*.) The goal of the organization was to promote the social-realist plays of the day at prices accessible to the common worker.

The *Volksbühne's* slogan was *"Die Kunst dem Volke"* (Art for the People). The theater's original building had been constructed in 1913–1914 on the eastern side of Berlin, but World War II reduced it to rubble. Construction of the Berlin Wall began in August 1961, dividing Berlin down the middle. Once it was completed, people from West Berlin were no longer able to cross over to see productions on the other side. East Berlin authorities decided to sponsor a new *Freie Volksbühne* in the western part of the city, to take care of that problem. It would present communist propaganda to viewers in West Berlin.

After several years of trying to find a permanent home, in 1962 Piscator succeeded in becoming director of West Berlin's *Freie Volksbühne*, which did not yet have a real stage of its own. He therefore opened the theater's first season with the production of *Der Stellvertreter* on the stage of the *Theater am Kurfürstendamm*, an established theater that could accommodate his requirements for dramatic theatrical effects.[36] The production, however, was selected to serve the purposes of the Communist Party.

19

THE PLAY

T
HE DEPUTY focuses on two main characters, Kurt Gerstein (based on a real person) and the fictional Father Riccardo Fontana. As a prisoner of the Allies after the war, the real Gerstein (a Nazi officer) set forth a written statement on which the broad outline of the play was later allegedly based. Gerstein's story may have been true, but he was a confused man who was found hanged in his cell (perhaps a suicide) before his story could be confirmed. As such, he remains an enigmatic figure.[1] The Fontana character is fictional, though Hochhuth has said it was based upon Fr. Maximilian Kolbe and Fr. Bernhard Lichtenberg (to both of whom his play was dedicated), and upon similar self-sacrificing priests.[2]

The basic plot of *The Deputy* involves a good Nazi (Gerstein) who tells a good priest (the fictional Fontana) about what the Nazis are doing to the Jews. Fontana, however, is continually thwarted in his efforts to get a message to the pope. When he finally succeeds, Pope Pius XII does not care about the victims. Fontana then sacrifices himself by putting on a yellow star and going to a concentration camp, thereby becoming the true deputy of Christ. Recurring themes include the idea that Hitler's war against the Soviet Union was a kind of papal crusade, and that Pius and the Jesuits were primarily concerned about their investments in the armament factories.

Although Hochhuth has gone back and forth on the issue, at least once he wrote that *The Deputy* had no imputation of anti-Semitism, because there was no evidence that Pius was an anti-Semite.[3] Obviously, the silence of any character cannot drive a theatrical production, so Pius is not onstage very long. Papal silence, however, is the subject of much dialogue in the final version of the play. Nearly all the other characters discuss among themselves, or at least mention, the pope's failure to speak out directly and forcefully against Hitler's treatment of the Jews, thus leading up to a direct confrontation consisting of a single pivotal scene. In some productions it is the only scene in which the pope himself appears onstage. In some versions, the pope's final act is to wash his hands, stained with ink from his editing of a statement that was never made, in a manner reminiscent of Pontius Pilate.[4]

If it were produced as written, *The Deputy* would take seven or eight hours to perform. Since that does not meet theatrical needs, the German producer, Erwin Piscator, edited the script into a more manageable length, making very substantial changes along the way.[5] In fact, considerable alterations were made to both plot and staging in every country where the play was produced,

A synopsis of Piscator's original play is as follows:

Act I: *The Deputy* opens with a discussion over whether Pope Pius XII should have abrogated the concordat to protest the actions of the Nazis. A cold-hearted Catholic industrialist—played by the same actor who plays Pius—defends his use of slave labor.

Act II: Hitler feared Pius more than any other world leader. Pius, however, has too many commercial interests that preclude him from condemning Hitler. A cardinal argues that the Nazis are the last bulwark to stand against Soviet domination of Europe.

Act III: As Jews are rounded up "under the Pope's windows," Riccardo Fontana, the fictional priest protagonist, declares, "Doing nothing is as bad as taking part . . . . God can forgive a hangman for such work, but not a priest, not the Pope!" A German officer comments that the pope has given friendly audiences to thousands of German soldiers.

Act IV: Pius, who has an "aristocratic coldness" and an "icy glint" in his eyes, expresses concern about the Vatican's financial assets and the Allied bombing of factories. He worries that the bombing will impoverish the Italian workers and they will ultimately become anarchists/communists. Pius reiterates his commitment to help the Jews while keeping silent to avoid greater evil. When angrily questioned by Fontana, Pius pontificates on the geopolitical importance of a strong Germany vis-à-vis the Soviet threat.

Act V: Fontana pulls open his shirt and reveals that he is wearing a yellow star out of support for the Jews. He joins deportees to die at Auschwitz, where the rest of the act takes place, ending with a quotation from German ambassador Ernst von Weizsäcker: "Since further action on the Jewish problem is probably not to be expected here in Rome, it may be assumed that this question, so troublesome to German-Vatican relations, has been disposed of."[6]

The Deputy was more noted for its charges against the pope than for its plot or theatric insight. The play does not develop Pius as a tragic figure, since he is neither tragically indecisive nor torn by his alternatives. Not only does he lack Christian charity, but he also lacks simple human decency. *Variety* wrapped it up in its own way: "It's hardly picture material, of course, and doubtful for the road or stock."[7]

A play is just a play, but Hochhuth, and others associated with *The Deputy*, wanted this to be something more. According to Hochhuth, the "main thesis" of *The Deputy* was "that Hitler drew back from the extermination program as soon as high German clerics . . . or the Vatican . . . forcibly intervened."[8]

In the "Sidelights" to *The Deputy* Hochhuth says: "Perhaps never before in history have so many human beings paid with their lives for the passivity of a single statesman."[9] In an editorial, the Jesuit magazine *America* responded: "perhaps never before in history have so many vicious, tendentious and mean imputations of motives been based on such flimsy, distorted and falsified historical arguments. *The Deputy* is character assassination."[10]

The general view of Pius XII, based on what had been widespread knowledge of him for two decades, suddenly and spectacularly flipped from lily white to coal black after *The Deputy* saw the light, without *any* new evidence being produced. That prompted *America* magazine to ask:

What has happened . . . to erase with one sweep these informed and unsolicited tributes to the memory of Pope Pius XII? Why do they count for nothing when *The Deputy* comes to town? By what dialectic, or through what human fickleness, has a great benefactor of humanity and of the Jews particularly, now become a criminal?[11]

Many students of the play have wondered where Hochhuth got his information, particularly relating to papal motives. As one author wrote:

> Where did Hochhuth get his facts? He was able to use the evidence presented at the Nuremberg trials and at the Eichmann trial, and to consult US and German historical records and contemporary documents. These provided him with material for his descriptions of the persecution of the Jews and for his concentration camp scenes. But for his main charges—the contemptible motives he attributes to Pope Pius XII for his silence—he quotes no documentary evidence at all.[12]

Hochhuth said he spent three months in Rome "studying the atmosphere, talking to Swiss Guards, Romans and Jews who had been hidden in Italian monasteries."[13] Since he never had access to any archive, Hochhuth claimed to rely upon answers to a series of questions he posed to "an elderly and experienced German-speaking bishop,"[14] but he refused to name the bishop.[15] Instead, he brought unwarranted suspicion on numerous Vatican officials.

Both my coauthor and I have visited the Vatican many times, armed with impressive official credentials, but neither of us has been able to push a bishop into a corner and persuade him to reveal secret Vatican documents. Maybe Hochhuth got lucky. Maybe he made the story up (his reputation for veracity is not good), or maybe he referred to the Vatican documents obtained by the three DIE agents involved in "Seat-12." In the end, these varied possibilities are irrelevant. The important point is that one play alone could not have changed the world's perception of Pius XII from an anti-Nazi pope into a pro-Nazi one. No single piece of literature could accomplish such a transformation. A full-blown KGB framing operation could, however, do just that.

Some of the factual mistakes regarding the Church that appear in *The Deputy* are not the kind that high clerics or a bishop would have made. Soviet *dezinformatsiya* experts might, however, make just such mistakes. Erik von Kuehnelt-Leddihn indentified the following mistakes (and others) in his 1969 book, *The Timeless Christian*:

> 1. Father Fontana is referred to as "Count Riccardo Fontana, a twenty-seven-year-old Jesuit, who works as a young attaché in the Berlin nunciature." First of all, the time needed to prepare for a Jesuit priesthood prevents anyone from becoming a Jesuit at that young age. Additionally, at that time there were no Jesuits in the diplomatic service. Perhaps most

obviously, Jesuits do not retain secular titles, like "Count"; they have to give them up.

2. The play mentions a concordat between the Vatican and Japan. No such agreement was ever signed.

3. The play also has Spanish court dress being worn in the Vatican— "the somber beautiful court dress of Henry II." It is simply not true.

4. According to the play, Hitler forbade all measures against the Church. Pastor Martin Niemoeller, president of the World Council of Churches (1961–84), who was sent to Dachau (1937–1945) for opposing the nazification of the Protestant Church, and lots of other religious victims of Hitler's Nazism wish that were true!

5. Pius XII was always alone at the table because he could not abide the sight of a human face. In actuality, Pius followed the Vatican custom of taking most meals alone, but he sometimes dined with guests, and he was known as a witty conversationalist.[16]

6. An officer of the Swiss Guard is depicted in full uniform in the center of Rome to summon a cardinal who was visiting Count Fontana. Swiss Guards, however, were not permitted to wear the uniform outside the Vatican.

7. The Society of Jesus is mistakenly referred to as the "Order of Jesus," and in the play the "Order of Jesus" supplied the Soviet Union with mercury from Spanish mines. That did not happen.

8. Contrary to the play, there was no papal legate in Washington at that time, only an apostolic delegate.

9. In the scene where Pius tried to forbid Fr. Fontana from pinning the Star of David on his cassock, the Pope says: "We forbid him to do it—forbid it ex cathedra!" This is absurd. Ex cathedra pronouncements can be made only in respect of dogmatic formulations.[17]

The historical aspects of *The Deputy* contain further circumstantial evidence that the show was produced by the KGB's framing experts. The printed play's appendix, entitled "Sidelights on History," has been described as follows:

Forty-five pages of demonstration and proof! But the quantity is deceptive. The materials are all mixed up higgledy-piggledy; seldom are we
told precisely where the arguments and quotations come from ... "Solid
collections of sources are mentioned only in isolated instances; but
evidence and witnesses of dubious value are mentioned frequently ....
The work is based on second and third-hand evidence, on popular books
which do not even claim to provide a final clarification ... "[18]

The "Sidelights" reveals a close association with postwar Soviet propaganda. As German scholar Michael Feldkamp noted: "In the summer of 1963
the Vatican pointed out 'numerous similarities' between Hochhuth's play and
'the usual communist propaganda against the Church and the Pope,' among
them the charge of a 'common crusade with Hitler against the Soviet Union,'
and the claim that the 'enormous economic power' of the Holy See and the
Jesuit order explained their abandonment of Christian moral principles."[19] The
West German government even expressed its "deepest regret" for such attacks
on Pius XII, since he had protested racial persecution by the Third Reich and
had "saved as many Jews as possible from the hands of their persecutors."[20]

More recently, Giovanni Maria Vian, editor of the Vatican's newspaper
L'Osservatore Romano, wrote that the play "took up many of the ideas
proposed by Mikhail Markovich Scheinmann in his book *Der Vatican in
Zweiten Weltkrieg* ("The Vatican in the Second World War"), first published
in Russian by the Historical Institute of the Soviet Academy of Sciences, a
propaganda instrument of Communist ideology."[21] Vian noted that Pius
XII's approach during the war had been "anti-Communist, and because of
this, already during the war, the Pope became the target of Soviet propaganda
as being in cahoots with Nazism and its horrors."[22]

Scheinmann's book, of course, was pure Soviet propaganda. Historian
John Conway explained:

Scheinmann's book is notable for its assiduous culling of source material
and the utter perversity of its conclusions. According to Scheinmann,
Pope Pius XII was obsessed by one thought alone, the need to organize a
crusade against the Soviet Union, and he sought every possible assistance
for this purpose. In consequence the acts of any anti-Soviet government,
however criminal, were to be ignored or even approved. Various aspects
of this "portrait" have been taken over by Hochhuth, though he explicitly
denies the charge that the Vatican was seeking to organize a crusade
against Bolshevism.[23]

Hochhuth had an advantage not available to Scheinmann. He— and his legion of promoters and defenders— could deflect any criticism by pointing out that it was a play; it was fiction. At the same time, especially with the historical appendix, *The Deputy* had a claim of historical honesty. It was a true highpoint for Soviet disinformation.

20

DISINFORMATION UNDER
EVERY ROCK

*T*HE DEPUTY ran for only a couple of weeks in Berlin, receiving mixed reviews at best, but it caused a political uproar.[1] Its negative view of Pius XII was denied by virtually every person who had firsthand knowledge of the pope's wartime activities. German chancellor Konrad Adenauer even apologized to the Vatican for Piscator's production.[2]

Despite its short and commercially unsuccessful debut, however, *Der Stellvertreter* was quickly translated and produced by some of the most prominent names in theater. All were Western communists or sympathizers. The first French production of *Der Stellvertreter* took place at the *Théâtre de l'Athénée* in Paris. The translator was Jorge Semprún, an award-winning novelist and playwright. He was also an active communist.[3]

Semprún had been a communist militant since his youth, and he joined a communist resistance group in France during World War II. After the war, while still in France, he also joined the exiled Communist Party of Spain (PCE). For nearly a decade in the 1950s and early 1960s, Semprún organized clandestine activities for the PCE.[4] In fact, at the time when he translated Hochhuth's play, he was still an active member of the party's top echelon, the Politburo. Only after being expelled from the Politburo in 1965 (over strategy differences) did Semprún truly focus on his legitimate writing career.[5]

The French production was codirected by Francis Darbon and noted

British director Peter Brook. Like Piscator, Brook was a theatrical legend. Unlike Piscator and Semprún, there is no documented evidence that he was a *member* of the Communist Party. As a young man, however, Brook wrote that his "political certainties" had been shaken when the Soviets reached an accord with the Nazis.[6] Furthermore, during World War II Brook produced a play (his first attempt at directing), with the proceeds going to the "Aid to Russia Fund."[7] In 1955, he made a very successful tour of the Soviet Union.[8] Discussing the Soviets' attraction to his work, Brook explained: "Above all, they kept commenting on what they termed our simplicity, austerity and economy. Suddenly they realized that they were using the very words with which Khrushchev had launched his new line of architecture."[9] Later, when Brook put together an anti-Vietnam play, *US*, the Lord Chamberlain complained that it was "bestial, anti-American, and Communist."[10]

Brook's production of *The Deputy* ran for about six months in Paris, and it went a long way toward establishing the so-called Theatre of Fact in France.[11] Brook, however, did not like the "Theatre of Fact" label. "You can never get to the facts," he said. "I'd rather call it the theatre of myth."[12]

In addition to working in France, Brook was one of the three permanent directors of the new, but highly regarded, Royal Shakespeare Company (RSC) at the Aldwych Theatre in London. This company was established by Peter Hall (later, Sir Peter Reginald Franklin Hall), another one of the most influential figures in postwar British theater.[13] He and Brook served as permanent directors along with French director Michel St. Denis.[14] Like many young directors at the time, Hall was deeply influenced by popular theatrical trends, and the RSC soon came "to be regarded as an avant-garde stronghold."[15]

In his book *Strategies of Political Theatre*, author Michael Patterson lists the 1961 establishment of the RSC and its expansion into the Aldwych Theatre (which permitted more modern productions) in a "brief chronology" of political theatre.[16] In 1962, a commentator wrote: "At the Aldwych . . . Peter Hall has offered incomparable opportunities to several dramatists of the new school in recent months."[17] On the other hand, "some London visitors [were] puzzled to find a Shakespeare company so relentlessly dedicated to introducing the newest and fartherest-out [sic] drama."[18] (A few years later, Emile Littler, a theatrical producer and a board member of the RSC, expressed moral outrage at the "dirt plays" that the company was producing at the Aldwych.[19])

Der Stellvertreter received its first English production in London by the Royal Shakespeare Company at the Aldwych Theatre in 1963 under the title *The Representative*.[20] Robert David MacDonald translated the play for the RSC.[21] He had worked as a translator for the United Nations Educational, Scientific and Cultural Organization (UNESCO) in the 1950s. At that time, UNESCO was perceived by many as a platform for communists to attack the West,[22] and the KGB used it to place agents around the world.[23] (UNESCO also assisted with the publication of the journal *World Theatre*, which praised Erwin Piscator's courage for bringing *Der Stellvertreter* to the stage.)[24]

While working at UNESCO, MacDonald met Piscator. Although he had no prior theatrical experience, MacDonald "immediately became involved in theatre as a director."[25] He worked with Piscator in Berlin, and the two men formed a close professional relationship. This led to MacDonald's translating (and reworking) *Der Stellvertreter* into English.[26]

The period 1963–64 was the highpoint in terms of Communist Party membership in Great Britain, and political theater was just beginning to take hold.[27] "Like shock waves expanding concentrically across all of Europe, interest in the epic theater of [German Communist playwright Bertolt] Brecht grew in direct proportion as the ideology of Communism gained respectability within Europe's intellectual classes."[28] Several new and talented playwrights "shared a laudable but strange conviction: that by writing plays and having them performed, they might help to change the way society is structured."[29] By 1978, *Performing Arts Journal* would report: "In general, the hope of political theatre groups is that, eventually, Britain will have a Marxist-based socialist government representing the working class, and that production and distribution will be worker controlled."[30]

The director who handled *The Representative* at the Aldwych was Clifford Williams.[31] He added a new scene at the beginning of the play and ended with a film of the Auschwitz victims being buried by bulldozer.[32] Newspaper clippings and other documents were also read over loudspeakers at different points in the play.[33] Of Williams it was written: "Hochhuth's play undoubtedly spurred Williams's interest—at a time of shifting social and theatrical perspectives in theatre that might provoke arguments or disturb complacency."[34] Of course, Williams had come to the RSC from the "Left-wing and indeed almost Communist" Theatre Workshop,[35] where he had trained under the noted communist director Joan Littlewood.[36]

The American publisher of *Der Stellvertreter* was Grove Press in New York. Grove Press belonged to Barney Rosset, a self-proclaimed communist, who purchased the company in 1951, and turned it into an influential alternative press. Among the radical political thinkers and writers Grove Press published in the 1960s were Malcolm X and Erwin Piscator's old partner, Bertolt Brecht. Grove Press also published Che Guevara's diaries, with an introduction by Fidel Castro. Che's diaries, of course, were produced by the Kremlin's *dezinformatsiya* machinery. His KGB-enhanced diaries were serialized in *Evergreen Review* and then released in book form by Grove Press. *Evergreen Review*, like Grove Press, was owned by Barney Rosset. In a 2006 interview, Rosset was asked about his religion. He replied that he never had a religion: "So I became a Communist. As a religion. And you better believe it."[37]

Evergreen Review also promoted *The Deputy*. In May 1964, just after the play opened on Broadway, *Evergreen Review* published an article written by Hochhuth.[38] In addition, not only did the magazine run advertisements for the book version of *The Deputy*; it used cross-marketing and advertised Rudolf Vrba's *I Cannot Forgive*, calling it "an eyewitness report— documenting *The Deputy*—by a man who escaped from Auschwitz."[39] In actuality, Vrba's account proved highly suspect, and he later admitted that he had taken "artistic license" in writing it.[40]

Herman Shumlin was the American producer who brought *Der Stellvertreter* to Broadway as *The Deputy*. While he was not of the same historic importance as Piscator or Brook, he had a long, successful career in film and on the stage. Among his Broadway productions were *The Last Mile* (1930), *Grand Hotel* (1930), *The Children's Hour* (1934), *The Little Foxes* (1939), *The Male Animal* (1940), *The Corn Is Green* (1940), *Watch on the Rhine* (1941), *The Searching Wind* (1944), *Inherit the Wind* (1955), and *The Deputy* (1964).

Shumlin was also an active communist. According to *Time* magazine (February 5, 1940), Shumlin was the only producer who advertised in the communist *Daily Worker*. The article went on to note that "Mr. Shumlin had almost no friends except Leftist Lillian Hellman." Hellman, with whom Shumlin had a professional and a romantic relationship, was outspoken in her support for communism. The notes for a play she authored (*The Little Foxes*) state that she was "known both for her mink coats and her outspoken support of the Communist Party and communist-affiliated organizations."[41]

Shumlin served as chairman of "the leftist Joint Anti-Fascist Refugee Committee" (JAFRC).[42] This organization was "originally formed by Communists to aid Stalinist refugees from Spain."[43] Although the JAFRC's charter was to raise money for relief causes, after World War II it sent funds to Yugoslavia, helping the communists win the first postwar elections. In 1947, JAFRC was investigated for communist infiltration by the House Committee on Un-American Activities. When JAFRC refused to turn records over, a federal judge held Shumlin and fifteen other members of JAFRC guilty of contempt of Congress. Shumlin was given a five-hundred-dollar fine and a suspended three-month jail term.[44]

In 1964, Shumlin received a Tony award for bringing *The Deputy* to Broadway. This was perhaps due in large part to the perceived bravery it took to stand up against all of those who objected to the play's characterization of Pius. Many critics did not like Shumlin's version of *The Deputy*, but it ran on Broadway for almost a year. That seems not to have been as a result of the play's theatrical quality. Discussing concern about violence from protestors at the opening, *New York Times* theater critic Frank Rich wrote: "The only bomb was on stage, but the publicity turned the show, now forgotten, into a quasi-hit and earned its producer a Tony for his courage."[45] Another critic said the play was "like one of those comic-strip versions of a literary classic."[46]

It is probably to be expected that Shumlin would write a magazine article about the play. His piece appeared in the February 1964 issue of *Jewish World*. Another of the early praises of *The Deputy* published in the United States was written by David Horowitz.[47] As the latter has since explained, he was at that time a practicing communist.[48] Before eventually becoming a leader of the conservative (or neoconservative) political movement, Horowitz spent time in various leadership positions at *Ramparts* magazine, which made its way from its founding in the early 1960s as a Catholic periodical to a far-Left magazine suspected of having Soviet funding.[49]

By the end of his life, syndicated columnist Max Lerner was viewed by many as a conservative, but that turn came late. As a younger man, he backed the communists in the Spanish Civil War, and he was reluctant to denounce the Moscow purge trials.[50] Prior to the Hitler-Stalin pact that preceded World War II, Lerner and other American leftist intellectuals, including Soviet agent I. F. Stone, signed a letter that appeared in *The Nation* magazine (where Lerner served as political editor). The letter was a "full throated defense of Stalinism," and it criticized fellow liberals for being anticommunist.[51] At the end of the Second World War, Lerner attended a gala banquet with Red Army generals. Later he took up permanent residence in Hugh Hefner's Playboy Mansion. Like so many other Americans with leftist ties, he wrote a piece promoting *The Deputy*.[52]

Michael Harrington, originally a follower of American Catholic Dorothy Day, "dropped Day's anarchism, pacifism and religion, in that order."[53] He praised *The Deputy* in *Midstream* magazine (December 1963). At this time, Harrington was the American Socialist Party's bridge to new student members. A "lifelong Socialist," Harrington was the chairman of Democratic Socialists of America and the leader of the American socialist movement until his death, in 1989.[54] Of course, many communists wrote under pseudonyms, making later identification impossible. [55]

In March 1964, as *The Deputy* was opening on Broadway, Susan Sontag, who throughout her career was criticized for repeating Marxist jargon,[56] highly praised *The Deputy* in "Book World," a section of the *New York Herald Tribune*.[57] This was about two years before Sontag emerged as an important American writer and political activist who marched "under the dual banners of modernism and Marxism."[58] In fact, as late as 1978—well after she recognized that Marxism was often used to support totalitarian regimes— she said: "I want to remain Marxist in a certain sense."[59]

Just months after *The Deputy* debuted in Berlin, Rowohlt of Hamburg, the far-left German publisher of the play, came out with a paperback book titled *Summa Iniuria, oder Durfte der Papst Schweigen?* ("The Height of Injustice, or Should the Pope Have Remained Silent?"). It contained "90 commentaries selected from more than 3,000 major articles, addresses, and brochures dealing with the play."[60] The compiler of the essays, Fritz J. Raddatz, was best known as a scholar of Karl Marx. He wrote *Karl Marx: A Political Biography*,[61] and he edited a collection of letters between Marx and Friedrich Engels.[62]

As a matter of fact, Raddatz very likely played a role in Rowohlt's publication of *Der Stellvertreter* from the outset. In the 1950s, Raddatz was head of the foreign department and deputy chief of the *Volk und Welt* (People and World) publishing house in East Berlin—positions that in my experience would have required him to have a relationship with the East German Stasi, and possibly with the KGB. In 1958, Raddatz crossed over into West Germany and settled in Hamburg, where by 1960 he had become the chief reader of the Rowohlt publishing house, as well as close associate and deputy to Heinrich Maria Ledig-Rowohlt, the head of the firm. He remained with Rowohlt until 1969.[63]

In the United States, the communist-owned Grove Press did the same thing as Rowohlt, publishing a book entitled *The Storm over the Deputy: Essays and articles about Hochhuth's explosive drama* just months after the play debuted on Broadway. This book was a collection of essays, reviews, and interviews related to the play and the issues it raised. The editor of this collection was Eric Bentley, best known for his work on the German communist playwright (and former Piscator collaborator) Bertolt Brecht— "the world's most famous communist."[64] Bentley also edited the Grove Press edition of Brecht's work, and he wrote a highly personal memoir of his years with Brecht and a play based upon Brecht's testimony before the House Committee on Un-American Activities.[65] Many of the reviews and essays included in *The Storm over the Deputy* were penned by authors with close ties to communism, but even those essays that defended Pius served the purpose of keeping this issue alive.

The Deputy finally made it to film in 2002, in the motion picture *Amen*. The screenwriter for the project was Jorge Semprún, the former member of the Spanish Communist Party's Politburo who had translated the play into French.[66] The film's accomplished director was Constantinos Gavras, better known as Costa-Gavras. After World War II, Gavras's Greek father was found to be a communist and sent to prison. Costa-Gavras was denied a visa to the United States over concern that he was also a communist. Some of his later politically charged films seemed to confirm that suspicion, but he also made films critical of totalitarian (Soviet) regimes. There is no proof that he was a member of the Communist Party.[67]

21

KGB FINGERPRINTS

A FEW MONTHS AFTER *THE DEPUTY* was launched on Broadway, an American journalistic icon, who is still compared to the likes of H. L. Mencken and William F. Buckley, published a powerful piece faulting the Catholic Church for its role in the rise of Fascism. Writing in his own influential weekly, I. F. Stone stated:

> Pius XII, in being friendly to Hitler [and to Mussolini] was only following in the footsteps of Pius XI . . . . More than the sin of silence lies on the consciences of God's "deputies." They were accessories in the creation of these criminal regimes . . . . It helps to heal our hearts that a young German should have written *The Deputy*. It is also a good sign that the play should have aroused such animosity—like a painful memory dragged unwillingly from the subconscious of a whole generation.[1]

Later that year, Stone wrote another piece, insinuating that Pius XII had feared Hitler.[2] Recently published KGB documents in the *Vassiliev Archive* show that I. F. Stone (né Isidor Feinstein) was a paid Soviet spy. He had originally been recruited by the NKVD in 1936 on ideological grounds and given the codename "Blin" (Russian for "pancake").[3] Venona intercepts of highly classified, Soviet-intelligence-enciphered communication from 1944 show that Stone then had a new NKVD handler, Vladimir Pravdin, whom he agreed to meet regularly and to whom he indicated that he would not be averse to having a "supplementary income."

In a cable sent to Moscow, Pravdin recommended to NKVD headquarters that if this "business" relationship were agreed upon, then Stone would have to do his part and really produce. Subsequent Venona intercepts show that by December 1944 the business relationship had worked out, and Stone was being secretly paid by the NKVD for producing articles on subjects recommended to him by Moscow. Throughout his career, Stone's articles indicate he continued to be used by Soviet intelligence as a *dezinformatsiya* outlet.[4]

Changing minds is what Soviet communism was all about. Changing minds was also Stone's main task as Soviet spy. He was prominent in his day, and he was certainly a prize asset for the NKVD/KGB. It is now known to be more than coincidental that his articles expressed the position of the Soviet Union on so many issues: demonizing the Korean policies of John Foster Dulles, General MacArthur, and President Truman; condemning US efforts to prevent communist expansion in Vietnam; belittling the FBI and embarrassing J. Edgar Hoover; maligning Pope Pius XII and faulting the Catholic Church—the KGB's archenemy—for the Nazi persecution of Jews; supporting the Kremlin's efforts to persuade the world that there was no Soviet involvement in the JFK assassination; and many, many similar issues. Even some of the issues for which he might be hailed today, including opposition to racial discrimination and McCarthyism, were right in line with the Soviet position at the time.

Stone's prominence and his caustic style played an immense role in calling attention to *The Deputy* and making it a *cause célèbre*. In addition, Stone's sister, leftist theater critic Judy Stone, contributed a friendly interview with Hochhuth, which was published in *Ramparts* magazine in the spring of 1964.[5]

In 1963, as *The Deputy* was beginning to create a stir in Berlin and cause a rift between Catholics and Jews, a KGB-sponsored publisher in the United States, the Liberty-Prometheus Book Club, republished an old book that mirrored the charges raised by *The Deputy*. The book was *Shylock: The History of a Character*, authored by Hermann Sinsheimer, and it focused on the mistreatment of Jews by popes and other Christians.[6] As the KGB had hoped, this book found its way into major media outlets, where authors sympathetic to *The Deputy* continued the play's promotion.[7]

Liberty-Prometheus Book Club was co-owned by Carl Aldo Marzani, an Italian-born American communist and very active Soviet *dezinformatsiya* agent, probably recruited before World War II.[8] After the war, he served thirty-two months in prison for concealing his membership in the Communist Party while working for the State Department. Upon his release he went into various leftist publishing ventures, for which he received KGB subsidies.[9]

Documents in the Mitrokhin Archive show that over the years Marzani (KGB codenamed "Nord," German for *north*), received substantial sums of money for having his Liberty Book Club publishing company (codenamed "Sever," Russian for *north*) produce pro-Soviet material. Marzani was also given an annual ten thousand dollars to advertise those books aggressively.[10] (Years ago, Soviet intelligence often used German words to designate its agents abroad, probably because many of its undercover handlers were from Central Europe and spoke that language. The fact that Marzani had a German codename supports the suggestion that he may have been a prewar recruit.)

In early 1960, the KGB station in New York, which was handling Marzani, sent an enciphered cable to Moscow recommending that he be given an additional six thousand to seven thousand dollars, in order to enable Liberty Book Club to continue publishing pro-Soviet material. The cable justified its request as follows:

> NORD is an extremely energetic person and is quite devoted to his task. Despite his financial difficulties, he is struggling to keep SEVER afloat. SEVER, together with its commercial bookselling network, the Prometheus Book Club, has been in existence for fourteen years. During this time it has published and distributed more than 200 titles of a progressive nature, by both American and foreign authors. The catalogue of the SEVER publishing firm lists around fifty titles, and the Prometheus Book Club has 7,000 members. Books are also sent to 8,000 addresses on an individual basis.

In May 1960, the International Department of the Soviet Communist Party's Central Committee, which was responsible for supplying the *dezinformatsiya* funds in this instance, approved a secret grant of fifteen thousand dollars, more than twice what the New York KGB station had requested.[11]

It was entirely unusual for the Communist Party's International Department to have been brought into the plans for what at first blush seems to have been a general and fairly routine disinformation operation that had been around for years. Moreover, although the New York station's cable was sent to KGB headquarters in Moscow, from the overblown wording of the request for funds it is clear in retrospect that the cable was actually addressed to the International Department—KGB headquarters had been funding Marzani for many years and did not need to be told what he did and how good he was at it. It is also particularly remarkable that more than double the requested amount was quickly approved.

The significance of the above cable exchange lies in when it took place—early 1960. It was in February 1960 that Khrushchev approved an all-out, very secret operational plan designed to destroy the Vatican's moral authority and at the same time to tarnish the reputation of the United States. The plan had been dreamt up by KGB chairman Aleksandr Shelepin together with Alexei Kirichenko, the Politburo member responsible for international policy. The operation was to be carried out jointly by the KGB and the Communist Party, i.e., the latter's International Department. The cable exchange is evidence that the KGB immediately tasked its stations abroad to contribute in whatever way they could to this offensive, just as my DIE was given the assignment to procure any and all possible Vatican documents.

In 1963, the first book about the Kennedy assassination to appear in the United States, *Oswald: Assassin or Fall Guy?*, was published by Marzani.[12] That book, written by a documented KGB agent, Joachim Joesten, alleged that the CIA had killed President Kennedy, but, as with *The Deputy*, it did not produce any evidence to support the charge.

The first review of Joesten's book was signed by an American journalist also paid by the KGB, Victor Perlo (identified as a Soviet agent by Elisabeth Bentley and Whittaker Chambers, and in the Venona electronic intercepts). Perlo's endorsing review was published in *New Times* (a KGB front, at one time secretly printed in Romania), which published nine more articles on the assassination, all accusing elements in the United States of the crime.

Perlo also wrote one of the first laudatory reviews of *The Deputy*, for the same KGB front, *New Times*.[13] Many people in the United States and around the world are still convinced, even today, that the CIA was behind President Kennedy's assassination. Many people around the world also continue to believe another of the Kremlin's lies: that Pius XII was "Hitler's Pope."

M. S. (Max) Arnoni, a Holocaust survivor, onetime editor of the *Encyclopedia Britannica*, and publisher of *A Minority of One*, a highbrow magazine for the liberal American elite, also jumped in to promote *The Deputy*. According to former KGB general Oleg Kalugin, now an American citizen, Arnoni received money from the KGB for promoting the Soviet line in the American media. Kalugin spent years spying in the United States for the KGB under the cover of a journalist.[14] One of his tasks was to recruit agents in American left-leaning magazines and newspapers.[15] Kalugin would even, on occasion, finance these magazines and newspapers and then plant stories reflecting the Soviet line, hoping that other news outlets would repeat them. Kalugin wrote: "I had no qualms about stirring up as much trouble as possible . . . . "[16] American communists were happy to help with such projects. As a recent commentator noted: "However loathsome and psychotic" J. Edgar Hoover's FBI may have been, it "got one thing right: The [Communist Party of the United States] was an arm of Soviet foreign policy, no more, no less."[17]

Kalugin developed close ties with Arnoni. At first, Kalugin simply relied on his friendship with the publisher of *A Minority of One* to place KGB-written articles into his magazine. As Arnoni's financial situation worsened, Kalugin first funded the publication of some letter/ads (often signed by several leftist journalists) in the *New York Times*. Eventually, Kalugin gave Arnoni ten thousand from the KGB. Arnoni hid the source of the funds. "Thus did the KGB infiltrate a small yet influential American publication."[18] Arnoni "unwittingly did the bidding of the KGB."[19]

Arnoni became a strong supporter of *The Deputy*. Not only did he write in support of the play in his own journal; he also wrote an article for another periodical, *American Dialog*.[20] Beyond discussing Hochhuth's drama, he made inflammatory "factual" assertions that are demonstrably false.[21] For instance, Arnoni wrote that "the man who was to become Pius XII was deeply involved in the politics of ultra-rightist German parties."[22]

The US Communist Party, secretly financed by the KGB, also joined in. When the *New York Times Book Review* decided to do a major, front-page article on *The Deputy*, it explained that it had turned to a Catholic scholar (George N. Shuster) and a non-Catholic scholar (Robert Gorham Davis).[23] It did not explain that Davis had been a member of the Communist Party, who had testified before, and "named names" to, the US House Committee on Un-American Activities.[24]

By early 1964, when *The Deputy* was about to open on Broadway, so many religious leaders, politicians, diplomats, and others had spoken against it that it was somewhat of an international scandal. New York's Cardinal Spellman called *The Deputy* "an outrageous desecration of the honor of a great and good man."[25] The National Council of Catholic Men and the American Jewish Committee tried to talk the television networks out of promoting the play.[26] Jewish War Veterans even marched on the play's opening day to boycott it and defend the pope's honor.[27]

With the play's ability to open in serious jeopardy, a little magazine from San Francisco, with Catholic roots and a communist future, took the lead in defending it. In fact, without *Ramparts* magazine, *The Deputy* might never have played on Broadway. (A few years later, similar concerns about the historical honesty of Hochhuth's next play, *Soldiers*, kept it from opening at the National Theatre in London.) Hochhuth repaid *Ramparts* by granting the magazine one of the very few interviews he gave in those days. It was conducted by Judy Stone, sister of "investigative journalist" and spy I. F. Stone.

Ramparts was founded in 1962 by Edward Keating as a liberal Catholic quarterly. Very quickly, however, Keating became disillusioned with the institutional Church.[28] After just a few issues he changed direction, saying: "From now on, it's no more Mr. Nice Guy."[29]

Keating started by soliciting an article from a Louisiana priest who had been critical of the Church's record on race relations. After the article was written, but before it went to press, the priest and his bishop both tried to recall it. Keating ignored their requests and published the piece anyway.[30] In the next issue, *Ramparts* called for a liberalization in the Church's teaching on contraception.

Ramparts soon explored the "natural" connection between Catholics and the John Birch Society. As *Ramparts* Editor Warren Hinckle explained, Keating went from a "respectfully orthodox convert to a brazen anti-cleric who would make jokes in public and even in the presence of nuns about 'taking a bite out of the Pope's ass.'"[31]

Of course, *Ramparts* found it handy to hold onto its "Catholic" image as long as it could. Hinckle said he talked Keating into defending *The Deputy* by telling him that "he could become famous overnight if he, a Catholic publisher, headed a committee to defend the Pope-baiting play." Keating agreed—with a vengeance.

In early 1964, Keating wrote articles supporting *The Deputy* for three different publications: *Ramparts, This World* magazine, and the *San Francisco Chronicle*.[32] He also made an important appearance on the WABC television program *New York, New York*. Keating's biggest contribution, however, came when he released a wartime letter that had been written by a prominent member of the Roman Curia, Eugene Cardinal Tisserant, to Emanuel Cardinal Suhard, the archbishop of Paris. In it, Tisserant wrote: "I fear that history will reproach the Holy See for having followed a policy of comfort and convenience, and not much else."[33]

As soon as Keating released the letter, Tisserant issued a statement explaining that it was not about Pope Pius XII or the Jews. Tisserant had written it in a fit of anger on the day after Italy joined the war, and he was mad that other clergy did not make calls for peace similar to those frequently made by Pius XII. "The pope's attitude was beyond discussion," he explained. "My remarks did not involve his person, but certain members of the Curia. In the dramatic period of the War, and what a period that was, Pius XII was able to guide the Church with invincible strength." Tisserant told the *New York Times*: "It seems evident to me that the principles, reaffirmed by Pope Pacelli in his first encyclical, and repeated forcefully at every circumstance, above all in the Christmas messages of the war years, constitute the most concrete condemnation of the Hitlerian type of absolutism."[34] In fact, the *Times* published excerpts from an address that Tisserant had given during the war in which he praised Pius XII's wartime conduct. Nevertheless, the timing of Keating's release garnered significant attention.

Tisserant's letter apparently had been seized from Cardinal Suhard's files by the Gestapo when the Nazis took Paris late in World War II. Precisely how it got from the Gestapo archives to Keating is unclear. It may have fallen into Soviet hands after the war and from there made its way to the magazine's headquarters. Throughout the 1960s, *Ramparts* came up with many documents and stories that cast the Soviet Union in a good light or its enemies in a bad one, and the sources of information were often hard to uncover. In his memoirs, editor Warren Hinckle acknowledged his own suspicion about the source of some of the information he received, suggesting that it was either the KGB or a rogue operation from inside of the CIA. He eventually took to setting up secret meetings and using coded language.[35]

Beyond convincing Keating to adopt *The Deputy* as a cause, Hinckle played a big role in seeing that the Broadway curtain went up on the play. By his own account, he invented an "ecumenical conspiracy" in support of the play. He formed a committee with a Soviet-sounding name: the Ad Hoc Committee to Defend the Right of *The Deputy* to be Heard. He found "a few prominent Protestants," like social activist John C. Bennett, to join the committee, but he had trouble finding any Catholic leaders who would do so.[36] Hinckle spoke to one auxiliary bishop, "highly regarded for his liberalism, who told me he would rather endorse a company that put the picture of Jesus Christ on packages of contraceptives than get involved on the side of the author of *The Deputy*." In desperation, he signed up some laymen he called "Catholic window dressing." The laymen, Gordon Zahn and John Howard Griffin, were rewarded by later being named associate editors of *Ramparts*.[37]

Hinckle also drafted two Jews: Rabbi Abraham Heschel of the Jewish Theological Seminary and Maxwell Geismar, a critic and literary historian. Of Geismar, Hinckle wrote: "a wonderful man about whom I cannot marshal enough superlatives, who, from our chance meeting during the white-heat controversy over *The Deputy*, was to become almost instantly my closest friend, confidant, foster father, and soul mate, and the most important intellectual influence on the developing *Ramparts*." This "most important intellectual influence" on Hinckle and *Ramparts* was an avowed Marxist who wrote the introduction to Eldridge Cleaver's book, *Soul on Ice*, a collection of essays written while Cleaver was in prison, serving time for drug dealing and rape. (Cleaver later became a senior editor at *Ramparts*. He also joined the Black Panthers, was arrested following a shootout, fled to various communist nations, became disenchanted with communism, and returned to face charges.)

Hinckle later admitted that his Ad Hoc Committee to Defend the Right of *The Deputy* to be Heard was "in the finest tradition of Potemkin villages." It "barely had as many members as words in its cumbersome title." It did, however, serve his purpose. As he later wrote: "Armed with press release, we marched out to do murder in the Cathedral."

Hinckle, who had never been to New York before, sent out provocative press releases and threw a catered press conference (likened by many to a party) in New York's *Waldorf Astoria* hotel. He sent long (and expensive) telegram invitations and followed up with telegram reminders to "everyone in New York City in possession of a pencil or camera." In length, according to Hinckle, the telegrams were "somewhere between the Gettysburg Address and the Declaration of Independence, and kept the Western Union lady on the telephone for nearly three hours, as I dictated to her the names and addresses of an eclectic group of invitees drawn at whim and whimsy from the Yellow Pages." Among the recipients of the telegrams were not only the major publications, but also *The American Organist, Bedside Nurse, Casket and Sunnyside, Detergent Age, Elementary Electronics, Floor Covering Weekly*, and dozens of similar trade and industry publications.[38]

It took far more money than a magazine like *Ramparts* would logically be able to devote to such a project to pull this off, but Hinckle attracted a huge crowd. One photographer said it was the biggest press conference he'd seen since Adlai Stevenson conceded in the presidential race. When a reporter questioned why no other members of the "blue ribbon committee" had shown up besides Hinckle and Keating, they said that the "room was too crowded."

Ramparts' defense of *The Deputy* overshadowed most of the news critical of the play in the final days before opening night and made sure the curtain went up. It was never really clear why the California-based *Ramparts* decided to promote the New York play or how it could justify the cost, but subsequent history sheds some light on the matter.

Ramparts dropped most of its Catholic identity shortly after *The Deputy* episode. In October 1964, Keating said *Ramparts* "more or less" came from a Catholic viewpoint, adding that the magazine could be described as catholic with a small c.[39] It soon, and routinely, published "no holds barred" criticisms of members of the Catholic hierarchy—unprecedented in the Catholic press at that time. In 1965, the president of the Catholic Press Association denounced the magazine as "unethical." In December of that year, the magazine described itself as "New Left," not Catholic. Hinckle explained: "there weren't enough Catholic laymen to write for and to buy the magazine. Besides, we got bored with just the church."[40]

In 1967, *Time* magazine editorialized: "no other left-wing publication in the United States pursues shock more recklessly or plays around more with facts."[41] As former *Ramparts* insider Sol Stern explained, "*Ramparts* would stretch or deny the truth to sell our counter narrative about America and the world." He also said: "The passions that moved us were not those that moved the Founders. We were not liberals. We were socialists and anti-imperialists...."[42]

Ramparts made a deal with the Cuban government to publish Che

Guevara's diaries, with an introduction by Fidel Castro. According to former editor Sol Stern, the agreement "required us to publish a Fidel Castro rant, filled with Communist propaganda and denunciations of American 'barbarism.'" Stern explained:

> We believed that the revolution was a great leap forward for the socialist cause. We followed the lead of one of our intellectual heroes, Columbia University sociologist C. Wright Mills, in arguing that Fidel Castro was a new breed of revolutionary leader—more humanist, more open, even more hip than old-style bureaucratic Communists. In fact, we imagined Fidel and Che as fellow New Leftists."[43]

Earlier, *Ramparts* managing editor Robert Scheer had coauthored a book defending Castro's Cuban revolution.

Ramparts was an early opponent of the Vietnam War. One of the magazine's best-known covers showed the hands of four of its editors burning their draft cards. Explaining the magazine's position in favor of withdrawing from Vietnam, Stern said:

> I suppose you might say that such a withdrawal would have let the Vietnamese people "make their own history." But the real reason that *Ramparts* was for total withdrawal of American troops was that we wanted the Communists to win and were sure that they would. In the view of most of the editors, the Communists were Vietnam's rightful rulers.[44]

Moreover, it was not just America's involvement in Vietnam that drew criticism from the magazine. "Instead of urging Americans to take pride in the founding ideals of the Republic, *Ramparts*' editors and writers were preoccupied with attacking America's liberal institutions."[45]

While it no longer claimed a Catholic identity, until at least 1969 *Ramparts* devoted special attention to the Catholic Church. According to former communist and onetime *Ramparts* editor Peter Collier, Hinckle encouraged articles on "the new spirit of dissent within the Catholic Church being." Articles from this era opposed Church teaching on sexuality (especially Pope Paul VI's teaching on birth control in *Humanae Vitae*), complained about abuse of authority by the Catholic hierarchy, and promoted leftist "liberation" theology. *Ramparts* religion editor James F. Colaianni identified priestly celibacy, authoritarianism, suppression of socially aware priests, lack of communication, absence of grievance procedures, and summary disciplinary actions as some of the greatest structural problems with the Church.[46]

Ramparts eventually adopted a communist operational model, but that proved unsustainable. David Horowitz, who was a communist when he edited the magazine late in the 1960s, later explained:

> Without a formal hierarchy at *Ramparts*, every issue that came up had to be debated. The need to justify decisions was not only time-consuming for us, but at times cruel to others, as I discovered when we attempted to reduce the mailroom budget at *Ramparts* and were met with a political revolt. The mailroom was staffed by members of Newsreel, a "collective" of radicals who had made promotional films for the Black Panthers and the Vietcong. They had no respect for our publication. The revolution's pecking order had again shifted to the left, and we could not overcome the view that *Ramparts* was part of the power structure that needed to be overthrown.[47]

When *Ramparts* collapsed once and for all in 1975, three of its principals formed the leftist magazine *Mother Jones*. They were supported in this effort by the Institute for Policy Studies, which has been linked to KGB disinformation campaigns.[48]

CIA documents released under the Freedom of Information Act confirm that by 1966, *Ramparts* was a reliable outlet for Soviet propaganda. The CIA eventually devoted twelve full-time or part-time officers to investigating *Ramparts*. They identified and investigated 127 writers and researchers, as well as nearly two hundred other people with some link to the magazine who were suspected of advancing the Soviet cause.[49] Many of those who were investigated have since admitted they were using *Ramparts* to advance communism. That is exactly what they were doing when they used the magazine to promote *The Deputy*.

22

THE DEPUTY'S ANTI-SEMITISM

WHEN *THE DEPUTY* DEBUTED, many reviewers and commentators noted its distinct anti-Semitic flavor.[1] Trude Weiss-Rosmarin noted that the "play has *not one* Jewish character of strength and nobility."[2] She continued: "Jews have as strong a case against *The Deputy* as the Vatican . . . . Mr. Hochhuth has placed upon stage 'negative Jews' exclusively, Jews who conform to the Nazi stereotype."[3] *Time* magazine reported: "Hochhuth, a Protestant who once belonged to Hitler's youth corps, has been denounced as a pro-Communist and an anti-Semite."[4] *Ramparts*, a friendly outlet with a favorable review, observed that Hochhuth had been "damned variously as a Nazi, a Communist and an anti-Semite."[5] One of Hochhuth's biographers noted that he had difficulty portraying Jews.[6]

The Broadway producer of *The Deputy*, Herman Shumlin, cut out scenes of Jewish collaboration and certain Jewish characters from the American production.[7] Of Hochhuth's depiction of Jews, Shumlin said: "Why, he doesn't even know what a Jew looks like . . . . He has a stereotype of them as short men with eyeglasses."[8] Weiss-Rosmarin said: "Mr. Hochhuth's ignorance of Jews shows in his choice of those whom he regards as 'typical' victims of the Nazis. 'The Manufacturer,' who spits in the face of a Jew to prove that he has nothing in common with Jews, is in fact the Jew-hater's image—and so are the other thoroughly unsavory Jews who appear in *The Deputy*."[9] Jewish war veterans even marched on the play's Broadway opening, though they reportedly were more concerned about the depiction of Pius than that of Jews.[10]

Jewish actor and director Otto Preminger, who had directed films dealing with Catholics and Jews,[11] was so outraged at Hochhuth that he accused the playwright not only of having been a Nazi, but of having been a particularly vicious one. Hochhuth responded by demanding a retraction and threatening to sue if one were not forthcoming.[12] Rather than retracting, Preminger reasserted his charge. Hochhuth eventually filed suit for five hundred thousand dollars in the Southern District of New York, but he allowed the case to be dismissed before depositions or any other discovery took place.

Some have tried to find elements of anti-Semitism in the works of the famous nineteenth-century satirist Wilhelm Busch that Hochhuth edited in the late 1950s. Busch's satires did sometimes make fun of Jews—but also of clerics and schoolmasters and just about everyone else. Hochhuth argued that Busch was not actually anti-Semitic, citing one occasion on which he wrote about an innocent Jew hanged for a crime committed by Christians. Moreover, in an edition of Busch that he knew would be read by children, Hochhuth said that he omitted depictions of Jews, "so that German children would not mock the Jews."[13]

Hochhuth's usual response to charges of anti-Semitism was: "Whoever reads my play and still maintains the opinion that I am an anti-Semite, or Nazi, or Communist, that person cannot be answered."[14] He has recalled "with grief" the visit to his parents' house during the war of a Jewish woman married to a cousin. "She was very sweet to us and grateful," but when she returned home she committed suicide upon being called in by the Gestapo.[15] In fact, Hochhuth has described the main thesis of *The Deputy* as an accusation of Pius XII and the Church for not having done what they could have for the Jews.[16]

How then does one account for the anti-Semitism of *The Deputy?* The most logical conclusion is that it was introduced by the strongly anti-Semitic KGB. Anti-Semitism permeated the Kremlin in those years, and the play fit perfectly into the spirit of West German *and* Soviet policy at that time.

Given the Jewish backgrounds of both Marx and Lenin, as well as the claimed equality with which a communist society would treat all people, many Jews were attracted to both communist ideology and to the Soviet Union, and many prospered there—for a while. When Stalin took over and sought to solidify his power by engaging in *political necrophagy*, fostering anti-Semitism suited his needs. Perhaps this was an honest reflection of his beliefs—after all, he was perfectly willing to throw in with Hitler, and he continued persecuting Jews throughout his reign—but it also served his political needs. Anti-Semitism has continued to be a feature of Russian society, though there are occasional ebbs and flows.

Just months before *The Deputy* was allegedly born, I ended my assignment as acting chief of Romania's Trade Mission to West Germany and head of Romania's intelligence station in that country. There was no longer much open or official anti-Semitism there. The last of the thirteen Nuremberg Trials ("The High Command Trial") had ended a couple of years earlier, but the hunt for Jew-haters continued with ferocity, and even unrepentant anti-Semites no longer dared to express their hatred for Jews in the Western sphere.

Assigned as a diplomat to West Germany, I was privy to various tales about violence directed at anti-Semites. One case was later documented by Benjamin B. Ferencz, the chief prosecutor for the United States Army at the *Einsatzgruppen* Trial in West Germany.[17] In a 2005 interview, Ferencz revealed that during the early postwar years, the US Army used to deliver low-ranking Nazi suspects to Displaced Persons Camps for the purpose of having the suspects executed by the so-called Displaced Persons (DPs). According to Ferencz:

> I once saw DPs beat an SS man and then strap him to the steel gurney of the crematorium. They slid him in the oven, turned on the heat and took him back out. Beat him again, and put him back in until he was burned alive.[18]

It seems most unlikely for Hochhuth, a sane, young, and entirely unknown playwright who lived in *that* post-Nazi Germany, and who was only fourteen when the war came to an end, to have openly expressed the kind of anti-Semitic elements that are found in the original version of *The Deputy*. Far more likely is it that those anti-Semitic touches were inserted by Soviet intelligence operatives who truly felt that way.

In 1960, when I returned from Germany, there was a strong anti-Semitic attitude both in the Kremlin and at the top of the KGB's intelligence community. Jews were being removed from the KGB. The Romanian DIE and its mother organization, the Securitate, were also in the process of quietly removing them.

Khrushchev loathed Jews even more than Stalin did. "It's in my blood—

my serf's blood!" I heard Khrushchev say during his six-day vacation in Romania.[19] On that occasion, Romanian ruler Gheorghe Gheorghiu-Dej informed Khrushchev that the Israeli foreign intelligence service was prepared to pay Bucharest secretly in dollars for each Jew that would be allowed to emigrate. As far as Dej knew, that was a first in the Soviet bloc, and he did not have the courage to approve such a delicate operation all by himself.

Initially, Khrushchev exploded in a deluge of invectives against the "swindler *jidani* usurers" who believed "they could buy us the way they bought America." (*Jidan* was the worst Romanian pejorative for a Jew, and Khrushchev relished using it.) During dinner, however, the Soviet ruler changed his mind. He insisted that Dej take products, not cash, from the *jidani*, so that even if the operation eventually leaked out, it would not look like a sale of slaves. Khrushchev's choice of quid-pro-quo barter object was livestock farms, as he considered himself an expert in the agricultural field.

"Pigs for pigs," was the conclusion of General Sakharovsky— the head of the all-powerful Soviet espionage service, who had accompanied Khrushchev to Bucharest. So Romania started getting pig farms from Israel in exchange for exit visas for Romanian Jews.[20]

In the early 1970s, when I became the deputy head of the DIE, General Sakharovsky—still my de facto boss—took me on a tour of the infamous KGB interrogation complex in Moscow, called Lefortovo, to see a secret exhibit entitled "A Hundred Years of War against Zionism." There, in that forbidding-looking prison built in 1881, I was shown the torture chamber used to extort confessions from the "Jewish anarchists" seized by the Okhrana (predecessor of the KGB) after Tsar Alexander II was assassinated in 1882. I set foot into the office where Martyn Latsis, one of Feliks Dzerzhinsky's deputies, signed the documents authorizing the *Cheka* to shoot tens of thousands of "bourgeois Jews" who were "sabotaging the people's revolution." I saw the cell where in 1938, the *Cheka*, now upgraded to GPU (*Gosudarstvennoye Politicheskoye Upravleniye*, or State *Political* Directorate, a revealing name change), forced the founder of the Third International (an international communist organization), Nikolai Bukharin, to write a confession of "dastardly crimes" committed on behalf of American Zionism.[21]

I also saw the cell where Swedish diplomat Raoul Wallenberg, who had saved thousands of Jews from the gas chambers during World War II, had been secretly held—and killed—by the KGB, after being kidnapped from

Hungary in 1945.

Over the years, the Russian/Soviet/Russian political police changed its name many times, from Oprichnina to *Preobrazhenskiy Prikaz*, to Okhrana to *Cheka*, to GPU, to OGPU, to NKVD, to NKGB, to MGB, to MVD, to KGB, to MSB, to FSK, to today's FSB. All the while, Lefortovo prison remained unchanged, as a monument to the organization's unchanging hatred of the Jews.

In 1992, the "new" KGB of the post-Soviet Russia arrested two Russian scientists of Jewish descent, Vil Mirzayanov and Dr. Vladimir Uglev. They were sent to Lefortovo. The charge related to their simultaneous publication of articles in the Russian *Moscow News* and the American press asserting that Russia was secretly working to develop a nerve gas, in violation of national laws and international commitments.[22] To help the "new" KGB prosecute the case against these two "Jewish spies," Russian Prime Minister Viktor Chernomyrdin (a long-time communist and former Soviet official), signed a retroactive decree in May 1993 that made the revelations of the two scientists a crime.[23]

In May 1993, Will Englund, an American correspondent in Moscow, was summoned by the same "new" KGB to be interrogated about his connections with the two scientists. The Western world was astonished when it learned that Englund was called to the infamous Lefortovo, which for seventy-five years had been the gateway to communist firing squads and gulags. Even more telling was the communist seal with hammer and sickle that still adorned the interrogation room.[24]

23

THE DEPUTY'S IDEOLOGICAL ROOTS

T*HE DEPUTY* is just another Potemkin village. Its producer, Erwin Piscator, matured politically and professionally in the service of the Soviet Union, where all forms of the arts, including theater, were supposed to dish up the Kremlin's *dezinformatsiya* needs. Soviet composer Dmitri Shostakovich explained: "By the late 1920s the honeymoon with the Soviet government was over for genuine artists . . . . In order to be in favor, to receive commissions and live peacefully, one had to get into state harness and plug away."[1] To be branded as one who did not conform to the Soviet line could be lethal.[2] "For many years, the most gifted and sensitive of the Soviet poets, novelists and dramatists either were silent or wrote 'for the drawer'—secretly, or only for the intimacy of family and trusted friends."[3]

In April 1932, the Soviet government and the Communist Party issued an epic decree for Soviet artists: "On the Reorganization of Art and Literary Organizations."

This decree placed artistic control into the hands of two new groups: the Union of Soviet Writers and the Union of Soviet Composers.[4] Through these unions, Stalin secured an unprecedented degree of control over the arts and the artists.

Stalin strengthened and perfected the system of "creative unions." Within the framework of this system, the right to work (and therefore to live as an artist) comes only to those officially registered and approved. The creative unions of writer, composers, artists, et al. were formed, beginning in 1923, as bureaucratic organizations with strictly defined ranks and with equally strong accountability and constant cross-checking. Every organization had a branch of "security services," or secret police, as well as innumerable unofficial informers . . . . Any attempt to circumvent one's union ended badly: various forms of pressure and repression were always ready. Moreover, obedience was rewarded. Behind this well-oiled and smoothly running mechanism stood the figure of Stalin, an inevitable presence that often gave events a grotesque, tragicomic coloration.[5]

That same year, on October 26, Stalin also coined the term "socialist realism."[6] As described by a Soviet author: "Socialist realism implies an art imbued with communist ideology, that is to say, its very core is a deliberate purposeful struggle for the victory of communism, an evaluation of life in the light of communist ideals."[7] An American scholar explained: "Socialist realism became an officially imposed esthetic standard which every art in the USSR, without a single exception, was forced to follow."[8]

In order for a literary work to pass the test of socialist realism, it had to coincide with the Kremlin's interests and to portray Soviet life in an optimistic manner, "showing 'positive heroes'—miners overfilling their production quotas, military heroes, or stalwart Soviet women heroically and literally laying the brick and mortar of a new society."[9] Inappropriate poetry could lead to the poet's arrest.[10] Stalin even had several painters shot.[11] Ballet was required to embody the ideals of heroism, duty, honor, comradeship, and other virtues of the new Soviet citizen.[12] The Soviets even took control over the development of circus performers.[13]

In early 1936, the Central Executive Committee and the Council of People's Commissars established an All-Union Committee for Affairs of the Arts in the Council of People's Commissars. All theatrical productions, the cinema industry, and all institutions fostering music, painting, sculpture, or any other form of art came under the authority of this group. At each venue, the theatrical director and the artistic director had to prepare a yearly repertoire plan of all productions and submit it to the committee for approval. The committee also evaluated each new production after dress rehearsal.[14]

Stalin and Andrey Zhdanov, the party ideologue for cultural matters, determined the official attitude toward various plays, ballets, literature, and other art forms. Zhdanov announced, "The central committee of Bolsheviks demands beauty and refinement from music."[15] Zhdanov argued that "the Soviet Army is victorious, we are advancing on Europe, and Soviet literature must be an aid in this, it must attack bourgeois culture, which is in a state of confusion and decay." Zhdanov wanted to strike a blow at "harmful influences" such as "the spirit of negative criticism, despair, and nonbelief."[16]

Grigory Yevseyevich Zinovyev, chairman of the Petrograd City Soviet, ordered all the opera houses in the city (today's St. Petersburg) to be closed. He explained that the proletariat did not need opera houses. "They are a heavy burden for the proletariat. We Bolsheviks can't carry the heavy burden any more."[17] Stalin also shut down at least one other opera house.[18]

One "typical episode" of the regime's approach to those who dared to defy it involved a popular director/actor/ composer named Vsevolod Emilyevich Meyerhold. In 1938, his theater was shut down on Stalin's personal command, and "an anti-Meyerhold campaign was smeared all over the pages of the press."[19] Later, Meyerhold "disappeared without a trace in the years of the 'great terror.'"[20]

Like everything else, radio was also heavily censored in the Soviet Union. "Everyone knows that you can't appear on radio if your text hasn't been passed by the censor. Not one, but almost ten censors, each of whom signs. If the papers aren't signed, no one will let you near a microphone. Who knows what you might say to the whole country?"[21]

Under this regime, many Soviet theatrical productions intentionally promoted anticlericalism.[22] For instance, when originally produced, the ballet *Paganini* depicted a tormented artist who sold himself to the devil in exchange for perfection in the ability to play the violin. When produced later, the choreographer purposely shifted emphasis, "to make the true forces of evil in the plot to be the Catholic Church, represented by black-clad hooded figures who pierce Paganini with their violin bows while a cardinal stands in the background, wielding a huge cross."[23] As author Mary Grace Swift explained:

> Closely linked with this element, an antireligious strain appears which tries to make religion look either silly or sinister, whether dealing with Moslems or Christians. Figures representing religion—knights, monks, or characters enforcing Moslem customs—are depicted as instruments of oppression against a heroine who stands for all the bright, patriotic virtues of her particular national group.[24]

If the art in question did not serve the party's interests, it was banned. "Beginning in 1946, one Party resolution after another was proclaimed, containing attacks on books, plays."[25] Moreover, reproduction of forbidden books was made virtually impossible, because all the printing presses were taken over by the state.[26]

Tikhon Khrennikov was appointed by Stalin to administer Soviet music. In 1948, at the first Composers' Congress, he proclaimed: "armed with clear Party directives, we will put a final end to any manifestations of anti-People formalism and decadence, no matter what defensive coloration they may take on."[27] The congress unanimously condemned several leading composers for being "formalists."[28] This, of course, led to many compositions praising Stalin and the Soviet Union. As one composer said: "They sang about Stalin the eagle . . . ; I think there must have been some twenty thousand [songs], maybe more. It would be interesting to work out how much money our leader paid out for songs about our leader."[29]

"Stalin, who had a superlative appreciation of the propaganda potential of art, paid special attention to film. He saw the Soviet movies had a powerful emotional effect."[30] Stalin "wanted our film industry to put out only master-pieces. He was convinced that under his brilliant leadership and personal guidance it would do so."[31] He did not hesitate to use his authority. "If he ordered a film made, they'd make it. If he ordered them to stop shooting, they stopped shooting. That happened many times. If Stalin ordered a fin-ished film destroyed, they'd destroy it. That happened more than once too."[32]

The Soviets were also happy to use American art forms to advance their cause in the United States. By the 1940s, American communists had fully embraced and significantly co-opted folk music. The American Communist Party was essentially an agency of the Soviet government. "Folk singers had become a ceremonial part of Communist Party meetings."[33] The effect that they wanted with the music was "national in form and revolutionary in content."[34]

Folk singers in the Soviet Union did not fare as well. Native art was con-sidered counterrevolutionary because, like most ancient art, it was religious in nature. As such it was rooted out in the 1920s and 1930s.[35] In some cases, this was done with great ruthlessness.

Since time immemorial, folk singers have wandered along the roads of the Ukraine. They're called *lirniki* and *banduristy* there. They were almost always blind.... and defenseless people, but no one ever touched or hurt them. Hurting a blind man—what could be lower?

And then in the mid thirties the First All-Ukrainian Congress of Lirniki and Banduristy was announced, and all the folk singers had to gather and discuss what to do in the future. "Life is better, life is merrier," Stalin had said. The blind men believed it. They came to the Congress from all over the Ukraine, from tiny, forgotten villages. There were several hundred of them at the Congress, they say. It was a living museum, the country's living history. All its songs, all its music and poetry. And they were almost all shot, almost all those pathetic blind men killed.[36]

The folk singers were killed because collectivization was under way, the Soviets had wiped out the kulaks as a class, and these singers were singing songs of dubious content. The songs weren't approved by the censors; they really could not even be submitted for approval. They were not written down. "You can't hand a blind man a corrected and approved text and you can't write him an order either. You have to tell everything to a blind man. That takes too long. And you can't file away a piece of paper, and there's not time anyway. Collectivization. Mechanization. It was easier to shoot them."[37]

Of course, by eliminating these bearers of oral tradition, the Soviet leadership also wiped out a significant part of their culture. "When they shoot a folk singer or a wandering storyteller, hundreds of great musical works die with him. Works that had never been written down. They die forever, irrevocably, because another singer represents other songs."[38]

Eventually, the Soviet leaders wanted to show the world that they had native culture, so they invented a new folk singer/poet. Dzhambul Dzhabayev's poetry was supposedly written in Kazakh and then translated into Russian. Children studied his work in school. The only thing was Dzhabayev did not write songs, and the translators did not read Kazakh. "The so-called translations of the nonexistent poems were written by Russian poets and they didn't even ask our great folk singer for permission."[39] Real oral tradition was replaced by stories and songs that served the party's needs, much as false histories of Catholic leaders would replace the truth about them.

In the 1950s, after Stalin's death, Soviet artists were often sent overseas to spread the Communist Party's message. In 1954, several well-known Russian performers put on a series of concerts in England to inaugurate

"British–Soviet Friendship Month." Their performances were "reminiscent of the old prerevolutionary 'meetings,' for the spectators were urged to buy certain newspapers; to begin certain societies; and the dancers performed against a background of British and Soviet flags, sharing the stage with various officials and members of the diplomatic corps, including . . . the Soviet Ambassador."[40]

"To Marx, religion was an opiate of the people, and the USSR theatrical world has stressed this concept. Certain ballet productions have purposely made religion appear both stupid and vile."[41] Of course, the choice of productions was political, not artistic.

> It is somewhat amazing that artists of the nation which produced *Swan Lake* or *Firebird* would voluntarily produce *Native Fields* or *Tatiana* without official urging. The example has been cited where the Ministry of Culture ordered in 1958 that each opera and ballet theatre should produce one contemporary ballet a year. If a theatre should have other plans, the Party chief is on hand, in the theatre, to see that such directives are enforced.[42]

There was no such thing as an independent journal in the Soviet Union. As the Anti-Defamation League explained in 1961, "Everything published in the USSR for popular consumption is rigidly controlled by the state, and every opinion expressed in a newspaper is equivalent to an official opinion."[43] One Soviet author complained: "tsarist censorship practices pale in comparison with the policy of the Soviet government."[44]

Erwin Piscator and his framing of Pius XII in *The Deputy* were products of this society.

24

ROLF HOCHHUTH

I N 1966, Erwin Piscator, who had transformed Hochhuth's eight-hour script about the Vatican into the explosive play called *Der Stellvertreter,* departed this world. Rolf Hochhuth needed a new researcher, and David Irving came into his life. Irving was an English writer who specialized in the military history of World War II, and he became Hochhuth's closest collaborator and lifelong friend.

In 1969, during a visit to Germany, Irving met Robert Kempner, one of the American prosecutors at Nuremberg. Later, in a letter submitted to FBI director J. Edgar Hoover, Kempner said Irving was a "young man, who made a nervous and rather mentally dilapidated impression," and who expressed many "anti-American and anti-Jewish statements."[1] In a speech delivered in Canada, Irving did indeed make a mentally dilapidated impression, vociferously articulating his contempt and hatred for people who spoke about the Holocaust:

> Ridicule alone isn't enough; you've got to be tasteless about it. You've got to say things like "More women died on the back seat of Edward Kennedy's car at Chappaquiddick than in the gas chambers at Auschwitz." Now you think that's tasteless, what about this? I'm forming an association especially dedicated to all these liars, the ones who try and kid people that they were in these concentration camps, it's called the Auschwitz Survivors, Survivors of the Holocaust and Other Liars, A-S-S-H-O-L-E-S. Can't get more tasteless than that, but you've got to be tasteless because these people deserve our contempt.[2]

Later Irving published *Hitler's War,* a book he said was aimed at cleaning away the "years of grime and discoloration from the façade of a silent and forbidding monument," to reveal the real Hitler, whose reputation, Irving claimed, had been slandered.[3] Irving portrayed Hitler as a rational, intelligent politician whose only goal was to increase Germany's prosperity.[4] Irving faulted Winston Churchill for the escalation of war,[5] claimed that Hitler knew nothing about the Holocaust, and offered £1,000 to anyone who could find any written command from Hitler ordering the Holocaust.[6]

In a footnote, Irving introduced the thesis that a letter sent by the president of the World Zionist Organization, Chaim Weizmann, to Neville Chamberlain on September 3, 1939, pledging to support the Allied war effort represented in fact a "Jewish declaration of war against Germany," which therefore justified the German "internment" of European Jews.[7] Irving's anti-Semitism went so far as to denounce *The Diary of Anne Frank* as a forgery.[8]

In 1967, a year after Hochhuth and Irving joined together, they produced a new show titled *Soldiers, Necrology on Geneva.* Like *The Deputy, Soldiers* also dealt with dead people unable to defend themselves (or so Hochhuth and Irving believed). The focal character was another strong anticommunist, Polish general Wladyslaw Sikorski. During World War II, Sikorski took refuge in London, joined the Allied forces, and became prime minister in exile of Soviet-occupied Poland, commander in chief of the Polish Armed Forces, and a staunch advocate of the Polish cause. He was killed on July 4, 1943, when his plane crashed into the sea immediately upon takeoff from Gibraltar.

People around the world speculated that he had been killed by Moscow, which considered Sikorski an enemy because he had requested the International Red Cross to investigate the slaughter of thousands of Polish prisoners at the Katyn massacre during the war. Stalin claimed that the Katyn atrocity had been committed by the Germans, but Sikorski refused to accept Stalin's explanation. Therefore, on April 16, 1943, Moscow broke relations with Sikorski's government-in-exile, and Stalin labeled Sikorski a traitor.[9]

According to *Soldiers,* however, Sikorski was murdered by *British* agents on the orders of Winston Churchill. The play claimed that the agents entered the plane Sikorski was on and killed him (and others, including his daughter, two members of Parliament, and a dozen other innocent people) prior to takeoff. The alleged reason was that Sikorski's war with Moscow was creating a problem for the Anglo-American-Soviet alliance. The assassins then abandoned the plane. The pilot, who was allegedly in cahoots with the killers, intentionally crashed the plane (after taking special precautions for his personal safety), making it look as though Sikorski had been killed by the impact. Hochhuth claimed that British agents later killed the pilot to keep him quiet.

Time magazine called this theory "a tenuous personal speculation indicative only of a common European fascination with conspiratorial-plot theories of history."[10] A leading Polish literary critic called the allegations "insane."[11]

At a press conference taking place at the Berlin première of *Soldiers*, Hochhuth was asked to expand on the "sources of his secret knowledge" about Sikorski's assassination. Hochhuth claimed to have a wealth of information, but he was evasive when asked about where it came from. Sometimes it was from a retired British intelligence man; other times it was from a Polish lady.

Central to Hochhuth's case, of course, was that the surviving pilot, Edward Prchal, had been in on the assassination. Hochhuth claimed that after five years of painstaking research, he had "conclusive evidence" that the pilot had survived the crash but died at the hands of the "Old Firm" (meaning a front organization for British intelligence) in a staged knife fight in Chicago. His theory was that Prchal, although in on the plans, had been killed by the "Old Firm" to ensure that he would not reveal the plot.

In December 1968, Sir David Frost, the famous British journalist, organized a television interview with the producers of *Soldiers*, which had recently opened in London. Frost had been hosting serious interviews with major political figures, the most notable being the one with Richard Nixon, which was the basis for the 2006 play and 2008 film *Frost/Nixon*. Hochhuth declined to appear in Frost's interview, citing his inability to speak English (despite Frost's offer of a translator), but David Irving and theater critic Kenneth Tynan were there as part of what Frost called "the Hochhuth contingent."

With persistence, Frost had located the pilot Prchal, still very much alive in the United States. Much to the chagrin of the Hochhuth contingent, Prchal appeared in the flesh on Frost's stage during the television interview. He said, "Mr. Hochhuth is producing a slander of the century."

According to Frost, "the credibility of the Hochhuth-Tynan-Irving case went from bad to worse." The Hochhuth contingent maintained that the man who appeared on the stage was an imposter. Frost proved that he was indeed the surviving pilot portrayed in *Soldiers*.

After the show, Frost asked the guests to return for a second show. Taping went so poorly for the Hochhuth contingent that they tried to stop the second show from being broadcast. Eventually Prchal won a £50,000 lawsuit against the playwright,[12] and later investigation would prove there was no substance to any of the wild claims in *Soldiers.* Hochhuth's biographer noted: "Hochhuth's ... accusation resulted in a libel action brought by the surviving pilot of the crashed aircraft which involved the author [Hochhuth] and the producers of the play in London in a costly financial settlement."[13]

A few perceptive people noted a similarity between *The Deputy* and *Soldiers,* in that both plays slandered famous heroic figures who happened to be already dead. Both plays also calumniated men who had been staunch anticommunists.

Soldiers, like *The Deputy,* caused quite a controversy. It was initially banned in England. It also led actor Carlos Thompson—who had admired Hochhuth and was at first interested in helping bring the play to the stage and perhaps film—to write a book exposing the shoddy research and ridiculous theories Hochhuth had set forth. After concluding his research, Thompson summed up how his attitude toward Hochhuth had changed. Sitting at his desk and looking out the window at the Swiss Alps, Thompson says he was:

> ... jolted to the final realization that my pin-up boy of yesterday, the enlightened "conscience of our society" in whom I had believed and who had shed light on the unimportance of my own writing—he, the "good" German *Geist,* the spokesman of the new Germany, was dead. From the ashes rose a man who asked me to stand before the world press and perjure myself on his behalf.[14]

Thompson's research showed Hochhuth as "semi-paranoid" and all-too-eager to believe anything he was told. Describing what he called a "sad example of Hochhuth's methods," Thompson wrote about the "tangled gyrations of Hochhuth's thinking," adding that the playwright's mind "worked along dangerously greased rails." Hochhuth was very quick to rewrite sections of his play and even to eliminate characters, and he would shift his premise based upon nothing more than (and often less than) a rumor.[15]

After a discussion with the British actor Laurence Olivier and others about suggested changes to *Soldiers,* including eliminating characters, Hochhuth readily agreed. Olivier's wife, Joan Plowright, who was present, remarked: "There is one thing we all agree on, I'm sure. We have never seen an author so little married to his words."[16] She was unaware that they may not have been his words to start with.

Hochhuth originally claimed that Churchill had caused Sikorski to be killed owing to the latter's strong stance against the Soviets, which was endangering Churchill's new alliance with Stalin. When an article in the Moscow *New Times* (an undercover KGB magazine published in English for Western consumption) made a different argument, he immediately adopted the Soviet line and suggested that Churchill had had Sikorski killed owing to his pro-Soviet policies. Hochhuth did another flip-flop when discussing the British government's desire to implicate a certain participant in the plane crash. He gave inconsistent answers not only about his theories and the source of his information, but even about why he was living in Switzerland instead of Germany. (Evidently he was afraid of being sued in West Germany, although he had been quick to sue others he believed had libeled him.)

Hochhuth's research for *Soldiers* was sloppy at best, and his analysis was even worse. Julius Firt, one of many witnesses interviewed by Carlos Thompson, said: "I find it difficult to understand what Hochhuth is really after. His play on the Pope was tendentious enough, but this one, marshalling non-existent evidence to prove that Britain killed Sikorski, is one big step further."[17] Polish Prince Lubomirski, another witness, said: "Hochhuth had nothing, and construes everything to his advantage."[18] Yugoslavian dissident Milovan Djilas (whom Hochhuth tried to invoke when questions arose about his honesty) said: "Hochhuth's quotation of me is a complete distortion."[19] Stanislaw Lepinowski said: "*The Sunday Times* quoted Mr. Hochhuth and through him, quoted me. What I had said to him was totally misrepresented."[20] Lepinowski went on to say that "after reading his play, I find that it is the exact opposite of what he told me."[21]

One witness said: "I have begun to ask myself if Hochhuth does not suffer from delusions. He remembers visiting me in my home, which he never did, and conversations between us that never took place."[22] Thompson wrote: "It was becoming difficult to follow Rolf's gyrations of theory-within-theory."[23] Another time he wrote: "Rolf was beginning to tire. He was forgetting his own invention."[24] When a witness came forth to contradict his theory, Hochhuth attributed it to British disinformation.[25] Another time he suggested that witnesses were faking amnesia.[26] Yet another witness said that

Hochhuth simply refused to consider the theory that the Soviets were behind the general's death.[27] Responding to allegations from Sikorski's countrymen that undercut his thesis, Hochhuth said: "all the Poles in London lie."[28]

When pressed on his sources, Hochhuth always dodged the issue. Rather than providing witnesses or documents, he claimed to have deposited his proof in a bank vault to be opened fifty years later. He said: "I know that in fifty years my play will be unassailable." Those fifty years will soon be up, but there is surely no one alive today who expects Hochhuth to produce any new revelations anytime in the future.

Anyone who carefully reviews Hochhuth's alleged justifications for the accusations that he has made must conclude that he simply does not care about the truth. *Time* magazine wrote of him:

> One cut above a crank and several cuts below a thinker, Hochhuth seems very much like those dedicated slaphappy few who insist that Bacon wrote Shakespeare.[29]

Of course, perhaps he kept shifting his story and misremembering facts because he did not write all the parts of his play. Moreover, there is no apparent reason to suppose that Hochhuth behaved any differently when writing *Soldiers* than he did when writing *The Deputy* or anything else.

In 1978, Hochhuth published *Eine Liebe in Deutschland* ("A Love in Germany"), a novel about an affair between a Polish prisoner of war and a German woman in World War II, which became the play *Juristen* ("Judges") and the film *Ein Furchtbarer Jurist* ("A Terrible Judge"). The novel stirred up a debate about the Nazi past of Hans Filbinger, a high-ranking member of West Germany's conservative Christian Democratic Union and the sitting minister president of Baden-Württemberg.

Filbinger, Hochhuth's target, was a lifelong Catholic and a strong anti-communist. He campaigned under the slogan "Freedom instead of Socialism." Filbinger had been a German Navy lawyer and judge during World War II. Hochhuth's writings asserted that Filbinger was responsible for the death sentence given to the German sailor Walter Gröger in a British prisoner-of-war camp when the war was already over. According to Hochhuth, Filbinger sentenced Gröger to death and then borrowed twelve guns from the British for the execution. On these points Hochhuth was demonstrably wrong.

The military records at the German Federal Archive, Kornelimünster bei Aachen, document the following facts relating to the Gröger case. The German sailor Walter Gröger was serving in Nazi-occupied Oslo, Norway when he tried to desert in December 1943. He was immediately caught and consigned to various military prisons as his case dragged out. In early 1944, the German Navy planned to sentence him to eight years imprisonment, but superior officers in the German Navy, including the commander, demanded the death penalty for him, after reviewing his file. It was at this point that Filbinger entered the case as a Navy judge, but only to process the decision that had already been made. On March 16, 1945, still during the war, Gröger was sentenced to death for desertion, and the sentence was carried out two hours later.[30]

The storm over Hochhuth's accusation forced Filbinger to resign from office, but the debate dragged on for the rest of Filbinger's life. When he finally passed away in 2007, Baden-Württemberg minister president Günther Oettinger said:

> There is no legal decision given by Hans Filbinger that caused a person to lose his life. And in the case of those legal decisions that are held against him, he either did not have the authority to make the decision, or else he was not free to make the decision that many people now allege he did.

In response to this, Hochhuth called Filbinger a "sadistic Nazi" who long after the capitulation had personally sentenced the sailor Gröger to death.

Two German newspapers said Hochhuth had lied. In his response, which appeared on April 13, 2007, in the *Süddeutsche Zeitung*, Hochhuth characterized their statements as "pure invention" and complained about the undermining of the "tragedy of the sailor Walter Gröger" whom Hans Filbinger "personally ordered to be killed while a British prisoner of war." The online version of Hochhuth's article, entitled "The Liar," was deleted by the *Süddeutsche Zeitung* one day after it appeared, with the following comment:

> The writer Rolf Hochhuth's claim that appeared in the *Süddeutsche Zeitung* of April 13, 2007 ("The Liar")—that Filbinger had sentenced Gröger to be killed while he was a British prisoner-of-war—is *false*. Hochhuth's well-known statement of 1978 that "even in a British prison camp [Filbinger] went after a German sailor with Nazi laws," actually is based on the Petzold case… Hochhuth could not be reached for comment.[31]

Hochhuth seems to have "confused" the Gröger case with that of an artillerist named Petzold, but even he was sentenced to only six months prison, not death. Filbinger was but one more victim of Hochhuth's imagination.

The Deputy, Soldiers, and *Eine Liebe in Deutschland* all became movies, making Hochhuth a very wealthy man. In Basel, Switzerland, he and his first wife, Marianne, bought and lived in the famous house that had belonged to the nineteenth-century German philosopher Friedrich Nietzsche. When his career obliged him to move to Vienna, Hochhuth lived a few hundred yards from the imperial Burgtheater, in an apartment on Burggasse in the house that had once been Sigmund Freud's.[32]

Hochhuth has lived a life of extravagant luxury, but he seems to have remained "noticeably paranoid and nervous." According to his friend and researcher, David Irving:

> Early in July 1966 ... he came to England for what was to prove his one and only visit. I wrote a whole page profile of him for the *Evening Standard*. He stayed with us in Paddington. Since my father was ... occupying the guest room ... we bedded Rolf down in our drawing room for a few days. At two o'clock one morning I had occasion to go down and look for a file—Rolf jack-knifed bolt upright in bed, terrified and shouting with fear at this unexpected intruder. "What is it? Who are you? What do you want?" He was pathologically fearful for his own safety.[33]

Hochhuth was constantly worried that he, Irving, and Thompson (while he was still working with Hochhuth) would be targeted by British intelligence agents from what he called "the Old Firm." He said: "The men who killed Sikorski still sit at the Old Firm. I am constantly worried."[34] Thompson thought to himself, "And well you must be, if you go about life in this fashion. How many lies had he told me already?"[35]

What do we really know about *The Deputy*'s purported playwright, who set off an enormous storm of controversy and was suddenly catapulted onto the world stage of fame and fortune? Rolf Hochhuth is generally described as a very leftist writer, but his statements about his beliefs are often completely contradictory.

Hochhuth was born on April Fools Day, 1931, in Eschwege, a small city in Hessen, which after World War II would lie on the western side of the border dividing West and East Germany. His father owned a small shoe factory, and the family was middle-class and Protestant. Rolf had been in a Nazi children's organization (*Jungvolk*), but that was what all children did, and there is no indication that the family was particularly pro- or anti-Nazi during the war. He graduated from secondary school (*Mittlere Reife*) in 1948 but did not go on to complete the academic *Abitur* (high school graduation).

Hochhuth reports that he attended a trade school to learn the book business, but that he essentially educated himself as he went along. He eventually came to consider himself something of an authority on postwar German literature. As a young man he began writing poetry and short stories. Between 1950 and 1955 he held jobs as an assistant in various book-related businesses in several West German cities, while auditing courses at nearby universities and starting to write poems and stories.

Hochhuth has been generally disdainful of professorial writers—those with an *Abitur* degree—but he developed a taste for exciting, well-written literature. In 1955 he got a job with the very large Bertelsmann publishing house, working as a reader in their *Lesering* department (a sort of book-of-the-month club). He edited several books and story collections, including a collection of the popular Wilhelm Busch. Hochhuth claims that in 1959 his Busch edition sold more than a million copies, so the publisher gave him a special three-month leave of absence, during which time he worked on some of his own writing and took his wife (the first of four) on a trip to Rome. It was on that trip that he claims to have met a secret, unnamed bishop who gave him the information that inspired *The Deputy*.

Hochhuth has said that as a young man he was extremely upset when stories of the Nazi killings began to come out, and he could not understand why so many good Germans had done nothing about it. Nevertheless, Hochhuth made a long partnership with, and did everything in his power to protect, David Irving, a fanatical denier of Hitler's Holocaust.

Irving raised again his profile as a Holocaust denier in 2000, when he sued Deborah Lipstadt of Emory University and Penguin Books over Lipstadt's book *Denying the Holocaust*. Irving complained that the book accused him of being "a Nazi apologist and an admirer of Hitler, who has resorted to the distortion of facts and to the manipulation of documents in support of his contention that the Holocaust did not take place." Irving said this was part of a "concerted attempt to ruin his reputation as an historian."

At trial, Irving invoked his correspondence with Hochhuth (who called to lend moral support) as evidence of his broadmindedness. The defense, however, rested on the "truth of the matter asserted." Legally, that more or less means "yes, we said it, but it's true."

Specifically, the defense argued that, "Irving is discredited as an historian by reason of his denial of the Holocaust and by reason of his persistent distortion of the historical record so as to depict Hitler in a favourable light." The British judge sided with the defendants:

> I find myself unable to accept Irving's contention that his falsification of the historical record is the product of innocent error or misinterpretation or incompetence on his part . . . . [I]t appears to me that the correct and inevitable inference must be that for the most part the falsification of the historical record was deliberate and that Irving was motivated by a desire to present events in a manner consistent with his own ideological beliefs even if that involved distortion and manipulation of historical evidence.

The *New York Times* proclaimed: "The verdict puts an end to the pretense that Mr. Irving is anything but a self-promoting apologist for Hitler."

Irving was again in the news and in court when he was arrested by Austrian authorities in 2005. According to the BBC, Irving was in Austria to "give a lecture to a far-right student fraternity" when he was picked up on charges stemming from talks he had given there in 1989. Other sources also noted that at the time of the arrest, Irving was returning from visiting Rolf Hochhuth.

Hochhuth defended Irving as he faced the charges. In a newspaper interview he called Irving "an honorable man," a "fabulous pioneer of contemporary history," and "much more serious than many German historians." He said descriptions of Irving as a Holocaust-denier were "idiotic." This caused German newspapers and Jewish groups to label Hochhuth an anti-Semite. In fact, the German publishing house *Deutsche Verlags-Anstalt* cancelled publication of Hochhuth's autobiography over this matter. (Irving, by the way, pleaded guilty and received a three-year sentence.)

This was not the only time Hochhuth had defended Irving. The playwright spoke very highly of him in his memoirs. When critics asked how anyone could write words of praise for someone like Irving, his answer was,

"Because I am Hochhuth."

It is not easy to pin down where Hochhuth stands on anything. For many years he carried on an intensive correspondence with the historian Golo Mann, who had initially supported leftist politicians and wrote a favorable review of *The Deputy*. In later life, Mann turned politically conservative, and on September 22, 1978, he sent Hochhuth an insightful letter—in effect a farewell letter, the break being caused by Hochhuth's defense of his anti-Semitic researcher David Irving. Mann explained that he did not have a clear grasp on Hochhuth's politics, but he noted a sympathy towards communism:

> I have never considered you a Communist, at least not in the usual meaning of the word. What I have wondered about for a long time is that the thrust of your dramas and plays has constantly gone in one direction, which would at least not be unwelcome to the Communists.[36]

Mann was perceptive.

25

A NEW LOOK AT *THE DEPUTY*

OLF HOCHHUTH'S CARELESS HANDLING of the facts in his *Soldiers* show raised serious questions about the credibility of his first play, *The Deputy*. Those doubts further deepened in 1971, when General Karl Otto Wolff, chief of staff to SS *Reichsführer* Heinrich Himmler and SS leader of German-occupied Italy, was released from prison and rattled the whole premise of *The Deputy*. In no way had Pius XII been "Hitler's Pope." In fact, Hitler had regarded Pius XII as one of his main enemies.[1]

As Wolff finally revealed, in the fall of 1943 the Führer had ordered him to abduct Pius XII from the Vatican. Hitler blamed the pope for sabotaging his racial purification of Germany and for overthrowing Mussolini. He wanted the kidnapping carried out immediately. Wolff informed Hitler, however, that the order would take at least six weeks to carry out. Eventually, Wolff persuaded Hitler that there would be a huge negative response if the plan were implemented, and the Führer dropped it.[2]

Documents later found in the Vatican's Secret Archive show that Wolff also managed to tip off the Holy See about Hitler's plan. Upon learning about it, Pius told his senior bishops that, should he be captured by the Nazis, his resignation would become effective immediately, paving the way for a successor who would continue his fight against the Nazis.[3]

A few months after Wolff's revelation, KGB chairman Yuri Andropov conceded to the Romanian DIE: "Had we known then what we know today, we would never have gone after Pius." By that, of course, he meant that, had the Soviets realized Hitler's hatred of Pius would be so easy to establish, they would not have framed Pius as "Hitler's Pope."

How did Moscow react to Wolff's revelation? Essentially by ignoring it, and by stepping up its efforts to frame Pius XII. Books and articles inspired by *The Deputy* continued to make headlines in the West, trying to convince readers that Pius XII was indeed "Hitler's Pope." In fact, the slander against Pius XII continues to rear its ugly head.

Today, however, a closer examination of *The Deputy* through the magnifying lens supplied by Wolff's revelation and by documents and first-hand testimonies leads to the inescapable conclusion that *The Deputy* was a product of *dezinformatsiya*. One such proof can be found in *The Deputy*'s treatment of the Katyn forest massacre. In 1940 the Soviets, using German weapons and ammunition, executed some twenty-two thousand Polish military officers, policemen, intellectuals, and civilian prisoners of war in and around the Russian town of Katyn, near the city of Smolensk. The victims were then buried in mass graves. During the Khrushchev years, when Gen. Ivan Serov was the KGB chairman, the Kremlin's publicly proclaimed version of this incident was that German soldiers had committed the murders.[4]

For a long time Germany and the Soviet Union blamed each other for the Katyn massacre. In March 1946, at the Nuremberg trials, Goering's defense tried to bring up Katyn, but the Soviet commission, led by that master of Kremlin framings, Andrey Vyshinsky, protested forcibly. Katyn was not discussed.[5]

Between 1939 and 1941, the brutal General Serov was in charge of deportations in the Soviet-controlled Baltic countries and Poland. He was the political police commissar for Ukraine, and he was in charge of the execution of thousands of Polish prisoners of war. At that time, the party boss in Ukraine was Khrushchev, who was responsible for the deaths of hundreds of thousands of Ukrainian peasants. He earned a nickname as "the Butcher of Ukraine."[6]

When Khrushchev ascended to the Kremlin, he appointed Serov to head the KGB, and together they built a deception operation to divert attention away from the belief that the Soviets were responsible for the Katyn massacre. Khrushchev ordered that a large memorial be built in a small village named Khatyn (chosen for the similar spelling of its name), located near Minsk in

Belorussia (now Belarus), in order to commemorate some Soviets who had allegedly been killed there by the Germans.

Khrushchev fell from grace several years before the Khatyn memorial could be completed, but it did eventually become a pilgrimage shrine. Leonid Brezhnev solemnly escorted President Richard Nixon to the Belorussian Khatyn in 1974, but it was all in furtherance of another framing.[7] The British *Daily Telegraph* (July 3, 1974) explained in an article entitled "Khatyn— Another Hoax":

> President Nixon's visit to the memorial in the Byelorussian village of Khatyn has caused a mistaken impression that Russia has erected a memorial to the victims of the wartime massacre of Polish officers in the Katyn forest. In fact, Khatyn and Katyn are two entirely different places; Khatyn, in which the 'kh' is pronounced as the English 'h' is a small village some 30 miles to the north-east of Minsk, the capital of Byelorussia. Katyn, which is pronounced as written, is a town about 15 miles west of Smolensk, a provincial city in Russia proper. Khatyn is about 160 miles west of Katyn . . . . The Russians have tried to erase Katyn from maps and history books. The reference to it in the 1953 edition of the Soviet Encyclopedia was dropped . . . . No visitors are allowed to the area, and no memorial has been erected. It was not until 1969 that the Russians announced the unveiling of a "memorial complex" on the site of the village of Khatyn. It was one of 9,200 Byelorussian villages destroyed by the Germans, and one of 136 of which all the inhabitants were killed.

Soviet lying went on until October 13, 1990, when Mikhail Gorbachev officially acknowledged Soviet guilt for the Katyn murders.[8]

In 1963, when *The Deputy* was first published, the KGB was still struggling to persuade the rest of the world that the Soviets had not been involved in the Katyn massacre. Hochhuth himself was certainly not in a position to know anything about the KGB's secret efforts to cover up the massacre. The KGB framing experts working on *The Deputy* would not, however, have missed a chance to score a point for their side in the text, and they didn't.

In the play, a Christianized Italian Jewish family living within sight of the pope's residence is packing in preparation for seeking asylum at a monastery. The father and grandfather argue about the Katyn massacre, which has been in the news. The older man claims: "I know the Germans better than you ... Stalin killed them." The son insists that the Germans did it, pointing out that "German ammunition was found in their bodies." Just then a German SS officer and two Italian Fascist militiamen burst in and haul the family off to a labor camp.[9] The message intended by this scene, which is entirely irrelevant to the play's action, seems to be that you can never trust the Germans and that they caused the Katyn massacre. This message was surely of no particular interest to Hochhuth, but Moscow would indeed have cared.

The historical aspects of *The Deputy* contain further circumstantial evidence that the show was produced by *dezinformatsiya* experts. The "Sidelights on History" published with the play seem to anticipate every anti-Pius XII argument that would be made for the next forty years. That fact, as much as anything else, seems to indicate a collective hand in authoring it. Moreover, one item in the "Sidelights" clearly betrays the Soviet hand and perfectly illustrates how to construct effective *dezinformatsiya*:

> Pius XII, a cold skeptic, also did not "believe" in history, as we know from a conversation he had with Adolf von Harnack. No doubt for this very reason he calculated in all sobriety that he had a good chance to be canonized, provided he helped the process along. Which he did. Not only his unpopularity in the Vatican was to blame for the sarcasms of Roman monsignori, who went so far as to say that he had canonized Pius X and instituted proceedings toward the canonization of Pius IX in order to establish precedents for his own elevation.[10]

In the above paragraph, not only is the reader gratuitously informed that Pius was "a cold skeptic," but we are also told that he was disliked by high-ranking priests at the Vatican, and that he schemed to get himself canonized. All of those allegations are not only slanderous and completely unsourced, but they are artfully clustered around the very respectable name of Adolf von Harnack, a leading Protestant German theologian who lived in Berlin after 1890, including from 1925 to 1929, when Pacelli was the nuncio there. Whether factually verifiable or not, it is entirely plausible that the two religious leaders might have met at the time when they were both living in Berlin. Harnack thus becomes the "kernel of truth" holding up the *dezinformatsiya* in this "Sidelights" paragraph.

In that pre-Internet era, Hochhuth was unlikely to have had access to any private statements made by Adolf von Harnack, who was a member of a prominent Berlin family and who died before Hochhuth was born. General

Agayants's researchers would, however, undoubtedly have come across Harnack's name when combing KGB secret archives for ideas on how to smear Pacelli in connection with his days in Berlin.

The one place from which the *dezinformatsiya* officers would have started their research surely would have been the voluminous reports from Arvid Harnack, whom the KGB considered to have been its most important German agent during World War II. Arvid lived in Berlin and was Adolf von Harnack's nephew. Originally recruited in the 1930s, Arvid lost touch with the Soviets during their purges, but he was reactivated on September 17, 1940, by the newly arrived deputy station chief of Soviet intelligence in Berlin, Aleksandr Mikhaylovich Korotkov, who gave him the new code name of "Korsikanets." Arvid handled a loose network of some sixty agents providing valuable economic and political intelligence.[11] On September 7, 1942, Arvid was arrested by the Gestapo, sentenced to death and executed three months later.[12]

It is entirely unlikely that any private comments made by Adolf von Harnack (who died in 1930) would have been available to Hochhuth. There might, however, have been reports in KGB archives from Arvid when he was first recruited, naming for his Soviet handlers all his family members and other people he knew—the kind of routine information new recruits are asked to supply to help their handlers direct their intelligence activities. The Harnack family dinner table was known for its interesting guests and conversations, and Arvid might even have boasted to the Soviets that his uncle had once met the papal nuncio—or not; it would not have mattered for the purposes of *dezinformatsiya*. The point is that Arvid's reports could very well have inspired General Agayants to create an "Adolf von Harnack" item for the "Sidelights." Almost any kind of slander could be tossed into such an item, which would be read as conversational reporting that needed no documentary sourcing.

In fact, the whole subject of precisely how Pius XII became the focus of *The Deputy* is still intriguingly nebulous. In an interview with Patricia Marx, first broadcast over the radio in New York in February 1964 and then printed in *Partisan Review* (Spring 1964), Hochhuth enlarged on the genesis of his play. He started with a disclaimer: "It all happened a long time ago, and it is very hard for me to reconstruct exactly how it all began." He then said that he took some notes on Kurt Gerstein, a Nazi officer who claimed to have tried to warn others about the Nazi extermination plan for the Jews.

"My idea was to write a short story about him—quite a long time ago," said the playwright. He continued:

> Later, however, in 1956, I met a man in Austria, who had helped with the gassing in Auschwitz ... and I read accounts which referred back to this old subject. Then it first became clear to me what the form of the play must be.
>
> Also, at that time, the book *The Third Reich and the Jews*, which contained the Gerstein report, was published. And then, in 1958, a book appeared containing the documents concerning the Vatican's attitude toward the deportation of Jews from Rome. ... I cannot say more than this. It is seven years ago. It all fitted itself together like a mosaic.[13]

Hochhuth has never identified this "man in Austria," who was so important in the development of the play, just as he never identified a chatty "bishop" at the Vatican who he would later claim gave him material on the pope. (Nor, for that matter, did he ever identify the "retired British Intelligence man" and/or the "Polish lady" who allegedly gave him information for his second play, *Soldiers*.[14])

Hochhuth said he suddenly realized that this material had the dramatic stuff of a play: "the argument of the play hardly had to be invented by me, but could be taken directly from actual events—I mean, Gerstein bursting in upon the Papal Nuncio, had to be the dramatic climax of a play." The Marx interview continued with the following exchange:

> Miss M: In the beginning, then, the Pope wasn't in the play at all?
>
> Mr. H: Well, there had appeared, as I said, some documents about the attitude of the Vatican, which already have a voice in the play. It simply developed in such a way that the most meaningful antagonist to [fictional Father] Riccardo [Fontana] could be none other than the highest moral authority—precisely because he makes a demand which only the highest moral authority can make.[15]

"A fish starts smelling from the head" had been the Kremlin's slogan during the Cold War years, and its propaganda machinery did everything it could to attack the leaders of its main enemy, the United States. Moscow portrayed President Harry Truman as the "butcher of Hiroshima," painted

President Dwight Eisenhower as a "shark" of the warmongering military-industrial complex, and described President John F. Kennedy as an arrogant millionaire who acted as if he owned the world. It was clear that "the highest moral authority," the pope himself, not only had to appear on the stage; he had to be the play's main protagonist. In fact, Hochhuth repeated the phrase "the highest moral authority" three times in his brief exchange with Patricia Marx, almost as if it were a mantra that had been hammered into his head: The play's main protagonist had to be Pope Pius XII. The evidence, however, suggests that this decision was made not by Hochhuth, but by the play's first producer, KGB influence agent Erwin Piscator.

How an unknown, uneducated writer like Rolf Hochhuth induced a famous producer like Erwin Piscator even to look at his play is a question in and of itself. Hochhuth claims to have shown his manuscript around his office. His boss, business manager Karl Ludwig Leonhardt, was impressed enough to set it in galley proofs, but he was also a good enough businessman to check first with *his* boss at Bertelsmann headquarters in Gütersloh. The latter supposedly told Leonhardt that the book was too provocative for them (they were very much a family-oriented publishing house). Leonhardt sent the galleys over to Rowohlt, a far-left publishing house with strong communist ties.[16]

Here is where one of the legends surrounding *The Deputy* says that Piscator got his hands on Hochhuth's play. According to one of Hochhuth's biographers, in February 1962 "an unknown thirty-year old author called on Piscator to discuss a play which their common publisher thought might be of interest. This was Rolf Hochhuth and the play *Der Stellvertreter* or *The Representative*."[17] That would be a fairly straightforward story.

Piscator, however, gives a more interesting version of how they first met:

When in the spring of 1962 I was chosen as the artistic director of the Freie Volksbühne in Berlin . . . a telephone call reached me from Mr. Ledig-Rowohlt: he had received a play from his friend, Karl Ludwig Leonhardt, acting as intermediary, the first work of a young German author, which was really more than "just" a play.... The play was sent to me, not in manuscript as usual, but in galley proofs, set not by Rowohlt publishers [the eventual German publisher of the play] but by a publisher who had to acknowledge, after typesetting, that he lacked the courage for publication."[18]

Piscator also said: "No one had any idea how the play could be staged, since it went beyond any and all dimensions."[19]

Piscator accepted the script presented to him. First, he had to reduce the mammoth dimensions of Hochhuth's play from eight hours to two. Piscator wrote:

> Of course, it is difficult to make a stage version of this "total" play, to cut a play out of the play. ... In any event, I have agreed with the Rowohlt publishing house that the book will reach the public at the same time as the initial Berlin production, as necessary underpinning and supplement.[20]

Note that Piscator promised that *he* would have the book ready for the public at the play's opening, apparently including the "documentary supplement," meaning the lengthy background material published as *Sidelights on History*.[21] According to a biography of Piscator:

> There was an entire year between the first contact with the text, which Piscator received in the spring of 1962, and the production. Piscator's careful and hands-on staging led to the fact that the feared scandal— at least in Berlin—did not come about.... The producer of the Berlin opening had cut the play in half, reduced the number of actors by half, and concentrated the dramatically multi-faceted work entirely on the attitude of Pope Pius XII toward the persecution of the Jews.[22]

As he had promised, Piscator delivered the script—including the *Sidelights*—to the Rowohlt publishing house in time for the book to be released together with the play's opening.

Hochhuth was "quite convinced that if Piscator had not staged the play at the *Freie Volksbühne*, he would never have had any of his works performed in the German theatre."[23] Hochhuth said: "*The Deputy* is politics,"[24] and in that play Piscator found his perfect vehicle for *political theater*, a school of drama that credits Piscator for its very name.

"Thanks to this play,'" Piscator said of *The Deputy*, "there is some point in working in the theatre."[25] It ended as the kind of "epic, political, theatre such as I have been fighting [for] for thirty years and more."[26] "I don't think I am devaluing those authors who worked with me in the 1920s if I say that the type of play I ideally had in mind at that time is only now being written...."[27]

Of course, if this were truly an artistic endeavor, and not a political

operation, it should have bothered Piscator that—as Hochhuth said—
The Deputy violated the tenets of its own theatrical genre.[28] The presentation
of Pius focused on his personality rather than on history.[29] The play tried to
make the case that Pius, if not necessarily pro-Nazi during the war, at least
feared communism more than he feared Hitler.[30] There was, of course, no
documentary evidence to back up such claims.[31] Piscator's play even introduced an allegorical figure, a nameless doctor (likened by some to Mengele)
who played an important role in the dramatic action.[32] That was certainly
outside the bounds of documentary theater.

In a letter Piscator wrote in August 1962, he told the set and lighting
designer: "While the scenic elements must be accurate in every detail, the
setting must assist me to go beyond documented reality."[33] As such, Piscator
and Hochhuth were not true to their own theatrical format. Instead they
simply used the play to further a political end.[34]

Piscator ultimately focused the play on Khrushchev's archenemy, Pius
XII. He was framed as—what else?—a Nazi collaborator. That is how all religious servants disliked by the Kremlin were being framed during those days.
The play ran in Berlin for only a couple of weeks, receiving mixed reviews
at best,[35] and its view of Pius XII was denied by virtually every person who
had firsthand knowledge of the pope's wartime activities. But, as previously
seen, the Soviet *dezinformatsiya* machinery further improved *The Deputy*,
translated it into several languages, gave it spectacular stage productions,
and reproduced it as a popular film, all the while ensuring huge publicity
every step of the way.

Once again, Piscator had triumphed, while serving Moscow's purpose.[36]

26

KHRUSHCHEV'S POLITICAL NECROPHAGY

K HRUSHCHEV'S POSTHUMOUS FRAMING of Pius XII as "Hitler's Pope" grew out of a very secret Soviet "science," which within the sanctum sanctorum of the Soviet bloc was known as *political necrophagy*. That "science," aimed at consolidating the seat of a new political ruler, has become a way of life for the Kremlin. Of course, the political heads of other countries also try to blame their predecessors for anything that goes wrong, but in Russia the blame has a tendency to get ugly, even lethal.

Khrushchev's political necrophagy evolved from the Soviet tradition of sanctifying the "supreme" ruler. Although the communists publicly proclaimed the decisive role of "the people" in history, the Kremlin—and its KGB—believed that only the leader counted. Change the public image of the leader, and you change history, I heard over and over from Khrushchev's lips.

Once Khrushchev was enthroned in the Kremlin, he changed Stalin's posthumous image from a Russian saint into a ruthless butcher. That changed Russia's history. Next, he changed the posthumous image of Pope Pius XII, and that changed the history of the Judeo-Christian world.

The "science" of political necrophagy was officially born on February 26, 1956, when Khrushchev exposed Stalin's crimes in a four-hour "secret speech" at the Twentieth Congress of the Soviet Communist Party.[1] The world press was taken in by this "new honesty." The *New York Times* veteran correspondent Harry Schwartz wrote: "Mr. Khrushchev opened the doors and windows of a petrified structure. He let in fresh air and fresh ideas, producing changes which time already has shown are irreversible and fundamental."[2]

Actually, Khrushchev's "secret speech" was just a cheap show intended to distract attention away from his own image as a callous political killer who had approved the infamous carnage at Katyn (where some fourteen thousand Polish prisoners had been shot), and who had become known as "the butcher of the Ukraine" because of the many hundreds of thousands of people executed there while he was Stalin's viceroy in Kiev.

A few days after Khrushchev had delivered his "secret speech," his new spy chief, General Aleksandr Sakharovsky (former chief Soviet intelligence adviser to Romania), slipped the text of it to my foreign intelligence service, the DIE. "This is the most secret document I have ever held in my hand," Sakharovsky said—with a wink. He asked the management of the DIE to pass the "secret speech" to the Israeli Mossad, which had just begun discussing a secret barter arrangement with the DIE to allow Romanian Jews to emigrate to Israel in exchange for US dollars. The DIE obediently leaked the secret speech to the Mossad, which at that time was closely cooperating with the American CIA.

In June 1956, Khrushchev's "secret speech" was published by the *New York Times,* which acknowledged that it had gotten it from the CIA. There are many public versions about how that speech ended up at the *Times.* I knew Sakharovsky well, and there is no doubt in my mind that he had also tried other ways to see that the speech was published. The Mossad is famous for obfuscating its operations. A few months later, however, Sakharovsky thanked DIE management—he had certainly thanked others as well—for having helped him to introduce Khrushchev's new "communism with a human face" to the world. Soon after that, Khrushchev's "secret speech" was debated in all Communist Party organizations and media throughout the Soviet bloc.

The framing of Pius XII was Khrushchev's second political necrophagy operation. Not only did it accomplish its original goal, but it also helped a suddenly crippled Khrushchev to survive in the Kremlin—for a while. In 1962, the West German Supreme Court publicly tried Bogdan Stashinsky, a KGB illegal officer, for killing two Russian émigrés in West Germany. After being heard initially with skepticism, Stashinsky convinced the court and the German public of his sincerity and remorse. What had started out as

Stashinsky's trial was soon transformed into one against Khrushchev, who had decorated Stashinsky for his work, as the world learned in great detail what kind of man and mentality were running the Kremlin.

The sanctified ruler, whose secret speech unmasking Stalin's crimes was fresh in everybody's memory, appeared to the Karlsruhe courtroom and the Free World to be just another butcher—and a flat-out liar. It was not at all true that after the Twentieth Party Congress Khrushchev had stopped the KGB's killings—he had merely turned its cutting edge abroad. It was not true that he wanted peaceful coexistence with the West—political assassination had clearly become a main tool of his foreign policy. It was not true that Khrushchev was innocent—*he* had ordered the killings committed by Stashinsky, and *he* had signed the decree rewarding the perpetrator with the highest Soviet medal.

At the end of his seven-day trial, Stashinsky stated, "I wanted to give worldwide publicity to the way in which [Khrushchev's] 'peaceful coexistence' really works in practice."[3]

Stashinsky did just that. He received the relatively light sentence of eight years, since the West German court declared him only an "accomplice to murder" and emphasized that the guilt of those from whom he had received his orders was far greater. "Murder is now carried out on express government orders," the judge explained. "Political murder has, so to speak, now become institutionalized."[4]

The flamboyant Khrushchev became a crippled ruler gasping for air. The first pages of most Western newspapers were now dedicated to his crimes and lies. A few months later, however, *The Deputy* came out. Suddenly, the Western media turned their attention away from Khrushchev's crimes, focusing instead on Pius XII's "crimes."

Khrushchev may have been booted out, but his *political necrophagy* survived. When Gorbachev came along, he accused Brezhnev of having milked the country for personal gain. Gorbachev even had some of his predecessor's relatives arrested, in an obvious attempt to prove that the Soviet Union had been devastated by individuals, not by Marxism. For his part Yeltsin accused Gorbachev of "leading the country to ruin," and Putin blamed Yeltsin for the "demise of the Soviet Union, the greatest catastrophe of the century."

Political necrophagy—blaming and condemning one's predecessor in office—is a dangerous game. It hurts the country's national pride, and it usually turns against its own user. When Khrushchev died, Brezhnev decreed that his predecessor had badly harmed the country's historical respect for the Kremlin, and that he was not worthy of being buried in the Kremlin Wall next to the other former leaders. The Soviet government even refused to pay for Khrushchev's gravestone.

In 1972, when I visited Khrushchev's grave in the Novodevichy Cemetery, there was only a small, insignificant marker identifying it. In 1989, when Romanian tyrant Nicolae Ceaușescu was executed, the Court that sentenced him to death decided that his outrageous cult of personality and his *political necrophagy* had dishonored Romania's traditional respect for its leaders, and that he did not even deserve a coffin and grave. Ceaușescu's corpse was therefore dumped into a bag and tossed away at a soccer stadium.

27

HITLER'S POPE, THE BOOK

STALIN HAD LONG SINCE DEPARTED from the battlefield; Khrushchev was *hors de combat* for a few years and then he also died. His political necrophagy disappeared into the fog of history, and the slanderous battle cry accusing Pius XII of being "Hitler's Pope" slowly faded into the mists of time. The Kremlin—correctly, as it turned out—was consumed with worry about problems that lay closer to home, such as the rise of the *Solidarity* movement in Poland.

On October 16, 1978, Cardinal Karol Józef Wojtyla —a Pole!—became Pope John Paul II. Andropov, the power behind the Soviet throne, must have asked himself: What would Stalin or Khrushchev do? An operation was eventually mounted by Soviet military intelligence—defending the Soviet bloc was a military assignment—through its friends in Bulgaria (as was established by an official Italian investigation).[1]

On May 13, 1981, a young Turk named Mehmet Ali Ağca—who proved to be a Bulgarian agent—shot and critically wounded the pope as he was entering St. Peter's Square. The pope was struck four times and suffered severe blood loss. Ağca was apprehended and later sentenced to life in prison. Later, the pope famously forgave Ağca for the assassination attempt. Italian president Carlo Azeglio Ciampi later pardoned the would-be assassin at the pope's request and deported him to Turkey, in June 2000.

Several investigations pointed to the Soviets,[2] but the Kremlin avoided most blame for the shooting, so they decided to take another run at the pope. This time they turned to a *dezinformatsiya* operation not far removed from the earlier effort to frame Pius XII with a phony history. In his book *The End and the Beginning: Pope John Paul II—The Victory of Freedom, the Last Years, the Legacy,* author George Weigel drew on newly opened archives pertaining to the intelligence departments of communist countries and revealed a fascinating story about an effort to smear the new pope's reputation.[3]

Using their counterfeiting experts, in 1983 Polish intelligence agents crafted a phony diary purportedly written by a former lover of Cardinal Wojtyla. They used the identity of a woman he would have known but who was now, of course, dead. The plan was to leave the diary hidden in an apartment where it would be found during a police raid. Western reporters would assume it was legitimate and report on it as such.

As it turned out, however, the agent assigned to plant the fake diary got drunk and was involved in an automobile accident. In an effort to avoid arrest and detention, he explained who he was and exposed the plan. One can only wonder what would have happened had the pope's credibility been damaged early in his pontificate by a disinformation scheme like this. Of course, the phony diary was only a variation on *The Deputy* and its "Sidelights on History" section.

Soviet bloc intelligence agents also conducted phony letter-writing campaigns against the pope. These hatchet jobs were often complemented with threats and blackmail operations directed against him. Pope John Paul's body and his reputation survived these attacks. The Soviet bloc did not survive, thanks in part to John Paul's support for Solidarity. The Kremlin's war on the Vatican again melted into the background.

In 1999, the fairly dormant question of Pope Pius XII's alleged support for Hitler's persecution of the Jews suddenly generated renewed interest with the publication of John Cornwell's book, *Hitler's Pope: The Secret History of Pius XII.* The thesis of Cornwell's book was that Eugenio Pacelli was a single-minded Vatican lawyer and diplomat who, from the earliest part of his career, set out to establish the absolute authority of Rome over Europe's Catholic populations.

There is no hard evidence that Cornwell was connected with the Russian intelligence services; their archives are still sealed—some 29 billion pages are hidden away in them. Nevertheless, Cornwell resorted to political necrophagy. He used Khrushchev-style tactics of framing and *dezinformatsiya* to distort the historical truth about Pius XII. The flyleaf to the cover of the American edition boldly declares a hard-hitting *new* war on the memory of Pius XII:

> *Hitler's Pope* is the previously untold story of the man who was arguably the most dangerous churchman in modern history: Eugenio Pacelli, Pius XII, Pontiff from 1939 to 1958 and long controversial as the Pope who failed to speak out against Hitler's Final Solution. Here is the full story of how Pacelli in fact prompted events in the 1920s and '30s that helped sweep the Nazis to unhindered power.... In 1930 he negotiated a treaty with Hitler, the Reich Concordat, which ensured that the Nazis would rise unopposed by the most powerful Catholic community in the world—sealing, by Hitler's own admission, the fate of the Jews in Europe.

There we have it. In Cornwell's view, Pius not only failed to speak up for the Jews; he was in fact responsible for Hitler's rise to power and for the whole Holocaust. The flyleaf continues, claiming that Cornwell provides "striking new evidence" that Pius XII "had a personal antipathy toward the Jews," and stating that Cornwell draws "on research from secret Vatican and Jesuit archives made available *only to the author.*"

The Vatican has examined and refuted the outrageous claims Cornwell makes, as my coauthor (Rychlak) has scrupulously documented and discussed in his book, *Hitler, the War, and the Pope.* Thus, the reader's attention in this book is called to only a few significant points. Those points demonstrate how Cornwell tried to revive the Kremlin's war on Pius XII by using typical KGB disinformation means and methods.

To support his conclusion that Pius was "Hitler's Pope," Cornwell selectively edited quotes from Western publications, a technique widely used by the "science" of disinformation. By this method, a clever writer can turn a quotation into the exact opposite of what was originally intended. To see how this works, let us take a look at a remarkable statement quoted in the introductory materials to *Hitler's Pope.* Cornwell offers a supposed quotation from Thomas Merton, a well-known contemplative monk whose writings have inspired many people. In Cornwell's hands, the quotation reads:

> Pius XII and the Jews ... The whole thing is too sad and too serious for bitterness ... a silence which is deeply and completely in complicity with all the forces which carry out oppression, injustice, aggression, exploitation, war.

This seems to be a shocking condemnation of the pope from an esteemed Catholic thinker. If Merton had written this, it would indeed give one pause. But Cornwell manipulated a text by Merton to create this quotation. (The Sulners, who fabricated the documents used to frame Cardinal Mindszenty, would have been proud!) Since Cornwell gives no citation for this Merton quote (although he did give references for the other two less controversial quotations used on the same page), it was not easy to document his trick.[4]

Below is the complete statement, which was written by Merton in his personal journal, and which is a complaint that *he himself* had been ordered not to publish *his essay* on nuclear war. The "silence" about which he complained was the "silence" that had been imposed upon *him*. It was unrelated to Pius XII. Here is Merton's complete text, with the parts extracted by Cornwell highlighted in italics:

> A grim insight into the stupor of the Church, in spite of all that has been attempted, all efforts to wake her up! It all falls into place. Pope *Pius XII and the Jews*, the Church in South America, the treatment of Negroes in the US, the Catholics on the French right in the Algerian affair, the German Catholics under Hitler. All this fits into one big picture and our contemplative recollection is not very impressive when it is seen only as another little piece fitted into the puzzle. *The whole thing is too sad and too serious for bitterness.* I have the impression that my education is beginning—only just beginning and that I have a lot more terrible things to learn before I can know the real meaning of hope.
>
> There is no consolation, only futility, in the idea that one is a kind of martyr for a cause. I am not a martyr for anything, I am afraid. I wanted to act like a reasonable, civilized, responsible Christian of my time. I am not allowed to do this, and I am told I have renounced this—fine. In favor of what? In favor of *a silence which is deeply and completely in complicity with all the forces that carry out oppression, injustice, aggression, exploitation, war.* In other words silent complicity is presented as a "greater good" than "honest, conscientious protest." It is supposed to be part of my vowed life, it is for the "Glory of God." Certainly I refuse complicity. My silence itself is a protest and those who know me are aware of this fact. I have at least been able to write enough to make that clear. Also I cannot leave here in order to protest since the meaning of any protest depends on my staying here.[5]

Cornwell selected the phrases that are italicized above, and linked them with ellipses. This is more than academic fraud. This is *disinformation* at its best.

Another KGB *disinformation* technique used in Cornwell's *Hitler's Pope* is revealed by the book's cover. The dust jacket of the original British edition represents a deliberate and nasty deception. The cover is a photograph showing Nuncio Pacelli leaving a reception given for German President Hindenburg *in 1927.* The caption given on the inside of the dust jacket of the British edition, however, dates the photograph as having been taken in *March 1939.*

This is not an honest mistake. This is intentional deception for a purpose. By March 1939 Hitler was Führer, and Pacelli had been elected pope on March 2, 1939. A naïve reader who had fallen for Cornwell's slander could easily conclude that Pius XII rushed off to visit Hitler as soon as he was elected. That never happened—neither Pacelli nor Pius XII ever met Hitler.

This dramatic photograph shows Nuncio Pacelli, dressed in formal diplomatic regalia (which could easily be confused with papal garments), as he exits a building. In front of him stands a chauffeur saluting and holding open the square-looking door typical of old-fashioned, ceremonial automobiles from the 1920s. On either side of the nuncio stand soldiers of the Weimar Republic. Those who do not recognize the differences in uniform details could easily confuse the Weimar soldiers with Nazi soldiers because of their distinctive helmets widely associated with Nazi-era German soldiers.

The American edition of *Hitler's Pope* (and its later paperback version) has the correct date—1927—for the cover photograph, but the picture is cropped to eliminate two important points of reference: the soldier nearest the camera and the square door of the automobile. Both of those images provide clues to the true date of this photo, which Cornwell apparently wanted to avoid—he has admitted that he approved the photo.[6] In the American edition, the photo's background has also been significantly darkened and blurred, making it unlikely for the observer to notice that the remaining soldier is wearing a Weimar uniform, not a Nazi one. The chauffeur, with the cropping of the car door and the blurring, takes on the appearance of a saluting SS officer. It all helped Cornwell establish his thesis.

The Soviet political police always had a large component that did nothing but manipulate photographs, as counterfeited photos were a favorite means of framing people—both for demotion and for promotion. During Stalin's reign, unwanted people were not only killed but also removed from photographs where their presence was no longer desired. In the early 1920s, the Soviet media abounded with pictures showing Lenin together with Trotsky—Lenin's closest collaborator. After Lenin died, however, the image of Trotsky was replaced in all these pictures by that of Stalin. Nikolai Yezhov, at one time the chief of the Soviet political police, suffered a similar fate. A very popular figure during the great purge, he was often seen in pictures together with Stalin. After Yezhov disappeared from the political scene, however, the pictures were doctored to show Stalin without Yezhov.

After I was granted political asylum in the United States, Ceauşescu sentenced me to death both by firing squad and in public opinion. In March and April 1978, during Ceauşescu's last visits to the United States and to Great Britain, the Romanian media were full of pictures showing me together with Ceauşescu and his wife at the White House and at Buckingham Palace. After I defected a few months later, my image disappeared from the copies of all those pictures. An example can be seen in my book *Red Horizons*, which reproduces the same photograph as it was published first before and then after being doctored.[7]

The *dezinformatsiya* continues. In the preface to his book, Cornwell says that the idea of writing a book on Pius XII occurred to him "several years ago . . . at a dinner with a group of postgraduate students," where there was a discussion on how "he had not done enough to save the Jews from the death camps." Claiming that his original intention was to portray the pope as a strong spiritual leader, Cornwell set off for Rome to conduct some background research.

While Cornwell was granted access only to the Vatican's open archives, he claimed that his book was based on "previously unseen material." He also said he spent "months on end" in a "windowless dungeon beneath the Borgia Tower," while a "silent factotum brought him Pacelli's files, which had been hidden from view for decades."

In fact, the files were simply in an underground storage vault; moreover, they were not secret, and they covered the years 1912–1922, before Hitler was running Germany and while Pacelli was nuncio to the Kingdom of Bavaria. Vatican records show that Cornwell visited those archives only from May 12 to June 2, 1997, that he did not come every day, and that he often stayed for very brief periods of time. Like Hochhuth, Cornwell apparently needed the Vatican merely as window-dressing for his own story. He later admitted that he was there only three weeks and that the files were not secret—but by then the damage was done.[8]

In his preface, Cornwell claimed that by mid-1997, "nearing the end of my research, I found myself in a state I can only describe as moral shock" over the evidence that Pacelli had an "undeniable antipathy toward the Jews" and that his "diplomacy in Germany in the 1930s" betrayed groups that "might have challenged Hitler's regime and thwarted the Final Solution." Inevitably one recalls Hochhuth's elusive bishop at the Vatican, who supposedly opened Hochhuth's eyes with gossip about Pius's failings.

Hochhuth's criticism of Pius is chamomile tea, however, compared to Cornwell's knockout slug of whiskey. Cornwell's mention of the Borgia Tower is also a nice—and irrelevant—touch, bringing to mind all the evils of the Borgia popes. One is again reminded of Hochhuth, in this instance with his mention of the Katyn massacres. Such touches are typical of KGB *dezinformatsiya* operations. As for Cornwell's research, his book relies mainly on secondary sources, such as Carlo Falconi's *The Silence of Pius XII*, which was based on documents counterfeited by the communist government of Croatia. When he does use original documents, he misrepresents them.[9]

In his books *Hitler, the War and the Pope* and *Righteous Gentiles*, Rychlak shows how Cornwell cited "original documents" to build his credibility, even though they did not actually support his case. This is the same technique used by the KGB, and it explains why my DIE was asked to keep producing documents, even though they were not incriminating.

In his original preface to *Hitler's Pope*, Cornwell makes a point of saying that, as a Catholic who had returned to the fold after an absence of twenty years, he originally wanted to write the full story of Pius XII so that his "pontificate would be vindicated." In the preface to the 2008 edition, Cornwell expands on this statement, saying he "embarked on this biography of Pius XII with an open mind, in fact with a large measure of sympathy." After all his research, however, he became convinced that Pius XII "was not a saintly exemplar for future generations."

The KGB's *dezinformatsiya* specialists in framing were experts at this old rhetorical device: If you really want to slander someone, just pretend you were completely impartial, even sympathetic, when you started your investigation into his character, and then proclaim your deep regret over being forced to admit his faults. Or vice versa. Almost all books on Ceaușescu published in the West—with money from my Romanian DIE—started with the author's supposed "belief" that he was a Soviet-style communist, and ended by presenting him as a uniquely Westernized one. Hochhuth used the same device in *The Deputy*, when he said in an interview after his play opened that he had originally simply intended to write a sympathetic story about Kurt Gerstein and his difficulties in getting the papal nuncio in Berlin to listen to his tales about the Nazi killings. It was only later that Hochhuth (or Piscator) introduced a coldly cynical pope into his play.[10]

A good example of Cornwell's research can be found in his discussion of a concordat signed by the Vatican and Serbia in 1914. Cornwell alleges that a power-driven Pacelli insisted on the concordat, despite the risk of war and over Vienna's objections, and that the concordat in fact led to World War I. Cornwell cites leftist newspapers and writers as the sources for his conclusions, but in fact, historians agree that the concordat had no effect on the outbreak of war whatsoever. In discussing this concordat, Cornwell ominously mentions that all the various materials were "once in the keeping of Eugenio Pacelli." There was, however, nothing sinister in that, because as a junior member of the Vatican team handling the negotiations it was Pacelli's job to take notes and keep the papers.

The most revealing insight into Cornwell's research methods lies in the fact that, citing a secondary source, he wrote that the papal nuncio in Vienna had warned Pacelli about the risks posed by the concordat. Remarkably, Cornwell made no mention of the original document from the Vienna nuncio, *which Cornwell is shown to have signed out* while doing research in the Vatican archives, and which directly contradicts the statement in his book.[11]

Eventually Cornwell qualified his criticism of Pius XII's handling of the roundup of Roman Jews in October 1943, and he also acknowledged the reality of the threat of an invasion of the Vatican, which he had previously downplayed. In 2008, however, Penguin Press released a new, paperback edition of *Hitler's Pope*. The only apparent change was a new preface in which Cornwell tried to withdraw many of these qualifications.

In the new edition, Cornwell still argues that Pacelli was "an ideal church leader" for Hitler to exploit, saying: "I am not inclined to alter this view despite the many citations of Pacelli's alleged deeds of mercy toward Jews and others, or his private criticism of Hitler, or his cautious, even-handed reproaches against both the Axis and the Allied powers."[12] According to Cornwell, Pacelli was a vain, beady-eyed, overwhelmingly ambitious careerist who dominated Vatican policy long before he was elected pope. The author tries to focus on the early 1930s, when Secretary of State Pacelli "entered into a series of negotiations with Hitler's government, culminating in the Reich Concordat."[13] He also says that Pacelli's postwar claim to have "on various occasions" condemned the "fanatical anti-Semitism inflicted on the Hebrew people," is "a blatant lie."[14]

This shifting from one argument (after it has been proven weak) to another, and continuing to do that without ever fully backing away from the original argument, is typical of a KGB *dezinformatsiya* operation. Promoters and supporters of *The Deputy* did the same. That does not necessarily mean Cornwell was an agent of the Kremlin, but it does mean that in addition to using their moniker for Pius XII, he employed the same methods that they did.

28

ANDROPOV'S COCAINE

"**[D**EZINFORMATSIYA] WORKS LIKE COCAINE," KGB chief Yuri Andropov used to preach. "If you sniff it once or twice, it may not change your life. If you use it every day, though, it will make you into an addict—a different man."

Turning the communist leader of Romania, Nicolae Ceauşescu, into the West's most favorite tyrant was based on Andropov's cocaine theory. "We should plant the image of the new Ceauşescu *in the West* like opium poppy seeds, one by one by one. And we should water these seeds day after day, until they bear fruit," Andropov told me in 1972, when the KGB boss had decided to make Ceauşescu a box-office success in the West, in a test run preparatory to trying the same trick with the ruler in the Kremlin. (Does anyone still remember the frenzy that greeted Mikhail Gorbachev on his trips to the West?)

Eventually, a "new" Ceauşescu emerged from the seeds planted in the West by the DIE and the KGB, just as a "new" Pius XII had emerged from *The Deputy*. Nobody in the West knew the real Ceauşescu, just as the West's new Cold War generation was entirely unaware of Pius XII's heroic struggle against the Nazis before and during World War II. Moreover, most public officials in the West were unfamiliar with the Kremlin's highly secret *dezinformatsiya* and framing operations.

On Christmas Day 1989, however, Ceauşescu and his wife were executed for genocide. Few looked back to speculate about how they had been so misled. By that time, piles of Mikhail Gorbachev's *Perestroika: New Thinking for Our Country and the World*, which apparently not many people read with care, had taken the place of Ceaușescu's memoirs in the bookstore windows. Gorbachev's book proposed a new utopia. The Soviet Union would now be a "Marxist society of free people." Life would be materially rich and spiritually uplifting. The people would attain their "democratic rights" and be treated with "trust and respect," and there would be "equal rights for all." Now the new man in the Kremlin, "Gorby," was touted as a nascent democrat and political visionary. So much for institutional memory.

The framing of Pius XII was the framing of Ceaușescu and Gorbachev in reverse. Over the years, the pro-Nazi image of Pius XII, which had been seeded in the West by the Kremlin and watered by KGB agents and Western communists, generated a flurry of books, movies, and articles denigrating the heroic pontiff and helping the framing to succeed.

Authors, including Garry Wills,[1] James Carroll,[2] Susan Zuccotti,[3] Michael Phayer,[4] David Kertzer,[5] and Robert Wistrich,[6] swallowed the Kremlin's framing and wrote highly distorted books about Pius XII. John Cornwell, who published the utterly defamatory *Hitler's Pope*, came back with a second book touching on the topic.[7] Robert Katz, author of two books promoting the Kremlin's lies about Pius XII back in the 1960s, authored a new book that largely combines his earlier laments.[8] Daniel Goldhagen combined the worst accusations made in all the other books and launched a broad-based attack on Christianity itself.[9]

Like Cornwell, many of these authors selectively edited real quotations in order to transform positive information about Pius XII into negative. Here is one example from Suzan Zuccotti's book *Under His Very Windows*. Pursuant to Pope Pius XII's request, Luigi Cardinal Maglione, the Vatican's secretary of state, met to lodge a protest with German ambassador Weizsäcker after the notorious October 16, 1943, roundup of Jews in Rome.[10] Weizsäcker was known to be a friendly voice within the German leadership in Rome, and he was embarrassed about the Nazi treatment of the Jews.[11] Cardinal Maglione began his memo about the meeting by writing:

> Having learned that this morning the Germans made a raid on the Jews, *I asked the Ambassador of Germany to come to me and I asked him to try to intervene on behalf of these unfortunates. I talked to him as well as I could in the name of humanity, in Christian charity.* The Ambassador, who already

knew of the arrests, but doubted whether it dealt specifically with the Jews, said to me in a sincere and moved voice: I am always expecting to be asked: Why do you remain in your position?

Zuccotti deleted the nonitalicized clauses above, thereby eliminating the cardinal's first two express references to the victims being Jewish. She also omitted the entire concluding paragraph, which recounted Maglione's last words to Weizsäcker:

> In the meantime, I repeat: Your Excellency has told me that you [Weizsäcker] will attempt to do something for the unfortunate Jews. I thank you for that. As for the rest, I leave it to your judgment. If you think it is more opportune not to mention our conversation [to the German high command due to fear of retaliation], so be it.[12]

So, even though Cardinal Maglione referred explicitly to "Jews" three times, Zuccotti's readers never saw those references. Similarly, Zuccotti quoted a report written by Nuncio Valerio Valeri to Cardinal Maglione, dated August 7, 1942. This report related to the deportation of Jews from France to unknown areas, probably in Poland. In her quote, Zuccotti deleted the crucial first line of Valeri's report, where he mentions that he had used his position to intervene *frequently* for Jews in the name of the pope.[13] This testimony, which would be hard to rebut, was simply omitted.

Zuccotti even mischaracterized Pius XII's first encyclical, *Summi Pontificatus*, saying that it "never mentioned Jews. Indeed, despite references to the unity of the human race, it seemed to single out Christians, or perhaps Catholics, for special consideration."[14] In fact, Pius did expressly use the word "Jew" in the context of explaining that there is no room for racial distinctions in the Church.[15]

This flurry of new lies supporting the original framing's lies about Pius XII has generated new allegations, many of which are hilariously inconsistent even with the earlier insinuations. Eventually, the argument reached beyond the pope and the Catholic Church, challenging the very foundation of Christianity, the New Testament itself.[16] Of course, as Rabbi David Dalin has noted, many of the critics are not honestly seeking the truth; they are instead distorting the truth in order to influence the future of the Catholic Church.[17]

Too many stories about Pius XII have not been properly traced back to the *original* source—just as nobody ever bothered to check out Ceaușescu's sudden love affair with democracy. In his book *Constantine's Sword*, for instance, excommunicated former priest James Carroll advanced a supposed deathbed condemnation of Pius XII by Pope John XXIII.[18] This is another repeated lie that has become the truth. No eyewitness has ever come forward to support Carroll's story. The Postulator of John XXIII's Cause for Canonization, Fr. Luca De Rosa, OFM, stated that Pope John was, in fact, "full of admiration and devotion" for Pius XII.[19] Archbishop Loris Capovilla, formerly private secretary to Pope John, called the Carroll story "a lie."[20]

In reality, John XXIII had a photograph of Pius XII on his desk, with a prayer on the back asking for Pius's canonization as a saint. The prayer called Pius "a fearless defender of the Faith, a courageous struggler for justice and peace ... a shining model of charity and of every virtue."[21] A million of these prayer cards were put in circulation by John XXIII's staff, and John (who prayed monthly before the tomb of Pius XII)[22] said in an audience that surely one day Pius would be raised to the Catholic altars.[23]

John XXIII even considered taking the name "Pius XIII."[24] In his first Christmas broadcast to the world after his election, John paid the high honor of saying that Pius XII's doctrinal and pastoral teachings "assure a place in posterity for the name of Pius XII. Even apart from any official declaration, which would be premature, the triple title of 'Most excellent Doctor, Light of Holy Church, Lover of the divine law' evokes the sacred memory of this pontiff in whom our times were blessed indeed."[25] Of course, only a saint can be declared a Doctor of the Church. Yet *Constantine's Sword* is at least the third publication in which Carroll has advanced the fabricated deathbed story, and he did so twice in that book!

The often-overlooked truth about why Carroll, Cornwell, and so many other post-Hochhuth liberal Westerners have fallen into the KGB trap and watered the poppy seeds of its framing of Pius XII, is that their works were ultimately not about Pius. They were part of a new offensive aimed at further dividing the Judeo-Christian world by discrediting the Vatican. They saw the end of John Paul II's anticommunist papacy coming, and they tried to help elect a leftist pope, by making people believe that Pius XII and John Paul II had led the Church in a bad direction.

According to these writers, John Paul and Pius were overly authoritarian, and just as Pius XII's leadership supposedly led to the Holocaust, John Paul's leadership was supposedly heading for another catastrophe. The only hope was to elect a very different kind of pope. The last chapter of *Hitler's Pope* was entitled "Pius XII Redivivus." In it, Cornwell argued that John Paul II represented a return to a highly centralized, autocratic papacy, as opposed to a more diversified Church. Cornwell wrote that there were early signs of a titanic struggle between the progressives and the traditionalists, with the potential for a cataclysmic schism, especially in North America.

Cornwell felt that John Paul II was leading the traditionalists as the Church moved toward this struggle, and he argued that "canonization of Pius XII is a key move in the attempts to restore a reactionary papal absolutism."[26] Any doubt about Cornwell's intent was resolved in March 2000, when Pope John Paul II made an unprecedented and historic trip to the Holy Land. At that time, as Christians and Jews were coming closer together, Cornwell described the Pontiff as "aging, ailing, and desperately frail as he presides over a Vatican that is driven by cliques, engulfed in scandal, and subject to ideological power struggles."[27]

To Cornwell, the Vatican was "a nest of nepotism and corruption, sexual depravity, gangsterism, and even murder." That is exactly how Khrushchev and Sakharovsky also depicted it—and the United States as well. Much like Hochhuth before him, Cornwell quoted an unidentified "Vatican insider," who described the Vatican as "a place of gossipy eunuchs . . . . The whole place floats on a sea of bitchery."[28]

In his 2001 book, *Breaking Faith*, Cornwell made charges against Pope John Paul II similar to those he made against Pius XII in *Hitler's Pope*. He argued that centralization of power under John Paul's authoritarian rule had brought about a fundamental breakdown in communications between hierarchy and laity. "Bullying oppression," Cornwell wrote, was driving people away from the Catholic Church. He blamed virtually all of the Church's modern problems on "the harsh centralized rules of Wojtyla's Church." He called John Paul a "stumbling block" for "a vast, marginalized faithful" and said the pope had "encouraged an oppressive intellectual culture."

Most of the world credited John Paul II with being instrumental in bringing down communism in Eastern Europe, by being the spiritual inspiration behind its downfall and a catalyst for "a peaceful revolution" in Poland. Despite having no armies under his command and no weapons to deploy, Pope John Paul II played a pivotal role in one of the twentieth century's greatest geopolitical dramas—the struggle against the Soviet Union's forceful dominance in Asia and Eastern Europe.[29] Cornwell, however, despised John Paul. He warned that if a conservative pope were to succeed John Paul II, the Church would "deteriorate" and push "greater numbers of Catholics toward antagonism, despair and mass apostasy."[30] It is safe to say that at the time, Cornwell was desperately trying to prevent a Ratzinger-style papacy.

Cornwell's book *The Pontiff in Winter* was his final shot at Pope John Paul II. The title of the American version of this book is *The Pontiff in Winter: Triumph and Conflict in the Reign of John Paul II*, but the British title is more telling about Cornwell's intent: *The Pope in Winter: The Dark Face of John Paul II's Papacy*. In this book, Cornwell argued that John Paul had "taken a bit of the Iron Curtain with him" to the Vatican to mold a rigid, authoritarian papacy. Cornwell not only blamed John Paul for the spread of AIDS and global terrorism (just as the Kremlin had blamed the United States); he also said that John Paul had developed a "medieval patriarchalism" towards women, and that his "major and abiding legacy . . . is to be seen and felt in various forms of oppression and exclusion." Cornwell criticized the pope's positions on the September 11 attacks, the clash between Islam and Christianity, and statements regarding Mel Gibson's motion picture *The Passion of the Christ*. Cornwell charged that the Catholic teachings voiced by the pontiff had "alienated generations of the faithful," and that "John Paul's successor will inherit a dysfunctional Church fraught with problems."[31]

Cornwell's clear intent was to prevent another conservative from becoming pope.[32] His continuing theme was that the Church needed to decentralize its authority. Mainly, however, he advanced the typical laundry list of liberal Catholic demands, including married clergy, women priests, a bigger role for the laity in running the Church, and inclusive language in the Mass.[33] He clearly was deeply offended by the Church's teachings on sexuality. Cornwell preached that contraception, homosexuality, divorce, and essentially all extramarital sex are matters to be decided by consenting adults, and he would like the Church to change its position on these matters. Instead of offering consistent arguments, Cornwell reviewed opinion surveys suggesting that most Catholics have difficulty with Church teachings on contraception, abortion, divorce, and homosexuality. He interpreted this as resistance to papal authority, and the only solution that made sense to him was to weaken the papacy and change the Church teachings. That, it seems, is the real motivation behind his writing, not the pursuit of the truth.

In other words, Cornwell recited the *dezinformatsiya*'s laundry list of accusations against the Catholic Church, and used *dezinformatsiya* techniques to further denigrate it.

Pope John Paul II, perhaps better than anyone else, recognized the parallels between his efforts and those of Pius XII. John Paul, of course, did not have a horrible world war to contend with, nor was he threatened with the possible invasion of Vatican City, but given those differences, the approach each leader took was similar. As John Paul II explained, "Anyone who does not limit himself to cheap polemics knows very well what Pius XII thought of the Nazi regime and how much he did to help countless people persecuted by the regime."[34]

No smoking gun has yet been found to prove the Kremlin's hand in this new war against the Judeo-Christian world, because the KGB archives are still, unfortunately, sealed. But swaying the Vatican into electing anti-American popes sympathetic to the Kremlin and its historical anti-Semitism has long been Moscow's dream. According to the *New York Times:*

> ... the forty-nine cardinals gathered in Rome [in October 1958] to elect Pius XII's successor were indignant over a Soviet attempt to influence their choice of the next Pope. The alleged attempt was made in a broadcast by the Moscow radio, entitled "Events in the Vatican" and beamed to Rome *in Italian.*[35]

Radio Moscow charged that under Pius XII's pontificate, the Vatican followed a policy of open support of "the most reactionary and aggressive imperialistic circles." That was, of course, "Zionist America" and its main ally, Israel. The Moscow broadcast also charged that Pope Pius XII had meddled in politics and so had "destroyed the principle of the universality of the Church's mission in the world." Echoing criticisms of Pius XII leveled by the Nazis, Radio Moscow concluded: "The hope has been expressed that the new pope may interest himself more in religious problems and less in political problems."[36]

In 1939 Hitler made a similar attempt before the enclave of the Sacred College of Cardinals. The then-German ambassador to the Holy See called on Eugenio Pacelli, cardinal secretary of state and camerlengo, or chamber-lain, and made known to him the wishes of the German *Reichskanzler*. But Cardinal Pacelli, the most strongly anti-Fascist of the cardinals, was elected pope anyway.[37]

The hopes of Cornwell and company were also thwarted in 2005, when the theologically conservative Cardinal Joseph Alois Ratzinger became Pope Benedict XVI. Not only did he continue policies in line with his predecessors; he also signed the papers to permit the sainthood cause of Pope Pius XII to advance, and he oversaw the beatification of John Paul II.

On October 9, 2008, Benedict affirmed that Pius "often acted in secret and in silence" to defend Jews during the Holocaust. Celebrating a Mass commemorating fifty years since Pius's death, Benedict said: "In light of the concrete situations of that complex historical moment, he sensed that this was the only way to avoid the worst and save the greatest possible number of Jews." Benedict said he prayed that the process of beatification "can proceed happily."[38]

PART III

FRAMING THE US GOVERNMENT AS A PACK OF ASSASSINS*

* This part of the book contains information published in *Programmed to Kill: Lee Harvey Oswald, the KGB, and the Kennedy Assassination* (Chicago: Ivan R. Dee, 2007) .

29

THE END OF AMERICA'S INNOCENCE

T HE ASSASSINATION OF PRESIDENT JOHN F. KENNEDY fifty years ago, at first seen by Americans as a random act of violence, sent the whole country into shock. The Camelot fairytale of youth and beauty came to an abrupt and violent end, graphically compounded two days later when Jack Ruby shot and killed Lee Harvey Oswald, Kennedy's accused assassin, on live television. The Dallas police and FBI quickly identified Oswald as the lone assassin of the president, but there was little evidence to support that conclusion.

There was, however, irrefutable proof that, just before killing President Kennedy, Oswald had traveled to Mexico under a false identity and there had secretly met with "Comrade Kostin," aka Valery Kostikov, a diplomatic official assigned to the Soviet Embassy. Kostikov has been identified by the CIA as an officer of the KGB's Thirteenth Department (assassinations abroad), which became known in KGB jargon as the Department for Wet Affairs (*wet* meaning *bloody*). There is also irrefutable evidence that Oswald's Soviet wife, Marina, had been in touch with the Soviet Embassy in the United States and that she concealed evidence from US authorities confirming her husband's secret trip to Mexico and meeting there with the KGB officer Valery Kostikov.

Lyndon Johnson, who had just been sworn in as president, looked upon the assassination as a criminal case for the police to solve. On November 25, 1963, he told J. Edgar Hoover it would be enough for the Texas attorney general to produce a report and for the FBI to work with Texas authorities and put together its summary report. Hoover agreed.[1] Johnson also pointed out to American journalist Joseph Alsop that the FBI thought it could do the "wisest, quickest and most effective" study.[2] But then, Johnson heard that the US Senate and House wanted to start their own investigations due to emerging international aspects to the case. He became afraid that any official suggestion of Soviet involvement in the assassination could lead to a nuclear threat from Moscow.

On November 29, Johnson was briefed by Dr. Glenn Seaborg, chairman of the Atomic Energy Commission. As Max Holland documented in *The Kennedy Assassination Tapes*, "With chilling precision Dr. Seaborg tells Johnson about the consequences of an all-out nuclear exchange with Moscow. The cost in American lives from a first strike alone is breathtaking: 39 to 40 million American casualties, not to mention untold dislocation and devastation that will take decades to overcome."[3]

Therefore, on that same day, Johnson, who was facing elections in a few months, created "a very high caliber, top-flight, blue-ribbon group" whose purpose was not to investigate the assassination, but primarily to invoke the collective integrity of its distinguished members and to issue a public report that would dispel all rumors of "foreign complications" stemming from Oswald's known connections with the Soviet intelligence and with communist Cuba. This group came to be called the Warren Commission after its chairman, Chief Justice Earl Warren.

The Warren Commission did not actually begin its field investigation until March 18, 1964, after the end of Jack Ruby's trial. Norman Redlich, the Warren Commission staff lawyer in charge of preparing the questioning of Oswald's Soviet widow, Marina, wrote in a memorandum that she had "lied to the Secret Service, the FBI and this commission repeatedly on matters which are of vital concern to the people of this country and the world." Chief Justice Warren, however, ruled out any attempt to test Marina's sincerity by using a lie detector or cross-examination, because, as he explained to his staff, it would make little sense for the commission to impugn the credibility of its chief witness on Oswald's character.

On June 15, the commission announced it had completed its investigation. The final report was written by three lawyers—Norman Redlich, Alfred Goldberg, and Lee Rankin—who had no experience in foreign counterintelligence, and who worked under "constant pressure from the commission 'to close doors rather than open them' because of the time pressure to complete the report before the coming presidential election."

The Warren Commission report was published by the Government Printing Office on September 24, 1964—six weeks before the elections. It consists of twenty-six volumes of haphazardly assembled testimonies to the commission and documents obtained primarily from federal and state authorities and from the Soviet government, plus one volume containing the summary report. The summary report is a disorganized hodgepodge of material assembled by various staff members, to which is attached an unsatisfactory index. Nevertheless, the twenty-six published volumes contain a wealth of factual but essentially raw information clearly showing the Soviet hand to an informed analyst with inside knowledge of Soviet intelligence operations and methods.

The commission's conclusion was that JFK was killed on November 22, 1963, by shots fired from the Texas School Book Depository by Lee Harvey Oswald, and that Oswald was killed two days later at the Dallas Police Department by Jack Ruby. The commission "found no evidence to indicate that either Lee Harvey Oswald or Jack Ruby was part of any conspiracy, domestic or foreign, to assassinate President Kennedy"; it further resolved that "there is no credible evidence that Oswald was an agent of the Soviet government," and that "he did not receive unusually favorable treatment in entering or leaving the Soviet Union or in returning to the United States." The commission "could not make any definitive determination of Oswald's motives," although it did discuss some of his asocial and anti-American character traits that might have contributed to his motivation.

In the late 1970s, the House of Representatives formed the Select Committee on Assassinations and conducted its own investigations. In 1979 it published twelve volumes of documents and hearings and one summary volume on the JFK assassination (Government Printing Office, with the summary reissued by Bantam). The committee's report does contain some important new and relevant factual material in the form of documents that had come to light after 1964 and interviews conducted by the committee pointing even more suggestively toward Moscow than the Warren Commission's materials. Again, however, because it lacked inside knowledge of Soviet intelligence, the House committee could not properly evaluate what it had uncovered.

In its final report, the committee excluded the possibility of a Soviet hand in the assassination by simply stating:

> In fact the reaction of the Soviet Government as well as the Soviet people seemed to be one of genuine shock and sincere grief. The committee believed, therefore, on the basis of the evidence available to it, that the Soviet Government was not involved in the assassination.[4]

Such credulity showed that the House committee, like the Warren Commission, understood nothing about the degree to which the Soviet government had always relied on disinformation and deception, to the point of even falsifying the Moscow street maps and telephone books. Evidently no one remembered that Khrushchev had boldly lied to President Kennedy in denying that the Soviets were putting nuclear missiles on Cuba.

During the years when I was the chief of Romania's espionage station in West Germany, I became involved in a joint Soviet KGB-Romanian DIE operation that would, eventually, crack open the dark window concealing the supersecret web of connections between Oswald and the KGB. In 1958, I was unexpectedly called to East Berlin for an emergency meeting. General Nicolae Doicaru, at that time acting chief of the DIE, and KGB Colonel Rudenko, the DIE's Soviet adviser for intelligence on military technology, were waiting for me at our embassy.

"We've gotten a brand new task for you from Moscow," Rudenko explained. He did most of the talking. On the table before me, the KGB colonel plunked down the Romanian translation of an American document. It was a press release (dated April 30, 1956) that had been distributed by the US National Advisory Committee for Aeronautics (NACA)—the forerunner of NASA (the National Aeronautics and Space Administration). The document reported that NACA had received a new type of airplane, the Lockheed U-2, that would make it possible to obtain the meteorological data needed for the jet transports of tomorrow, which would be flying at altitudes far higher than those then used by all but a few military aircraft.

"Even the American media knew it was a lie," Rudenko added, handing me a newspaper clipping. It was an article (from the *Los Angeles Times* of April 14, 1957) concerning the same Lockheed U-2 plane that the US government was claiming would be used to conduct scientific research. According to the article, the U-2 was actually a spy plane, which was then flying out of Europe and Japan under top-secret classification. The fact that the U-2 planes themselves were heavily guarded day and night was hard proof that they were highly classified and were being used for extremely secret missions.

"CIA's latest tool," Rudenko concluded, handing me a Russian document and its Romanian translation. It was a requirement issued by the Soviet military intelligence service, the GRU (*Gosudarstvennoye Razvedyvatelnoye Upravleniye*), which asked for data on the U-2 plane. After listing what the GRU had already learned about the U-2, the order asked for "everything," including rumors about the flight altitude of this "black lady of espionage." According to that requirement, the Soviet Defense Ministry knew that U-2 planes had flown over the Soviet Union several times, but its Air Defense Command (the *Voyska protivovozdushnoy oborony*, or V-PVO) had not been able to track them for certain because of their ultrahigh altitude.

Acknowledging that the flight altitude of the U-2 should be a highly classified secret known to very few people, the GRU indicated an indirect way to obtain this information, and that was by learning the maximum operating range of the American radar gear used to monitor the flights of the U-2. The GRU requirement indicated that most of the U-2 flights over the Soviet Union originated at the US Air Force bases in Wiesbaden, West Germany and Atsugi, Japan, both manned by the Marine Corps, and it asked for any kind of information on the radar gear existing at those airports.

In the summer of 1959, I got a new directive from DIE headquarters. According to the requirement, it was believed, based on "unconfirmed" information just obtained by the KGB, that the U-2 spy plane could fly at altitudes of "about 30,000 meters" (roughly 90,000 feet). My station was asked to make a special effort to check out that information and expedite to headquarters any confirmation or expansion of it.

I had already sent headquarters data obtained from the US base in Wiesbaden, which clearly showed that the U-2's flight altitude was one of the most highly classified American military secrets, known only to persons directly involved in its flights and to a few specially cleared air traffic controllers and radar operators at that base. Unless an unexpected miracle occurred, I was sure that my station could produce nothing more on the subject. From the new request, I realized that the KGB must have been luckier. Evidently, one of its other stations had been able to get its hands on a traffic controller or radar operator assigned to the Marine Air Force base in Wiesbaden or in Atsugi.

It would not take long for me to learn that that was true. On June 19, 1960, Nikita Khrushchev landed in Bucharest as head of a large party delegation to attend the Third Congress of the Romanian Communist Party (at that time called the Workers Party), and he remained there for eight days. Khrushchev's spy chief and expert on Romanian matters, General Sakharovsky, had come with him, although he was not formally included in the party delegation. The Congress was dedicated to Romania's rapid industrialization, and as I was by then head of Romania's technological espionage department, I became the liaison officer with General Sakharovsky.

Khrushchev spent most of the evenings sipping vodka and telling stories about the downing of the first U-2 spy plane on May 1, 1960, and about the subsequent Paris summit meeting, where he had just finished "humiliating" Eisenhower. According to what I learned during those eight days when I was in Sakharovsky's company, the Soviets had been able to shoot down the U-2 only because the KGB had obtained reliable information on the plane's flight altitude. I understood that the intelligence had been received somewhere toward the end of the previous year, but that the Soviet Air Defense Command (V-PVO) had for some time found no opportunity to verify it, because there had been no more U-2 flights until April 9, 1960. Observing that flight, the V-PVO became convinced that the KGB intelligence was accurate, and it therefore adjusted its radar and missiles so as to be prepared when the next flight came over. That happened on May 1, 1960.

"The most valuable May Day present we've ever given the Comrade," Sakharovsky said. He told me that from the moment the U-2 had entered the Soviet airspace until it had been shot down, he had been in constant contact with the V-PVO commander, Marshal Sergey Semyonovich Biryuzov. That evening Sakharovsky had dined with the Comrade, and a couple of weeks later he received the Order of Lenin.

Naturally, I toasted Sakharovsky on his success. "Bottoms up to the *serzhant*, too!" I ventured.

In those days, *serzhant* was the broken record being played by our Soviet *razvedka* (foreign intelligence) advisers, who placed a high priority on recruiting American servicemen. Of course the KGB wanted us to recruit high-ranking American officers, but in Soviet experience it had proved true that sergeants were much easier to approach and recruit. They might never be colonels or even captains, but some were extremely productive intelligence agents. That was why Sergeant Robert Lee Johnson, who had been stationed in West Germany in the 1950s, was secretly awarded the rank of Red Army major and received written congratulations from the Soviet Council of Ministers and from Khrushchev himself.[5] (Years later, Vitaly Yurchenko, a high-ranking KGB officer who defected to the CIA in 1985—and soon redefected—reported that the KGB regarded the case of Chief Warrant Officer John Anthony Walker—another *serzhant*—as the greatest success in KGB history, "surpassing in importance even the Soviet theft of the Anglo-American blueprints for the first atomic bomb" and causing "devastating consequences for the United States" in the event of war. John F. Lehman, who was the US secretary of the Navy when Walker was arrested, agreed.[6])

"Well, he wasn't even a *serzhant*," Sakharovsky said.

As was normal, the Soviet general did not elaborate on the details of the operation that had ended with the downing of the U-2 and the capture of its pilot, Francis Gary Powers. A few weeks after the U-2 plane had been shot down, however, the DIE's *razvedka* advisers added a new wrinkle to their constant refrain about our need to recruit a *serzhant*—now we were also told to start looking for a "defector."

At that time we were not interested in the *razvedka* advisers' demand— what American *serzhant* would defect to Romania anyway? Soon after President Kennedy was shot, however, we began focusing on the advisers' recommendation about a defector. To our surprise we learned that before defecting to Moscow Lee Harvey Oswald had been stationed as a radar operator at the supersecret Atsugi Air Base outside of Tokyo, and that some of the U-2 planes that flew over the Soviet Union took off from that Marine base.

At about that same time, in the United States the writer Edward Jay Epstein was conducting his own investigation of the Kennedy assassination, published as *Legend: The Secret World of Lee Harvey Oswald* (Reader's Digest/McGraw-Hill, 1978). This book introduced new and useful material on Oswald, which Epstein had managed to dig up and carefully document. Epstein claimed to have interviewed over four hundred persons who had been, in one way or another, associated with Oswald. Among them were "about seventy Marines Oswald had served with in Japan and the Far East," most of whom "had never been previously interviewed by the FBI or

Warren Commission."

Zack Stout, one of the Marines who was stationed at Atsugi Air Base with Oswald, stated that Oswald had gotten involved with an attractive Japanese girl who "worked" as a hostess at the Queen Bee, one of the three most expensive nightclubs in Tokyo and one that catered to American senior officers and U-2 pilots. Stout and other enlisted Marines marveled that such a high-class hostess would go out with Oswald at all. They also wondered how he could afford her, since an evening with such a girl should have cost Oswald roughly the equivalent of a month's pay.[7] Such an expense was also totally out of character for Oswald, who had consistently been described as a penny pincher throughout his whole life.

Who would have paid for Oswald's girl from the Queen Bee? Epstein's book is centered around suspicions that Oswald had ties to Soviet intelligence, and it provides significant information indicating that the KGB must have been financing and manipulating that Queen Bee hostess who began spending her days and nights with Oswald.

Sometime after returning to the United States from the Soviet Union, Oswald would claim in a radio debate on the subject of Cuba that, as later reported by the organizer, New Orleans journalist William Stuckey, "It was in Japan that [Oswald] made up his mind to go to Russia and see for himself how a revolutionary society operates, a Marxist society."[8] Oswald is said to have confided to his new American friend George de Mohrenschildt that, "I met some Communists in Japan and they got me excited and interested, and that was one of my inducements in going to Soviet Russia, to see what goes on there."[9]

On October 18, 1957, Oswald learned that his unit was to be shipped out to the South China Sea and the Philippines because the civil war in Indonesia was heating up. According to Stout, Oswald seemed unhappy about having to leave Japan. According to George Wilkins, another Marine serving with Oswald at Atsugi, on October 27, just before departure, Oswald shot himself in the arm with a derringer pistol he had ordered, in violation of Army regulations, from a mail-order house in the United States. The wound did not appear to be serious, and several of the Marines believed that Oswald had deliberately shot himself in order to remain in Japan. He stayed in the hospital for almost three weeks but was released just in time to board the USS *Terrell County* with his unit on November 20 and head for the Philippines.[10]

After three months at sea, Oswald and his unit returned to Atsugi, where he was court-martialed for having had an unregistered weapon, the derringer with which he had shot himself. He was sentenced to twenty days at hard labor, forfeiture of $50 in pay, and reduction to the rank of private (thus nullifying his having passed the examination for corporal). Although Oswald received a suspended sentence, he was put on mess duty instead of being returned to radar duty. Immediately he put in for a hardship discharge, hoping, according to the other Marines, to be discharged in Japan, where he had made friends. His request was turned down, whereupon he picked a fight with the sergeant who had put him on mess duty, and that landed Oswald in the brig for nearly a month. When he was finally released on August 13, 1958, several of the Marines found him to be a changed man: cold, withdrawn, and bitter.

According to Joseph Macedo, a fellow radar operator, Oswald complained: "I've seen enough of a democratic society here in MACS-1. When I get out I'm going to try something else." After that Oswald seemed to associate less than ever with the other Marines, often disappearing on passes to Tokyo.[11]

Oswald finally left Japan on November 2, 1958, on board the USS *Barrett*. Upon arrival in San Francisco, he took thirty days' leave to visit his mother and go squirrel hunting with his brother. Then on December 22, 1958, he reported for radar duty at the Marine Air Control Squadron No. 9 (MACS-9) at El Toro Air Base in Santa Ana, California.[12] John Donovan, the officer in command of Oswald's radar crew, described him as "competent, very competent" in any job he saw him handle. Like the other Marines assigned there, Oswald had a much higher than average IQ, but Oswald was different in that he was almost solely interested in international affairs, not in women and sports the way the others were. He liked to ask a passing officer about some matter of foreign affairs, then afterwards remark to Donovan: "If men like that are leading us, there is something wrong—when I obviously have more intelligence and more knowledge than that man." He knew the names of many philosophers, but his knowledge did not go much beyond the names. He expressed particular interest in Hegel and the subject of social revolutions. When he talked with people, however, he did not seem to be seeking information but rather wanting to show how much he knew—"He had his mind made up and was willing to discuss that point of view with anyone."[13]

According to the Marines in his unit, the work at El Toro was not demanding, and Oswald spent much of his spare time studying Russian. He subscribed to a Russian-language newspaper and would answer with *da* and *nyet* when his fellow Marines teased him about his interest in the Russian language and in communism. He seemed to enjoy having the nickname "Oswaldovich" and being jokingly called a "Russian spy." On February 25, 1959, he took a test in the Russian language and received an overall grade of "poor," which while low did show he had achieved some proficiency in that difficult language.[14]

During the period when he was stationed at El Toro, the KGB operational pattern required that the communications plan for every important agent in the United States be based on *impersonal* means of transmitting their information. The KGB favored the use of dead drops for agents who were able to provide intelligence on unprocessed film. In the few cases where agents had large volumes of documents to turn over, such as agents involved in scientific and technological intelligence (S&T), the KGB also used lockers at train and bus stations.

Nelson Delgado, Oswald's bunkmate at El Toro, said that toward the end of Oswald's tour of duty there he noticed a stack of "spotter" photographs showing front and profile views of a fighter plane among Oswald's papers. Oswald stuffed the photographs into a duffel bag along with some other things, and Delgado agreed to deposit the bag in a locker at the Los Angeles bus station for him and bring him back the key. For this Delgado believed Oswald had given him two dollars.[15] Assuming Delgado's recollection is accurate, there can hardly be any other explanation than espionage for a duffel bag containing classified material to be placed in a public locker.

It is quite possible that Oswald included in such duffel bags some of the new information on the height at which the U-2 planes were flying in their practice runs over that part of Southern California. According to Francis Gary Powers, the U-2 pilot whom the Soviets shot down on May 1, 1960, at El Toro Oswald had had access "not only to radar and radio codes but also to the new MPS-16 height-finding radar gear," and the height at which the U-2 flew was the most highly classified secret about it.[16]

On February 15, 1962, after having defected to the Soviet Union, Oswald would write his brother Robert: "I heard over the voice of america [sic] that they released Powers the U2 spy plane fellow. That's big news where you are I suppose. He seemed to be a nice, bright american-type [*sic*] fellow, when I saw him in Moscow."[17]

It would have been normal procedure for the KGB to take Oswald to observe the Powers trial as one of the rewards given him for having helped the Soviet Union to shoot down the U-2. Otherwise, there is little reason Oswald would have seen him in Moscow.

It is significant that the pilot of the U-2 plane was not interrogated by Soviet military intelligence, as would have been normal if the downing of the plane had been simply the result of a military operation. Colonel Oleg Penkovsky, a GRU (Soviet military intelligence) officer who was in clandestine contact with the CIA, reported on April 23, 1961, that since Powers had been downed in a military operation, the GRU had selected him, Penkovsky, because he spoke good English, to talk to Powers when he was brought to Moscow. Penkovsky said that, however, KGB chairman Aleksandr Shelepin had interfered with the GRU's plans. "Shelepin got an interpreter and picked Powers up."

Powers himself would later write that he was secretly interrogated at the Lubyanka, the KGB headquarters, and that means that it was actually the KGB, not the Red Army, that had played the first violin in the whole operation.

According to Powers, his interrogation began the same day he was shot down, and it was witnessed by about a dozen people, some in uniform but most in civilian dress—the latter evidently important KGB officials who had come to see the show. During one session, which was conducted by a general rather than the usual two majors, "a short, thin, chain-smoking man of about forty monitored the proceedings." Later, Powers would learn that this was Shelepin, the chairman of the KGB.[18]

A substantial part of Powers' interrogation centered on the flight altitude of the U-2.[19] He was asked if he had ever been stationed at Atsugi, and he answered truthfully that he had not. His interrogators specifically asked him about U-2s at Atsugi, showing him articles in Japanese about a U-2 that had crash-landed there.[20] (The Soviets would not have wanted Powers to suspect they might have had a source at Atsugi, and newspaper articles could conveniently explain their interest in that base. In September 1959, the Japanese magazine *Air Views* had published a detailed account of a U-2's emergency landing at a glider-club strip near Atsugi and suggested that the U-2s might be conducting other reconnaissance besides weather.[21])

Epstein's well-documented book, which is centered around suspicions that Oswald had secret ties to Soviet intelligence, provides significant information indicating that Oswald had indeed been manipulated by Moscow. Epstein even collected sufficient data to cause him correctly to suspect that George de Mohrenschildt, the wealthy American oilman who had reportedly come from the old Russian nobility and who became Oswald's "best friend" after Oswald returned to the United States, was in fact Oswald's KGB "handler."

In 1977, Epstein had a meeting with de Mohernschildt at the Breakers Hotel in Palm Beach, Florida. The meeting had been arranged by the *Reader's Digest* magazine. Epstein and de Mohrenschildt broke for lunch and decided to meet again at 3 p.m. When the latter arrived at the Palm Beach home where he was staying, he found a card telling him that he had to testify under oath to the House Select Commission on Assassinations. De Mohrenschildt's body was found later that day. He had committed suicide by shooting himself in the mouth.[22]

Unfortunately, Epstein lacked the inside background knowledge that would have helped him to fit his bits and pieces together into one whole picture, and to reach a firm conclusion. His very well-documented story is left hanging in midair.

30

KHRUSHCHEV: A MONUMENT TO DISINFORMATION

TODAY, PEOPLE MIGHT REMEMBER KHRUSHCHEV as a down-to-earth peasant who corrected the evils of Stalin. That is the result of another successful disinformation campaign. The Khrushchev who was my *supreme* boss for nine years—during which time I was promoted up to the top of the Soviet bloc intelligence community—was brutal, brash, and extroverted. He tended to destroy every project he got his hands on, and he ended up with an even more personal hatred for what he called the "Western bourgeoisie" than Stalin had.

Many times I heard Khrushchev say, both when he was sober and when he was drunk, that Stalin had made one inexcusable mistake—he had turned his political police against the Soviet Union's own people. "Our enemies" were not in the Soviet Union, Khrushchev would explain. America's millionaires were the ones who were determined to wipe communism off the face of the earth. They were "our deadly enemies." They were the "rabid dogs" of imperialism.

After the U-2 spy plane was shot down over Soviet airspace on May Day 1960, Khrushchev demanded a meeting of the United Nations Security Council to tell his side of the story. That meeting began May 23, continued for four days, and ended with the decision to arrange a four-power Paris Summit aimed at calming the waters.

Khrushchev's handling of the Paris summit illustrates his nefarious nature.

According to what I learned from General Sakharovsky, once Khrushchev was in the plane flying him to Paris, he became consumed with the idea that Eisenhower had deliberately sent his U-2 plane over the Soviet Union a few days before the summit for the express purpose of sabotaging any resolution of the Berlin crisis, and Khrushchev began boiling over with a "vitriolic hatred" for his adversary. During that very flight to Paris, Khrushchev therefore decided to withdraw his—already accepted—invitation for Eisenhower to visit Moscow, unless Eisenhower declared from the summit meeting's podium that he would cancel the U-2 program. Just as the summit meeting was about to open, Khrushchev additionally decided to demand an apology from Eisenhower. In the end, Khrushchev opened the four-power summit by publicly announcing that the Soviet Union would no longer deal with Eisenhower, and that there would be no more summits as long as Eisenhower was still president.

At the beginning of 1962, the management of the DIE learned that Khrushchev wanted to go down in history as the Soviet leader who had exported communism and Soviet nuclear power to the American continent. According to General Sakharovsky, that was now almost a done deed. Khrushchev predicted that the new US president, John Fitzgerald Kennedy, would suffer a heart attack when he realized Soviet nuclear rockets were only ninety miles away from him.

During the critical days of the Cuban crisis, Romanian leader Gheorghe Gheorghiu-Dej happened to be visiting the Kremlin. On the morning of October 23, 1962, returning home from a state visit to Indonesia and Burma, Dej stopped off in Moscow for a couple of hours to inform Khrushchev about the results of his visits. And there he stayed. Just before that, Kennedy had publicly warned Moscow to refrain from any dangerous adventure in Cuba, and Khrushchev—who at critical moments always reached out for an audience—needed somebody around to whom he could vent his anger. This time that was Dej.

According to Gheorghiu-Dej, the Soviet leader was unusually irascible, and although their meeting was held before noon, Khrushchev already reeked of vodka. Shortly after Dej entered Khrushchev's office, Marshal Rodion Malinovsky, the Soviet minister of defense and an old friend of Dej's (after WWII Malinovsky had become the Soviet gauleiter of Romania), came in and reported that the American Navy had been put on alert, and that according to Soviet electronic monitoring the Pentagon was preparing a blockade of Cuba. Khrushchev flew into a rage, yelling, cursing and issuing an avalanche of contradictory orders. Without asking Dej what his program for the day was, Khrushchev commanded a state luncheon and festive evening at the opera to be held in Dej's honor, ordering both events to be attended by the whole Presidium of the Communist Party and to be widely publicized by the Soviet media as a display of communist unity.

The rest of that day, Khrushchev acted more irrationally than Gheorghiu-Dej had ever seen him before, his mood changing from one minute to the next. During the state luncheon, Khrushchev swore at Washington, threatened to "nuke" the White House, and cursed loudly every time anyone pronounced the words *America* or *American*. At the end of the opera performance, however, he went out of his way to extend personal congratulations to an American singer who had performed in *Boris Godunov*.[1]

The next morning, Gheorghiu-Dej was having breakfast with Khrushchev when General Vladimir Yefimovich Semichastny, the new chairman of the KGB, presented the Soviet leader with a freshly decoded KGB cable from Washington stating that Kennedy had canceled his official visit to Brazil and ordered a naval "quarantine" to prevent the eighteen Soviet cargo ships heading toward Cuba from reaching their destination. According to Dej's account, when Khrushchev finished reading that cable his face was purple. He looked inquiringly at Semichastny, and, when the terrified general nodded, Khrushchev "cursed like a bargeman." Then he threw Semichastny's cable on the floor and ground his heel into it. "That's how I'm going to crush that viper," he cried. The "viper," Dej explained in telling the story, was Kennedy.

Goading himself on, Khrushchev grew increasingly hysterical, for whole minutes in a row uttering violent threats against the "millionaire's whore" and his CIA masters. "If Kennedy had been there, the lunatic would have strangled him dead on the spot," I heard Dej telling, when he was back in Bucharest.

As I later learned, no sooner had Dej left Moscow than Khrushchev found a new victim in William Knox, the president of Westinghouse Electric International, who also happened to be visiting Moscow that same day. Khrushchev summoned him to the Kremlin "for three hours of threats, complaints, and peasant jokes." As the scene was described by former US official William Hyland:

Khrushchev appeared in a state near exhaustion, but he warned that if a Soviet ship were sunk, Soviet submarines would go into action. Perhaps Khrushchev thought Knox would sound the alarm to the American Embassy, which in turn might warn Washington to veer from its perilous course.[2]

On the night of October 25, 1962, Khrushchev received a joint PGU/GRU report stating that the conventional and nuclear forces of the United States had been put on worldwide alert, and that "the largest invasion force mounted since World War II" was massed in Florida. That intelligence report (Sakharovsky showed it to me a few years later), concluded that there were serious indications that an attack on Cuba could take place within the next two or three days. I also learned from Sakharovsky that early on the morning of October 28, 1962, Khrushchev received a cable from Anatoly Dobrynin, the Soviet ambassador in Washington, containing the text of a message handed to him by Attorney General Robert Kennedy, the president's brother. The message warned that time was running out, and that the United States was prepared to take strong and overwhelming retaliatory action by the end of the week if Moscow did not immediately agree to withdraw its missiles from Cuba.

It did not take Khrushchev long to make up his mind. At around midnight Moscow time, about a dozen of the Soviet ships turned away from the confrontation. The Kremlin also publicly announced that all Soviet missile bases in Cuba were to be dismantled and that inspections would be permitted.

On the evening of that same Sunday, October 28, 1962, I went to Gheorghiu-Dej's residence in Bucharest to report the end of the Cuban crisis. "That's the greatest defeat in Soviet peacetime history," Dej said. That day also happened to be my birthday, and Dej celebrated both events with caviar and champagne. Although it was true that Kennedy had won, Dej remarked, he would not give a penny for his skin. "He won't die in his bed," Dej predicted. Though he took secret pleasure in Khrushchev's "apocalyptical" humiliation, Dej was also troubled. "The lunatic could easily fly off the handle and start a nuclear war!"

Nikita Sergeyevich Khrushchev was certainly the most controversial Soviet to reign in the Kremlin. He unmasked Stalin's crimes, but he made political assassination a main instrument of his own foreign policy; he authored a policy of peaceful coexistence with the West, but he pushed the world to the brink of nuclear war; he repaired Moscow's relations with Yugoslavia's Tito, but he destroyed the unity of the communist world.

Even though they were political heretics, Lenin and Stalin genuinely strove to build a paradise for the workers, filling the country with gigantic industrial complexes, erecting huge hydroelectric power plants, and even changing the course of some rivers. Khrushchev, on the other hand, had an eminently destructive nature: he smashed Stalin's statues, shattered the Soviet Union's image as the workers' paradise, and broke up the Sino-Soviet alliance, all without building anything new to fill the vacuum he had created. On September 11, 1971, Khrushchev died in ignominy, but not before seeing his memoirs published in the West giving his version of history.

Everything in Khrushchev's life deviated considerably from the path taken by his Soviet predecessors. Unlike Lenin and Stalin, who had come from the very thin layer of Russia's middle class, Khrushchev belonged to the meanwhile heroicized proletariat, an insignificant social category made up of urbanized Russian peasants—the most backward peasantry in all of Europe. The grandchild of a serf and the son of an indigent miner, Khrushchev grew up in a deeply ignorant peasant environment and started his working life as an unskilled manual laborer. He became a member of the Communist Party in 1918, joined the Red Army a year later, and served as a junior political commissar in the campaigns against the Whites and the invading Polish army. Unlike Lenin, who was a lawyer, and Stalin, who had studied at a theological seminary, Khrushchev had no formal education whatsoever when he became a party activist. "When we saw postcards of ballerinas, we thought they were simply photographs of women wearing indecent costumes," Khrushchev wrote disarmingly in his memoirs.[3]

I learned about Khrushchev's start down the path of power mostly from General Sakharovsky, who became one of his closest collaborators. Of course, Sakharovsky described a good Khrushchev while he was reigning in the Kremlin, and a bad Khrushchev after the controversial Soviet leader was demoted, but I have done my best to corroborate or refute Sakharovsky's claims independently.

Vladimir Lenin, Leon Trotsky, Nikolay Bukharin, Grigory Zinovyev, Lev Kamenev, and even Iosif Stalin all rose to the leadership of the Soviet Union because they had become intellectually infatuated with Marxism and had dedicated their lives to it. Khrushchev climbed to the top because he was a bellicose bureaucrat. He started his rise to power in a period when Stalin was in the process of eliminating the Old Bolshevik intelligentsia and replacing it with rough, ignorant peasants or factory workers who pledged allegiance to him. Khrushchev fitted that mold perfectly and was soon absorbed by the new communist bureaucracy. In 1931, after being hastily indoctrinated during a two-year course at the Stalin Industrial Academy, Khrushchev was assigned as a full-time activist with the Moscow Regional Committee. Two years later he became its second secretary and was given the job of politically supervising the construction of the Moscow metro. Stalin had noticed him in 1934 during a visit to the metro construction site, where Khrushchev had fawned over the "Little Father" in the Kremlin.

Khrushchev's show of devotion, along with the brutality he was using in driving the workers building the metro, made such a strong impression on Stalin that he instantly catapulted Khrushchev to the position of first sec-retary of the Moscow party committee and made him a full member of the seventy-man Central Committee of the Communist Party. Less than a year later, Stalin made Khrushchev an alternate member of the ruling Politburo.

Khrushchev matured politically in a period when Lenin and Stalin produced what historians now term the greatest peacetime mass-terror in European history, a period in which many millions of Soviet people lost their lives. That left a strong imprint on Khrushchev's formation— he became impulsive, violent and brutal, and he ended up with a deep hatred for what he called the "bourgeoisie." I was present at several meet-ings between Romanian leader Gheorghiu-Dej and Khrushchev, and there I repeatedly heard Khrushchev actually brag about his hatred: "It is in my blood—my serf's blood!" After hearing such outbursts, Gheorghiu-Dej, who had himself authorized many thousands of killings, repeatedly expressed uneasiness over Khrushchev's bloodthirstiness.

Khrushchev became a party activist in a period when Soviet policy was carried out through heavy-handed propaganda and disinformation. Hence, he matured into a compulsive political chatterbox who had no objective appreciation of facts and filled his speeches with distortions, deliberate omissions, and flat-out lies. According to Sakharovsky, many times the interpreters Khrushchev used while traveling abroad (all of whom were Sakharovsky's officers) had to change the sense of Khrushchev's statements or to ignore some entirely, because they were filled with vulgarities, inexactitudes, deceptions, and self-contradictions.

Khrushchev's close association with Stalin's killings made him aware of what political crime could accomplish and gave him a taste for the simple criminal solution. In 1936, Stalin unleashed his Great Purge aimed at eliminating all competition and opposition to himself. In the ensuing slaughter, some 7 million people lost their lives, including most of the high-ranking Soviet communists.

Of the seven men who formed Lenin's Politburo at the time of the October Revolution, Stalin alone outlived the purges. Among provincial party secretaries, only three who had zealously supported Stalin's purges survived the executions. The flamboyant Khrushchev, who as party boss in Moscow had ardently and vociferously upheld Stalin's new purges from the first day, was one of those three. As a supplementary reward, in 1938 Stalin appointed him first party secretary of Ukraine and gave him the task of organizing a similar purge in his new territory. There Khrushchev proceeded to carry out his master's wishes with savagery and brutality.

The habit of resorting to political assassinations remained with Khrushchev for the rest of his career. His addiction to political crime is well illustrated in the person he chose as his new chief of the secret political police. In 1954, Khrushchev reconstituted that organization as the Committee of State Security (KGB) and installed at its helm a man who was even more bloodthirsty than Beriya had been. General Ivan Serov, the first chairman of the "new" KGB, had already become infamous for the brutality with which, during Stalin's rule, he had forcibly deported people from the Caucasus, crushed the anticommunist opposition in the Baltic states, and murdered, in the Katyn forest, near Smolensk, an estimated 22,000 "bourgeois" Polish officers taken prisoner by the Red Army. Referring to his choice, Khrushchev said: "Beriya's deputies were Kruglov and Serov. I hardly knew Kruglov, but I knew Serov well, and I trusted him. I thought, and still think, Serov is an honest man. If there are a few dubious things about him, as there are about all Chekists [*i.e.,* members of the political police], then let's just say he was a victim of Stalin's general policy."[4]

Lenin and Stalin had called themselves internationalists and had indiscriminately murdered foreigners as well as Soviet citizens. Khrushchev's peasant origins had, however, molded him into such a nationalistic Ukrainian that after Stalin died he gave up the gray tunics buttoned to the neck, which had become a kind of international communist uniform, and instead started wearing peasant-proletarian outfits he invented. That was approximately the period when Khrushchev softened the repression of Soviet citizens and moved the cutting edge of his violence abroad.

When Khrushchev became the head of the Soviet Union, he had not yet set foot abroad, nor had he been given an opportunity to discuss foreign affairs with Stalin, for the latter had laid personal claim to that field. All Khrushchev knew about capitalism was therefore solely what he had learned from Soviet propaganda. He was utterly convinced that the West was the world's deadliest enemy, and he truly believed that the centerpiece of Soviet foreign policy necessarily had to be the struggle against the "millionaires" and their "bourgeois" countries. In his memoirs, he wrote: "Right up until his death, Stalin used to tell us, 'You'll see, when I'm gone the imperialistic powers will wring your necks like chickens.'"[5]

Khrushchev's total ignorance about the civilized world, together with his irrational hatred of the "bourgeoisie" and his propensity to offend people, made him believe that disinformation and threats were the most efficient and dignified way for a Soviet leader to deal with "bourgeois" governments. In the spring of 1956, he went to London together with Premier Nikolay Bulganin in response to an invitation from Prime Minister Anthony Eden. According to what I learned from Sakharovsky, Khrushchev's main goal on that trip was to persuade Eden quietly to sell prohibited technologies and equipment to the Soviet Union. Khrushchev's decision to take the chairman of the KGB, General Serov, along with him to London set off a storm in the British press, however, and it got the visit off to a bad start. The reason the talks ended badly was that Khrushchev began bragging about Moscow's hydrogen bomb arsenal, after Eden had refused to circumvent the Western embargo on strategic goods to the Soviet Union.

Toward the end of 1957, Moscow learned that the United States was ready to establish bases for intermediate-range ballistic missiles on the territory of its NATO partners. In an attempt to prevent that move, Khrushchev sent a threatening note to the head of each NATO country. The note to Great Britain, which was formally signed by Premier Bulganin but fully reflected Khrushchev's style, stated:

I say frankly that we find it difficult to understand what, in taking part in such a policy, guides the government of such a country as Great Britain, which is not only in an extremely vulnerable position by force of its geographical situation but which according to the admission of its official representatives has no effective means of defense against the effects of modern weapons. Nor can there, it is true, be such defense.[6]

At the beginning of November 1959, following the nationalization of the Suez Canal by Egypt's President Gamal Nasser, Great Britain and France sent an expeditionary force to capture Port Said and gain control of the canal. On November 4, one day after the Soviet invasion of Hungary, Khrushchev impertinently threatened the Western "aggressors." A letter Moscow sent to the British government stated, for instance:

If rocket weapons were used against Britain and France, you would doubtless call that a barbarous act. But how does this differ from the inhuman attack carried out by the armed forces of Britain and France against practically unarmed Egypt? . . . We are fully resolved to use force to crush the aggressors and to restore peace in the East.[7]

Disinformation had always been a main component of Soviet foreign policy. That fit Khrushchev like a glove, although he would soon learn that deceiving the West was considerably more difficult that lying to his fellow Soviets. Khrushchev, who had spent World War II as a general, considered himself an expert in military disinformation; therefore, once in the Kremlin he made military disinformation a main pillar of his foreign policy. According to what I learned from the *razvedka* advisers, Khrushchev started by trying to persuade the West that the Soviet Union's air force had acquired superiority over the United States. "Walnut" was the codename under which this KGB operation, coordinated by Khrushchev himself, was known in the DIE.

Just as I was leaving for my assignment as Romania's spy chief in West Germany, the DIE adviser for intelligence on military technology, KGB Colonel Rudenko, told me that in July 1955, Nikita Sergeyevich had organized a "spectacular" Aviation Day, on which wave after wave of the brand new MYa-4 strategic bombers had flown over Moscow. In actual fact, it had been the same squadron reappearing every few minutes. "That was all we had," Rudenko explained.

That endless air show had caused a shock explosion in the Western media, the KGB adviser claimed, which had immediately been followed up by an avalanche of data "leaked by us" showing that Moscow had outdistanced Washington in strategic bomber strength. "Now this just came in," Rudenko said during that same discussion, handing me a "documentary" study. His material had been prepared in Moscow and contained comparisons between the Soviet long-range TU-20 and MYa-4 strategic bombers and the American B-47 and B-52. The bottom line of the study was that the Soviet Union now had more and better strategic bombers that the United States did, and my station's task was to leak these comparisons to the West German media.

As I later learned, the United States government was only temporarily deceived by Khrushchev's bomber disinformation. In the spring of 1957, soon after the U-2 became operational, Director of Central Intelligence Allen Dulles wrote to Senator Stuart Symington:

> The estimate of Soviet heavy bomber strength as of April 1, 1956, which was given in my testimony before your subcommittee, was largely based on an estimated build-up rate which rested upon earlier evidence. Subsequent to my testimony before your committee in April 1956, the intelligence community acquired new and better evidence on Soviet heavy-bomber production and strength in operational units and we undertook a complete review of our estimates on this subject, [which] revised downwards the estimated total production on Bison (the Russian equivalent of the B-52).[8]

A few months after I arrived as station chief in Frankfurt, I was informed by DIE headquarters that the KGB had launched "Operation Walnut II," aimed at making the West believe that the Soviet Union had also become the world's largest rocket power. Once again, Khrushchev made the first move by telling James Reston of the *New York Times*: "Now we have all the rockets we need: long-range rockets, intermediate-range rockets and short-range rockets."[9] The disinformation departments of the Soviet bloc intelligence community followed step, and soon the West was laboring under the widespread impression that there was a growing missile gap in favor of the Soviet Union, which, in addition to a large variety of offensive rockets, also possessed sophisticated antimissile rockets able to defend its territory. Three years later, however, the Eisenhower administration was in possession of strong evidence obtained by its U-2 reconnaissance planes that the Soviets had in fact only two ballistic missile bases.

The film captured by the Soviets from the U-2 plane shot down over the Soviet Union on May 1, 1960, showed that Washington had seen through Moscow's lies, but Khrushchev evidently could not understand that his game had been compromised. New instructions from Moscow asked the DIE to redouble its efforts to deceive the West about the "missile gap," and also to spread the rumor that by then Moscow possessed antimissile systems as well. It was only in his memoirs that Khrushchev allowed himself indirectly to acknowledge that his claims to Soviet rocket superiority had been a bald-faced lie: "I used to say sometimes in my speeches that we had developed an antimissile that could hit a fly, but of course that was just rhetoric to make our adversaries think twice."[10]

In the end, Khrushchev's missile deception turned against him, just as most of his foreign policy adventures did. Temporarily convinced that there really was a missile gap in Moscow's favor, the United States engaged in a massive arms buildup that soon gave it overwhelming rocket superiority over the Soviet Union. At the same time the Chinese, who took Khrushchev's "missile deception" at face value, could not understand why he had failed to use his advantage, and they therefore branded him "soft" on imperialism and accused him of abandoning communist principles.

The fuse was lit that would eventually set off the blast ousting Khrushchev from the driver's seat. On October 14, 1964, less than a year after Kennedy was assassinated, Khrushchev was accused of "harebrained schemes, hasty decisions, actions divorced from reality, braggadocio, and rule by fiat," and he was dethroned.[11]

Many years later, Khrushchev in his grave suffered the ultimate indignity when his son Sergei became a citizen of the United States, the country his father had dedicated his life to destroying. In 2000, Sergei Khrushchev published a lengthy book in which he tried to put a human face on his father.[12] I found it sincere and convincing, but it deals with an entirely different Khrushchev—a serene, peaceful, loving one. Then again, if my daughter, who is now also an American citizen, should someday decide to write a book about her father, she would not know anything about my real career in Romania. Even though she visited me at my cover office and I often took her to the Generals' Club of the *Securitate*, she had never been able to get even a glimpse of my real work as Romania's spy chief. That was another of those strictly enforced rules inherited from Moscow.

Unfortunately, we continue to cope with the legacies of the Khrushchev I knew—not the one his son describes.

31

OPERATION "DRAGON"

O N NOVEMBER 26, 1963, four days after President Kennedy was killed, General Sakharovsky landed unannounced in Bucharest, in what proved to be his first stop on a blitz tour of the main "sister" services. From him, we in the DIE learned that the KGB had already launched a worldwide disinformation operation aimed at diverting public attention away from Moscow in respect to the Kennedy assassination, and at framing the CIA as the culprit. "The Comrade" himself—Khrushchev—wanted to make it clear to all "our sister services" that this was by far our first and most important task.

"The Comrade" was afraid, Sakharovsky told us, that if the American media and public opinion should start pointing the finger at Moscow, that could end in a nuclear confrontation. Time was of the essence. It was crucial, Sakharovsky emphasized, to spread our version about the assassination before Washington could spread its own, so that our disinformation machinery could plant the idea on virgin soil that the CIA was responsible for the crime.

We in the DIE knew better than to ask Sakharovsky questions. But we knew.

Blaming the CIA for the KGB's own assassinations and kidnappings abroad was a disinformation tactic that had been introduced by Khrushchev after the Twentieth Congress, where he had "unmasked" Stalin's crimes.

In spite of the KGB's penchant for bureaucratic paperwork, Khrushchev ordered that from then on, all operations connected with assassinations and kidnappings abroad must be handled on a strictly oral basis. They were never to be committed to paper, and they had to be kept totally secret from the Politburo and every other governing body. Only the Comrade himself could approve assassinations and kidnappings abroad. Regardless of any evidence that might be produced in foreign investigations, the KGB was never to acknowledge its involvement in assassinations and kidnappings abroad; any such evidence was to be dismissed out of hand as a ridiculous accusation.

Finally, after each operation the KGB was surreptitiously to spread "evidence" in the West, accusing the CIA or other convenient "enemies" of having done the deed, thereby if possible killing two birds with one stone. We learned about Khrushchev's new strategy soon after the Twentieth Congress from General Ivan Anisimovich Fadeyev, the new chief of the rebaptized and widely expanded KGB department for assassinations abroad, who came to Bucharest for an "exchange of information."

General Fadeyev was known to the DIE management from the years when he had headed the KGB *rezidentura* in East Berlin, which became an infamous mechanism for assassinating people in, and kidnapping people from, West Germany. He had also been instrumental in the brutal June 1953 suppression of anti-Soviet demonstrations in East Berlin, when his KGB troops opened live fire against the German demonstrators. That had been too much even for the bloodthirsty Stalin, as Fadeyev was recalled to Moscow. Not for Khrushchev, however.

In 1957, General Fadeyev began his exchange of experience in Bucharest by playing Khrushchev's broken record, according to which Stalin had made an unpardonable mistake by aiming the cutting edge of the state security apparatus against the Soviet Union's own people. Fadeyev said that when Khrushchev delivered his "secret speech," the only thing he had in mind was to correct that aberration. In December 1917, when Lenin founded the *Cheka*, he gave it the emblem of a shield and a sword to symbolize its duties: to shield and protect the communist revolution, and to put its enemies to the sword. Lenin never intended, Fadeyev said, to use "us" against "our own people." Ten million Soviet citizens gave their lives to defend "our" political system during World War II—what more evidence did one need to prove their devotion to communism?

Fadeyev explained that "our enemies" were not in the Soviet Union. America's bourgeoisie and our own traitors who had defected from their motherland and were now attacking it from abroad were our "deadly enemies." We should direct the cutting edge of our sword against them, and only them, to fulfill "our historic destiny" as the gravedigger of capitalism. That was what Nikita Sergeyevich had really wanted to tell us in his "secret speech."

In fact, Fadeyev explained, one of Khrushchev's first foreign policy decisions after settling down on the Kremlin throne had been his 1953 order to have one such "deadly enemy" secretly assassinated. Fadeyev was referring to a KGB operation aimed at killing Georgy Okolovich, a Ukrainian émigré who was the leader of the National Labor Alliance (*Natsionalnyy Trudovoy Soyuz*, or NTS), one of the most aggressively anticommunist Russian émigré organizations in Western Europe. Although born in the Crimea, Khrushchev had spent years as Stalin's viceroy for Ukraine and considered himself a Ukrainian—he would soon incorporate the Crimea into Ukraine—and it was quite normal for him to inaugurate his foreign policy by planning to "neutralize" the leaders of the anticommunist organizations run by Ukrainian émigrés.

The KGB execution team arrived in West Germany in February 1954. Unfortunately, in Fadeyev's view, the team's head, KGB officer Nikolay Khokhlov, "betrayed his country" by defecting to the CIA. Because troubles never come alone, Fadeyev added, two other officers from the KGB assassination unit defected at about the same time: Yury Rastvorov in January 1954, and Petr Deryabin in February 1954.

According to Fadeyev, all those setbacks led to drastic changes. First of all, Khrushchev ordered the KGB to spread the rumor worldwide that he had dismantled the KGB's assassination component. Then he baptized kidnappings and assassinations abroad with the euphemism "neutralization" operations. Finally, he rechristened the Ninth Department—as the assassination component had been called up to then—as the Thirteenth Department, buried its existence in even deeper secrecy, and put it directly under his own supervision. Having done all that, Khrushchev then introduced a new pattern for the KGB's "neutralization" operations.

Before Fadeyev left Bucharest, the DIE had acquired its own ultrasecret component for kidnappings and assassinations abroad. The new unit was given the name "Group Z," because the letter Z was the final letter in the alphabet, representing the "final solution." Only the head of the DIE had knowledge of its operations, but we understood that its structure was virtually identical to that of its "sister" units recently created in the East German, Hungarian, and Bulgarian foreign intelligence services. In accordance with another new KGB pattern, all four "sister" units had their operational components in East Berlin, and all were equipped by the KGB with a complete arsenal of supplies ranging from powerful soporifics to trusted agents living in the West who had previously been used in terrorist operations by the various bloc services, thus allowing for the standardization of operational methods.

In fact, one of the first operations conducted under Khrushchev's new rules was jointly carried out by the KGB, the DIE and the East German *Stasi* in September 1958, when anticommunist Romanian émigré leader Oliviu Beldeanu was secretly kidnapped from West Germany. The official East German newspaper, *Neues Deutschland*, and the Romanian equivalent, *Scînteia*, placed the onus for this crime on the CIA's shoulders by publishing official press communiqués stating that he had been arrested in East Germany after having been secretly infiltrated there by the CIA in order to carry out sabotage and diversion operations.

Now, in late November 1963, a special KGB courier notified the management of the DIE that within the Dragon Operation we should include mention of a jealous President Johnson as the instigator of the CIA plot, which he, allegedly, had personally arranged to take place in Texas on his home turf. By December, as part of the plot, the KGB added the "sharks" of the American "military-industrial complex," who were allegedly furious at Kennedy for wanting to cut back on the American military presence abroad and therefore on arms spending (and the sharks' profits).

The Dragon Operation has become one of the most successful disinformation operations in contemporary history. According to *JFK*, a 1991 movie made by Oliver Stone, the assassination of President Kennedy was the result of a conspiracy at the US government's highest level, implicating members of the military-industrial complex, the CIA, the FBI, the Secret Service, the Mafia, and Lyndon Johnson. The movie was nominated for eight Academy Awards and it won two. According to a later Gallup poll, between two-thirds and three-quarters of Americans believed there had indeed been a CIA conspiracy to kill John F. Kennedy.[1]

For many years, a satisfactory explanation of Oswald's motivation had yet to be offered, because the whole important dimension of Soviet foreign policy concerns and Soviet intelligence practice in the late 1950s and early 1960s had not been addressed in connection with Oswald by any competent authority.

In 2007, I published *Programmed to Kill: Lee Harvey Oswald, the Soviet KGB, and the Kennedy Assassination*, a book in which I was primarily concerned with documenting and explaining the events leading up to the assassination. I did include everything I knew about the subsequent disinformation campaign from the Romanian perspective, but I could just barely touch on what has now become an avalanche of insistent lies, off-the-wall opinions, and amateur analysis flooding through the public media in every country over the course of all these years. As that very clever master of deception Yuri Andropov once told me, if a good piece of disinformation is repeated over and over, after a while it will take on a life of its own and will—all by itself,—generate a horde of unwitting but passionate advocates.

Let me summarize my book's analysis of what led up to the assassination, presenting the Soviets with such an enormous headache in November 1963. The KGB recruited Oswald for ideological reasons when he was a US Marine stationed in Japan. When he insisted on defecting to the Soviet paradise, the KGB kept him there for three years and then persuaded him to return to the United States temporarily, in order to assassinate President Kennedy, who had badly humiliated Oswald's idol Khrushchev before the whole world. During this time, Oswald was intensively indoctrinated, trained in agent communications and weaponry, given a Soviet wife who was trained to assist him, and then dispatched off to Texas. Once there, an American businessman, George de Mohrenschildt, helped Oswald settle into his new surroundings.

De Mohrenschildt has been an enigma for most assassination researchers and even for his friends. A good part of *Programmed to Kill* deals with de Mohrenschildt. Here let me just say that he was a long-time Soviet illegal officer whose biography had frequently changed in order to accommodate his Soviet intelligence tasks. De Mohrenschildt became an American citizen in the 1930s, during the Nazi era, when he was documented by Moscow as Baron George *von* Mohrenschildt, son of a German director of the Swedish "Nobel interests" in the Baku oilfields. Toward the end of World War II, when it became clear that the Nazis would be defeated, the German baron became the French George *de* Mohrenschildt, who had attended a commercial school in Belgium founded by Napoleon. After World War II, he claimed that his father had been a Russian engineer in the Ploiesti oilfields in Romania, captured there by the Soviet Army and executed. No wonder de Mohrenschildt committed suicide when he was summoned to testify under oath to the House Select Committee on Assassinations in 1977.

By the time Oswald was settled in Texas, Khrushchev had changed his mind about killing Kennedy. In October 1962, Khrushchev had been revealed as a political murderer at a spectacular public trial held by the West German Supreme Court. The defendant was Bogdan Stashinsky, an officer of the KGB's Thirteenth Department, who had defected to West Germany in 1961. He confessed to having assassinated two leading Ukrainian émigrés in 1957 and 1959 at Khrushchev's order, for which afterward he was personally decorated by Khrushchev. What had started out as Stashinsky's trial soon transformed into one against Khrushchev.

The flamboyant, impulsive, and unpredictable ruler in the Kremlin, whose "secret" speech unmasking Stalin's crimes was still fresh in everyone's memory, now appeared to be just another odious butcher—and a flat-out liar. It was not at all true that after the Twentieth Party Congress Khrushchev had stopped the KGB's killings; he had merely turned the focus abroad. The West German Supreme Court declared Stashinsky only "an accomplice to murder."

"Murder is now carried out on express government orders," the judge explained. "Political murder has, so to speak, now become institutionalized."[2] Any revelation of a Soviet hand in an assassination of the widely popular American president would fatal to Khrushchev.

Oswald had arrived in the United States shortly before Stashinsky's well-publicized trial, after which the KGB tried to turn Oswald off. The KGB sent him many messages, and then he had secret meetings in Mexico City with "Comrade Kostin," the KGB assassinations expert who had been assigned to that nearby country where clandestine meetings could safely be conducted. Oswald had unfortunately been so well indoctrinated for his mission that he insisted on going through with it by himself, convinced he knew what his idol Khrushchev really wanted.

Here are a few extremely important pieces of evidence that were found in various places after Kennedy's assassination. These points have never been seriously considered by US investigators, who were unfamiliar with the KGB modus operandi. They are, however, crucial for understanding Oswald, his secret connection with the KGB's supersecret unit for assassinations abroad, and the reason he acted alone in the end.

The Warren Commission concluded that Oswald had *no* secret ties with the KGB and *no* connection with its Thirteenth Department, which was responsible for assassinations abroad. During the long holiday weekend of November 9-11, 1963, however, Oswald wrote a letter for the Soviet Embassy in Washington, in which he described the meeting he had just had with "comrade Kostin" in Mexico City, whom he also names elsewhere as Comrade Kostikov. As previously noted, the CIA identified "comrade Kostin," aka "Comrade Kostikov," as Valery Kostikov, an officer of the KGB's Thirteenth Department for assassinations abroad, who was assigned under diplomatic cover at the Soviet Embassy in Mexico.

After the assassination, a handwritten draft of Oswald's above-referenced letter was found among Oswald's effects in the garage of Ruth Paine, an American at whose house Oswald had spent that weekend. Ruth testified under oath that Oswald rewrote that letter several times before typing it on her typewriter. It was important to him. A photocopy of the final letter Oswald sent to the Soviet embassy was recovered by the Warren Commission. Let me quote from that letter, in which I have also inserted Oswald's earlier draft version in italics within brackets:

> This is to inform you of recent events since my meetings with comrade Kostin [*of new events since my interviews with comrade Kostine*] in the Embassy of the Soviet Union, Mexico City, Mexico. I was unable to remain in Mexico [crossed out in draft: *because I considered useless*] indefinitely because of my Mexican visa restrictions which was for 15 days only. I could not take a chance on requesting a new visa [*applying for an extension*] unless I used my real name, so I returned to the United States."

The fact that Oswald used an operational codename for Kostikov indicates to me that both his meeting with Kostikov in Mexico City and his correspondence with the Soviet Embassy in Washington were conducted in a KGB operational context. The fact that Oswald did not use his real name to obtain his Mexican travel permit confirms this conclusion.

Now let us juxtapose this *combined* letter against the free Mexico City guidebook *Esta Semana—This Week* for September 28—October 4, 1963, and against a Spanish-English dictionary, both found among Oswald's effects, but given no attention whatsoever. The guidebook has the Soviet embassy's telephone number underlined in pencil, the names *Kosten* and *Osvald* noted in Cyrillic on the page listing "Diplomats in Mexico," and checkmarks next to five movie theaters on the previous page.[3] In the back of his Spanish-English dictionary, Oswald wrote: "buy *tickets* [plural] for bull fight,"[4] and the Plaza México bullring is encircled on his Mexico City map.[5] Also marked on Oswald's map is the Palace of Fine Arts,[6] a favorite place for tourists to assemble on Sunday mornings to watch the Ballet Folklórico.

Contrary to what Oswald claimed, he was not observed at the Soviet Embassy at any time during his stay in Mexico City, although the CIA had surveillance cameras trained on the entrance to the embassy at that time.[7] All of the above facts taken together suggest to me that Oswald resorted to an unscheduled or "iron meeting"—*zheleznaya yavka* in Russian—for an urgent talk with Kostikov in Mexico City. The "iron meeting" was a standard KGB procedure for emergency situations—*iron* meaning ironclad or invariable.

In my day, I approved quite a few "iron meetings" in Mexico City— a favorite place for contacting our important agents living in the United States—and Oswald's "iron meeting" looks like a typical one. That means: a brief encounter at a movie house to arrange a meeting for the following day at the bullfights (in Mexico City they were held at 4:30 every Sunday afternoon); a brief encounter in front of the Palace of Fine Arts to pass Kostikov one of the bullfight tickets Oswald had bought; and a long meeting for discussions at the Sunday bullfight.

Of course, I cannot be sure that everything happened exactly that way— every case officer has his own quirks. But however they may have connected, it is clear that Kostikov and Oswald did secretly meet over that weekend of September 28-29, 1963. The letter to the Soviet embassy that Oswald worked so hard on irrefutably proves that.

It seems that no one in the Warren Commission had ever heard about the KGB's *zheleznaya yavka*, however. Therefore, all these strong pieces of evidence showing that in Mexico City, Oswald had an "iron meeting" with "comrade Kostin," an identified officer of the KGB's department for assassinations abroad, were lost within the twenty-six volumes of chaotically assembled documents and testimonies of the *Warren Commission Report*.

We should not blame the Warren Commission for missing the significance of the espionage proof sitting right in their hands. None of its members had any background in counterintelligence analysis. And because I suppose most of this book's readers are equally unfamiliar with the fine points of counterintelligence technique, let me put it this way: You cannot expect a plumber to perform heart surgery.

The Warren Commission's unfamiliarity with the KGB codes caused it to miss other pieces of conclusive evidence. After September 11, 2001, the FBI told members of the National Commission on Terrorist Attacks Upon the United States that only a native Arabic speaker could catch the fine points of an al-Qaida telephone intercept, especially one containing intelligence double-speak and codes. I spent twenty-three years of my other life double-speaking in codes. Even my own identity was codified. In 1955, when I became a foreign intelligence officer, I was told that my new name would be Mihai Podeanu, and Podeanu I remained until 1978, when I broke with communism. All my subordinates—and the rest of the bloc foreign intelligence officers—used codes in their written reports, when talking with their sources, and even in conversations with their own colleagues. When I left Romania for good, my espionage service was the "university," the country's leader was the "architect," Vienna was "Videle," and so on.

By that time, I was also managing Romania's equivalent of the National Security Agency, and I became relatively familiar with the KGB code and cipher systems. In an April 10, 1963, note Oswald left for his wife, Marina, before he tried to kill American General Edwin Walker in a dry run before going on to assassinate President Kennedy, I found two KGB codes of that time: *friends* (code for support officer) and *Red Cross* (code for financial help).

In this note, Oswald tells Marina what to do in case he is arrested. He stresses that she should contact the (Soviet) "embassy," that they have "friends here," and that the "Red Cross" (written in English, so that she'll know how to ask for it) will help her financially. Particularly significant is Oswald's instruction for her to "send the [Soviet] embassy the information about what happened to me." At that time the code for embassy was "office," but it seems that Oswald wanted to be sure Marina would understand that she should immediately inform the Soviet Embassy.

It is noteworthy that Marina did not mention this note to US authorities after Oswald's arrest. It was found at the home of Ruth Paine, the American friend with whom Marina was staying at the time of the assassination, and it also got lost inside the twenty-six volumes of the *Warren Commission Report*.

When the KGB realized that Oswald could not be reasoned with, they brought Fidel Castro peripherally into the case, asking him to get one of his agents in the United States to kill Oswald, if the latter could not be prevented from going ahead with the assassination when Kennedy made his scheduled visit to Dallas.

Oswald's killer, Jack Ruby, testified under oath to the Warren Commission that he had visited Cuba only once, as a tourist, in August 1959. Fourteen years later, however, the House Select Committee on Assassinations obtained records of the US Immigration and Naturalization Service "indicating that Ruby left Cuba on September 11, 1959, traveling to Miami, returned to Cuba on September 12, and traveled to New Orleans on September 13, 1959." These documents were later supplemented by tourist cards the committee obtained from the Cuban government, which showed "Ruby also entered Cuba on August 8, 1959, left on September 11, reentered on September 12 and left again on September 13, 1959."[8]

In connection with these newly discovered trips, the chief counsel of the House Select Committee on Assassinations, Robert G. Blakey, wrote: "We established beyond reasonable doubt that Ruby lied repeatedly and willfully to the FBI and the Warren Commission about the number of trips he made to Cuba and their duration."[9]

In its final report, the House Select Committee concluded that "vacationing was probably not the purpose for traveling to Havana, despite Ruby's insistence to the Warren Commission that his one trip to Cuba in 1959 was a social visit."[10] The official US investigation of Ruby stopped there, however.

32

NEW HARD PROOF OF
THE KGB'S HAND

SINCE THE PUBLICATION of *Programmed to Kill*, a good deal of unimpeachable information has become available, providing fascinating insights into the KGB's disinformation operation aimed at framing the CIA as the behind-the-scenes perpetrator of President Kennedy's assassination. Not only are we now better able to envision the KGB's thinking and projected aims for the postassassination period, but many of the players have also been identified as KGB agents, and some of the techniques have been exposed as tried and true KGB ploys—agents and operational tricks that have turned up in other KGB disinformation operations, some of which have been discussed earlier in this book. (The Soviet intelligence officers whom I knew in my previous life generally recommended that we continue to use operational scenarios that had worked in the past.)

The first piece of irrefutable evidence proving the KGB had launched a disinformation offensive with respect to the Kennedy assassination aimed at diverting public attention away from Moscow was released by Boris Yeltsin, Russia's first freely elected president. In his memoir, *The Struggle for Russia*, Yeltsin revealed a letter to the Central Committee of the Communist Party of the Soviet Union dated November 23, 1963—the day after Kennedy's assassination—signed by KGB chairman Vladimir Semichastny, which recommended publishing, in a "progressive paper in one of the Western countries," an article "exposing the attempt by reactionary circles in the

USA to remove the responsibility for the murder of Kennedy from the real criminals, [i.e.,] the racists and ultra-right elements guilty of the spread and growth of violence and terror in the United States." Semichastny's request was approved. Two months later, R. Palme Dutt, the editor of a communist-controlled British journal called *Labour Monthly*, published an article that raised the specter of CIA involvement without offering a scintilla of evidence. "[M]ost commentators," Dutt wrote, "have surmised a coup of the Ultra-Right or racialists of Dallas ... [that], with the manifest complicity necessary of a very wide range of authorities, bears all the hallmarks of a CIA job."[1]

The CIA is by far the world's best intelligence organization. It decisively contributed to America's Cold War victory, and it became the world's first line of defense against terrorism and nuclear proliferation. By portraying it as a criminal organization, the KGB hoped to diminish its ability to recruit human assets able to see what satellites could not—what Soviet bloc despots were *thinking,* and what their most secret war plans were.

Much of the reliable new information that documents the Kremlin's disinformation operation blaming the CIA for killing Kennedy has come from defectors. In 1992, the British smuggled Colonel Vasili Mitrokhin, a KGB archivist, out of the Soviet Union, along with some 25,000 highly classified documents he had stolen from KGB foreign intelligence archives over the course of many years. Those documents represent a minuscule part of the whole KGB archive. Nevertheless, the FBI described the *Mitrokhin Archive* as "the most complete and extensive intelligence ever received from any source." In the view of the CIA, this archive is "the biggest counter-intelligence bonanza of the postwar period."[2]

Mitrokhin reported on the Kennedy assassination conspiracy stories promoted by the KGB, and his material identifies a number of the agents in the West who were engaged in promoting those conspiracy theories. Among the most important revelations provided by the *Mitrokhin Archive* are the highly classified KGB documents proving that the so-called Kennedy assassination conspiracy, which to this day has generated thousands of books all around the world, was born in the KGB, and that some of it was financed by the KGB.

Equally significant are the documents in the *Mitrokhin Archive* showing that the KGB had constructed this conspiracy using some of the same paid KGB agents who were called upon to promote the disinformation operation designed to frame Pius XII as having been pro-Nazi: Carlo Marzani, codenamed Nord, who received a significant amount of money from the KGB to produce pro-Soviet books; I. F. Stone, codenamed Blin (Russian for "pancake"), who began receiving the Kremlin's money in 1944; and Victor Perlo, codenamed Raid or Raider, identified as a Soviet agent in the Venona electronic intercepts, as well as by defectors.

That should come as no surprise. After all, both operations took off in 1963 (*The Deputy* hit the Berlin stage in February, and Oswald shot the president in November), both would have been dreamt up by Khrushchev with the help of his spy chief, General Sakharovsky—the former chief Soviet intelligence adviser for Romania—and both would have been carried out by the same disinformation experts on the desk at KGB headquarters at that time.

According to documents in the *Mitrokhin Archive*, the first book on the assassination published in the United States, *Oswald: Assassin or Fall Guy?*, was authored by a former member of the German Communist Party, Joachim Joesten, and published in New York by KGB agent Carlo Aldo Marzani.[3] The publisher Marzani was regularly and generously paid by the KGB (and by the Communist Party's Central Committee) to promote books of a progressive nature by both American and foreign authors.[4] Until the *Mitrokhin Archive* documents began appearing in 1999, it was not known that Joesten's publisher, Marzani & Munsell, received subsidies totaling $672,000 from the Central Committee of the Communist Party in the early 1960s.[5]

Shortly before publishing Joesten's book on Oswald, Marzani supported the KGB's attack on Pius XII. As noted in an earlier chapter discussing Hochhuth's *The Deputy*, when that anti-Pius XII play debuted in Berlin in 1963, Marzani was able on short notice to republish *Shylock: The History of a Character*, an early book describing the mistreatment of Jews by popes, which helped to advertise Hochhuth's play.

It is noteworthy that Joesten's book saw the light of day just a couple of days before the *Warren Commission Report* was published, conforming to the KGB's instructions that we in the DIE received in the Dragon Operation. In his book, Joesten also follows what we knew as Dragon Operation guidelines by describing Oswald as an FBI agent provocateur with a CIA background, who was used to shield the real assassins, an unnamed group of American right-wing conspirators.

No one knows how Joesten became such an instant authority on the assassination. He has said that he spent five days in Dallas "investigating" the tragedy and that he then, on December 11, 1963, returned home to his wife. But she said he failed to show up for dinner that evening, instead leaving her a note saying he had gone to Europe. And gone he was for several months. Later that year, Joesten began publishing articles and books on the Kennedy assassination.[6]

As discussed earlier, when people asked Rolf Hochhuth where he got his outrageous stories about Pius XII, he would say he had spent three months in Rome chatting up a talkative German bishop, but that the source material had to remain sealed for fifty years. The public has not been satisfied with either five days in Dallas or three months in Rome.

The first review of Joesten's book, which praised it to the skies, was signed by KGB agent Victor Perlo and was published on September 23, 1964, in *New Times*, which I knew was a KGB front at one time printed in Romania.[7] In the 1930s, Perlo was the head of a group of important agents run by the communist underground in the United States. In 1944, Perlo and his group were turned over to the KGB predecessor organization and handled by Elizabeth Bentley, who defected a year later. That transfer, incidentally, took place at the New York apartment of the lawyer John Abt, a lifelong member of the American Communist Party, who—according to the *Vassiliev Archive*—regularly helped the party underground, the KGB and the GRU with funding and legal matters.[8] After his arrest, Oswald stated he wanted to be represented by John Abt and tried to reach him by telephone, but Abt was away for the weekend.[9] The *Vassiliev Archive* also documents that Perlo frequently wrote articles for various communist fronts, signing them with assorted pseudonyms. In the 1940s, he helped the writer I. F. Stone compile material for various exposés.[10]

On December 9, 1963, I. F. Stone (KGB codename "Blin") published a long article in which he tried to justify why America had killed its own president. He called Oswald and Ruby "rightist crackpots," but put the real blame on the "warlike Administration" of the United States, that was trying to sell Europe a "nuclear monstrosity."[11] Stone was another paid KGB agent who a few months later joined in the attack on Pius XII. As noted in an earlier chapter, on March 9, 1964, Stone signed an article in his own weekly publication that praised Hochhuth's play *The Deputy* and attacked Pius XII as having been "friendly to Hitler" and to Mussolini.[12] That same month, Stone's sister,

Judy Stone, published a friendly interview with Hochhuth in *Ramparts*[13] which, as will be seen below, would play significant role in promoting the KGB disinformation connected with the Kennedy assassination as well.

So again we see the KGB rounding up the "usual suspects," both in order to smear Pius XII as pro-Hitler and to blame the CIA and other American targets for the death of President Kennedy.

Joachim Joesten dedicated his book *Oswald: Assassin or Fall Guy?* to Mark Lane, an American leftist who in 1966 produced the bestseller *Rush to Judgment*, alleging Kennedy was assassinated by a right-wing American group. Documents in the *Mitrokhin Archive* show that the KGB indirectly sent Mark Lane money ($2,000), and that KGB operative, Genrikh Borovik, was in regular contact with him. Another KGB defector, Colonel Oleg Gordievsky (former KGB station chief in London), has identified Borovik as the brother-in-law of Col. General Vladimir Kryuchkov, who in 1974 became head of KGB foreign intelligence, in 1988 chairman of the KGB, and in August 1991 led the anti-glasnost coup in Moscow.

The year 1967 saw the publication of two more books attributed to Joesten: *The Case Against Lyndon Johnson in the Assassination of President Kennedy* and *Oswald: The Truth*. Both books insinuated that President Johnson and his CIA had killed Kennedy. They were soon followed by Mark Lane's *A Citizen's Dissent* (1968). According to assassination researcher Vincent Bugliosi, Mark Lane has been "by far the most persistent and audible single voice" in making Americans believe that reactionary elements in the United States killed Kennedy.[14] Lane has also intensively traveled abroad to preach that America is an "FBI police state" that killed its own president.

Mark Lane helped New Orleans District Attorney Jim Garrison arrest a local man (Clay Shaw), whom Garrison accused of conspiring with elements of US intelligence to murder Kennedy in order to stop the latter's efforts to end the Cold War. Garrison's book, *On the Trail of the Assassin*, inspired Oliver Stone's movie *JFK*, which, as I mentioned prior, claims the assassination of President Kennedy was the result of a conspiracy at the highest level of the US government.

Thus, the Kennedy assassination conspiracy was born, and it has never stopped. All kinds of people with any sort of remotely related background expertise joined the party, each viewing events from his own narrow perspective. Some witnesses to the JFK assassination have claimed to have heard more shots and seen more assassins and observed different wounds than those described in the *Warren Commission Report,* even though the latter's forensic conclusions have repeatedly been declared accurate by responsible analysts. For example, a ballistics expert supplied the information that led to Bonar Menninger's *Mortal Error: The Shot that Killed JFK* (St. Martin's, 1992), which concludes that a Secret Service agent probably killed JFK by accident. Gaeton Fonzi's *The Last Investigation* (Thunder's Mouth, 1993) was written by a journalist who had worked with the House committee and claimed to have personal knowledge of a CIA/Oswald link through investigations he conducted in places like Miami. Computer expert David S. Lifton wrote *Best Evidence: Disguise and Deception in the Assassination of John F. Kennedy* (Macmillan, 1980), in which, on the basis of his own examination of photographs, concludes that JFK's wounds had been altered before he was buried, although no purpose for such an alteration is offered. Dr. Charles A. Crenshaw also wrote a book questioning the wounds: *JFK: Conspiracy of Silence* (Signet, 1992).

All such books divert the public's attention away from the real case. Unfortunately, serious publishing houses continue to accept books of this kind, which are based on nothing more than each author's viewing some aspect of the story through his own narrowly focused lens and then letting his imagination run wild.

Another extremely significant new piece of information provided by the *Mitrokhin Archive* revolves around a short, handwritten and apparently naïve note that starts, "Dear Mr. Hunt," in which "Lee Harvey Oswald" politely asks for "information concerning my position ... before any steps are taken by me or anyone else." In 1975, photocopies of this document were mailed in the United States to three of the most active conspiracy advocates, along with a note alleging that the head of the FBI had the original.

According to Mitrokhin, the note had been fabricated by the KGB using words and expressions taken from actual letters handwritten by Oswald during his stay in the Soviet Union, and had been twice authenticated by the KGB's Technical Operations Directorate. (Remember that the KGB insisted on using photocopies of forgeries, as that made them more difficult to detect.) The KGB intended the "Dear Mr. Hunt" note to be an allusion to Texas oil tycoon H. L. Hunt, who was part of its original plan to implicate wealthy Texans in the assassination. In 1977, the note was published in a small Texas newspaper. (The owner of the newspaper was the late Penn Jones, Jr., a "mysterious-deaths" conspiracy advocate, who self-published several books on the Kennedy assassination and was supported by the leftist *Ramparts* magazine.[15] As discussed earlier, *Ramparts* actively attacked Pius XII and was instrumental in seeing Hochhuth's anti-Pius XII play *The Deputy* produced in New York. *Ramparts* also published numerous articles on the Kennedy assassination, often implicating US government officials.) The "Dear Mr. Hunt" note was then picked up by the *New York Times*, which claimed it had been authenticated by three handwriting experts and by Oswald's widow.

The KGB forgery had been "validated."

In connection with the above "Dear Mr. Hunt" forgery, it is instructive to recall the forgeries created by the Hungarian communists in an effort to compromise Cardinal Mindszenty (discussed earlier). In 1949, right in the middle of his trial, the handwriting experts Lázlo and Hanna Sulner, who had fabricated documents used against Mindszenty, escaped to Vienna. Once safely in the West, they explained how they had copied words and phrases from some of the manuscripts stolen from Mindszenty's office, and then had strung them together to create perfect forgeries, such as his alleged confession. Hanna said her father had invented a machine that could produce foolproof copies of handwriting and that Lázlo had become very proficient at using it. She added that the Hungarian security police officers had been very interested in the machine, eventually confiscating it so that they themselves could make their own (rather sloppy) forgeries. (Here, I again recall how mystified I was when the KGB kept asking me to have my agents search the Vatican archives for more and more innocuous documents written by Pope Pius XII. Now we know why.)

In April 1977, the KGB informed the Communist Party's Central Committee that it was orchestrating additional "active measures" to expose the supposed role of the "American special services" in the Kennedy assassination. By 1980, E. Howard Hunt, a former CIA officer who had been caught up in the Watergate scandal, was publicly complaining that people were accusing *him* of having had some role in the Kennedy assassination.[16]

Several authors have recently published meticulous books on the Venona intercepts. Although the decryption of Soviet intelligence broadcasts from the period 1940 to 1948, known as the Venona material, does not directly apply to our knowledge of the disinformation operation that took place in the post-Kennedy assassination period, it does provide documentary background information on some of the KGB agents involved. I. F. Stone is one of them.

Another source of KGB foreign intelligence documents is known as the *Vassiliev Archive*. In the 1990s, the Kremlin authorities briefly allowed some of the KGB's foreign intelligence archives, covering the 1930s and 1940s, to be made available to former KGB officer Alexander Vassiliev, so that he could make notes on the documents for a projected joint Russian/American publication in the West. In the end, this window of opportunity was shut down before anything was published, but Vassiliev and his notebooks made it out to London in 1996. In 2009, the so-called *Vassiliev Archive* was published without Russian censorship and augmented by more complete Venona decryptions and other material made possible with the help of Vassiliev's notes. This archive provides new information on some of the Soviet intelligence agents used in connection with the Kennedy assassination and other disinformation operations.

One other book provides some surprisingly significant new information from the Cuban perspective. Entitled *Castro's Spies* and published in 2012, it is authored by Brian Latell, a writer and former CIA officer, who has collected factual information from defectors and overt sources. His most important source is Florentino Aspillaga, a radio intercept officer with Cuban intelligence who defected in Vienna in 1987. Latell interviewed him in 2007, and describes him as the most valuable defector ever to come from Cuba.

In October 1963, having just finished his training as a communications technician, the sixteen-year-old Aspillaga was assigned to sit alone in a commo hut on the shore near Havana and monitor CIA transmissions from Virginia, Miami, and offshore ships, looking for spies. Only once in the dozen years he held that job did his routine vary, and that was on November 22, 1963. At about 9:00 or 9:30 that morning, he got a coded radio message telling him to call his headquarters, which he did from another hut with a secure telephone. He was ordered to stop all CIA tracking for that day and instead to listen for communications from Texas, and to report anything of importance back to headquarters.

About three or four hours later, Aspillaga began picking up messages on amateur radio bands about the shooting of President Kennedy in Dallas, which he reported to his headquarters on the secure telephone. (Kennedy was shot at about 12:30 p.m. Dallas time, which would have been 1:30 p.m. Havana time.)

Aspillaga told Latell: "Castro knew. They knew Kennedy would be killed." Aspillaga did not try to embroider this story or to accuse Fidel of the killing, and his story remained the same even after going over it again and again. He said that, fearing for his life, he never told this story to anyone until after his defection in 1987. Latell checked and found he had included this information in the Spanish-language memoirs he wrote for his original debriefers in 1990. It did not become publicly available until the appearance of Latell's book in 2012.[17]

The significance of this small item lies in the fact that it supports the *Programmed to Kill* analysis of Fidel Castro's peripheral role in the KGB's damage-control measures and disinformation operation orchestrated in connection with Oswald and his assassination of the president. After Oswald's secret meeting with "comrade Kostin" in Mexico City, the Kremlin evidently informed Castro about Oswald's intention to assassinate President Kennedy during his visit to Dallas, and asked for Cuba's help. Castro's DGI provided its agent, Jack Ruby, who was given a cover story about why he might have to kill Oswald, and the KGB briefed Castro on the role he should play in the ensuing disinformation operation should it all become necessary.

As soon as news of the assassination hit the airwaves, the Kremlin and its friends rushed to disseminate their version of who was responsible before anyone else dared to do so. Fidel Castro was among the first to react.

Because of Oswald's public support for Cuba and visit to the Cuban Embassy in Mexico City, Castro knew he had to act quickly to deflect any suspicion that he was responsible for Kennedy's death. As was his wont, he made many long speeches in Cuba and over Radio Havana, beginning on November 23. In all his speeches, he consistently said only nice things about Kennedy, whose death Castro said could only benefit "ultra-rightist and ultra-reactionary sectors" in the United States. At first he even denied that he had ever heard of Oswald. However, when his consular officers said they had reported to Castro on Oswald's visit to their office in Mexico City, Castro admitted it but improved on the story, saying not only that Oswald had gotten angry over not receiving a Cuban visa, but that he had stormed out, threatening to kill Kennedy and slamming the consulate door behind him. The consulate employees denied Oswald had threatened to kill Kennedy, and no one seems to have wondered what connection such a remark could have had anyway with the refusal of a Cuban visa. Castro was apparently just trying to improve on the disinformation suggestions he had undoubtedly received from the KGB. As time went on, Castro, like the KGB, settled for simply blaming the CIA for the assassination.[18]

When I was working for Nicolae Ceauşescu , I always tried to find a way to help him reach a decision on his own, rather than telling him directly what I thought he should do about something. That way, both of us were happy. From our KGB advisors, I had learned that the best way to put over a deception was to let the target see something for himself, with his own eyes. Not surprisingly, there are two cleverly executed and spectacularly successful examples of this tactic that turn up as part of the KGB disinformation operation connected with the Kennedy assassination.

In November 1963, Morris Childs, the number two man in the American Communist Party (which he had joined in 1919!), was on his annual visit to Moscow for the purpose of requesting money and receiving policy instructions. On November 22, as news of the assassination broke, Morris was summoned to the office of Boris Ponomarev, the powerful chairman of the International Department of the Central Committee of the Communist Party. The two men had just begun discussing how the American party should react when a couple of party underlings burst in, their faces ashen. In Russian, which Morris had never admitted to understanding, they breathlessly briefed Ponomarev on Oswald's arrest, blurting out that he was a former US Marine who had defected to the Soviet Union, but that after he had attempted suicide, Soviet psychiatrists had concluded he was unbalanced, so the Soviets were glad to be rid of him when he asked to go back to the United States. The storytellers excitedly added that the KGB had just sworn to the Kremlin that it had never had any operational relationship with him.

Suddenly the storytellers noticed Morris—"the American"—and asked what he should be told. Ponomarev vouched for him and said he should be told the truth. The talented actors then retold the same story, which was relayed to Morris through an interpreter. The Soviets beseeched Morris to believe they had nothing to do with the assassination.

In fact, since 1951, Morris Childs had been a very sensitive FBI agent, whose reporting was considered to be completely reliable and whose identity was never revealed to anyone until 1995, when John Barron received permission to publish *Operation Solo: The FBI's Man in the Kremlin*, from which the above account is taken.

In 1993, before the publication of *Solo*, my wife and I had enjoyed a long lunch with John Barron, hosted by Alfred Regnery, who had published my book *Red Horizons* and had just read the outline of a book on the Kennedy assassination I was writing. At lunch, the discussion centered around Morris's diary, which Barron had just obtained from Morris's widow, and around Al Regnery's intention to publish it as a book. During that lunch, I learned that Morris's information was regularly and anonymously distributed to top members of the US government on an "eyes only" basis. Barron's book, published in 1995, contains convincing evidence that Morris was a very trusted FBI agent and that the information he provided to the FBI played a decisive role in the decision of the Warren Commission—and later, of the House Committee on Assassinations—*not* to consider any Soviet bloc hand in President Kennedy's assassination.

There is no question that Morris Childs, as well as his brother Jack, who had both once been loyal members of the American Communist Party, were by 1951 and for the rest of their lives absolutely reliable and devoted FBI sources. Morris was mainly involved with policy guidelines and Jack with funds, both of which commodities they obtained from the Soviet Communist Party and passed on to its American subsidiary. Even after 1963, both brothers continued to meet with their communist contacts and both remained confident the Soviets trusted them.[19]

According to the *Mitrokhin Archive*, however, in 1974, the KGB component responsible for operations in the United States became suspicious of Morris Childs because of certain anomalies in his background. Jack, then, also fell under suspicion for similar reasons. Both brothers had been leading figures in the American party since its early days and both had switched their allegiance to the FBI in 1951. (Morris was the number two man in the overt party and Jack an important member of the underground party, who picked up the funds for the party through clandestine meetings with KGB officers.

By the 1970s, the working-level KGB officers responsible for espionage in the United States had wondered if the brothers might be reporting to the FBI, especially because the brothers had experienced no ill effects from the anticommunist "witch-hunts" of the 1950s.)

Although in the 1970s the working level of the KGB periodically recommended that the party replace both brothers, the party dragged its feet and took no action for various reasons, mostly saying the head of the party in the United States was happy with them. Morris finally retired from his party position in 1981, and Jack died that same year. Both brothers had been highly decorated by the Soviets in the 1970s—in 1977 the party even threw a special birthday party for Morris, attended by KGB chairman Andropov, party International Department chairman Ponomarev, Soviet leader Leonid Brezhnev, and about half the Politburo. Brezhnev pinned the Order of the Red Banner, a high honor, on Morris's lapel. (At the same time, Jack was given the same award, which he would receive the next time he went to Moscow.)[20]

Putting all of the above information on the Childs brothers together, we must inevitably conclude that the top levels of both the KGB and the Soviet Communist Party had long understood—since at least 1963 and probably much earlier— that Morris and Jack Childs were reporting to the FBI. Instead of dumping or even arresting them, the KGB and party leadership realized they could use the brothers as unwitting conduits for disinformation. The brothers would not only pass the Kremlin's political messages to the American party, but they would also act as superbly credible sources for the disinformation the Kremlin wished to convey to the American government. When the incredible happened and Oswald did succeed in killing President Kennedy, the Kremlin went into overdrive to convince both Childs brothers separately that the Soviets had nothing to do with it.

The show put on for Morris on November 22, 1963, was unquestionably a farce, deliberately staged as part of the Kennedy assassination disinformation operation. The Soviets certainly knew that Morris spoke Russian as he had spent the first nine years of his life in tsarist Russia, and later three years at the Communist Party's Lenin School in Moscow, where he had even been recruited by the KGB predecessor as an informant. Moreover, it is incredible that any party flunkies would have dared to break into Ponomarev's meeting with an American, to say nothing of their having spoken freely about such extremely sensitive matters as Oswald's background or KGB file records.

As a marvelous bonus, the *Mitrokhin Archive* completes the picture. Although the First (US) Department of the KGB's foreign directorate spotted weak points in the backgrounds of the Childs brothers and kept urging the party to drop them, the top KGB and party leaders knew perfectly well that the brothers were reporting to the FBI. The interruption of Ponomarev's meeting with Morris on November 22, was clearly planned deliberately, so that he would convince the FBI (and thus also the top level of the American government) of the lie that the Soviets had had absolutely nothing to do with Kennedy's assassination.

Remarkably, another staged performance took place in Cuba on that very same day of November 22, 1963—an "amazing coincidence," as Fidel Castro would call what happened. On that afternoon, Fidel hosted a luncheon at his Varadero beach house outside of Havana, to honor Jean Daniel, the distinguished French correspondent of the Parisian weekly *L'Express*. The latter had been visiting Cuba for several weeks and had already spent a couple of days with Castro. About a dozen people—Castro, Daniel and his wife, and nine or ten other Cubans—were sitting around a table, when Cuba's figurehead president called on the telephone with preliminary news of the Kennedy assassination attempt. Fidel took the call in the presence of his guests, who heard him exclaim in astonishment: "*¿Como? ¿Un atentado?*" (What? An assassination attempt?). Fidel seemed genuinely shocked, but he had the presence of mind to ask immediately who the vice president was. When it was shortly thereafter learned that the president was dead, Castro expressed alarm, saying: "They will have to find the assassin quickly, otherwise you watch and see, they will try to blame us." Brian Latell, after reporting the above story in his book, perceptively points out that Castro may have had an ulterior motive for arranging that luncheon with such care, "and with the expectation that Jean Daniel would write one or more widely circulated articles." Indeed, two articles by Daniel soon appeared in the *New Republic* describing the above scene. Because Daniel was a journalist of impeccable reputation, no one would ever question where Castro was when he heard the news, or his surprise over it.[21] But why did Fidel worry about who the vice president was, even before the president was reported mortally wounded? And why was he afraid people would blame Cuba, before anyone knew who the assassin was? In any case, it seems clear that Fidel Castro was doing his best to support the KGB's disinformation operation by denying any Cuban involvement in the assassination and by trying to peddle some of the KGB's suggested solutions to the crime.

Jack Childs also played a role in the disinformation operation mounted after the assassination. The Communist Party had introduced Jack to Fidel Castro in May 1963, during the latter's first visit to Moscow. The two seemed to get along well together, so in May 1964, the Soviet Communist Party sent Jack from Moscow to Havana, after coaching him in how to deal with Castro, who allegedly needed someone to talk to. After cooling his heels for nine days, on the tenth day Jack was finally summoned by Fidel. They were discussing party relations between the United States and Cuba, when out of the blue Fidel asked: "Do you think Oswald killed President Kennedy?" Castro then answered his own question, saying his people had experimented with a gun similar to the one Oswald had used, and they had concluded it was impossible for one person to have fired the three reported shots in such short succession—it had to have been a conspiracy. He also told Jack Childs that Oswald had stormed out of the Cuban Embassy in Mexico City after being refused a visa, saying "I'm going to kill Kennedy for this." Jack, of course, reported this back not only to the American party, but especially to the FBI, which did give it to the Warren Commission, although FBI director Hoover trivialized it, convinced there had been no conspiracy.[22]

Now we can understand why Morris and Jack Childs were both awarded the Order of the Red Banner with great ceremony at the Kremlin in 1977.

The jewel in the crown of Soviet disinformation connected with Oswald's story is the recently published revelation that the U-2 spy plane flown by Powers over the Soviet Union was not shot down by Soviet rockets, as the Russians have always claimed, but by a Sukhoi Su-9 plane that had been especially modified to achieve higher altitudes by having its weapons removed. According to the recently published revelations of Soviet Capt. Igor Mentyukov, the pilot of that airplane, he had caught the U-2 in the slipstream of his unarmed Su-9, causing the U-2 to flip over and break its wings. The salvo of Soviet rockets had indeed scored a hit, downing a pursuing MiG-19, but not the U-2.[23] (In an article about the downing of Powers's U-2 plane, published in the US in 2000, Khrushchev's son Sergei acknowledged that the Soviets fired three SA-2 rockets, but only one ignited. Unsure about their success, the Soviets fired thirteen further antiaircraft missiles, but the later rockets hit a pursuing MiG-19 piloted by Sr. Lt. Sergey Safronov, who was posthumously awarded the Order of the Red Banner.[24])

According to Captain Mentyukov, the U-2 flight altitude was higher than the altitude the Soviet rockets could reach. He also noted that the pilot of the U-2 plane would have certainly died if his frail plane had been hit by a rocket.[25]

It seems that, after Oswald provided the KGB with the highly secret flight altitude of the U-2 plane, the KGB prepared a specially modified airplane, keeping it ready to intercept the US spy plane. This measure provided an additional bonus: the U-2 pilot was captured alive. Khrushchev did indeed parade Powers and used him as propaganda.

"The most valuable May Day present we've ever given the Comrade," I heard Sakharovsky say.

PART IV

UNRAVELING TODAY'S
WEB OF DECEIT

33

FROM DISINFORMATION TO TERRORISM

I
N DISCUSSING YURI ANDROPOV'S LEGACY, Western Sovietologists usually focus on his brutal suppression of political dissidents, his role in igniting the violent suppression of the 1956 uprising in Hungary (where he was ambassador at the time), his role in preparing the 1968 invasion of Czechoslovakia, and his pressure on the Polish regime to impose martial law. In contrast, the leaders of the Warsaw Pact intelligence community, when I was one of them, looked upon Andropov as the father of a new disinformation era, which revived anti-Semitism and generated international terrorism against the United States and Israel.

The grisly decapitation and dismembering of *Wall Street Journal* reporter Daniel Pearl in 2002 symbolizes Andropov's legacy. The mastermind of the September 11, 2001, attacks, Khalid Sheikh Mohammed, gruesomely murdered Pearl solely because he was an American Jew. The Kremlin's continued silence about the framing of Pius XII, who was politically decapitated in part because he had protected the Jews, symbolizes another Andropov legacy.

Andropov was the first head of the KGB to be enthroned in the Kremlin. As a former ambassador and afterward head of the Soviet Communist Party's department responsible for relations with the ruling parties in communist countries, his interests lay abroad, and that is where he directed the cutting edge of the KGB sword. Andropov extended Khrushchev's policy of individually framing religious and political leaders disliked by the Kremlin, such as Pius XII and US presidents, to framing entire religious movements and whole countries. Zionism, Israel, and the United States were his main targets.

Andropov began his unprecedented fifteen years as KGB chairman only a couple of years after the framing of Pius XII, and just months before the 1967 Six-Day Arab-Israeli War, in which Israel humiliated the Soviet Union's most important allies in the Arab world at that time—Egypt and Syria. In those days, the governments of those two countries were in effect being run by Soviet advisers.

The new KGB chairman decided to repair the Kremlin's prestige by humiliating Israel. Toward the end of that year, Andropov introduced a new arrow into the KGB's quiver—presenting Zionism as Nazi-style racism, and hijacking "Zionist" El Al airplanes. Before 1969 came to an end, Palestinian terrorists trained at the KGB's Balashikha special-operations school east of Moscow had hijacked their first "Zionist" El Al plane and landed it in Algeria, where its thirty-two Jewish passengers were held hostage for five weeks. The hijacking had been planned and coordinated by the KGB's Thirteenth Department, known in Soviet bloc intelligence jargon as the Department for Wet Affairs (*wet* being a KGB euphemism for *bloody*). To conceal the KGB's hand, Andropov had the Popular Front for the Liberation of Palestine (created and financed by the KGB) take credit for the hijacking.

The media frenzy generated by that terrorist operation convinced Andropov that airplane hijacking was the weapon of the future. He therefore extended the hijackings from Israeli planes to any other "Zionist" flying target of opportunity. During the next two years, various Palestinian terrorists (trained by the KGB) took credit for hijacking thirteen Israeli and Western passenger planes and for blowing up a SwissAir plane in flight, killing forty-seven passengers and crewmembers.

The huge political "success" brought about by the hijacking of "Zionist airplanes" prompted Andropov to expand into organizing "public executions" of "Zionists" in airports, train stations, and other public places. Andropov's puppet Dr. George Habash, leader of the Popular Front for the Liberation of Palestine and a fanatical Marxist, mirrored the true colors of the new terrorist tactic: "Killing one Jew far from the field of battle is more effective than killing a hundred Jews on the field of battle, because it attracts more attention."[1]

The most important "anti-Zionist" operations for which the KGB took secret credit while I was still in Romania include:

December 1968, attack on an El Al plane in the Athens airport

February 1969, attack on the El Al office in Zurich

November 1969, armed attack on the El Al office in Athens, leaving 1 dead and 14 wounded

May 30, 1972, Ben Gurion Airport attack, leaving 22 dead and 76 wounded

September 1973, Vienna train attack

December 1974, Tel Aviv movie theater bomb, leaving 2 dead and 66 wounded

March 1975, attack on Tel Aviv hotel, leaving 25 dead and 6 wounded

May 1975, Jerusalem bomb, leaving 1 dead, 3 wounded

July 4, 1975, bomb in Zion Square, Jerusalem, leaving 15 dead and 62 wounded

April 1978, Brussels airport attack, leaving 12 wounded

May 1978, attack on an El Al plane in Paris, leaving 12 wounded

By 1972, Andropov's disinformation machinery was working around the clock to persuade the Islamic world that Israel and the United States intended to transform the rest of the world into a Zionist fiefdom. According to Andropov, the Islamic world was a petri dish in which the KGB community could nurture a virulent strain of America-hatred, grown from the bacterium of Marxist-Leninist thought. Islamic anti-Semitism ran deep.

The message was simple: The Muslims had a taste for nationalism, jingoism, and victimology. Andropov pontificated that "we" should make them feel sick to their stomachs just thinking about that "Council of the Elders of Zion" (meaning the US Congress), the aim of which was to have the Jews take over the world. We should whip up their illiterate, oppressed mobs to a fever pitch. Terrorism and violence against Israel and America would flow naturally from the Muslims' anti-Semitic fervor, Andropov explained.[2]

The Kremlin has always been a strong advocate of *divide et impera*. The split between the Judeo and the Christian worlds generated by the framing of Pius XII proved that this archaic strategy of divide and conquer worked in modern times as well. In 1972, Andropov launched Operation "SIG" (*Sionistskiye Gosudarstva*, Zionist Governments). This was the code name for a "socialist division of labor" aimed at turning the Islamic world into an "explosive" enemy of the United States. The Romanian DIE's sphere of influence for the operation embraced Libya, Iran, Lebanon, and Syria, where Romania was involved in building hospitals, schools, and roads and maintained large colonies of builders, doctors, and teachers. The DIE's task was to scour Romania for trusted Communist Party activists belonging to Islamic ethnic groups, train them in *dezinformatsiya* and terrorist operations, and infiltrate them into its target countries. They would be charged with the task of implanting a rabid, demented hatred for American Zionism by manipulating the ancestral abhorrence for Jews felt by many people in that part of the world.

Before I left Romania for good, in 1978, the DIE had sent about five hundred undercover agents to its Islamic target countries—and, as I later learned, it continued to send such agents until the Soviet bloc collapsed, in 1989. Most of them were engineers, medical doctors, teachers, and art instructors. According to a rough estimate received from Moscow, by 1978 the Soviet bloc intelligence community had sent some four thousand such agents of influence into the Islamic world. The assumption was that about 70–75 percent of those assets would end up being really useful.

In 1972, the DIE received from the KGB an Arabic translation of the *Protocols of the Elders of Zion* along with "documentary" material, also in Arabic, "proving" that the United States was a Zionist country whose aim was to transform the Islamic world into a Jewish fiefdom. The DIE was ordered to "discreetly" disseminate both "documents" within its targeted Islamic countries. During my later years in Romania, every month the DIE disseminated thousands of copies throughout its Islamic sphere of influence. In the meetings I had with my counterparts in the Hungarian and Bulgarian services, with whom I enjoyed particularly close relations at that time, I learned that they were also sending such influence agents into their own Islamic spheres of influence.

On one of my visits to Budapest, I met János Kádár, the Hungarian leader. Operation SIG was one of the subjects in which Kádár was particularly interested. I was aware that Kádár had founded Hungary's foreign intelligence service, but that had been in 1949. By the time we met, I assumed Kádár would surely have thousands of more important things on his mind, but that proved wrong. Operation SIG was uppermost in the minds of Soviet bloc leaders in those days. A few years later, when I became Ceaușescu's national security adviser (in addition to my DIE duties), the Romanian leader asked me to report periodically on the number of influence agents sent to the Arab and Islamic countries.

How much influence did all those operations have? No one can say for sure, just as no one can exactly measure how much damage the framing of Pius XII has generated. Nevertheless, over the course of twenty-plus years, the cumulative effect of sending out thousands of influence agents and hundreds of thousands of copies of the *Protocols of the Elders of Zion* into the Islamic world certainly made some dent. Witness the 1979 takeover of the US Embassy in Tehran, the 1983 bombing of the US Marine barracks in Beirut, the 1993 bombing of the World Trade Center in New York, the 1998 destruction of the US embassies in Kenya and Tanzania, and, of course, the attacks on the World Trade Center and the Pentagon on September 11, 2001.

Soon after launching Operation "SIG," Andropov unleashed Operation *"Tayfun"* (Russian for *typhoon*), aimed at expanding international terrorism into Western Europe. As was usual for such international operations, the KGB established another "socialist division of labor" to mobilize the entire bloc intelligence community in support of its extended terrorist war. The Soviet Union would assume the most difficult tasks, those of creating new terrorist organizations, indoctrinating their members, and providing intelligence, money, and political support for terrorist operations—which Andropov called "armed struggle."

The Czechoslovakian foreign intelligence service was charged with supplying terrorists with an odorless plastic explosive (Semtex-H) that could not be detected by sniffer dogs at airports. In 1990, Czechoslovakian president Václav Havel acknowledged that the communist regime of his country had secretly shipped a thousand tons of this odorless plastic explosive to Palestinian and Libyan terrorists. According to Havel, a mere two hundred grams was enough to blow up a commercial plane in flight. "World terrorism has supplies of Semtex to last 150 years," Havel estimated.[3]

The East Germans had to provide the terrorists with arms and ammunition. According to secret documents found after the fall of the Berlin Wall in the archives of the East German Ministry for State Security, colloquially known as the Stasi, in 1983 alone its foreign intelligence service provided the PLO with $1,877,600 worth of AK-47 ammunition.[4]

The Cubans mass-produced concealment devices for transporting the plastic explosive and weapons into the target countries. In 1972, I spent a "working vacation" in Havana as the guest of Raúl Castro, at that time head of Cuba's military and security forces, and visited what proved to be the Soviet bloc's largest factory for manufacturing double-walled suitcases and other concealment devices for use in secretly transporting weapons. General Sergio del Valle Jiménez, Cuba's minister of interior, told me that smuggling arms to "anti-Zionist terrorist organizations" was one of his main jobs.

Romania's task in that joint venture was to produce false Western passports needed by Andropov's "freedom fighters." During my last six years in Romania, the DIE became the Soviet bloc's main manufacturer of forged West German, Austrian, French, British, Italian, and Spanish passports, which were regularly provided to international terrorist organizations and groups. The DIE also handcrafted a large collection of entrance visa stamps from all around the world, needed by terrorists to travel to their target countries.

In the mid-1970s, a wave of terrorism inundated Western Europe. *Tayfun*'s first major accomplishment was the assassination of Richard Welch, the CIA station chief in Athens, on December 23, 1975. That was followed by: a bomb attack on Gen. Alexander Haig, commander of NATO in Brussels, who was not injured although his armored Mercedes limousine was damaged beyond repair; a rocket attack against Gen. Frederick J. Kroesen, commander of US Forces in Europe, who also escaped alive; a grenade attack against Alfred Herrhausen, the pro-American chairman of the Deutsche Bank, who was killed; and an assassination attempt on Hans Neusel, a pro-American state secretary at the West German Ministry of Interior responsible for internal security affairs, who was wounded.

When the Soviet bloc collapsed in December 1989, those terrorist operations went *poof!* and scores of KGB-sponsored terrorists were arrested in the former East Germany. Peter Michael Diestel, who became East Germany's interior minister after the fall of its communist government, acknowledged in 1990 that Schönefeld Airport in East Berlin had for years been "a turntable for terrorists of all kinds." Christian Lochte, a senior official in the West German counterintelligence service,[5] stated that the KGB and the *Stasi* had done "everything possible to destabilize this country and the rest of Western Europe as well."[6] Moreover, the West German government uncovered evidence that the *Stasi* had also trained Palestinian terrorist groups in East Germany and in southern Yemen and that it had been involved in the 1986 Libyan bombing of the La Belle discotheque in West Berlin, which killed two American soldiers and wounded 229 other people.[7]

In November 1982, Yuri Andropov became the first KGB officer to head the Soviet Union. Once on the Kremlin throne, he used the foreign intelligence machinery to introduce himself to the West as a "moderate" communist and a sensitive, warm, Western-oriented man. He was depicted as someone who enjoyed an occasional drink of Scotch, liked to read English novels, and loved listening to American jazz and the music of Beethoven. I knew him well. Andropov was none of the above.

Already terminally ill when he seized power, Andropov did not have time to do much more than project his new image. He did, however, promote the fortunes of his protégé, a vigorous and callous young professional communist who, as the world would soon learn, shared his mentor's views on the importance of deception and influence operations: Mikhail Gorbachev.

Gorbachev began his career, as had Andropov, in Stavropol, and Andropov soon engineered Gorbachev's appointment to the Soviet Politburo. One Gorbachev biographer says that Gorbachev was Andropov's "principal organizer and his 'crown prince.'"[8]

Gorbachev's glasnost and its unplanned, spectacular outcome in Eastern Europe made him an instant hit in the West, for a while. Public opinion in the Soviet Union, however, was a different matter. Able to speak freely after enduring almost three- quarters of a century with their mouths metaphorically wired shut, the Soviets spent most of their time venting their pent-up angers and frustrations. Everybody began fighting everybody else and waiting for another miracle. In real life, of course, economic miracles do not happen by themselves. The stores became emptier than ever, and millions of Soviets started blaming the man who had allowed them to voice that blame.

Suddenly, the privileged Moscow *nomenklatura* decided that the president of the Soviet Union, Mikhail Gorbachev, looked like a loser, and it sought help from the political police and its "science of *dezinformatsiya*," the usual way out of a tight spot in a Kremlin balance-of-power struggle.

On June 22, 1991, Vladimir Kryuchkov, the chairman of the KGB, informed the Soviet parliament that the motherland was on the brink of catastrophe. He then revealed "reliable" KGB information showing that Western intelligence services were drawing up plans for the pacification and even occupation of the Soviet Union. By remarkable coincidence, his speech was "clandestinely" videotaped and broadcast on Soviet television that same evening. Two months later, the world was horrified by news of a coup d'état in Moscow. On August 18, 1991, following a pattern similar to the one it had used to oust Nikita Khrushchev, the KGB arrested a vacationing Gorbachev at his summer residence in the Crimea, took over the Kremlin, and paraded its own military might on the streets of Moscow.

On the orders of the self-proclaimed "State Committee on the Emergency Situation," created by the coup's leaders, who included Vladimir Kryuchkov, KGB troops also surrounded the headquarters of the first freely elected president of the Russian Republic, Boris Yeltsin. Thousands of unarmed citizens gathered to defend the building. A small insurgent tank unit switched sides, and President Yeltsin, standing on one of these tanks, made a passionate appeal to the people of Moscow to preserve the "Soviet order."[9] That speech, televised worldwide, constituted the birth certificate of a new Soviet star.

34

PUTIN TIME

B Y 1999, President Yeltsin's ill-conceived privatization had enabled a small clique of predatory insiders to plunder Russia's most valuable assets. The looting had become so outrageous that people attending auctions of state-owned businesses started carrying banners with a slogan that would become commonplace: *privatizatsiya* (privatization) = *prikhvatizatsiya* (grabbing).[1] "They are stealing absolutely everything and it is impossible to stop them," said Anatoly Chubais, the Yeltsin-appointed tsar of this privatization, who acquired a good part of Russia's energy industry and became a billionaire himself.[2] The corruption generated by this widespread looting penetrated every corner of the country, and it eventually created a Mafia-style economic system that threatened the stability of Russia itself.

During this time, a small number of businessmen and investors were able to make large fortunes by recognizing and taking advantage of imperfections in the developing markets. Most of these oligarchs, as they came to be known, are now in prison or in exile. Only a few have managed to thrive under Putin.

Much has been made of the fact that in this anti-Semitic nation, of the seven oligarchs who controlled 50 percent of Russia's economy during the 1990s, six were Jewish. Ironic as it seems, anti-Semitism actually made it easier for them to make their billions. As reported in the British press, since the Soviet Union restricted Jews' ability to assimilate and rise up in society,

"Jews who wanted to get ahead were forced into the black market economy. When communism collapsed and the black market was legalized as free market capitalism, the Jewish entrepreneurs had a head start."[3]

Of course, since Putin took power, most of the original Jewish oligarchs have fled the nation.

By July 1998, the ruble had lost 75 percent of its past year's value, short-term interest rates had climbed from 21 percent to 60 percent, and the stock market had slumped by more than 60 percent. Petropavlovsk, the capital of Kamchatka, and a few other smaller towns were deprived of electricity as a result of unpaid bills.[4] Yeltsin unsuccessfully tried to solve the crisis by sacking two prime ministers within six months—Viktor Chernomyrdin in March, and Sergey Kiriyenko in August.

As of 1999, the Kremlin was reporting more and more frequently that Russia's first freely elected president, Boris Yeltsin, was suffering from a "cold." When the Russian media recalled that, in the past, "colds" had proved lethal for some of the country's rulers (former presidents Konstantin Chernenko and Yuri Andropov were dead within weeks after catching "colds"), the Kremlin shifted course and said that Yeltsin had the "flu," which later proved to be a euphemism for a heart problem that necessitated a multiple bypass operation. Soon after that, Yeltsin came down with one more "cold"— this time allegedly the result of a postsauna chill—which metamorphosed into a two-month bout of pneumonia and created another presidential stagnation.[5] To top it all off, an influential Moscow newspaper was already reporting that a putsch against the ailing Yeltsin was in the making.[6]

There is reason to conclude that his failing health, combined with the fear that he might be thrown out of power and accused of stealing billions and of dismembering the Soviet Union, eventually convinced a weakened Yeltsin to place his fate in the hands of Russia's historically powerful political police.

At the end of December 1999, Yeltsin unexpectedly abdicated. "I shouldn't be in the way of the natural course of history," he explained, speaking in front of a gaily-decorated New Year's tree and a Russian flag with a golden eagle. "I understand that *I must do it* and Russia *must* enter the new millennium with new politicians, with new faces, with new intelligent, strong, energetic people."[7] Yeltsin then signed a decree stating that, under Article 92 Section 3 of the Russian Constitution, the power of the Russian president would be temporarily performed by the recently appointed Prime

Minister Vladimir Putin. Yeltsin also announced that a special presidential election would be held around March 27, 2000, and he made a strong appeal for people to vote for Putin—a former KGB general—who was "a strong person worthy of becoming president."[8]

For his part, Putin signed a decree pardoning Yeltsin—who was reportedly connected to massive bribery scandals—"for any possible misdeeds" and granting him "total immunity" from being prosecuted (or even searched and questioned) for "any and all" actions committed while in office. Putin also gave Yeltsin a lifetime pension and a state dacha (summer home).[9]

This had all the appearances of a behind-the-scenes KGB putsch. The events that preceded and those that followed Putin's sudden promotion strongly suggest that it was. Yeltsin made history by outlawing the Communist Party and dissolving the Soviet Union. Putin, however, began to rebuild the country's confidence in its Soviet institutions. He spoke publicly and with fondness about his years in the KGB, claiming to have inherited his desire to work for this institution from his grandfather, who was a cook at one of Stalin's dachas, and from his father, who had "links" of some kind to the KGB— meaning at the least that he reported on his friends and neighbors. Putin asked his nation to understand that the secret police agency "works in the interest of the state." He argued for patience, pointing out that "90 percent" of all KGB intelligence was collected with the collaboration of ordinary citizens.[10]

This spin worked with the Russian people, who regarded Putin as disarmingly honest. Their admiration for him began in December 1999, when as prime minister he viciously lashed out at Soviet defectors, calling his former colleague General Oleg Kalugin, who had quit the KGB after the August 1991 coup and settled in the United States, a "traitor" and an "absolute loafer."[11] Soviet people were still highly addicted to Soviet anti-Americanism. Putin then went to the Lubyanka, the building that has headquartered the Soviet Union's political police since its creation, to celebrate the birth of the *Cheka*, the first Soviet political police organization, founded on December 20, 1917. "Several years ago, we fell prey to the illusion that we have no enemies," Putin told a meeting of top security officials. "We have paid dearly for this. Russia has its own national interests, and *we* have to defend them."[12]

The next day, December 21, 1999, Putin organized a closed-door reception in his Kremlin office, allegedly for politicians who had won seats in the Duma. By coincidence, that was also Stalin's 120th birthday, and Putin took the opportunity to raise a glass to good old Stalin.[13] According to the Russian magazine *Novaya Gazeta*, his toast was addressed to "Dzhugashvili." Stalin, meaning *man of steel*, was the dictator's nom de guerre; Iosif Vissarionovich Dzhugashvili was his real name.[14]

A couple of days later, in a fourteen-page article titled "Russia on the Threshold of a New Millennium," Putin defined Russia's new political future: "The state must be where and as needed; freedom must be where and as required."[15] In the same article, Putin labeled the Chechens' effort to regain their independence as "terrorism," and he pledged to eradicate it: "We'll get them anywhere—if we find terrorists sitting in the outhouse, then we will piss on them there. The matter is settled."[16]

In March 2000, Putin was officially elected president, but people did not know who he really was. His framers introduced into Russian schoolbooks a page of purple prose dedicated to the young Volodya Putin, depicting him as a national hero:

> This is your president, the one responsible for everything in this country. He is not afraid of anything. He flies in fighter planes, skis down mountains and goes where there is fighting to stop wars. And all the other presidents of other countries meet with him and respect him very much. And they show this on television and write about it in newspapers. Then he had so many friends—the entire country of Russia—and they elected him president. Now every one says: Russia, Putin, Unity![17]

The cover of some of these schoolbooks, released in September 2000, carried a drawing of a boy resembling Putin who was pointing an accusing finger, apparently at a dishonest bureaucrat, and saying: "Comrade children! Be vigilant, know your rights."[18] The media in Russia were also still largely state-controlled. They described the unknown Putin as a man of the people, someone who did not mince words but who, like regular folks, said what was on his mind.[19]

By 2002, Russia was also mass-producing official portraits and busts of Putin—just as Romania had produced Ceaușescu's when he was still unknown. Putin passed them off as mere state symbolism, like the flag or the national anthem, adding that he would be charmed if the portraits and busts would remain on people's desks and walls after his term of office.[20] Russians will have to wait and see if there is going to be an "after" to his term of office.

Once installed in the saddle, Putin ordered that the statue of Yuri Andropov be reinstated at the Lubyanka, from where it had been removed after the KGB coup in 1991.[21] Andropov was the only other KGB officer to have been enthroned in the Kremlin, and it was therefore logical for Putin to pay homage to him.

Putin took another page from Andropov's book and started filling the most important Kremlin positions with undercover KGB officers, many of whom came from St. Petersburg—where Putin had most recently been assigned.[22] They would become known as "Putinburgers."[23] He signed a decree creating a new structure to increase central Kremlin control over Russia's ninety-eight administrative regions; he divided the country into seven "super" districts, each headed by a "presidential representative,"[24] and he gave five of these seven new posts to former KGB officers.[25] He also appointed former KGB general Viktor Ivanov as the deputy head of his administration.[26]

Soon after that, former KGB officers became Russia's ministers of foreign affairs and defense. Numerous others became high-ranking members of the government. In a brief interview with Ted Koppel of the ABC News program *Nightline*, Putin acknowledged that he had brought KGB officers to the Kremlin, but he explained that it was because he wanted to root out graft. "I have known them for many years and I trust them. It has nothing to do with ideology. It's only a matter of their professional qualities and personal relationship."[27]

In reality, filling the most important government positions with undercover intelligence officers was another Russian tradition. The tsar's Okhrana security service had its undercover agents planted everywhere, as Andropov pointed out to me in the early 1970s, when the Kremlin decided to Sovietize that traditionally Russian concept. Until 1913, *Pravda* itself was edited by such an agent, Roman Malinovsky, who had been recruited by the Okhrana while serving a jail term for theft and burglary. After he was released, the Okhrana covered up his criminal record and placed him in Lenin's Communist Party, where he gradually rose to become the editor of *Pravda* and later Lenin's deputy for Russia and chairman of the Bolshevik faction in the Duma.[28] According to Andropov, he was also one of Lenin's best friends. The Okhrana's framing of Malinovsky worked wonders.

From Andropov, I also learned that all Soviet bloc citizens responsible for running the diplomatic, foreign trade, economic, technological, and even religious activities in the West should now be made undercover intelligence officers. It was something like the wartime militarization of the government, but it had to be accomplished by the foreign intelligence service rather than the army. Ceaușescu's Romania followed step.

By 1978, when I broke with communism, the lines separating the top leadership of the country from the intelligence apparatus had become blurred. A couple of weeks after I was granted political asylum in the United States, the Western news media reported that my defection had unleashed the greatest political purge in the history of communist Romania. Ceaușescu fired one third of his cabinet members, demoted four Politburo members, and replaced twenty-two ambassadors. All were undercover DIE officers on whose military documents and pay vouchers I had regularly signed off.

On December 31, 2000, President Putin, celebrating his first anniversary as president, announced that Russia had a new national anthem. In fact, the law signed by Putin restored the melody of Stalin's national anthem, which had been prohibited after the collapse of the Soviet Union. Those original lyrics, written by the poet Sergey Mikhalkov, praised Stalin, Lenin, the Communist Party, and the "unbreakable" Soviet Union. At Khrushchev's request, Mikhalkov wrote a second version of the lyrics, removing Stalin's name, after his memory had become politically unpalatable. Mikhalkov has now again rewritten his lyrics, this time to satisfy Putin.[29]

Yelena Bonner, the widow of the Nobel Peace Prize winner Andrey Sakharov, denounced Putin's actions in this matter as a "profanation of history." Putin disagreed, explaining: "We have overcome the differences between the past and the present."[30]

In April 2000, just seven days after Putin had been overwhelmingly elected Russia's president, American businessman Edmund Pope was arrested by the FSB. He was charged with espionage, but his trial evolved into a farce. Professor Anatoly Babkin, the main FSB witness against Pope, recanted his testimony and stated that he had been forced to sign it. The FSB threatened to put Babkin in jail, but he still withdrew the charges. The Russian research institute where Babkin worked provided the court with documents showing that all the technical material given to Pope was unclassified and had been legally sold to him. Nevertheless, Pope was found guilty and was sentenced to twenty years in prison based on a verdict that was written in just two and a half hours.[31]

Once again, the United States had been framed to look like an enemy of Russia. Then, on December 12, 2000, Pope was magnanimously pardoned by President Putin,[32] just as other Americans ludicrously framed by the KGB had been pardoned by Putin's predecessors. By that time the damage was done, however. Particularly for domestic consumption, the United States had once again been shown up as an enemy of Russia. Most Russians started looking at Putin with admiration—standing up to the almighty America was not a small matter.

According to a March 2001 Russian government press release, a series of trumped-up, closed-door espionage trials against the United States were underway in Moscow on charges "so lacking in evidence and so far-fetched in their suppositions that at least three of them have been thrown out by Russian appeals courts."[33] Those setbacks did not discourage Putin's government, however, which, in each instance, responded to the not-guilty verdict by reopening the case against its target.

In March 2001, for instance, Vladimir Moiseyev, a career Russian diplomat, was on his third trial for the same charge—spying for the United States and its main ally in Asia, South Korea. The "incriminating" document presented by the FSB turned out to be a copy of a speech that Moiseyev, an expert on South Korea, had delivered publicly. Nevertheless, since July 1998 he had been jailed by the FSB, whose then-chairman, Gen. Vladimir Putin, had publicly declared that the case "was proven beyond a doubt."[34]

Throughout its existence, the Soviet Union was deeply anti-American, and most Russians grew up hating the United States. That hatred now made them fall for Putin's anti-Americanism.

Putin is a difficult read, but the Russians are enthralled with him, partly for that very reason. The night of November 20, 1998 was shattering for millions of Russians: Galina Starovoitova, the country's leading female political dissident, was shot dead in St. Petersburg. Her most trusted aide, Ruslan Linkov, was also shot but survived. During the Soviet years, Galina had worked with Nobel Prize-winner Andrei Sakharov, and she was still fighting the KGB, now rebaptized as FSB, which faced credible allegations that it had authored the assassination. While some ten thousand mourners gathered to pay their respects to Galina and to demand that the killers be brought to justice, Linkov was visited by his worst nightmare—Vladimir Putin, the head of the FSB. Putin held Linkov's hand for more than an hour and kept reassuring him: "It's all going to be okay. It's all going to be okay."[35]

Putin's co-workers call him the "Gray Cardinal" for his secrecy and Vatican-like mastery of intrigue. The Russian people admire his icy-blue eyes as indicative of the strong, silent type, a real man, who chooses his few words with great care. Russians also love Byzantine deception—generations of them have kidded themselves about the glorious state of their country—and Putin makes them feel clever again. In 2000, for instance, while Putin was dining with King Juan Carlos in Madrid, word came out that the FSB had arrested Vladimir Gusinsky, Russia's biggest media mogul. Putin originally pleaded ignorance. The next day, though, he revealed a surprising familiarity with the arrest. A week later, in Berlin, Putin condemned as "excessive" the measures taken against Gusinsky. Back in Moscow, Putin launched the rumor that the arrest was a provocation against himself. Eventually, the Kremlin-controlled MOST radio station insinuated that Gusinsky's arrest was an unfortunate retaliation for President Clinton's public support for Gusinsky during his recent visit to Moscow.[36] Case closed.

When you get right down to it, Putin's magic derives from his following the tradition of cloaking himself in secrecy. Soviet rulers did not become known until after they were gone. It is true that one might get a glimpse of Putin's love of karate through occasional carefully managed appearances, or by seeing pictures of him showing off as an older "Tarzan," half-naked with a knife under his belt or a rifle in his hand, but on the whole Putin looks even less three-dimensional than his caricature-like Soviet predecessors did.

Why should Putin be so secretive about himself in today's Internet age? For one thing, he spent most of his working life as a spy and has secretiveness in his blood—no one was supposed to know what he did. Nor is Putin an "ideologue," whose work and speeches can be scrutinized in a search for the man behind them. He is not a creator, but rather a creation. He is a product of the KGB, not a Lenin who built that KGB. He is a product of the Kremlin's anti-Americanism, not a Stalin who spawned that anti-Americanism. He is a product of the Kremlin's nuclear proliferation and anti-American terrorism, not a Khrushchev who authored both.

During the old Soviet days, the West invented Kremlinology, a discipline of trying to decode whatever was going on behind the Kremlin's wall of secrecy by, for instance, comparing the annual photos of the May Day parade to see which Politburo member stood closest to the ruler. Now we have Putinologists, like Prof. Stephen White of Glasgow University, Prof. Michael McFaul of Stanford University, and the Hoover Institution's John Dunlop. They do their best with the meager information available on their subject, but it is nearly impossible for an outsider to put himself in the shoes of a man whose career was spent in the darkness of Soviet espionage and who has deception in his bones.

35

FROM "HITLER'S POPE" TO SEPTEMBER 11, 2001

W ITH THE FRAMING OF PIUS XII as "Hitler's Pope," the Kremlin began to make anti-Semitism an international movement. The low point came in 1975, when Yuri Andropov used the United Nations to officially brand Zionism as evil. The Soviet bloc *dezinformatsiya* machinery worked around the clock to persuade the leaders of Third World countries to adopt a UN resolution declaring that Zionism was "a form of racism and racial discrimination." Officially presented as an Arab initiative, the resolution had actually been drafted in Moscow and was supported by Palestine Liberation Organization leader and KGB puppet Yasser Arafat, along with several friendly Arab governments, Cuba's Fidel Castro, and most of the Soviet bloc.

The KGB community disseminated hundreds of anti-American and anti-Semitic cartoons around UN headquarters in New York. Andropov used to preach that, in the Third World, cartoons were much more convincing than documentary materials. By 1975, the clandestine distribution of cartoons around the premises of UN headquarters had become such a common Soviet bloc occurrence that my DIE had to assign a graphics expert (Maj. Gheorghe Roşu) to its station in New York. Coauthor Rychlak interned at the United Nations in 1979, and he remembers seeing such propaganda at that time.

That so-called Arab initiative was adopted as UN Resolution 3379 by seventy-two countries—actually only a slight majority, considering that thirty-five nations voted against it and thirty-two abstained. Soon after that, the Soviet bloc intelligence community unleashed a vitriolic *dezinformatsiya* campaign portraying the United States and Israel as Zionists. In December 1991, only a few months after the Soviet-led voting bloc disintegrated, that anti-Semitic resolution was repealed by the large margin of 111 to 25. Nevertheless, the UN continued to treat Israel as an enemy. By 2002, the United Nations General Assembly had passed 408 resolutions condemning Israel,[1] the only UN member prohibited from holding a seat on the Security Council.[2] The total number of votes cast against Israel up to that same date: 55,642.[3] And on November 29, 2012, the UN General Assembly voted overwhelmingly—138 to 9 (with 41 abstaining)—to upgrade the PLO's status to a "non-member observer state."

No Arab terrorist state or organization had been condemned by the UN. The reason? The Soviet bloc had successfully turned a significant part of this organization against Israel and its main supporter, the United States—the very country that had formulated its motto: "We the People of the United Nations, United for a Better World." During my last ten years in Romania, the Soviet bloc intelligence community poured millions of dollars and thousands of people into this gigantic project. When I defected, virtually all UN employees and representatives from the communist countries (comprising one-third of the world's population) and their Arab allies were secretly working, in one way or another, for the bloc's espionage services. Their main task was to portray Israel and the United States as Zionist countries whose aim was to transform the rest of the world into a Jewish fiefdom.

In August 1998, one of Andropov's pupils, KGB General Yevgeny Primakov, who rose as Russia's spy chief after the Soviet Union collapsed, became prime minister. Under Primakov—who converted to rabid anti-Semitism during the years he spent as Soviet adviser to Iraq's Saddam Hussein—anti-Semitism threatened to become a national policy in Russia.

In October 1998, retired General Albert Makashov, then a member of the *Duma*, called for the "extermination of all Jews in Russia." He insinuated that the Jews were being paid by American Zionism to ruin the motherland. Over and over again Russian television replayed Makashov screaming in the Duma: "I will round up all [the Jews] and send them to the next world."[4] On November 4, 1998, the Duma defeated a parliamentary motion censuring Makashov's hate-filled statement by a vote of 121-107. Eighty-three of the

Communist Party's 132 members in the Duma voted against censure, and of the remainder, all but one declined to vote. At the November 7, 1998, demonstration marking the eighty-first anniversary of the October Revolution, crowds of former KGB officers showed their support for the general, chanting "Hands off Makashov!" and waving signs with anti-Semitic slogans.[5]

On August 3, 2001, *ninety-eight* US senators sent a letter to President Putin expressing concern about the rise of anti-Semitism in the Russian Federation:

> In years past, the US Senate has been united in its condemnation of such virulent anti-Semitism, which, unfortunately, has been present during much of Russia's history. Your remarks last year publicly condemning anti-Semitism assume special significance against a backdrop of centuries of tsarist and Stalinist persecutions. We strongly encourage you to continue to publicly condemn anti-Semitism whenever it manifests itself in the Russian Federation. We also believe that it is important to back up the rhetoric of condemnation with the substance of action.[6]

A few days later, however, a new KGB-style operation aimed at spreading hatred for Zionism and the Jews around the world mushroomed up. On August 31, 2001, a UN "World Conference on Racism, Racial Discrimination, Xenophobia and Related Intolerance" opened in Durban, South Africa. A main objective was to approve another resolution asserting that Zionism was a brutal form of racism, and that the United States and Israel were its main supporters.[7] Yasser Arafat, Fidel Castro, and the same gaggle of Arab and Third World governments that had supported the UN anti-Semitic Resolution No. 3379 in 1975, urged participants to condemn Israel and the United States as Zionist powers who wanted to conquer the Islamic world.[8]

Of course, at that very moment, Russia's federal and local governments were being run by former officers of the same Soviet political police that had vandalized Jewish cemeteries in Germany and France, framed Pius XII as "Hitler's Pope," portrayed the United States and Israel as mortal enemies of the Islamic world, and been the ghostwriters of the UN's anti-Semitic Resolution No. 3379. The proceedings at the Durban conference reveal an unmistakable Soviet *dezinformatsiya* pattern. The day after Arafat's speech, anti-Semitic cartoons carpeted the conference grounds.

On September 3, 2001, the United States withdrew its delegation from Durban, charging that the UN conference had been "converted into a forum against Israel and Jews."[9] The Israeli government followed suit. On September 4, 2001, Congressman Tom Lantos, a member of the US delegation, told reporters, "This conference will stand self-condemned for yielding to extremists." He added, "I am blaming them for hijacking this conference."[10]

The September 11, 2001, attacks came eight days later. On that same day the KGB was celebrating 124 years since the birth of its founder, Feliks Dzerzhinsky. The weapon of choice for that horrific act of terrorism that has changed the face of our world was the hijacked airplane, a concept that had been invented by the KGB.

The anti-Semitism revived through Soviet disinformation has been transformed into bloody hatred for "American Zionism." This is another legacy of Khrushchev's and Andropov's *dezinformatsiya*. After September 11, 2001, thousands of people in the Islamic world danced in the streets for days to celebrate the glorious victory over the American evil. Killing Americans, Jews, and their allies became a way to energize Islamic extremists by giving them "victories" to celebrate. In March 2002, a stream of Palestinians lined up in a Fatah-controlled refugee camp to pay their congratulations to the father and brother of eighteen-year-old Mohamed Daraghmed, who had just killed five children and four women in a suicide bombing attack in Israel.[11]

The imam of the leading mosque in New York (the Ninety-Sixth Street Mosque) claimed, in an interview published in Egypt, that the Jews were responsible for the World Trade Center and Pentagon attacks.[12] "It was Mossad and Israel that perpetrated those horrible crimes," agreed Mohamed Ali Eliah, the imam of the Islamic House of Wisdom in Dearborn Heights, Michigan. "How else do you explain that four thousand Jews didn't show up for work at the Twin Towers the morning of September 11?"[13]

The twenty-six-year-old Mohammad Junaid told Britain's ITN television network: "My mother was in the north tower of the World Trade Center, but I still feel absolutely no remorse for what happened on September 11." He added: "I may hold an American passport, but I am not an American— I am a Muslim." Soon after that, Junaid, whose mother had been led to safety from the blazing World Trade Center by New York firefighters, bought a one-way ticket to Pakistan to sign up with the Taliban. "I will kill every American that I see in Afghanistan. And I'll kill every American soldier that I see in Pakistan."[14]

Eventually, Andropov's new anti-American and anti-Jewish terrorism seems to have grown into a kind of a nefarious "science" threatening the whole civilized world. A seven-thousand-page *Encyclopedia of Jihad* (circulated in the form of a CD-ROM), was found in 1999 in the home of Arab terrorist Khalil Deek when he was arrested for allegedly plotting to bomb Jordan's main airport on the eve of the millennium. The book's eleventh volume (which is on a separate CD-ROM) details how to poison water and food supplies with ricin, a highly toxic chemical used by Moscow in terrorist actions, most notoriously in the umbrella-tip murder of Bulgarian dissident Georgi Markov, carried out in London by Andropov's KGB and its Bulgarian puppet in 1978.[15]

36

THE KREMLIN'S NUCLEAR
TERRORISM

WAS IT MERE COINCIDENCE that the September 11, 2001, terrorist attacks on New York's World Trade Towers and the Pentagon took place on the very day that the KGB was celebrating the birthday of its founder, Feliks Dzerzhinsky? That is hard to know. By their very nature, foreign intelligence operations are secret, arcane and duplicitous undertakings. In the words of a former head of the British foreign intelligence service MI6, Stella Rimington, unraveling them is "like the unraveling of a knotted skein of wool. You get hold of an end and you have to follow it through until you are near enough to the heart of the knot to see what it consists of."[1]

Let us try to unravel the skein tangled around September 11. During the years I was at the top of the Soviet bloc intelligence community, I knew that symbolism constituted a very important secret message for the "initiated." The Kremlin had a penchant for symbolism, another weapon of the emotions successfully wielded by all Russian tsars and their communist successors. The emblem of the Soviet Union consisted of a hammer and a sickle, to symbolize the alliance between the proletariat and the peasants. The emblem of the Kremlin's political police was a sword and a shield, symbolizing its duties: to put the country's enemies to the sword, and to shield and protect the communist revolution. Most of the KGB-financed international terrorist organizations were called "liberation" movements, to symbolize the

Soviet bloc's commitment to liberating the rest of the world from American imperialism/Zionism.

Andropov and his East European viceroys raised a glass of champagne to celebrate the terrorist bomb that exploded in Jerusalem's Zion Square on July 4, 1975, leaving fifteen dead and sixty-four wounded. That was clearly a slap at the United States, whose national day is the Fourth of July. It was also significant that the first attack on the World Trade Center, which was intended to knock the North Tower into the South Tower and to generate mass killing, took place on February 26, 1993, when the Kremlin was celebrating forty-one years since the first Soviet nuclear test. The suicide attack against the US Navy destroyer USS *Cole*, in which seventeen sailors were killed and 39 injured, took place on October 12, 2000. That was the anniversary of the beginning of Israel's major offensive of 1973, which was decisive in Israel's winning the Yom Kippur War. The significance of the failed bombing attempts over Detroit and New York on Christmas Day 2009 needs no explanation.

There are many other "coincidences" in the course of Russia's recent policy decisions strongly suggesting that they were not accidental. In 2002, for instance, Putin and the ex-KGB officers who are now ruling Russia began openly moving their country back into the encampment of the former Soviet Union's traditional clients—which had been the deadliest enemies of Zionism and the United States. Putin started out with the exact same three terrorist governments named by President George W. Bush as an "Axis of Evil"—Iran, Iraq, and North Korea.

In March 2002, Putin quietly reinstituted the sale of Russian weapons to Iran. In August 2002, he concluded a $40 billion trade deal with Saddam Hussein's tyrannical regime in Iraq. Then, just before September 2002, while the United States was preparing to mourn its victims of the previous year's terrorist attack, Putin received Kim Jung Il, North Korea's despicable dictator (who has since passed away) in Moscow with grand honors.[2] At the same time, Putin began quietly helping the highly anti-Semitic government of the Islamic Republic of Iran to construct a 1,000-megawatt nuclear reactor at Bushehr, with a uranium conversion facility able to produce fissile material for nuclear weapons. The West stood silent, just as it had stood silent. No one wanted to remember Ayatollah Khomeini's dire threat of 1980:

We do not worship Iran, we worship Allah. For patriotism is another name for paganism. I say let this land burn. I say let this land go up in smoke, provided Islam emerges triumphant in the rest of the world.[3]

During the first decade of the 21st century, a wave of new books violently asserting that Pius XII was "Hitler's Pope" inundated the West.[4] These books, beginning with John Cornwell's 1999 book, *Hitler's Pope*, are being used to persuade young people to abandon Christianity and to move toward Islam. Rychlak has received letters from prisoners who complain that this is rampant in American penitentiaries.

The revival of Pius XII's image as "Hitler's Pope" is also pushing the world toward a nuclear midnight, prepared by Iran. Its first target is Israel. The rest of the Judeo-Christian world will come next. The 1945 nuclear bombs dropped on Hiroshima and Nagasaki caused the immediate deaths of an estimated 80,000 people. When factoring in the deaths from the long-term effects of radiation, the total toll is estimated at 120,000. Today's nuclear weapons are many times stronger.

Khrushchev and his political necrophagy are to blame for the nightmare of the new Holocaust now facing us, carried out by a deeply anti-Semitic Iran armed with nuclear weapons and a dangerous North Korea. Khrushchev liked to portray himself as a peasant, but that was misleading. Everywhere in the world, peasants have a sense of property. Khrushchev did not. As previously noted, he matured politically in a period when Soviet communists were bent on eradicating private property, and he developed an eminently destructive nature. Khrushchev smashed Stalin's statues, shattered the Soviet Union's image as a workers' paradise, demolished international communist unity, destroyed the reputation of Pius XII, revived anti-Semitism and generated today's international terrorism, all without constructing anything new to fill the vacuum he created.

Khrushchev also overturned Stalin's policy of nonproliferation of his nuclear weapons. I never met Stalin, but I heard plenty of stories about him from Khrushchev and Igor Kurchatov, an undercover intelligence officer who headed the Soviet equivalent of the Manhattan Project. According to them, Stalin was a kind of Geppetto, the Italian carpenter who carved a piece of wood that could laugh and cry like a child. Stalin's Pinocchio was his first nuclear bomb. He baptized it "Iosif-1." On September 29, 1949, when Beriya called him from the Semipalatinsk test site in Kazakhstan to say that "Iosif-1" had produced the same devastating mushroom cloud as the American "Fat Man," Stalin was sitting on top of the world.

"That day, Stalin swore to keep nuclear power to himself," I heard Fré-déric Joliot-Curie say in August 1955, when I was a member of the Romanian delegation at the United Nations Geneva Conference on the Peaceful Use of Atomic Energy. The French nuclear physicist and prominent communist claimed he had been with Stalin in his office when Beriya called him from the Semipalatinsk test site.

Everything changed after Stalin died. After killing off the leaders of the Soviet Union's political police and his potential rivals, Khrushchev needed a positive boost, so he decided to repair Stalin's smoldering rift with China with a big bang. At the beginning of 1955, he approved Mao's request to help his country produce nuclear weapons. That, together with Khrushchev's political necrophagy, opened a Pandora's box and unleashed an international nightmare.

In April 1955, Khrushchev set up a joint venture aimed at helping China produce nuclear weapons. The KGB, which had—and still has, in its current incarnation—custody of all the Soviet Union's nuclear weapons, coordinated the operation. KGB-sponsored experts began building the essentials of China's new military nuclear industry, which was expressly designed to target "American Zionism."

Five years later, however, the relations between Khrushchev and Mao Zedong started to sour. The Chinese leader grew increasingly unhappy with Khrushchev's de-Stalinization and took at face value his proclaimed policy of peaceful coexistence with the West. He branded Khrushchev "soft on imperialism" and accused him of abandoning communist principles.

Mao's prime minister, Zhou Enlai, made several visits to Romania, where I repeatedly heard him say that Mao had gotten tired of Khrushchev and had started openly displaying his discontent—in a Chinese way. Zhou, speaking fluent French,[5] described for his Romanian hosts how Mao "smoked like a locomotive" during his meetings with Khrushchev, even though he knew of the Soviet leader's aversion to cigarettes. Even worse, during a 1958 meeting in Beijing, Mao, who was an Olympic-class swimmer, took his guest over to his Olympic swimming pool, even though he knew Khrushchev could not swim. It was hilarious, Zhou said, to see Khrushchev bobbing around in an inner tube while the Chairman swam rings around him, like a fish.

I did not know if all Zhou Enlai's stories were true—communist leaders were famous for their lies. Neither do we know any better now, since the secret archives of the Soviet Union and Red China are both still sealed. But when Khrushchev attended the Third Congress of the Romanian Workers Party in Bucharest in June 1960, he publicly attacked Mao. In return, he received a blistering response from the chief of the Chinese delegation. I observed the confrontation between the Ukrainian flowered shirt and the Chinese high-buttoned uniform, and I heard the Romanian leader, Gheorghe Gheorghiu-Dej, say that the incident might assume catastrophic dimensions in the volatile mind of "the peasant"—meaning Khrushchev.

A few weeks after the Third Congress, the Soviet bloc was indeed treated to a sample of Khrushchev's political necrophagy and his destructive tendency to tinker with every decision. Khrushchev suddenly withdrew all Soviet advisers from China and terminated all important joint projects. According to the Chinese, Moscow pulled out 1,390 experts, tore up 343 contracts, and scrapped 257 cooperative projects in just a few weeks.[6] The joint nuclear weapon project was among them, but by then the Chinese had learned enough to continue it on their own. Data provided by various US intelligence agencies attest that by the mid-1980s, China was producing at least 400 kilograms of plutonium-239 per year. The exact strength of the Chinese strategic force is still relatively unknown—at least outside the CIA— but in 1996 the number of warheads was estimated at 2,500, with 140–150 more being produced each year.[7]

Khrushchev did not survive his own efforts at nuclear proliferation. Nevertheless, he did light the fuse that ignited the production of Stalin's "Iosif-1" in North Korea and generated Ahmadinejad's nuclear Iran.

37

A KGB EMPIRE

DURING THE TWENTY YEARS Aleksandr Sakharovsky was my de facto boss, the Soviet general, who was a Russian to the marrow of his bones, repeatedly said, "Every society reflects its own past." Sakharovsky believed that someday "our socialist camp" might wear an entirely different face. Marxism might be turned upside down, and even the Communist Party itself might become history, but that would not matter. Both Marxism and the party were foreign organisms that had been introduced into the Russian body, and sooner or later they would have to be rejected in any case. One thing, though, was certain to remain unchanged for as long as the Russian motherland was still in existence: "our *gosbezopasnost*" (the state security service).

Sakharovsky used to point out that "our *gosbezopasnost*" had kept Russia alive for the past five hundred years; "our *gosbezopasnost*" would guide her helm for the next five hundred years, would win the war with "our main enemy, American Zionism," and would eventually make Russia the leader of the world.

So far, Sakharovsky has proved to be a dependable prophet. His successor at the PGU, Vladimir Kryuchkov—who later became chairman of the whole KGB and authored the August 1991 KGB coup that briefly deposed Gorbachev—clearly shared the same fanatical belief in Russia's *gosbezopasnost*. Kryuchkov's successor, Yevgeny Primakov, who had been an undercover KGB officer under Sakharovsky, rose to become Russia's prime minister. Most notably, Vladimir Putin was the very chief of the entire *gosbezopasnost* before being appointed (not elected!) Russia's president.

On September 11, 2002, large numbers of ranking *gosbezopasnost* officers gathered at the Lubyanka. They had not congregated to sympathize with the United States on the first anniversary of its national tragedy as a victim of terrorism, but to celebrate the 125th birthday of Feliks Dzerzhinsky—the man who had created the Soviet political police, one of the most anti-Christian and anti-Semitic institutions in history. A few days later, Moscow's mayor reversed his previous opposition and said he wanted to restore Dzerzhinsky's bronze statue to its former place of honor on Lubyanka Square.[1] The next year, the slogan "Russia for the Russians" started making noise in Russia, and a nationwide poll showed that 42 percent of the population believed that Jews ought to be barred from power.[2]

The Cold War is indeed over, but unlike other wars, that one did not end with the defeated enemy throwing down its weapons. The barbarous KGB, which in the course of its existence slaughtered at least 20 million people at home and another 70 million throughout the communist world, not only survived, but it also transformed today's Russia into the first intelligence dictatorship in history.

Now Putin and his ex-KGB cronies own Russia. According to the respected British *Guardian,* Putin has secretly accumulated more than $40 billion, becoming Russia's—and Europe's—richest man. He is said to own at least: 37 percent of the stock (worth $18 billion) of Surgutneftegs, Russia's third-largest oil producer; 4.5 percent of the stock (worth $13 billion) of Gazprom, the largest extractor of natural gas in the world; and 75 percent (worth $10 billion) of Gunvor, a mysterious oil trader based in Geneva.[3] Putin's puppet, Dmitry Medvedev—who was the Russian president until Putin (who had faced term limits) won it back in 2012—was chairman of Gazprom, which accounts for 93 percent of Russian natural gas production and controls 16% of the world's reserves. Putin's first deputy prime minister, Igor Sechin, is chairman of Rosneft, the biggest oil company in the world.[4]

Oil and gas account not only for Putin's exorbitant wealth, but for 50 percent of the Russian budget and 65 percent of its exports as well. When the price of oil went over $122 a barrel on May 6, 2008, analysts pointed to attacks on pipelines in Nigeria and turmoil in Iraq. Russia, however, made a fortune. Other disruptions of foreign oil supplies may give Russia—and Putin—other fortunes. Putin's Kremlin seems to be well aware of that possibility.

On July 12, 2006, militants of Hezbollah ("Party of God"), a deeply anti-Semitic Muslim fundamentalist group based in Lebanon but armed by Putin's Russia, launched a powerful rocket attack against Israel. That attack was followed by a thirty-four-day Israeli offensive against the attacker. Most of the Hezbollah weapons cases captured by the Israeli military forces during that offensive were marked: "Customer: Ministry of Defense of Syria. Supplier: KBP, Tula, Russia."[5]

In October 2010, the same Russian-supported Hezbollah conducted a drill simulating the takeover of Israel. The European Union-sponsored Gulf Research Centre, which provides journalists an inside view of the Gulf Center Region, found out that Hezbollah's military forces were armed with a large quantity of the "Soviet-made Katyusha-122 rocket, which carries a 33-lb warhead." Hezbollah was also armed with Russian-designed and Iranian-made Fajr-5 rockets which can reach the Israeli port of Haifa, and with the Russian-designed Zelzal-1 rockets, which can reach Tel Aviv. Hezbollah also possessed the infamous Russian Scud missiles, as well as Russian antitank missiles AT-3 Sagger, AT-4 Spigot, AT-5 Spandrel, AT-13 Saxhorn-2, and AT-14 Spriggan Kornet.[6]

With the passage of time, evidence has begun to reveal that Putin's Kremlin was involved in igniting, and then stealing, the 2011 Islamic revolutions. In Egypt, the most pro-American Islamic country, antigovernment demonstrations started on January 25, 2011, when people took to the streets to protest poverty, unemployment, and government corruption. Over the next few days, Cairo's Tahrir Square filled with a sea of Hezbollah's green flags mixed with red hammer-and-sickle banners. Some of the young people there who were allegedly demanding democracy could be seen burning the flag of the very country that symbolizes democracy for most of the world—the United States.

According to news media reports, on January 30, 2011, "a joint Hezbollah-Hamas unit used the rebellion's havoc in Egypt to storm the Wadi el-Natroun prison north of Cairo, and break out 22 members of Hezbollah's spy-cum-terror network led by Sami Shehab, who had been convicted for plotting terrorist attacks in Cairo, the Suez Canal and Suez cities, and on Israeli vacationers in Sinai in 2007–2008.[7] The plan was to release these terrorists and as many Muslim Brotherhood inmates as possible, in order to "organize" and "boost" the street protests.[8]

The leader of the Russian-armed Hezbollah, Sayyed Hassan Nasrallah, admitted to sending Sami Shehab to Egypt as head of a twenty-two-man force charged with carrying out terrorist operations aimed at destabilizing the country's pro-American government.[9] In a speech delivered to the rebels immediately after Shehab was freed from prison, Nasrallah said:

> I want to apologize to the youth of Tunisia and Egypt because we were late in announcing this message of support, which was not delayed due to hesitation or confusion . . . . If we addressed you before, it would have been said that Hezbollah cells were behind your mobilization—or Hamas or Iranian Revolutionary Guard cells."[10]

On February 20, 2011, the Meir Amit Intelligence and Terrorism Information Center released a report, published by the Egyptian daily *Al-Masri Al-Tawm*, stating that the real name of the just-freed Hezbollah terrorist leader Sami Shehab was Muhammad Yussuf Ahmed Mansour, that he was a trained operative in Unit 1800 of the Russian-armed Hezbollah, and that he had entered Egypt on a forged passport showing him to be an Egyptian.[11]

To an informed eye, the secret conversion of the Hezbollah operative Muhammad Mansour into the Egyptian Sami Shehab looks just like the KGB creation of the PLO chairman Yasser Arafat—but in reverse. The KGB, when I was still connected with it, went to great lengths to transform an Egyptian-born Marxist, Mohammed Yasser Abdel Rahman Abdel Raouf Arafat al-Qudwa al-Husseini, *nom de guerre* Abu Ammar, into a Palestinian-born Yasser Arafat. It took the KGB—and my DIE—many years to endow Arafat with a credible Palestinian birth certificate and other identity documents, to build him a new past, and to train him at the KGB Balashikha special-operations training school east of Moscow.[12] But as Andropov said, it was worth every minute. In 1994, the KGB-born-and-trained Arafat was awarded the Nobel Peace Prize. Yet in 2002 alone, there were a recorded 13,494 incidents of terrorism against Israelis, committed by Arafat's PLO. More than six hundred civilians had lost their lives.[13] Six months later, the number of Israeli civilians killed by Arafat's "martyrs" passed seven hundred.[14]

During the old Cold War, the KGB was a state within a state. Now the KGB, rechristened FSB, *is* the state. In 2003, more than six thousand former officers of the KGB—an organization that had in the past implicated and shot millions after framing them as Zionist spies—were running Russia's federal and local governments, and nearly half of all top governmental positions were held by former officers of the KGB. The Soviet Union had one KGB officer for every 428 citizens. In 2004, Putin's Russia had one FSB officer for every 297 citizens.[15]

Symbolic of this new era in Russia's history is the barbaric assassination of KGB defector Alexander Litvinenko in London in 2006, after he was framed as an "enemy of Russia" for exposing—in his book *Blowing Up Russia: The Secret Plot to Bring Back KGB Terror*—domestic crimes committed by the Putin administration. British intelligence documented that the crime was committed by Moscow, that it was "a 'state-sponsored' assassination orchestrated by Russian security services," and that it was perpetuated with Russian government-produced polonium-210.[16] The suspected killer, Russian citizen Andrey Lugovoy, was captured on cameras at Heathrow as he flew into Britain, carrying on him the murder weapon, polonium-210.[17] On May 22, 2007, the Crown Prosecution Service called for the extradition of Lugovoy to the UK on charges of murder.[18] On July 5, 2007, Russia declined to extradite Lugovoi.[19]

Also during 2007, the Russian KGB/FSB assassinated Ivan Safronov, a Russian military expert for the magazine *Kommersant* (and framed his death as a suicide) to prevent him from publishing an explosive article about the Kremlin's secret sale of SU-30 fighters to anti-American Syria. Safronov was the twenty-first journalist critical of the Kremlin to be killed since the progeny of Andropov's political police took over the Kremlin on December 31, 1999.[20] Well over 120 more Russian journalists have been killed since.[21]

Moreover, the little window into the KGB archives that had been cracked opened to Russian researchers by former president Boris Yeltsin was quietly closed. The fate of the tens of millions framed and killed by the KGB is still securely locked up behind the Lubyanka's walls. The KGB involvement in the war against religion—all religions—similarly continues to be shielded by a veil of secrecy.

On December 5, 2008, Aleksi II, the fifteenth Patriarch of Moscow and All Russia and the primate of the Russian Orthodox Church, died. He had worked for the KGB under the codename "Drozdov" and was awarded the KGB Certificate of Honor, as was revealed in a KGB archive accidentally left behind in Estonia when the Russians pulled out.[22] For the first time in its history, Russia had the opportunity to conduct the democratic election of a new patriarch, but that was not to be.

On January 27, 2009, the seven hundred Synod delegates assembled in Moscow were presented with a slate listing three candidates: Metropolitan Kirill of Smolensk (a secret member of the KGB codenamed "Mikhaylov"); Metropolitan Filaret of Minsk (who worked for the KGB under the code name "Ostrovsky"); and Metropolitan Kliment of Kaluga (who had the KGB codename "Topaz").[23]

When the bells at Christ the Savior Cathedral tolled to announce that a new patriarch had been elected, Kirill/"Mikhaylov" proved to be the winner. Regardless of whether he was the best leader for his church, he certainly was in a better position to influence the religious world abroad than were the other candidates. In 1971, the KGB had sent Kirill to Geneva as a representative of the Russian Orthodox Church to that Soviet propaganda machine the World Council of Churches. In 1975, the KGB infiltrated him into the Central Committee of the WCC, which had become a Kremlin pawn. In 1989 the KGB appointed him chairman of the Russian patriarchate's foreign relations as well. He still held those positions when he was elected patriarch.

In his acceptance speech as the new patriarch, "Mikhaylov" announced that he planned to take a trip to the Vatican in the near future. He also spoke about his intention to establish religious television channels in Russia that would broadcast to audiences abroad.

In Russia, the more things change, the more they seem to stay the same. The science of disinformation has proven to be such a wonder weapon that the Russians remain addicted to it. There is no end in sight to the Kremlin's manipulation of religions for the ultimate goal of consolidating its own power by widening the gap between Christianity, Judaism, and Islam.

38

KEEPING THE LIE-MACHINE GOING

FTER VLADIMIR PUTIN and his former KGB colleagues took over the Kremlin, the war against Zionist America exploded in Western Europe with the same fury as at the peak of the Cold War. Soon after we set foot in the new millennium, millions of Europeans began taking to the streets, not to celebrate the freedoms they enjoy because America liberated them from under the Nazi and Soviet boots, but to *condemn* the United States for its new war on terrorism. Once again the European left mobilized against its archenemy, Zionist America, persuading others around the world to join in gatherings conducted with all the passion of religious revival meetings. In 2001, when Osama bin Laden's terrorists declared war on the United States with their suicidal airplane attacks, those graying European Marxists who had taken to the streets to demonstrate against Americans when they were young Sorbonne students now took up their pens to condemn Americans once more.

The Russian backers supplying ideological instigation for this new anti-American offensive have become even more disturbing than the Kalashnikovs the al-Qaeda terrorists were pointing at us. French philosopher Jacques Derrida, who claimed he had broken with Marxism but still choked up with emotion whenever he heard "The Internationale,"[1] now began preaching that the Islamic war against the United States was justified because the United States was culturally alienated. Derrida therefore called for a "new Internationale" to unite all the environmentalists, feminists, gays, aboriginals, and other "dispossessed and marginalized" people who were combatting American-led globalization.[2]

Antonio Negri, a professor at the University of Padua who once was the brains behind the Italian Red Brigades—one of the KGB-financed leftist terrorist groups of the 1970s—and who served time in jail for his involvement in kidnapping and killing former Italian prime minister Aldo Moro, has now coauthored a virulently anti-American book entitled *Empire*. In it, Negri justifies Islamist terrorism as being a spearhead of "postmodern revolution" against American globalization—the new "empire"—which he claims is breaking up nation-states and creating huge unemployment.[3] The *New York Times* (which omitted any mention of Negri's involvement in terrorism) went so far as to call his modern-day *Communist Manifesto* "the hot, smart book of the moment."[4]

On December 14, 2002, the (Soviet-style) Secretariat of the (Soviet-created) World Peace Council, still headed by (KGB asset) Romesh Chandra, convened a meeting of its (Soviet-style) Executive Committee, which strongly "condemned the extremely dangerous escalation of US aggressiveness on the global level." An international appeal issued by the "WPC Secretariat" on the same day stated that "it is significant and encouraging to see large, unprecedented mobilizations against war and the problems of globalization that have been taking place in the recent period. Many and multiform movements that contest today's situation have been forming and growing. Demonstrations have been held in USA, Great Britain, Florence, Prague, and in many other European capitals as well as in other countries."[5]

The WPC document acknowledged that "the World Peace Council has participated in or co-organized these mobilizations," and it called on "peace movements to strengthen their struggle, take initiatives to mobilize the people and form links with the growing popular movement, at the same time boosting their autonomous action as WPC members and helping to form a broad and militant peace movement against the new world order."[6] The WPC official communiqué published at the conclusion of that meeting stated, in typical old Soviet-style: "The criminal Bush administration is intensifying readiness for the unilateral attack on Iraq, and this unilateralism of hegemony is becoming the biggest threat to world peace." The communiqué also called "upon the peoples and movements of the world aspiring to peace and justice to unite their voices and actions against the US war on Iraq."[7]

In early 2003, the same KGB-appointed Chandra, now honorary chairman of the World Peace Council, declared April 12 "international mobilization day" and called upon people throughout the world to organize demonstrations demanding that all governments "stop all support to the US and British murderers" and insisting that the UN General Assembly convene in order to stop the war in Iraq. WPC branches in at least fifty-seven countries joined in, calling for anti-American demonstrations. Over the April 12–13 weekend, more peace demonstrations were staged simultaneously around the world, with the largest in Athens and Moscow.

The Workers World Party (WWP) joined the fray. That was another KGB front known to me from when I served at the top of the Soviet bloc intelligence community. The WWP, which is headquartered in the United States, called for anti-American demonstrations on April 12, 2003 in Washington, Seattle, San Francisco, and Los Angeles, to condemn the "colonial occupation of Iraq" and to demand "regime change in Washington."[8]

The WWP was created by the KGB community in 1957, with the initial task of helping the Kremlin create a favorable impression of the 1956 Soviet invasion of Hungary among the trade unions and the "colored" population of the United States. It was run by a Soviet-style secretariat whose members were secretly indoctrinated and trained by the KGB, which also financed its day-to-day operation. In 1959, the WWP got its own newspaper, *Workers World*, which was edited by the KGB's disinformation department and was, for a while, printed in Romania together with the Cominform magazine (*For Lasting Peace, for Popular Democracy*). To camouflage Moscow's hand and to give the paper a broader appeal, the early issues showed both Lenin and Trotsky holding up a banner saying, "Colored and White Unite and Fight for a WORKERS WORLD."

Currently, the WWP has a national office in New York (55 W. Seventeenth Street) and eighteen regional headquarters across the United States, the addresses of which are posted on the Internet. Now the WWP represents itself as a "national Marxist-Leninist party promoting socialism, supporting working class struggles and lesbian/gay/bi/trans liberation, organizing protests, and denouncing racism and sexism." Two of its leaders, Larry Holmes and Monica G. Moorehead, repeatedly ran for president of the United States on the WWP ticket. Both portrayed the United States as a country run by warmongering governments, and both charged that America was full of political prisoners.[9]

The WWP newspaper *Workers World* is also still around and maintains its Cold War rhetoric. Its website states: "We're independent Marxists" whose "goal is solidarity of all the workers and oppressed against this criminal imperialist system."[10]

Over the years, the WWP created several front organizations along Soviet lines, such as the Youth Against War and Fascism, the United Labor Action, and the American Servicemen's Union. Most recently the WWP spawned a front called ANSWER, standing for Act Now to Stop War and End Racism. ANSWER is a United States–based umbrella group consisting of many Marxist antiwar and civil rights organizations. Formed in the wake of the September 11, 2001, attacks, ANSWER has since helped organize many of the largest antiwar demonstrations in the United States,[11] including demonstrations of hundreds of thousands against the Iraq war. It is supported by numerous foreign Marxist bodies (the Lebanese Communist party, the New Communist Party of the Netherlands, the Partido Comunista de la Argentina) and by other anti-American organizations (the Italian Tribunal on NATO Crimes, the Green Party USA, the Canadian-Cuban Friendship).[12]

ANSWER was the main organizer of the large anti-American demonstrations that took place in the United States on April 12–13, 2003. Its website contained numerous ready-to-use anti-American flyers (among them "Surround the White House" and "Vote to Impeach Bush") that could be downloaded, printed, and posted. ANSWER also provided dozens of buses to transport the "spontaneous" demonstrators from more than one hundred cities around the United States to Washington, San Francisco, and Los Angeles, where the main anti-American demonstrations were scheduled. Its website contained the names, phone numbers, and e-mail addresses of the contacts in charge of handling each bus, as well as detailed instructions for reaching those buses. For instance: "Buses from Detroit and Ann Arbor depart 9 P.M. Friday, April 11; return by 6 A.M. Sunday, April 13. Ann Arbor bus leaves from Michigan Union (State St. and S. University). Be there at 8:30. Detroit bus leaves from southeast corner parking lot at Temple St. and Third Street. Enter parking lot from south side of Temple, just east of Third. Security, free parking all weekend from Detroit departure point."[13]

It is noteworthy that the end of the Iraq Summit organized by President Putin in St. Petersburg and attended by the German chancellor and by the French president coincided with the April 12, 2003, anti-American demonstrations organized by the World Peace Council and its American offshoot, the Workers World Party. It is also noteworthy that in 2005, after he stepped down as chancellor, Gerhard Schröder accepted a high position at the Russian Gazprom company.[14] In an editorial titled "Gerhard Schroeder's Sellout," the *Washington Post* also expressed sharp criticism, reflecting widening international ramifications of Schröder's new post.[15] Democrat Tom Lantos, chairman of the United States House Committee on Foreign Affairs, likened Schröder to a "political prostitute."[16]

American politicians and media have offered various explanations for the current wave of European America-bashing: Europe feels irrelevant because Washington did not ask its permission to start the war against terrorism; for the past twenty years Europe poured all its wealth into welfare and social programs, and now it is ashamed to admit that its military is not up to snuff; Europe has always favored appeasement; the European Community is too self-absorbed in its own internal integration and does not want to be distracted by fighting terrorism—just as it did not want to be involved in its own Balkan conflict; the United States failed to solve world poverty and that made the Arab and Islamic countries mad.

Although there is some truth in all those explanations, there is another more cogent reason that is universally ignored: the survival of the KGB's Cold War *dezinformatsiya* machinery, which spent more than forty years running anti-American operations for the purpose of discrediting the Kremlin's "main enemy."

In the 1970s, during my last meeting with Andropov, the KGB chairman told me that "now all we have to do is keep this machinery alive." Andropov was a shrewd judge of human nature. He understood that in the end, the Soviets' original involvement would be forgotten, and then the *dezinformatsiya* machinery would take on a life of its own. That was just the way human nature worked.

In Russia, the more things change, the more they seem to stay the same. Of course the French, those clever diplomats, have the perfect saying for this: *Plus ça change, plus c'est la même chose.* And so it goes.

39

THE ANTIWAR MOVEMENT

IN MARCH 2008, the whole world watched in disbelief as the Reverend Jeremiah Wright, the spiritual adviser of a prominent US senator running for the White House as the Democratic Party's candidate, screamed at the television screen, "God damn America!" He accused the United States of America, the country that had defeated Nazism and its Holocaust, of deliberately spreading the AIDS virus to kill black people. He also insinuated that America, the only country on earth that had declared war on terrorism, had actually brought about the 9/11 attacks with its own "terrorism."

I expected the leaders of the Democratic Party to strongly censure Reverend Wright's poisonous anti-Americanism for the disinformation that it was. Instead, the Democrats' damage-control machine simply brushed away Wright's statement, calling it "a staple of black churches."

But "God damn America" was not born in black churches. I have many black friends and they all love and revere America. Nor is the phrase—and sentiment—of Islamic, French, German, or Mexican origin. The millions around the world waiting in line to be admitted into the United States do not hate America. They admire it—that's why they want to live here.

"God damn America" is a slogan launched many years ago by a religious movement dubbed "liberation theology," whose creation by the KGB *dezinformatsiya* machinery was described in a previous chapter.

I have good reason to believe that the Democratic Party's tolerance of Rev. Wright's anti-American profanity is the result of that party's growing tendency to swallow *dezinformatsiya* operations and to give them American cover. Back when I was granted political asylum, I was unable to tell the difference between the Republican Party and the Democratic Party. To my eyes of that time, both parties epitomized the embodiment of freedom and anticommunism. That was, until the memorable day of July 19, 1979, when President Jimmy Carter affectionately and repeatedly kissed the brutal Soviet ruler Leonid Brezhnev during their first encounter in Vienna.

Tyrants despise appeasers. On April 12, 1978, I was in the car with Ceaușescu driving away from an official ceremony at the White House. He took a bottle of alcohol and splashed it all over his face, after having been affectionately kissed by President Carter in the Oval Office. "Peanut-head," Ceaușescu whispered disgustedly. Five months after the infamous Carter-Brezhnev kiss, a KGB terrorist squad assassinated Hafizullah Amin, the American-educated prime minister of Afghanistan, and replaced him with a Soviet puppet. Then the Red Army invaded the country.

President Carter's feeble protest consisted merely of boycotting the Olympic Games in Moscow, a compromise that gave rise to the Taliban regime. I am grateful to President Carter for signing off on my political asylum, but in truth, it was he who laid the groundwork for the expansion of today's international terrorism. His presidential weakness in abandoning the pro-Western shah of Iran led directly to the birth of the modern Islamist revolution, which has since metastasized into far-flung terrorist organizations like al-Qaeda that have directly attacked America.

Another KGB *dezinformatsiya* launched the political career of the 2004 Democratic Party nominee for the White House, Senator John Kerry. On April 22, 1971, the former Navy lieutenant testified to the Senate Committee on Foreign Relations that American soldiers told him that in Vietnam they had "raped, cut off ears, cut off heads, taped wires from portable telephones to human genitals and turned up the power, cut off limbs, blown up bodies, randomly shot at civilians, razed villages in fashion reminiscent of Genghis Khan."[1]

Although Senator Kerry never fully revealed the source of those outrageous accusations, I recognized them as being the product of another KGB disinformation operation. In the 1960s and '70s, when I was a leader of the Soviet bloc intelligence community, the KGB spread those same vitriolic accusations, almost word for word, throughout American and European leftist movements. They were part of a KGB disinformation operation aimed at discouraging the United States from protecting the world against communist expansion.

I do not question Senator Kerry's patriotism. He surely loves this magnificent country as much as I do. Nevertheless, I have strong reason to believe that when he was young, he was deluded by Moscow's *dezinformatsiya*. During my years as an intelligence officer, I was many times involved in creating anti-Americanism out of whole cloth, and I could see how easy it was to make young people hate the almighty America.

In July 1953, I was charged to help organize an international congress of the *Fédération Mondiale de la Jeunesse Démocratique* (World Federation of Democratic Youth) held in Bucharest. The task of this youth congress was to denigrate American efforts to stop North Korea's expansion of communism. My boss of that time, General Penteleymon Bondarenko—Romanianized as Gheorghe Pintilie—put the final touches on my preparation. As previously mentioned, he was a Soviet citizen of vague Romanian ancestry who had become the first chief of the Romanian *Securitate*, where he was universally known as Pantyusha, his Russian nickname. He spoke hardly any Romanian, and what little he did was seasoned with a strong Russian accent and came out as an outdated working-class argot larded with vulgarities.

Pantyusha explained to me that "those f*cking students easily got excited about f*cking injustices and had a f*cking short fuse when it came to violent protests." That made them "putty in our hands, and we could mold them into any f*cking thing we wanted." My main task was to mold them into anti-American protesters.

As an intelligence officer, I was still green, but I eventually had to agree that Pantyusha knew his students. The young people attending the congress were put up at student hostels set aside for them in Bucharest, and I bunked with them. The walls of the hostels were plastered with articles and photographs supposedly documenting the abominable crimes committed by America's Genghis Khan–style military, generating violent anti-American reactions from the young visitors. Free alcohol was available in the hostels, which helped fuel the rioting.

At night, most of the young people, led on by the Swedish delegates, wandered buck naked from room to room, looking for sexual adventures.

In short, the congress was one colossal, uninhibited party, and the only price of admission was the special fun of yelling out anti-American epithets.

On July 27 of that year, while the youth congress was running full steam ahead, Romanian radio announced that an armistice in the Korean War had been reached that day. "American imperialism has been soundly defeated," the radio blared. Wild celebrations broke out. The debauchery born in the youth hostels spread to the streets, building up into night-and-day, anti-American hysteria. I was part of it. The next day, the Romanian government organized a "popular" meeting in Bucharest to celebrate the occasion. It was the first American defeat in the international arena and was royally feted. I remember joining in, shouting "Yankees go home!"

In retrospect, I recall that no mention was made during the youth congress of the fact that the war had actually been started when North Korean troops in Russian T-34 tanks crossed the 38th parallel on June 25, 1950, in an attempt to export the communist revolution. As usual, the actual history was entirely changed. No one wanted to hear that communist China had decided to enter the war the following October, although that event had turned the tide of the war. Instead, the World Federation of Democratic Youth congress spent the whole time loudly condemning America's war "atrocities," as displayed in the fabricated horror scenes posted all over the meeting hall and the youth hostels.

Looking back on that time in my life, I realize how much easier it is to change your political views at twenty-five than at fifty. Five decades later, as I watched the televised spectacle of thousands of young people demonstrating in Paris and Berlin against "America's criminal war" in Iraq, I could picture myself among them. They belonged to a new generation, but there they were condemning the same kind of carefully fabricated "American atrocities" that I had back in 1953, and they were just as many thousands of miles away from the real America as I had been.

Today, it is considered bad manners to point to any Soviet source of American anti-Americanism. But throughout their history, Americans had never before been anti-American. They voluntarily came to the United States. They were always a proud and independent people who loved their country and who won every military conflict up until its wars against communist expansion—

the Korean and the Vietnam Wars.

From 1776 to 1782, the Americans faced off against Great Britain, the most powerful empire in the world at that time—and won. In the War of 1812, the United States again forced the British to retreat back across the Atlantic. After the United States annexed Texas, whose independence the Mexicans refused to accept, in 1846 Mexico attacked the US and was soundly defeated. In 1898, the United States went to war to support Cuba's desire for independence from Spain, decimating the Spanish fleet and forcing Spain to sue for peace. During World War I, in which more than 40 million Europeans were killed, the United States quickly put together an army of 4 million and became instrumental in defeating the German aggressor.

During World War II, almost half a million Americans died to defeat Nazism and the Holocaust, and their country remained sturdily united around its commander in chief. The United States held national elections during that war, but no one running for office even thought to harm American unity in a quest for personal victory. Republican opponent Thomas Dewey declined to criticize Democratic President Franklin Roosevelt's foreign policy during a time of war.[2] When the war ended, a united America rolled up its sleeves and helped rebuild her vanquished enemies. It took seven years to turn Hitler's Germany, Mussolini's Italy and Hirohito's Japan into prosperous democracies, but that effort made the United States the uncontested leader of the world.

Then, suddenly, a number of Americans began turning *against* their country's own wars. By 1968, the anti–Vietnam War protesters in the United States numbered almost 7 million. They came to regard their own government, not communism, as the enemy.[3] It reached the point that today the Washington elite believe bashing the US commander in chief in time of war is as American as apple pie.

How did America's venerable patriotism arrive at this point?

"Democrats under Roosevelt, Truman and Kennedy forged and conducted a foreign policy that was principled, internationalist, strong and successful," said Sen. Joseph Lieberman on May 27, 2008, explaining the problem in a nutshell. "Now, the Democratic Party sees America as the main danger to the world's peace. The Soviets and their allies were our enemies, not because they were inspired by a totalitarian ideology fundamentally hostile to our way of life, or because they nursed ambitions of global conquest.

Rather, the Soviets were our enemies because we had provoked them, and because we failed to sit down and accord them the respect they deserved. In other words, the Cold War was mostly America's fault."[4]

Sen. Lieberman was right on the money, but he knew only one side of the coin. Here is the other.

The general perception in the United States is that America's antiwar movement has been a homegrown product. In reality, it is the result of a still very secret *dezinformatsiya* operation ignited by the KGB during the Vietnam War for the dual purpose of counteracting American efforts to protect the world against communist expansion, and of creating doubt around the world about American power, judgment and credibility. Unfortunately, it has fulfilled both aims.

KGB chief Yuri Andropov, a former ambassador and by far the best educated chairman the KGB ever had, baptized this *dezinformatsiya* operation with the codename "Ares," after the Greek god of war. Ares was usually accompanied in battle by his sister Eris (goddess of discord) and by his two sons, Deimos (fear) and Phobos (terror).

Andropov was convinced that the war in Vietnam provided a once-in-a-lifetime chance to make Europe *fear* America's military *terror* and instill *discord* between the Old Continent and its own leader at that time, the United States. Therefore, Andropov made Operation Ares a foremost priority from almost the first days of the Vietnam War.

In order to conceal its hand, the KGB created the so-called Stockholm Conference on Vietnam and staffed it with undercover KGB officers. This new *dezinformatsiya* front organization received an average of $15 million yearly from the International Department of the Soviet Communist Party— which in addition provided $50 million annually to Chandra's World Peace Council. The money—for both organizations—was delivered by the KGB in the form of laundered cash dollars in order to hide its origin. Nevertheless, Moscow's fingerprints were all over the new organization.

Copying the World Peace Council, Stockholm's smaller *dezinformatsiya* sister established a Soviet-style secretariat to manage its general activities, created Soviet-style working committees to conduct its day-to-day operations, generated Soviet-style bureaucratic paperwork, used Soviet-style vocabulary, and launched Soviet-style slogans. Moreover, it resorted to the same modus operandi as the World Peace Council. The DIE's operational program for 1968, for instance, included the task of obtaining one hundred thousand signatures worldwide on the "stop-the-Vietnam-War" appeal just launched by the Stockholm Conference. For the same year, the DIE was also tasked to set up émigré meetings in every major Western country, condemning America's "criminal aggression" in Vietnam.

The so-called Stockholm Conference held annual international meetings through 1972. During the five years of its existence, it spread around the world countless vitriolic *dezinformatsiya* articles and photographs supposedly depicting the debaucheries committed by the Genghis Khan–style American military against Vietnamese civilians. All these materials were produced by the KGB's disinformation department and contained basically fabricated descriptions of American atrocities committed against civilians in Vietnam, as well as counterfeited pictures supporting the allegations. "Even Attila the Hun looks like an angel when compared to these Amis," a West German businessman reprovingly told me after reading one such report in German ("Amis" was the German nickname for American GIs). These forgeries made quite an impression, however, within the Italian, Greek and Spanish communist parties.

In 1972, I had a long discussion with Andropov about Operation Ares. "It turned America against her own government," Andropov started off in his soft voice. It damaged America's foreign policy consensus, poisoned her domestic debate, and built a credibility gap between America and European public opinion that was wide and deep. It also transformed the world's leftists into deadly enemies of American "imperialism." Now all we had to do was to continue planting the seeds of "Ares" and water them day after day after day. Eventually, American leftists would seize upon our Ares and would start pursuing it of their own accord. In the end, our original involvement would be forgotten and Ares would take on a life of its own.

Sadly, Andropov seems to have been right. The US elections of 1974 brought in a new Congress dominated by leftist Democrats who immediately restricted the financing of the war in Vietnam, and in 1976 cut the funding altogether. As US forces precipitously pulled out of Vietnam, the victorious communists massacred some 2 million people in Vietnam, Laos and Cambodia. Another million tried to escape by sea, but many died in the attempt.

Ares has changed the United States as well. Today it is not only hotheaded young Americans like the young Navy lieutenant John Kerry, who scream out accusations of war crimes allegedly committed by the American military. The 2004 Democratic National Convention focused almost exclusively on the Vietnam days, giving new dimensions to Andropov's old "Ares" and throwing more mud on our military forces and their commander in chief than Andropov and his satraps had ever dared to imagine. One after the other, the convention participants denigrated America's armed forces by portraying their commander in chief as a "renegade," a "liar," a "deceiver," and a "fraud" who had concocted the war for personal gain.[5] The United States had some 140,000 soldiers engaged in a grueling war, fighters who needed political support from all sides—but all they got from that Democratic Convention was insults and hatred.

After the convention, one of the participants, Martin O'Malley, who later became governor of Maryland, even claimed to be more worried about the actions of the George W. Bush administration than about al-Qaeda.[6]

A few days after the convention ended, Teresa Heinz Kerry, wife of the Democratic contender for the White House, stated that four more years of the Bush administration meant four more years of hell for America.[7] Like her husband, she also had bought into the Ares *dezinformatsiya*.

I am also an immigrant like Teresa Kerry (born to Portuguese parents in Mozambique and naturalized American citizen twenty-five years later), and I have spent my thirty-four American years under six presidents—some better than others—but I have always felt I was living in paradise.

Yet by 2007, most leaders of the Democratic Party were engaged in a frantic campaign to condemn the United States for its war in Iraq, and to withdraw our troops unconditionally. Senator Harry Reid, the Democratic majority leader, famously declared, "the war is lost." House Democratic Leader Nancy Pelosi announced, "this war has been a grotesque mistake," adding that wealthy corporate interests would get a windfall and the middle class would get the bill. That is exactly what the "Ares" *dezinformatsiya* also preached.

On October 9, 2008, Sen. John Kerry, who in 2009 became chairman of the powerful Senate Foreign Relations Committee, stated in a televised interview with PBS's Jim Lehrer:

> Well, let me just say quickly that I've had an extraordinary experience of watching up close and personal that transition in Russia, because I was there right after the transformation. And I was probably one of the first senators ... to go down into the KGB underneath Treblinka Square and see reams of files with names on them. It sort of brought home the transition to democracy that Russia was trying to make.[8]

First of all, if Senator Kerry does not know that Treblinka was a Nazi death camp in Poland, whereas the KGB headquarters was, and still is, the Lubyanka, what should we suppose he learned from seeing all those files—written in a language he could not read anyway?

Unfortunately, Sen. Kerry and quite a few other top US political leaders now consider the Soviet Union and its KGB to be ancient history. They bought another Kremlin *dezinformatsiya,* according to which the nefarious Soviet legacy was uprooted in 1991 with the disintegration of the Soviet Union, just as the Nazi legacy was eradicated in 1945 with the end of World War II. They also believe Russia has become an ally who is as sincere a friend to the United States as is today's Germany.

Make no mistake: since the Soviet borders have been thrown open, Russia indeed has been transformed in unprecedented and positive ways. Young generations of intellectuals are now struggling to develop a new national identity. There are, however, substantial differences between post-Soviet Russia and post-Nazi Germany.

After Germany surrendered in 1945, Hitler's Third Reich was demolished, its war criminals put on trial, its Gestapo and military forces disbanded, and the Nazis removed from public office. In the 1950s, when I was acting chief of Romania's Mission in West Germany, I saw how West Germany's economy was being rebuilt with the help of Marshall Plan money, and how the country had become a multiparty democracy and a close friend of the United States.

None of these things have happened in the former Soviet Union. No individual has been put on trial, although its communist regime killed, *in peacetime,* 94 million people all around the world.[9] Most Soviet institutions, under new names, have been left in place and continue to be run by many of the same people who guided the communist state. The military and the political police forces, instrumental during the Cold War, have also remained in place but with new nameplates on their doors.

During most of the last century, the world's foreign and military policies were heavily centered around the Soviet Union, which dispossessed a third of the globe's population, deeply divided the world, and repeatedly brought it to the brink of nuclear war. Yet no American political figures talk about Russia any more, even though that country still has more than six thousand nuclear missiles.

Indeed, in August 2008, the deputy chief of the General Staff of the Armed Forces of Russia, General Anatoly Nogovitsyn, threatened to attack Poland with a new generation of nuclear weapons. By hosting a US antimissile shield, he said, Poland "is exposing itself to a strike 100 percent." Any new US assets in Europe, the general warned, could come under Russian nuclear attack.[10]

This new generation of Russian nuclear weapons, if it truly exists, must have been developed in one of the KGB-managed nuclear cities hidden throughout Russia. In the late 1970s, when I was still in Romania, the KGB's nuclear component alone had eighty-seven supersecret nuclear cities, such as the ones on Vozrozhdeniye and Komsomolsk islands in the Aral Sea. At that time, I coordinated Romania's technological intelligence and knew these nuclear cities quite well. They were built and run by the KGB. Not a single such city was ever listed anywhere, not even on the Soviet Union's most highly classified military maps.

For instance, Chelyabinsk City in the Urals was on a map of the Soviet Union, but Chelyabinsk-40, a city of 40,000 people also located in the Urals, was not. Nor did any maps show Chelyabinsk-65, Chelyabinsk-70, Chelyabinsk-95, and Chelyabinsk-115, all in the Urals.[11] Krasnoyarsk city in eastern Siberia was shown on maps, but there was no mention anywhere of Krasnoyarsk-25, Krasnoyarsk-26, and Krasnoyarsk-45. However, after a nuclear accident at the east Siberian city of Tomsk-7 in April of 1993, ten other "secret cities" located in that part of the country were disclosed.[12]

These secret cities are so enormous, they almost cannot be disassembled, and nothing so far indicates that they have been. Knowledge of them may persuade America in general, and its leaders in particular, to stop fantasizing that a Russia run by the KGB is our sincere friend—a Russia that, as we have seen, framed Pius XII as Hitler's Pope in order to divide and conquer the world.

In World War II, 405,399 Americans died because Neville Chamberlain fantasized that Hitler was a friend. We must not repeat such a mistake.

"Trust, but verify," was the famous signature phrase defining President

Ronald Reagan's foreign policy. The current US policy toward Vladimir Putin's Russia, however, is called "Reset" (erroneously translated by the State Department as "Peregruzka," which means "overcharged"). There is just one meaning for "trust, but verify." There are quite a few meanings for "reset" in dictionaries, but all tend to signify "restore"—except in Scotland, where "reset" is the legal term for knowingly and dishonestly receiving stolen goods.[13]

Russia's intelligence dictatorship is a new political phenomenon, and we need a new foreign policy to deal with it. Otherwise, we may face a new Cold War, one that threatens to be not only cold, but also bloody. I do not know what our new policy toward Russia should be. I have no access to classified information and no wish to play the armchair general. The know-it-all talking heads in the American media are no wiser than I am. I do, however, have reason to suggest that our administration and Congress take a serious look at President Truman's NSC 68 (1950).

That report of the National Security Council, a down-to-earth, 58-page document, described the challenges facing the United States of that day in realistic terms. "The issues that face us are momentous," NSC 68 stated, "involving the fulfillment or destruction not only of this Republic but of civilization itself."[14]

Therefore, NSC 68 focused on creating a "new world order" centered on American liberal-capitalist values, and it contained a two-pronged political strategy: superior military power and a "Campaign of Truth," defined as "a struggle, above all else, for the minds of men." President Harry Truman argued that the propaganda and disinformation used by the "forces of imperialistic communism" could be overcome only by the "plain, simple, unvarnished truth."[15] The Voice of America, Radio Free Europe, and Radio Liberation (soon to become Radio Liberty) became part of Truman's "Campaign of Truth."[16]

If you still wonder how the United States was able to win the Cold War without firing a shot, here is one explanation from Romania's second post-Ceausescu president Emil Constantinescu:

> Radio Free Europe has been a lot more important than the armies and the most sophisticated missiles. The "missiles" that destroyed Communism were launched from Radio Free Europe, and this was Washington's most important investment during the Cold War. I don't know whether the Americans themselves realize this now, seven years after the fall of Communism, but we understand it perfectly well.[17]

In July 2007, Russia's President Putin predicted a new Cold War against the West. "War has started," he announced on August 8, 2008, minutes after Russian tanks crossed into pro-Western Georgia.[18]

Dezinformatsiya became secret policy once more. This invisible weapon is again sustained by military threats, as it was during the Cold War. President Putin took pains to announce that Russia had test-launched a missile system that could maneuver in mid-flight, allowing it to dodge defenses. The chief of the General Staff of the Armed Forces of the Russian Federation, General Yury Baluyevsky, added: "We can build weapons which will render any anti-missile system defenseless." He also stated that Russia was ready to use nuclear missile systems to "defend the sovereignty of Russia and its allies."[19]

40

MARX'S GHOST LIVES ON

N A 2008 RASMUSSEN POLL, only 53 percent of Americans preferred capitalism to socialism, with another 27 percent unsure, and 20 percent strongly opting for socialism. One of the most popular nightclubs in New York City's East Village is the KGB Bar, jammed with Marxist writers who read from their literary works extolling the need to redistribute America's wealth.[1] Ironically, today's Russian *Pravda* chaffed: "It must be said, that like the breaking of a great dam, the American descent into Marxism is happening with breathtaking speed, against the backdrop of a passive, hapless sheeple, excuse me dear reader, I meant people."[2]

Why is the United States of America, which built the most successful free-market economy in history, now toying with Marxism? History will certainly provide a definitive answer to this question. Meanwhile, I suggest considering the explanation provided by the French philosopher Jacques Derrida, who claimed he had broken with Marxism but confessed to still being choked with emotion whenever he heard "The Internationale."

Just before he died, Derrida reminded us that the first noun in Marx's *Communist Manifesto* is "specter": "A specter is haunting Europe, the specter of Communism." According to Derrida, Marx began *The Communist Manifesto* with "specter" because a specter never dies.[3]

Derrida was on to something.

"Of only one fact do I feel certain, and it is that no thinking man can imagine that the ultimate result of the Great War can be anything but disastrous to humanity at large," stated Alfred Mosley, one of Europe's most celebrated economists, in 1915.[4] He was prophetic. The Great War brought Marx's specter to life in the shape of the Soviet Union. Marx's specter continued to come to life after each long war in another corner of the world.

The Soviet Empire, which transformed Eastern Europe into dismal feudalism, was created soon after World War II ended. My native country is a case in point: Four years of war on Germany's side had squeezed Romania like a sponge, and what little remained had been stolen by the vindictive "liberating" Soviet Army, which had laid waste to the land worse than a plague of locusts. Many young Romanian intellectuals who had grown up under the influence of the postwar patriotic fervor were willing to try anything, Marxism included, to rebuild their homeland. I was one of them.

In 1945, the young British voters, also tired of five years of war and ignorant of world history, turned to Marx's specter for help as well. Two months after World War II ended, they kicked out of office the legendary Winston Churchill—who was instrumental in winning that war—and brought in Clement Attlee, an undercover Marxist leader of the Labor Party. Attlee started his reign by nationalizing the healthcare system. His appetite for socialism thus whetted, Attlee went on to nationalize the finance, auto, and coal industries, communication facilities, civil aviation, electricity, the steel industry—just as many leaders of the Democratic Party in the United States have indicated they also intend to do.

The British economy collapsed and the powerful British Empire passed into history, providing a stern—but evidently ignored—warning to all who later might be tempted to look at Marx's Specter as savior. Even the most famous British brand names, like Jaguar and Rolls-Royce, had to be rescued from oblivion by auto companies in other countries.

In 1950 the British voters repented and brought Churchill back to Downing Street, but it took Great Britain eighteen years of conservative governments to repair the catastrophe generated by Attlee's government in a mere six years. In the process of recovery, the Labor Party was fortunate enough to acquire non-Marxist leaders, such as Tony Blair, who normalized the party again.

Researchers at the Max Planck Institute for Human Cognitive and Brain Sciences in Leipzig, Germany, have recently discovered a genetic factor, the A1 Mutation, that supposedly affects one's ability to learn from past mistakes. If true, then perhaps many people in South America carry the A1 mutation. They brought various Atlee-style *Partidos dos Trabalhadores* (Workers Party) leaders to power in Venezuela, Nicaragua, Honduras, and Argentina, and moved these countries into the Marxist fold. Russian military ships and bombers are now back in Cuba—and in Venezuela—for the first time since the Cuban missile crisis. Brazil, the world's tenth largest economy, even installed a former Marxist guerrilla fighter, Dilma Rousseff, as that country's president.

After forty-five years of Cold War, and still more years of war in Iraq and Afghanistan, millions of young Americans, unaware of history or unable to learn from it, have come to believe that capitalism is their real enemy, and that it should be replaced with socialism. They found a home in the Democratic Party, whose primary 2008 election theme was the promise to redistribute America's wealth.

But the United States of America spent too many years fighting Marxism, and its free population of independent entrepreneurs will never succumb to that heresy. Be that as it may, Marx's *Manifesto of the Communist Party* has endured to turn 165 years old this year, and the remaining Marxists of the world seem to be still clamoring to see their fantasy finally come to pass: the eradication of capitalism.

At the end of World War II, at a time when I knew nothing about Marxism, I also believed the Marxist disinformation about the marvels redistribution of wealth can perform. During those early days, I never suspected that by helping Marxism to grab Romania I was committing a crime against my own country, just like millions of Germans who supported Hitler's National Socialism because they were convinced that they were also helping their country.

Early on, millions of other Romanians were also persuaded, thanks to the Soviet "science" of *dezinformatsiya,* to believe that Marx's redistribution of wealth would rescue their country. There were quite a few well-to-do people in Romania, and the government-controlled media launched powerful disinformation offensives to persuade everyone, in every social stratum, that Romania could be *changed* into a prosperous country just by confiscating their wealth.

Stealing became a national policy on December 30, 1948, when the Kingdom of Romania was abolished and the Popular Republic of Romania was born. The new Marxist government confiscated the king's wealth, seized the land owned by the rich Romanians, nationalized Romanian industry and banking, and sent most of the property owners to gulags. Then in 1949, the Marxist government turned its covetous eyes in the opposite direction, toward the poorest elements in the country. By forcing the peasants into collective farms, it stole their land along with their animals and agricultural tools. Within a few years, virtually the entire Romanian economy was running on stolen property.

"Stealing from capitalism is moral, comrades," I heard Nikita Khrushchev repeatedly say. "Don't raise your eyebrows, comrades. I intentionally used the word *steal*. Stealing from our enemy is moral," he used to explain.

"Stealing from capitalists is a Marxist duty," my former boss, Romania's president Nicolae Ceaușescu, used to sermonize during the years I was his national security adviser.

Both men rose to lead their countries without ever having earned a single penny in any productive job. Neither man had the slightest idea about what made an economy work, and each passionately believed that stealing from the rich was the magic wand that would cure all his country's economic ills. Both were leading formerly free countries, transformed into Marxist dictatorships through massive wealth redistribution, which eventually made the government the mother and father of *everything*.

Both Khrushchev and Ceaușescu, however, died before learning that in the long run Marxist stealing does not pay, even when committed by the government of a superpower, as the economic collapse of the Soviet Union devastatingly proved.

41

DISINFORMATION IN
TODAY'S AMERICA

N 2008, veteran *Washington Post* journalist David S. Broder candidly compared Sen. Barack Obama's tactics for hiding his past to the tactics military pilots use to protect themselves when flying over a target heavily defended by antiaircraft guns: "They release a cloud of fine metal scraps, hoping to confuse the aim of the shells or missiles being fired in their direction."[1] This is also a good characterization of *glasnost*, which, as I explained earlier, is an old Russian term for polishing the ruler's— or would-be ruler's—image.

One of the overriding purposes of every *glasnost* I have known has been to hide the leader's past by giving him a new political identity. Stalin's *glasnost* was designed to conceal his horrific crimes by portraying him as an earthly god. Khrushchev's *glasnost* was to create a peaceful international façade for the man who brought the Kremlin's political assassinations to the West (as proved by the West German Supreme Court in October 1962, during the public trial of Bogdan Stashinsky, a KGB officer who had been decorated by Khrushchev himself for assassinating enemies of the Soviet Union living in the West).[2] Ceaușescu, who attained the rank of general after secretly attending a Red Army school for political commissaries in Moscow, focused his *glasnost* on hiding that past by portraying himself as a Romanian Napoleon—another five-foot-three tyrant—who hated Russia. Gorbachev, recruited by the KGB when he was studying at Moscow State

University,[3] designed his *glasnost* to veil his KGB past by portraying him as a magician-like leader who displayed a flirtatious "Miss KGB" to Western correspondents while pledging to transform the Soviet Union into a "Marxist society of free people."[4]

Thus it was that in America, the 2008 election campaign for the White House was, for me, a major case of déjà vu. It felt as though I were watching a replay of one of those election campaigns of Ceaușescu's in which I was involved during my years in Romania. Ceaușescu's media painted the Romania of his predecessor, Gheorghiu-Dej, as a decaying, corrupt, economically devastated country and demanded it be *changed* by redistributing the country's wealth. It was a disinformation campaign.

In the same way, the establishment US media painted America as a decaying, racist, predatory capitalist realm unable to provide medical care for the poor, rebuild her "crumbling schools," or replace the "shuttered mills that once provided a decent life for men and women of every race,"[5] and promised all this could be *changed* by redistributing the country's wealth. That also was a disinformation campaign.

Just as Ceaușescu loved to remind everyone that someone as great as he "is born once every five hundred years," so did Sen. Barack Obama portentously proclaim, "We are the ones we have been waiting for," artfully substituting the regal "we" to convey his actual meaning: *I am the One you have been waiting for.* Meanwhile, Obama's Houston campaign headquarters had a large poster of communist idol Che Guevara hanging on the wall, as revealed by that city's Fox News affiliate.[6]

The Democratic Party and the media both portrayed Obama an American messiah, and the senator agreed: On June 8, 2008, during an electoral speech in New Hampshire, he stated that the beginning of his presidency would be "the moment when the rise of the oceans began to slow and our planet began to heal."[7]

Once elected, during his first 231 days in the White House, Obama gave 263 speeches,[8] all of them essentially focused on himself. His 2010 State of the Union speech contained the word "I" 76 times. In 2011, when announcing that brave US military forces had killed Osama bin Ladin, Obama used the words "I", "me," and "my" a combined thirteen times in his short 1,300-word speech."[9] "I directed the director of the CIA . . . I met repeatedly with *my* national security team . . . I determined that we had enough intelligence to take action . . . At *my* direction, the United States launched a targeted operation against that compound in Abbottabad, Pakistan."[10] President Obama's 2012 State of the Union address contained the word *I* forty-five times and the word *me* thirteen times. By that time, he had been in the White House for 1,080 days and had given 726 speeches.[11] *USA Today* notes that, by the end of his first term, President Obama had given 1,852 speeches, public remarks and comments.[12]

Self-serving speeches have always been an important facet of *glasnost*. In fact, with the passage of time, Marxism has become a mere vehicle used by the "Marxist" rulers to build *glasnost* speeches aimed at promoting themselves, demonstrating Marxism's prodigious adaptability. Lenin's *glasnost* speeches changed Marxism so much that his followers ended up calling it "Leninism." Stalin put Marxism, Leninism, Hegel's dialectics, and Feuerbach's materialism into one *glasnost* bowl and came up with his own simplified political doctrine, which he dubbed "Marxism-Leninism-Stalinism." Ceaușescu's *glasnost* speeches were a ludicrous mixture of Marxism, Leninism, Stalinism, nationalism, Roman arrogance, and Byzantine fawning called Ceausism. All were focused on Ceaușescu; each contained hundreds of instances of "Me," "Myself," and "I." And all were so slippery, undefined, and everchanging that he filled twenty-four volumes of his collected works without ever being able to describe what his Ceausism really meant!

In Obama's case, when he was first running for president in 2008, his preferred policies and voting record clearly revealed him to be "the hardest-left candidate ever nominated for president of the United States."[13] And who can forget his unvarnished Marxist remark to "Joe the Plumber" three days before the final presidential debate, that "when you spread the wealth around, it's good for everybody"?[14]

President Obama is a brilliant young politician who was bitten by the Marxist bug, and who evidently believes that the change from capitalism to socialism is what the US really needs. Running for president as a secret socialist, however, meant sailing on uncharted waters, and it seems the senator decided to cover his radical ideology by comparing himself to Ronald Reagan,[15] and after his election, to Abraham Lincoln[16] and Teddy Roosevelt.[17]

Of course, people everywhere want their political leaders to be better than their predecessors. But the quintessence of Marxism is *change*, which is built on the dialectical materialist tenet that *quantitative changes generate qualitative transformations.* Thus, *"change,"* through the redistribution of the country's wealth, became the electoral slogan in all Soviet bloc countries.

Alas, *change* through wealth redistribution also became the electoral slogan of the Democratic Party during America's 2008 electoral campaign. People always love a free lunch. No wonder the Democratic Party easily filled entire stadiums with people who demanded that the wealth of the United States be redistributed. Some of those electoral gatherings looked like Ceaușescu's revival meetings—more than eighty thousand people were gathered in front of the now-famous Greek temple resembling the White House that had been erected in Denver, to demand that America's wealth be redistributed. It was a superb show of disinformation.

According to a March 12, 2008, amendment introduced in the US Senate by Sen. Wayne Allard (R-Colorado), funding just 111 of the 188 tax increases proposed thus far by the Democratic Party would steal $1.4 trillion from businesses and other taxpayers over the next five years. This huge redistribution of America's wealth would cause the tax bill of people earning $104,000 to rise 74 percent ($12,000) and that of people earning more than $365,000 to rise by 132 percent ($93,500),[18] but it would also heavily affect the average taxpayer earning $62,000, whose tax bill would rise 61 percent ($5,300).[19]

Millions of young Americans who were not yet paying taxes cheered, as did most of the people belonging to the 38 percent of households exempted from paying taxes at that time. They were, of course, galvanized by the prospect that a Democratic administration would force America's rich people to pay part of their own healthcare, mortgages, loans and school tuition, and they rushed to support Democratic candidates.

The Democratic Party won the White House and both chambers of the United States Congress. Soon the new political leaders of the United States began changing into a kind of a Ceaușescu-style *nomenklatura* (in the Soviet bloc, the special elite class of people from which appointees for top-level government positions were drawn) with unchecked power. This new *nomenklatura* started running the country secretly, just as Ceaușescu's *nomenklatura* did. "We have to pass the bill so that you can find out what is in it," then-leader of the US House of Representatives *nomenklatura*, Nancy Pelosi, once told the media.[20] That was a first in American history. It didn't take long before this *nomenklatura*—this arrogant, new elite class—began to take control of banks, home mortgages, school loans, automakers and most of the healthcare industry.

When tens of thousands of Americans disagreed with this transfer of wealth from private hands into those of the government and stood up for traditional American values, the congressional *nomenklatura* called them "extremists" and potential "terrorists."[21] That was what Ceaușescu's *nomenklatura* had also called its critics.

On February 7, 2009, the cover of *Newsweek,* at that time the second-largest weekly newsmagazine in the US, proclaimed: "We Are All Socialists Now."[22] That was exactly what Ceaușescu's newspaper *Scînteia* proclaimed after he changed Romania into a monument to himself. *Newsweek's change* produced the same results as *Scînteia's change*—on a US scale. More than 14 million Americans lost their jobs and 41.8 million people got food stamps. The GDP dipped from 3-4 percent to 1.6 percent. The national debt rose to an unprecedented $13 trillion that year, and is projected to reach $20 trillion by 2019.

Scînteia went bankrupt. In 2010, *Newsweek* was sold for one dollar (and even under new ownership and with a massive cash infusion, published its final print edition in December 2012). Also during 2010, a member of the congressional *nomenklatura*—and a stout admirer of and visitor to Fidel Castro's Cuba—Rep. Maxine Waters began preaching that the future of America's oil industry was socialism. While grilling oil company executives during a congressional hearing, Waters actually blurted out her intention to socialize the entire oil industry, quickly backtracking into more subdued language once she realized what she had said: "And guess what this liberal will be all about? This liberal will be all about socializing, uh, uh, would be about basically about taking over the government running all of your companies."[23] In 1948, when the Romanian *nomenklatura* nationalized the oil industry, that country was the second oil exporter in Europe. Thirty years later, when I broke with Marxism, Romania was a heavy importer of oil, gasoline was rationed, the temperature in public spaces had to be kept under sixty-three degrees, and all shops had to close no later than 5:30 p.m. to save energy.

A few conservative political commentators, like Rush Limbaugh, Sean Hannity, Glenn Beck, and Bill O'Reilly, warned that Marxism was infecting the United States. Unfortunately, with rare exceptions, leaders of both the Democratic Party and Republican Party have failed to warn the country about this danger. It seems no one believes it possible that the United States of America, the leader of the Free World, could be vulnerable to the virus of Marxism. That is another consequence of disinformation.

After winning the 2008 elections, the Democratic Party began changing the United States into a monument to its leader as well. Heaven forbid I should be understood as comparing President Obama to Ceaușescu or any other Soviet bloc monsters—I strongly believe that the first black American president should have a place of honor in our country's history—but I do note a few coincidences that should serve as food for thought. Following is a partial list of projects and places already named after President Obama:

California: Obama Way, Seaside; Barack Obama Charter School, Compton; Barack Obama Global Preparation Academy, Los Angeles; Barack Obama Academy, Oakland.

Florida: President Barack Obama Parkway, Orlando; Barack Obama Avenue, Opa-locka; Barack Obama Boulevard, West Park.

Maryland: Barack Obama Elementary School, Upper Marlboro.

Missouri: Barack Obama Elementary School, Pine Lawn.

Minnesota: Barack and Michelle Obama Service Learning Elementary, Saint Paul.

New Jersey: Barack Obama Academy, Plainfield; Barack Obama Green Charter High School, Plainfield.

New York: Barack Obama Elementary School, Hempstead.

Pennsylvania: Obama High School, Pittsburgh.

Texas: Barack Obama Male Leadership Academy, Dallas.

Change—in the direction of greater "fairness"—was still the Democratic Party's theme for the 2012 elections, but now the target was American capitalism. This new crusade was reflected in the article "Why isn't capitalism working?" by Lawrence Summers, former head of President Obama's National Economic Council. According to Summers's essay, Americans have been disillusioned with market capitalism: Only "50% of people had a positive opinion of capitalism, while 40 percent did not." The reasoning: "[Capitalism produces] inequality and declining social mobility . . . The problem is real and profound and seems unlikely to correct itself untended. Unlike cyclical concerns, there is no obvious solution at hand." The "problem's roots," according to Summers, "lie deep with the evolution of technology." Capitalism was a profit-driven economic system that cared more about enriching its owners than about modernizing the country's economy. The solution was government-financed research and production facilities.[24]

Solyndra! Remember that cute glass-and-steel factory built with $535 million of government money, which on August 31, 2011, went bankrupt, laying off eleven hundred employees and shutting down all operations? That was the solution. That was the future, in Summers's view.

Robert Reich, former secretary of labor under Bill Clinton, added his own two-cents' worth, calling American capitalism "Casino Capitalism," which uses "other people's money to make big bets which, if they go wrong, can wreak havoc on the economy . . . . It's been terrible for the American economy and for our democracy."[25]

The Republican candidate for the White House, Mitt Romney, happened to be a "capitalist," and the Democratic Party/news media's disinformation machinery ramped up a brutal campaign to crucify America's most "heinous" capitalist, Mitt Romney. In addition to constantly demonizing his private equity firm, Bain Capital—which in reality is one of the most respected companies in the venture capital field—the disinformation team got creative. For example, in a five-thousand-word piece published on May 10, 2012— at the same time as a rave report on President Barack Obama's public embrace of gay marriage—the highly influential *Washington Post* depicted Romney as an anti-gay bully who had psychologically murdered one John Lauber, an allegedly gay classmate in their prep school days, by forcefully chopping off a shock of his bleached hair. According to the *Post*, Lauber was a fragile young man, and four decades later his body collapsed around a spirit broken by Mitt Romney.[26] Wow! How dare that brute Romney now presume to run for president?

A few days later, the whole *Post* story was shown to be a disinformation campaign, but by then the damage was done. Stu White, who had been featured by the *Post* as an eyewitness to Romney's brutal assault on Lauber, told ABC News that, in fact, he had never even heard about the hair incident until contacted by the *Post*. Lauber's sister, Christine, confirmed that her brother had "never uttered a word about Mitt Romney or the haircut incident."[27] Nor was Lauber a broken spirit. He was a tough guy, who took dressage lessons in England and toured the world with the Royal Lipizzaner Stallion riders. Moreover, Lauber did not die because his spirit was broken by Romney. He died of cancer. According to his obituary published in the South Bend Tribune at the time of his 2004 death, "Lauber led a full life, graduating from Vanderbilt and becoming a member of the British Horse Society. He earned seaman papers, was licensed in three states as mortician, and was head chef of the [upscale] *Russian Resort* in California. He also served as a civilian contractor in Iraq."[28] According to his sister, Lauber kept his hair blond until he died. "He never stopped bleaching it."[29]

For people who dared to start their lives again from scratch in order to become citizens of this great country—as I did, and as did those millions who have patiently waited in line for their immigration papers—America is "the Canaan of capitalism, its promised land," as prescient German economist Werner Sombart called it in 1906.[30] This "Canaan of capitalism" was not created by Jeremiah Wrights; it was created by a long procession of American presidents who were capitalists like Mitt Romney, men who were daring enough to become successful in business and to earn sizable fortunes.

George Washington's assets are estimated in today's dollars at $525 million, Thomas Jefferson's at $212 million, Theodore Roosevelt's at $125 million, Andrew Jackson's at $119 million, James Madison's at $101 million, Lyndon Johnson's at $98 million, Herbert Hoover's at $75 million, and Franklin Delano Roosevelt's at $60 million. John Fitzgerald Kennedy may not have earned his own fortune, but he inherited an estimated $1 billion. Bill Clinton's estimated wealth is $80 million. Some of these presidents were better than others; but none has ever been called a "heinous capitalist."

The 2012 election ended that American tradition. Capitalism lost elections for the first time in the history of the United States. The Democratic Party's disinformation machinery was able to distort Romney's capitalist past to such a degree that he was always on the defensive, always portrayed as a greedy capitalist predator, when by all accounts his personal history was one of extraordinary generosity and humanitarianism.

The United States won the Cold War because Ronald Reagan was elected president long after he had purged himself of his own youthful infatuation with Marx's socialism. President Reagan was thus able to see through Marx's seductive ideology and to identify it as the political swindle it really is. Then he could subdue it. Let us hope that President Obama will also change himself.

42

FROM DISINFORMATION
TO ASSASSINATION

HE 2012 ASSASSINATION of John Christopher Stevens, the US ambassador to Libya, by Islamic terrorists vividly reminded me of the 1973 public assassination of Cleo A. Noel Jr., the US ambassador to Sudan. Both were killed by armed Islamic terrorists who stormed and occupied our diplomatic offices—an act of war against the United States, according to international law. Both coordinators of these assassinations became known to the US government, which chose to keep their identities a secret for political reasons.

Let me take you back in time four decades and provide an insider's view of what really went on, because I believe there are some important lessons to be learned about handling today's crises.

In 1973, PLO leader Yasser Arafat's liaison officer for Romania, Hani al-Hassan (nom de guerre Abu Hasan), let us Romanians know that Arafat had sent a commando to Sudan headed by his top deputy, Abu Jihad (né Khalil al-Wazir), to carry out an operation codenamed "Nahr al-Barad" (Cold River), after a Palestinian training camp destroyed by Israeli fighter jets eleven days earlier. Abu Jihad's task was to take hostage a few American diplomats in Khartoum whom Arafat wanted to use as exchange pieces for "freeing" Sirhan Sirhan, the Palestinian assassin of Robert Kennedy.

"S-s-top h-him!" Romanian dictator Nicolae Ceaușescu yelled when I reported the news. Because of his close relationship with Arafat, Ceaușescu was afraid that his own name might be implicated in that awful crime. "S-s-stop h-him!" Ceaușescu repeated.

It was too late. A few hours later we learned that, after President Richard Nixon refused the terrorists' demand, the PLO commando executed three of their hostages: US ambassador Cleo A. Noel Jr.; his deputy, George Curtis Moore; and Belgian chargé d'affaires, Guy Eid. According to Hassan, the PLO chairman himself ordered, via radio, that the hostages be shot.

In 2002, I learned quite a few more details about Arafat's personal involvement in this brutal assassination from James Welsh, a retired US Navy officer and former intelligence analyst for the National Security Agency (NSA) during 1972–1974. Welsh gave me original documents and intercept transcripts showing that in February–March 1973, NSA had secretly recorded the radio communications between Arafat and Abu Jihad during the PLO operation "Nahr al-Barad," which ended with the killing of Ambassador Cleo Noel. These conversations were recorded by Mike Hargreaves, an NSA officer stationed in Cyprus, and the transcript was kept in a file code-named "Fedayeen."[1]

According to Welsh's documents, Arafat used a Racal single sideband radio tuned to 7150 kHz to communicate with Abu Jihad. On March 2, 1973, at around 8 p.m. local time, Abu Jihad radioed the order to execute the hostages taken in operation "Nahr al-Barad." Because an hour later the international media had still not reported the killing, Arafat himself reiterated the order, via his radio, to kill the hostages. Later that same day, Arafat radioed his gunmen again, telling them to release Saudi and Jordanian diplomats and to surrender to Sudanese authorities. "Explain your just cause to [the] great Sudanese Arab masses and international opinion. We are with you on the same road."[2]

To the best of my knowledge, the United States government never accused Arafat of this unequivocally proven crime—either in a court of law, or even in the "court of public opinion." Nor did Arafat publicly acknowledge it, although he regarded that atrocious assassination as a badge of honor. I learned from Romania's former prime minister Ion Gheorghe Maurer that in May 1973, during a private dinner with Ceaușescu in Bucharest, Arafat excitedly bragged about this cold-blooded assassination. Maurer, a Western-educated lawyer who had just retired as Romanian prime minister, attended that dinner. "Be careful," Maurer told Arafat. "No matter how high-up you are, you can still be convicted for killing and stealing." Although a fanatical communist, Maurer had a kind of prurient, superstitious fear of being caught breaking what he called those two most fundamental laws of civilization.

"Who, me?" Arafat said, winking mischievously. "I never had anything to do with that operation."

Yasser Arafat was a product of the Kremlin's "science" of disinformation, and he ultimately became an expert in manipulating this invisible weapon. Arafat – whose real name was Mohammed Yasser Abdel Rahman Abdel Raouf Arafat al-Qudwa al-Husseini, and his nom de guerre Abu Ammar— was actually a bourgeois Egyptian nationalist-turned–Palestinian-terrorist by a KGB disinformation operation in the mid-1960s. As a first step, the KGB destroyed the official records of Arafat's birth in Cairo, Egypt, replacing them with fictitious documents attesting that he had been born in Jerusalem and was indeed a Palestinian by birth. In the early days of his rise to prominence, many Arabists viewed Arafat's new birthplace with skepticism. Even twenty-two years later, one of the best-documented books on the PLO stated that Arafat "was born in Cairo or Gaza on 27 August 1929."[3] Eventually, however, it seems that his fictitious birth certificate manufactured by the KGB came into its own, for today the international media generally portray him as a Palestinian by birth. As Mao Zedong famously said, "a lie repeated a hundred times becomes the truth."

Next, the KGB gave Arafat an "ideology" and an "ideological image," just as it gave them to Indian communist Romesh Chandra, the chairman of the undercover KGB organization portentously named the World Peace Council. In Europe, most of such people officially came across simply as peace activists, women's rights promoters, environmentalists, and the like. Those kinds of ideological orientations did not, however, have mass appeal in the Arab world. Therefore, the KGB disinformation machinery portrayed Arafat as a rabid anti-Zionist—an image that was not at all difficult. For him the KGB also selected a "personal hero"—the Grand Mufti Haj Amin al-Husseini, who had visited Auschwitz in the late 1930s and reproached the Germans for *not being more determined in exterminating the Jews*. (In 1985, Arafat is on record as having paid the mufti homage, saying he was "proud no end" to be walking in his footsteps.[4])

Even while I was still in Romania, I did not know the name of the KGB officer handling Arafat—that was the normal practice. Although the KGB knew the identities of all DIE officers, it never disclosed the identies of its own officers—even the head of the Soviet foreign intelligence service, General Sakharovsky, traveled to Romania under an operational alias (Aleksandr Sakharov). Many years later, however, Oleg Gordievsky, a former KGB officer who defected to Britain, revealed that in the 1970s, Arafat's KGB case officer was Lt. Col. Vasily Fedorovich Samoylenko. The latter was also responsible for secretly bringing Arafat's terrorists into the Soviet Union to be trained at the KGB's Balashikha special-operations training school east of Moscow.[5]

The KGB disinformation department tasked Arafat to create and head a terrorist group named Fatah, and in the aftermath of the 1967 Six-Day Arab-Israeli War it maneuvered to catapult him up as chairman of the PLO. Egyptian ruler Gamal Abdel Nasser, who was also a Soviet puppet,[6] publicly proposed the appointment.[7] The rest is history.

In 1978, Soviet leader Leonid Brezhnev and his KGB chairman, Yuri Andropov, involved my former boss, Nicolae Ceaușescu, in a disinformation plot, the goal of which was to get the United States to establish diplomatic relations with Arafat. The idea was simple: Have Arafat pretend to transform the terrorist PLO into a government-in-exile that was willing to renounce terrorism. Brezhnev and Andropov believed that newly elected US President Jimmy Carter would swallow the bait. Moscow gave Ceaușescu the job, because by 1978 he had become Washington's most favored tyrant. Ceaușescu accepted it, because he envisioned that this disinformation plot might bring the Nobel Peace Prize to both Arafat and himself.

"But we are a revolution," Arafat exploded, after Ceaușescu explained what the Kremlin wanted from him. "We were born as a revolution, and we should remain an unfettered revolution." Arafat postulated that the Palestinians lacked the tradition, unity, and discipline to become a formal state. That statehood was only something for a future generation. That all governments, even communist ones, were limited by laws and international agreements, and he was not willing to put any laws or other obstacles in the way of the Palestinian struggle to *eradicate* the state of Israel.

However, my former boss was able to persuade Arafat to focus on tricking President Carter. Although Ceaușescu sympathetically agreed that "a war of terror is your only realistic weapon," he also told Arafat that if he would transform the PLO into a government-in-exile and pretend to break with terrorism, the West would shower him with money and glory. "But you have to keep on pretending, over and over," my boss emphasized.

In April 1978, I accompanied Ceaușescu to Washington, where he convinced President Carter that he could persuade Arafat to transform his PLO into a law-abiding government-in-exile, if the United States would establish official relations with him. Three months later, I was granted political asylum by the United States, and Romania's tyrant lost his dream of getting the Nobel Peace Prize. In 1994, however, Arafat was granted the coveted prize because he promised to transform his terrorist organization into a kind of government-in-exile (the Palestinian Authority) and pretended, over and over, that he would abolish the articles in the 1964 PLO Covenant that call for the destruction of the State of Israel and would eradicate Palestinian terrorism.

In 1995, however, the number of Israelis killed by Palestinian terrorists rose by 73 percent compared to the two-year period preceding Arafat's Nobel Peace Prize.[8] At the end of the 1998–99 Palestinian school year, all 150 new schoolbooks used by Arafat's Palestinian Authority described Israel as the "Zionist enemy" and equated Zionism with Nazism.

In September 2000, Arafat started a second intifada. By June 2002, there were already a recorded 13,494 incidents of Palestinian terrorism against Israelis, in which more than six hundred civilians had lost their lives.[9] Six months later, the number of Israeli civilians killed by the PLO's "martyrs" exceeded seven hundred.[10]

Of course, people can change over the years, but only if they cut the ties to their past. I did just that. It was a wrenching experience, but it gave me an entirely new perspective. Arafat was never motivated to change, because well-meaning Western heads of state kept telling him what a great leader he was. At the signing of the Wye Accord at the White House on October 23, 1998, for instance, President Bill Clinton concluded his public remarks by thanking Arafat for "decades and decades and decades of tireless representation of the longing of the Palestinian people to be free, self-sufficient, and at home."[11]

Let us hope that the killer of Ambassador John Christopher Stevens in Benghazi will not get the Nobel Peace Prize, nor be given a red-carpet reception at the White House.

Yasser Arafat died in Paris on November 11, 2004, following a short illness. The cause of death was not clear. In July 2012, Swiss reports on tests on

Arafat's clothing indicated that he may have died of poisoning with Polo-nium-210. In November 2012, an international team of forensic pathologists opened Arafat's tomb in Ramallah on the West Bank and took samples from portions of his body, to carry out further investigation.[12]

So far, as mentioned earlier, there has been just one other known case of death by poisoning with Polonium-210, that of former KGB officer Alexander Litvinenko (2006), who had defected to Great Britain and revealed some earth-shattering KGB/FSB secrets to the British foreign intelligence service, MI6. One of those secrets, which became public, was that Ayman al-Zawahiri, the current leader of al-Qaeda, was trained for half a year by the KGB/FSB in Dagestan in 1997.[13] Another of Litvinenko's extremely damaging disclosures that became public knowledge was that Romano Prodi, a former prime min-ister of Italy and the tenth president of the European Commission, had been a longtime intelligence agent of the KGB/FSB. Litvinenko reported that he had learned this information from KGB General Anatoly Trofimov during the period when he, Litvinenko, was still working for the KGB/FSB. Trofimov was shot dead in Moscow in 2005.[14] In 2002, the Mitrokhin Commission, a parliamentary committee set up in 2002 by the Italian Parliament to investigate alleged KGB ties to Italian politicians, concluded that Prodi was "the KGB's man in Italy,"[15] and that he had been peripherally involved in the 1978 assassi-nation of Italian Prime Minister Aldo Moro, who was kidnapped and murdered by the KGB-financed terrorist organization known as the Red Brigades.[16]

On November 1, 2006, Litvinenko suddenly fell ill—like Arafat—and was hospitalized. Litvinenko's illness was later attributed to poisoning with Polonium-210, a highly toxic isotope known to be used by the former Soviet Union as neutron trigger, or initiator, for nuclear weapons. Litvinenko died on November 22, 2006. The Crown Prosecution Service, on May 22, 2007, called for the extradition to the UK of Russian citizen and resident Andrey Lugovoy (a former KGB officer), on charges of having murdered Litvinenko. On July 5, 2007, Russia declined to extradite Lugovoy. Overnight, he remarkably became a member of the Russian Duma, thus receiving parliamentary immunity!

At the time of this writing, no one knows if Polonium-210 will be found in the samples of Arafat's bones taken from his exhumed body. Nevertheless, there is solid ground for postulating that the KGB/FSB may have gotten tired of Arafat and decided to get rid of him. Arafat had become the symbol of today's disinformation and terrorism, and he had started being known as the KGB's man—at the top of the KGB community he was nicknamed *"Cheyadbom"* (from *Chelovecheskaya Yadernaya Bomba,* or human nuclear bomb). Original documents sneaked out of KGB/FSB archives after the collapse of the Soviet Union have added fuel to the fire.

Documents in the Mitrokhin Archive describe Arafat's close collaboration with my Romanian DIE and with the KGB in the early 1970s. Other documents disclose the KGB's secret training provided to Arafat's guerrillas, and reveal the supersecret channels used by the KGB to provide arms shipments to the PLO. Some of these documents even reveal the supersecret KGB dacha, code-named "Barvikha-1," used by Wadie Haddad, the head of Arafat's front organization in charge of smuggling weapons from the Soviet Union. Other KGB documents smuggled out by Mitrokhin show that KGB chairman Andropov sought Brezhnev's approval to use Haddad for kidnapping the CIA's deputy station chief in Lebanon.

On May 25, 1970, Brezhnev approved the kidnapping, and the new chief of Department V (kidnappings and assassinations), Gen. Nikolay Pavlovich Gusev, assigned Haddad to the task.[17] Fortunately, that operation ended in failure.

Other secret KGB information that became public showed that, during a visit to Moscow in May 2001, Arafat forged a secret alliance with Iran, involving Iranian shipments of heavy weapons to PLO terrorists. This new partnership was arranged at a clandestine meeting in Moscow between two of Arafat's top aides (Fuad Shobaki, the chief financial officer for military operations, and Fathi al-Razem, the deputy commander of the Palestinian naval police) and an Iranian government official whose name was not disclosed. In exchange for Iran's help, Arafat agreed to provide Iran with access to Palestinian intelligence on Israeli military positions.[18]

Seven months later, on January 4, 2002, Israeli navy and air force units captured a freighter in the Red Sea carrying some fifty tons of offensive weapons that had been loaded in Iran. The ship, the *Karine A,* was owned by the Palestinian Authority (PA) and captained by a PA naval policeman. The Israeli military took the captured ship to Israel, where the Israelis publicly exhibited the arms found on it. Most of the weapons displayed were prohibited to the PA by the Oslo accord agreed to by Arafat in 1993. Among the latter were long-range, Soviet-built Katyusha rockets, long-range mortars, antitank missiles, and a large quantity of Semtex-type explosive. Lt. Gen.

Shaul Mofaz, the chief of the Israeli Army, said that if this warfare equipment "had reached the hands of [Palestinian] terrorists," it might have "drastically increased the terror activity" in the Middle East.[19]

It is significant that, although Israel and the United States published undeniable written evidence proving that Arafat was personally involved in the above *Karine A* affair concerning smuggling prohibited arms from Iran, Arafat had stubbornly denied, including in a widely publicized personal letter to President George W. Bush, that he had had any knowledge of it.

In 2002, Arafat carried out yet another mass deception, the operational details of which indicated he still had KGB/FSB disinformation advisers helping him. By the spring of 2001, deadly suicide bombings within Israel had become an almost daily occurrence. These attacks culminated with the "Passover Massacre" of March 27. A Palestinian terrorist walked into the dining room of the Park Hotel in the coastal city of Netanya and exploded a bomb, killing 29 people and injuring 140 others.[20] Unwilling to further tolerate the daily murder of its civilians, Israel launched operation "Defensive Shield" (March 29–April 21, 2001). Its purpose was to dismantle the PLO terrorist infrastructure, concealed in the city of Jenin, which had become a terrorist headquarters complete with bomb factories.[21]

When the Israeli troops rolled into the PLO's Jenin terrorist camp in April 2002, they found a whole network of tunnels and bunkers filled with explosives set to detonate when Israeli troops entered the site. Thirteen Israeli soldiers died when a fourteen-year-old Palestinian suicide bomber sparked a series of explosions that demolished such a building while the soldiers were searching it.[22] Thereupon, Arafat's Palestinian Authority successfully launched a three-pronged disinformation plan that precisely followed the KGB rules for minimizing a national disaster: deny direct involvement in it, minimize the damage, and when the truth comes out, insist that the enemy was at fault.

First, Arafat denied any responsibility in that tragedy. Next, he refused to acknowledge that any Israeli soldier was killed in that disaster. And when the truth finally came out, Arafat's disinformation machinery launched the false rumor that the Jenin catastrophe had been caused by the Israeli soldiers, who had allegedly killed more than a thousand Palestinian civilians, who were still buried in the rubble.[23]

In May 2002, however, after all the bodies had been recovered from the Jenin camp, the deputy chief of the UN office in Jenin, Charles Kapes, reported that only fifty-four Palestinians had in fact been killed. The Israelis reported that they had found only forty-six dead in the rubble, including a pile of five bodies that had been booby-trapped.

"No matter whose figures one accepts," concluded David Holley, a British military expert working for Amnesty International, "there was no massacre."[24] US Secretary of State Colin Powell also officially announced there was no evidence of any Israeli massacre in Jenin, as alleged by the Palestinians.[25]

In April 2002, former director of central intelligence James Woolsey dismissed PLO claims that its chairman had been democratically elected. "Arafat was essentially elected the same way Stalin was, but not nearly as democratically as Hitler, who at least had opponents," Woolsey stated.[26] He knew what he was talking about, for he was at the CIA's helm when Arafat's PLO began making its grand conversion from an organization of bloody terrorists to an alleged governing body ostensibly holding fair elections. The exposure of the Jenin deception, which had the fingerprints of a KGB-type disinformation operation all over it, seems to have been the last drop in Arafat's glass. It was time for him to go.

A new, more Western-looking leader was poised to replace the blood-stained, old-fashioned, compromised Arafat. Few people noticed that Mahmoud Abbas, who took Arafat's place and continues to be president of the (newly named) Palestinian National Authority, was also educated in the former Soviet Union. Abbas graduated from Patrice Lumumba University in Moscow, a KGB-controlled school whose secret task was to create a new generation of foreigners dedicated to promoting the Kremlin's interests in their home countries. The first 288 students from forty-seven countries graduated in 1965. Soon after that, General Aleksandr Sakharovsky, who had been chief Soviet adviser to Romania's Securitate before becoming the Soviet Union's foreign intelligence boss, requested my DIE to help find "friendly foreigners" who could be granted scholarships at Lumumba. To the best of my knowledge, all foreign students at Lumumba were cooperating, in one way or another, with the foreign branch of the KGB.

Furthermore, few people realized that soon after Arafat's death, the United Nations itself turned into an open KGB/FSB puppet. On December 2, 2004, UN Secretary-General Kofi Annan endorsed the proposals of the "High-Level Panel on Threats, Challenges and Change," commissioned by him to build a UN "for the twenty-first century."[27] The panel recommended that the United States and Israel be further isolated by establishing the rule that only the UN could authorize preemptive wars against terrorism or any other threats. It is hard to believe, but true, that the main member of Annan's blue-ribbon panel was former KGB general Yevgeny Primakov, a former Soviet intelligence adviser to Saddam Hussein, who rose to head Russia's espionage service for a time—and to sing opera ditties with US secretary of state Madeleine Albright while secretly running the infamous Aldrich Ames spy case behind her back. Another prominent member was Qian Qichen, a former Red Chinese intelligence officer, who had worked under diplomatic cover abroad, had belonged to the Central Committee of the Communist Party when it ordered the bloody Tiananmen Square repression in 1989, had afterward risen to the Politburo, and in 1998 had become vice chairman of China's State Council. And then there was Amr Moussa, the secretary-general of the Arab League, who "misses the balance of power provided by the Soviet Union"[28] and is still unable to condemn—let alone prevent—terrorism.

43

MARXIST PERSONALITY CULTS AND HEAVY WATER

T HE LAST SUNDAY IN JUNE was the first really summery day of the year 1978, enticing almost all of Romania outdoors to enjoy the warm sun. Even the country's workaholic president, Nicolae Ceauşescu, cut short the meeting he was holding with his closest collaborators and pushed his entourage out for a game of volleyball.

"Let's go home," Elena announced to her husband, after his team had, as usual, won the game. She cackled like a mother hen—and walked like a duck—but her tone of voice left no room for argument.

As soon as the Ceauşescus had safely disappeared, I hopped into my car. "Home," I commanded. "Home," the driver repeated mechanically, slamming the navy blue Alfa Romeo into gear and taking off with tires squealing. "It's been a while since you last saw your house in the daylight, hasn't it, General?"

In Ceauşescu's Romania, as in all former Soviet bloc countries, the supreme leader was god, and his intelligence service was the magic wand that he hoped would transform the country into his temple. During the previous months I had been more enslaved to my job than ever before, and I now felt a sudden urge to do something, anything, for myself.

It had been a hectic few weeks. Ceauşescu, who wanted to be portrayed to the world as an independent nationalist who would breach the wall surrounding the Soviet bloc, had tasked my DIE with launching the lie in the West that he had been courageous enough to execute one of his senior generals, Ion Serb, after catching him red-handed passing secret documents to the Soviets. The general was neither charged with espionage nor executed; nevertheless, soon a stream of articles on the "courageous" Ceaușescu appeared in Western Europe and the United States.

Once that fable had been floated, Ceaușescu had rushed me off to Bangui to prepare a new visit for him to the Central African Republic, although my real task was to persuade President Jean-Bédel Bokassa that Ceaușescu had not only anti-Soviet but also anti-American leanings and thereby to charm Bokassa into granting the "independent" Ceaușescu concessions for operating some of his diamond mines. As it turned out, that task proved to be a breeze compared to my efforts to find a beauty salon there for Elena. During her last visit to Bangui, her Romanian hairdresser had come down with an intestinal bug, so this time I—unsuccessfully—had to scour those equatorial rain forests for a beauty salon that would do Elena's hair. It was all part of my job.

Afterward I had accompanied my boss to Cairo, and even before we had returned to Bucharest, he packed me off to West Germany to give a new push to his Fokker gambit. Then the Soviet KGB's recruitment of the commander of the Bucharest military garrison was secretly recorded on tape by Romanian counterintelligence, and all hell had broken loose. Overnight I had to bring Western medical experts to Bucharest to revive the prostrate Ceaușescu. The following week I had to ensure that the West was flooded with the rumor that the hardline communists in Romania had, under Moscow's manipulation, rebelled against Ceaușescu's policy of independence and had forced him to ask for a secret vote of confidence, which he had barely won through the promise of higher wages, a shorter workweek, and larger pensions.

"Scare the [Western] idiots into thinking they might lose me," he instructed.

In short, this particular Sunday was the first time I would have a chance to spend a couple of hours all to myself, and I felt a sudden urge to indulge myself, even if it was only by watering the flowers in my garden. As we sped down Kiseleff Chaussee, the fancy Bucharest avenue leading to my villa, my mind wandered off, musing that in a few minutes I would be home. I could already picture myself jumping into the swimming pool—a long, refreshing swim to begin with.

"Did you change the water?" I asked the driver. There was no chlorine available in Bucharest during those years, so the handful of elite *nomenkla-tura* people who were lucky to have a swimming pool had to keep replacing the water.

"I'm sorry, General," the driver said, nervously pumping the brake even though the street ahead was as clean as a whistle. "I forgot." He mopped his forehead with his sleeve. Even after driving me for five years, he still broke into a sweat whenever he had done something wrong, although I cannot remember ever having raised my voice at him. Maybe that was just the trouble.

The awkward silence in the car was broken by a female voice blaring out over the radio telephone: "Sixty-two, report to zero-one. Repeat, sixty-two report to zero-one." Sixty-two was my code in Ceaușescu's private radio telephone network, and zero-one was Ceaușescu's. "Sixty-two reporting to zero-one," I answered. So much for my swim.

Without waiting to be told, the driver spun the car around to the left with a squeal of the tires and floored the accelerator. Magically, all the traffic lights stretching out before us at once turned green, as the militia officers manning them recognized my car.

"Too bad, Comrade General," my driver sympathized.

Ceaușescu was in his enormous library pacing around in circles, hand inside his lapel, and going as fast as his stubby legs could propel his short frame. He had spent many hours in front of the mirror, perfecting his Napoleonic walk. Napoleon, also five-foot-three, was his idol.

"Who slept with whom last week?" Ceaușescu shouted across the room the moment he spotted me. Keeping tabs on the private lives of Romania's highest dignitaries was another of my secret assignments.

To become the unquestioned leader, one must know the weaknesses of one's subordinates—that constituted the "kernel of truth" in disinformation operations aimed at demoting uncomfortable people. The typically Soviet— or perhaps historically Russian—tendency of the ruler to distrust everyone around him, and to misuse his intelligence apparatus to learn the human foibles of the country's top bureaucrats, gave rise to supersecret bugging units assigned to monitor the top *nomenklatura* in the Soviet Union and some of its closest satellites. Among those secretly bugged by Ceaușescu were the country's prime minister and his deputies, the members of the Politburo, and the most important members of the cabinet, such as the ministers of defense, foreign affairs and foreign trade. Eventually, Ceaușescu even went so far as to monitor his own children and all the members of his and his wife's families.

"What's new with our man in Dunărea?" Ceaușescu asked, after I had filled him in on the latest juicy gossip.

I had been waiting for that too. There were few things in life more important to Ceaușescu in those days than his project for heavy water, which he himself had baptized with the codename "Dunărea," the Romanian name for the Danube. Ceaușescu dreamed of building himself into the leader of the Third World by making his "independent" Romania a nuclear country, and heavy water was the first step toward attaining that dream. Our man in Dunărea was a DIE illegal officer documented as a Western engineer who had allegedly never even heard of Romania. He had gotten himself hired by Atomic Energy of Canada Limited, where he had been given a top-secret clearance.

Fortunately, I did have some good news about him that I could use to stave off another of Ceaușescu's legendary outbursts of wrath whenever he disliked what he was hearing. The week before, I reported, we had brought the man into Romania "black," in order to give him Ceaușescu's latest orders. The cover for his absence from work, I explained, had been a long getaway weekend on the Spanish island of Majorca, and now he was already back in Canada.

"No slipups?" Ceaușescu asked. Espionage was his hobby.

I reported that one of my illegal officers had taken the man's place vacationing in Palma de Mallorca, and that the tips he had given the hotel personnel had been fat enough for them to remember him by. The two illegal officers, I pointed out, could pass for twins.

Ceaușescu allowed a smile to cross his sallow face. Any deception gave him a high. I said the fellow was as gung-ho as ever, and in two weeks he would be dead-dropping the first batch of undeveloped films containing blueprints for Dunărea.

"Go-o-od!" Ceaușescu stopped in front of me, grabbed one of the buttons of my jacket, and lowered his voice. "Would it be dangerous to have the Dunărea plant built in Scornicești?" He giggled, evidently excited by the idea of seeing his otherwise unremarkable little native town elevated to become the heart of Romania's nuclear program.

As I remember, I paused for a moment, pretending to admire the twenty-four-volume sets of his collected speeches lining the library walls. Four months earlier, when Ceaușescu had made me responsible for Dunărea, he had signed a top-secret presidential decree charging the Ministry of

Chemical Industry to produce heavy water industrially before the end of that five-year plan. Nobody, however, had dared to tell him that in all of Romania there was only handful of engineers who had even heard about heavy water, and I was thinking this might be a good day for me to break the bad news to him.

"There's just one little problem, though," I ventured.

"Out with it!" Ceaușescu's beady eyes shot me a wary look. "Where's the shit?" he asked nervously, anxious to get the bad news out in the open, where he could deal with it. "Did the Canadian police spot our man in Dunărea?"

By then I had learned that with Ceaușescu the best tactic was to let him guess for himself what the bad news was, rather than hit him over the head with it. Ceaușescu loved to watch whodunit movies, but only those in which he could anticipate the next move—he despised Hitchcock, whom he could never outguess.

The problem was not with our man in Dunărea, I answered. He was as clean as a hound's tooth. I tried to set the scene to help Ceaușescu along. The Canadians, I said, needed several hundred experts only to design their heavy water installations, and that was without counting the ones involved in constructing, and now in managing, their heavy water plant.

"Got it!" Ceaușescu exclaimed, snapping his fingers. "You want to say we don't have experts, right?" His expression took on a sly glint. "Well, that's why I torture myself by putting up with you, *mon cher.*"

Time to get it out, I thought, when I saw Ceaușescu winking in complicity. It would take Romania, I explained, a lot less time to build the factory as a joint venture with the Canadians than if we tried to do it all by ourselves based only on stolen technology. Here I stopped to read my boss's face. Taking the offensive was a good tactic to use with him, but only up to a certain point. The trick was not to go beyond that point.

For a moment, Ceaușescu looked puzzled. Then he let go of my jacket button. "N-No j-joint v-venture!" he finally yelled. "N-Never! If the C-Canadians could do it, we should be able to do it b-better!" Canada was only three hundred years old, he reasoned, raising his voice to a full-throated scream, while Romania had been around for more than two thousand years.

Ceaușescu's increased stuttering betrayed a towering rage, which had, as usual, blown up with the suddenness of a summer thunderstorm. High time to beat a retreat: "I've got a new movie for you this evening, if you like—

one about Napoleon."

"Where is it?" Ceaușescu asked, dropping his stutter.

"In the trunk of my car."

"What are we waiting for?" Ceaușescu led the way to his movie room with eager step and vigorously swinging arms. The rhythmic *clickety-click* as his heel taps hit the marble floor echoed down the corridor after him.

It was long after midnight when I reached my home again. Ceaușescu had been unable to sleep, and he had kept me there for a second movie. Saluting the security officer guarding my house and the Polish Embassy, I stared ahead at my dark windows. Mechanically I unlocked the front door and hung up my jacket. I grabbed up one of the classified telephones on my desk and dialed four digits. "You're free to go home," I growled at my executive officer, Lt. Col. Vasile Pop. I banged down the receiver, immediately feeling sorry for the poor fellow on the other end of the line. His life was certainly worse than mine, as he could never leave the office until after he had learned that I had arrived safely home, and in the morning he had to be at his desk at least half an hour ahead of me.

I was eating a sandwich in the kitchen when a loud jangling noise shattered the silence. It was the ring of the red telephone connecting me with Ceaușescu. Involuntarily I gave a shudder. "No, Comrade Ceaușescu, I'm not asleep . . . . No, I'm not f*cking anybody. Of course I'll be there in the morning . . . . Nine o'clock? . . . Yes, Comrade, I'll be there at nine."

In February 2006, I wrote about that final Sunday I had spent with Ceaușescu in an article titled "Leftwing Monster: Ceaușescu."[1] He did indeed end up as an egocentric monster, but he was not a monster when he came to power. I knew him well. Ceaușescu was transformed into a monster by Marxism and its disinformation machinery.

The Socialist Republic of Romania has been defined, both within its borders and in the West, as a dictatorship based on the mass appeal of Marxist ideology and on the strong arm of the Communist Party. In other words, Socialist Romania—like the other Soviet bloc countries—has been wrongly regarded, both at home and abroad, as having a form of government that, although dictatorial, ruled through a political party and through decisions based on a political ideology. That was *disinformation*.

Only a handful of people working in extremely close proximity to the Romanian leader and other Soviet bloc rulers, as I was, knew that over the years the Communist Party became a grab-bag of bureaucrats who, as a matter of fact, played no greater role in running those countries than did Lenin's embalmed corpse languishing in the Kremlin mausoleum.

Seen in its historical perspective, Marxism was such a raw, ill-defined and malleable system of government that one could make of it whatever one wished. Had it succeeded in France or Germany, Marxism would have certainly evolved into another Paris Commune or neo-Prussian military dictatorship, and it would have come to an untimely end like those other precedents. There was no way for any horde of bureaucrats or even for a huge military machine to sustain—for seventy long years—a form of government that utterly denied the motivational forces that have kept mankind alive throughout history: private property, competition and individual incentive.

It so happened that Marxism triumphed in feudal Russia, defined by its own luminaries as "a whole separate world, submissive to the will, caprice and fantasy of a single man, whether his name be Peter or Ivan."[2] There, Marxism gradually devolved into a secret and complicated, but essentially uncontaminated *samoderzhaviye*, the traditional Russian form of totalitarian autocracy in which a feudal lord ruled the country with the help of his personal political police. Floods of government publications, agitprop agents and community organizers worked around the clock to persuade the rest of the world that their country, although dictatorial, was governed by a political party that based its decisions on an idealistic political philosophy. In reality, every Marxist country ended up being run by one man, who transformed that country into a monument to himself.

The outrageous Marxist cult of personality was born. In some Marxist countries, this cult of the ruler has over the years even come to give him the right of life and death over his people. Stalin killed millions with impunity in order to transform Russia into a monument to himself. After his Red Army "liberated" Romania, Stalin transformed that country into a monument to himself as well. Stalin portraits, Stalin statues, Stalin streets, Stalin boulevards, Stalin plazas, and Stalin factories sprouted up like mushrooms all over the country. Romania even got its own Stalin city.

In 1947, Stalin forced Romania's heroic King Michael to abdicate, decreed that Romania should become a Marxist country, and installed on its throne a little Romanian Marxist god named Gheorghe Gheorghiu-Dej. Soon after that, every Romanian town also acquired its Gheorghiu-Dej monument, Gheorghiu-Dej street, Gheorghiu-Dej boulevard, Gheorghiu-Dej plaza, and Gheorghiu-Dej square. Before long, quite a few industrial and agricultural organizations boasted similar names. That outrageous cult of personality worked for the illiterate Gheorghiu-Dej, who was able to keep his throne until he died in 1956. It did not work for Romania, however, which became a kind of European Ethiopia, whose lack of freedom and depth of poverty aroused worldwide pity and compassion.

Ceaușescu "unmasked" Dej's "unprecedented" cult of personality, and allowed the plebs to cast their eyes on the opulence of Dej's palace. It was not long, however, before Ceaușescu proclaimed himself a "lay god" and began alternately residing in twenty-one lavishly furnished palaces, forty-one "residential villas," and twenty hunting lodges. Grandiose arches inscribed "The Golden Age: The Age of Nicolae Ceaușescu" appeared at the entrances to most Romanian cities. The Romanian media—Ceaușescu's main disinformation instrument—did its part, naming Ceaușescu the "Most Beloved Son of the People," the "Guarantor of the Nation's Progress and Independence," and the "Visionary Architect of the Nation's Future."

By 1989, Ceaușescu had seized all the top-level positions in the country and pinned them onto his own chest like war decorations, thereby establishing a dismal new feudalism in the middle of the twentieth century. Among them: president of Romania, leader of the Communist Party, supreme commander of the armed forces, chairman of the Supreme Council for Economic and Social Development, president of the National Council of Working People, chairman of the Socialist Democracy and Unity Front. By that time, the personality cult was extended to Ceaușescu's wife as well. Elena Ceaușescu became the country's first deputy prime minister, chair of the National Council on Science and Technology, and head of the National Council for Science and Education. Her national prominence had grown to the point that her birthday was celebrated as a national holiday, as was her husband's.

In 1978, when I broke with Ceaușescu, his portraits were hanging on the walls of every government office—and in Ceaușescu's Romania everything, from factories to schools to theaters, to movies and churches, were owned by the government.

44

HOW I BECAME A
"FILTHY JEW TRAITOR"

AFTER I HAD BEEN GRANTED political asylum by President Carter, the Romanian Supreme Court finally, on July 7, 1999, unanimously adopted Decision No. 41, canceling the two death sentences given to me by Ceaușescu in 1978. Decision No. 41 also ordered the Romanian government to restore my judicial and political rights, citizenship, military rank and all my properties confiscated by Ceaușescu. The chairman of the Supreme Court publicly stated that I had done in 1978 what all of Romania had done eleven years later—namely, sentenced Ceaușescu to death.

To the best of my knowledge, I became the first, and only, high-level Soviet bloc defector to the United States to be rehabilitated by his native country's Supreme Court (my Polish equivalent, Col. Ryszard Kukliński, was rehabilitated by the Polish government). I believe I am also the first, and only, "case" in which the government of a country belonging to the European Union has *refused* to implement a decision of its own Supreme Court.

Here's what happened. In 2003, the Romanian ambassador to Washington, Sorin Ducaru (now Romania's ambassador to NATO), informed the government of the United States and the American media (through Arnaud de Borchgrave, at that time editor-at-large of the *Washington Times* and *United Press International*) that Supreme Court Decision No. 41 had been implemented. It was a lie. Soon after, the *Washington Times* and *UPI* reported that, as of January 20, 2004, "Romania's border points still had arrest warrants out for General Pacepa, should he try to return."[1]

In Romania, my case is just the tip of the iceberg. In 2009, that country's Supreme Court, in Decision No. 293, declined to cancel a 1974 death sentence given by Ceaușescu to another intelligence defector, Constantin Răuță, who also committed the "crime" of "betraying" Ceaușescu's political police and helping the United States to defeat the Soviet evil.[2] Răuță, now an American citizen, became a reputable NASA scientist, who over the past thirty years worked on important US aerospace projects such as Hubble, EOS, and Landsat. He was also involved in the development of various space defense systems, making a substantial contribution to the security of the United States and her NATO allies. At the time of this writing, Răuță is still sentenced to death in Romania, a country that will soon be protected by a ground-based ballistic missile defense system in the development of which, ironically, Răuță himself played a role.[3] Construction of that US interceptor missile facility at a former air base in Deveselu, Romania, is scheduled to be finished in 2014. Yet, absent a miracle, Răuță will be still sentenced to death in that country.

Today's Romanian government may still consider anticommunism a crime, but it is nevertheless a NATO country. On November 23, 2002, when the Romanians were officially informed their country was being seated at the NATO table, a rainbow appeared in the sky over Bucharest. President George W. Bush, visiting Romania's capital at the time, told a cheering crowd, "God is smiling at us." God was indeed smiling at Romania. From one day to the next, that country, which has endured a long and dark history of Roman, Ottoman, Phanariot and Soviet occupations, no longer had to fear foreign domination. American soldiers, now stationed in Romania, are committed to defending that country's territorial integrity with their lives.

Yet Romania's justice system seems incapable of facing up to the fact that the country has been admitted into NATO. At the same time, its top justice representatives—mostly former communist judges or officers of Ceaușescu's *Securitate*—are chauffeured around in limousines imported from NATO countries.

In the past five years, 6,284 people sentenced by the communists for, in one way or another, helping the United States and NATO demolish the Soviet empire have asked to have their sentences canceled, but only three have succeeded—because of media pressure.[4] More than 500,000 patriots killed or terrorized by the communists have yet to be rehabilitated. At the same time, thousands of former *Securitate* officers and hundreds of thousands of its informants and collaborators who wrote the bloodiest era in Romania's history are still shielded by a veil of secrecy.

Professor Tom Gallagher, one of the world's leading experts on contemporary Romania, who teaches the evolution of postcommunist states at Bradford University in the UK, concluded that Romania had moved from rigid egalitarianism to superinegalitarianism run by ex-communists who pay lip service to democracy. This new elite has "widened the gap between a parasitic state and a demoralized society."

In Gallagher's view, Romania is not yet a democracy, because "a functional democracy cannot be based on lies, denial and amnesia." This is also the subject of his book *Theft of a Nation: Romania since Communism* (London: Hurst, 2004), which concludes that "a Romania under the control of corrupt ex-communists threatens to be a dangerous force for regional instability."

I'll put it my own way: Today we know all too well how a democracy can be transformed into a communist tyranny, but we are still learning how to reverse that nightmare.

In the 1950s, when I was acting chief of Romania's Mission to West Germany, I witnessed how the Third Reich was demolished, how West Germany's economy was rebuilt, and how that country became an established parliamentary democracy whose *Wirtschaftswunder* (economic miracle) made it the leading power in Europe to this day.

But not until 1998 was the Bundestag able to adopt a law canceling the sentences given to Claus von Stauffenberg, who continued to be considered a traitor for having led a plot to assassinate Hitler. Horst Heyman, president of the *Bundestag* commission that initiated this law, apologized to the German people because their parliament had needed fifty years to arrive at that point. Now the Germans who fought Nazism are honored in the grandiose *Haus der Geschichte der Bundesrepublik Deutschland,* the country's new museum of history.

Post-Ceaușescu Romania has changed for the good in many positive ways. The barriers the Soviets spent over seventy years erecting between themselves and the rest of the world, as well as between individual Soviet-bloc citizens, are slowly coming down. Romanian culture is reviving and a new generation of intellectuals is struggling to develop a new national identity. In 2004, Romania joined NATO, and in 2007 it was accepted into the European Union. Nevertheless, it may be that Romania must wait for a new generation, as was the case in the former Nazi Germany, to look back on communism's crimes with objective eyes.

Condemning the heresies of the past and rehabilitating its victims seems to be the most difficult step in the transition from tyranny to democracy. The former communist ruler of Poland, General Wojciech Jaruzelski, explained why: "If the victims should become heroes, what would *we* be?"

Romania's close proximity to Russia may not help either. In the 1970s, when I was Romania's national security adviser, I accompanied our prime minister on a visit to Pope Paul VI in Rome. If he could grant us one wish, the pope asked, what would that one wish be? "Change our geographical location," the clever prime minister replied.

Indeed, Romania was the only East European country not sharing a border with any Western country, and Ceaușescu, the snake-oil salesman who had seized the communist scepter in 1954, had compounded the problem with decades of news blackouts and outrageous disinformation operations.

Even when the Berlin Wall collapsed in November 1989, Romania was still so isolated that within two weeks Ceaușescu succeeded in pulling off a grandiose party congress that, to the fanfare of trumpets, reelected him and his illiterate wife as the country's benevolent rulers.

The 1989 fall of the Kremlin's East European viceroys was, for the most part, so peaceful that it enriched our vocabulary with the new term "velvet revolution." The exception was Romania, where the upheaval cost 1,104 dead and 3,352 wounded. Romania was also the only Soviet bloc country whose leader was executed by its own people. Ponder these differences with reluctant admiration for Romania, and you will realize that it may have a long way to go before becoming a truly Westernized country.

Here's where it gets personal. Currently there is a hard-hitting disinformation operation being conducted in Romania to rehabilitate Nicolae Ceaușescu and, in the process, to discredit the American CIA by discrediting *me*—for whom the CIA arranged asylum in 1978. The story goes that, according to some undisclosed documents allegedly found in CIA archives, Ceaușescu was really and truly a pro-Western leader who had intended to break Romania away from the Soviet bloc. Unfortunately, the story continues,

Ceaușescu was executed in 1989 because the CIA had concealed the truth about him to avoid having to admit it had granted me political asylum even though it knew all along that I had actually been a KGB agent all my life. (If this tale seems convoluted, that is just the nature of many disinformation stories. They just have to be constructed around some "kernel of truth"—the political asylum I received in 1978.)

History does repeat itself, and the annals of disinformation campaigns provide no exception. Recall the case of Pope Pius XII—originally highly praised by Roosevelt, Churchill, Einstein, and millions of others for his righteous outrage against the Nazis and his defense of the Jews during the Holocaust years, but who was then demonized by the *next* generation which bought into the Kremlin's disinformation that he had supported Hitler. Well, maybe now it's my turn to be demonized by the next generation.

The current disinformation campaign to rehabilitate Ceaușescu purports to be based on a "revelation" made by former director of Central Intelligence James Woolsey, according to which I had confessed to him, in his CIA office, that I was a KGB agent. This purported "revelation" was published in the violently anti-Semitic but very popular newspaper *Bursa,* which also alleged that I was a *Jidan* (in Romanian, the worst pejorative for a Jew) who hated the Romanians, as well as a homosexual and a womanizer.[5] Former head of the Securitate Lt. Gen. Iulian Vlad—who was in charge of assassinating me in the West after I broke with communism, and who was jailed three years for political homicide after communism collapsed—now has thrown more fuel on the fire by stating that I had been recruited by the CIA when I was ten years old.[6]

Anyone who may have read former director of Central Intelligence Woolsey's public endorsements of me and my bona fides over the years (including his enthusiastic introduction to this book!) would quickly have realized the statements about me made in *Bursa* and by General Vlad are bold lies crafted in fantasyland. But soon after *Bursa* launched the rumor that I was a KGB agent, a self-styled "American historian" named Larry Watts appeared in Romania to tell more stories about me. Watts had made something of a name in Ceaușescu's Romania and a fortune there post-Ceaușescu, and not long ago began traveling around that country to promote the so-called Romanian translation of a book he had allegedly written in English, in which he claims to "document" Ceaușescu's intention to break away from the Soviet bloc. But, you see, the noble Ceaușescu was unable to do so because his closest adviser, Lt. Gen. Ion Mihai Pacepa, was secretly working for the KGB—whence the title of Watts's book, *With Friends Like These*. It has become a bestseller in Romania.

It is noteworthy that Watts's "original" book in the English language was published only in Romania and appeared only *a year after* its Romanian "translation" had seen the light. That pretty much proves its role as disinformation. Clearly, Watts's book was first written in Romanian, for Romanian readers.

With Friends Like These is the second book Watts has written for Romanian consumption. His first, *Romanian Cassandra*, is an anti-Semitic harangue intended to rehabilitate Ion Antonescu, an earlier Romanian dictator under the Nazis, who was executed in 1946 as a war criminal. Antonescu was instrumental in the killing or deportation of some two hundred thousand Romanian Jews and gypsies, and his atrocious crimes are powerfully exposed in the US Holocaust Museum. *Romanian Cassandra* is another far-fetched disinformation project. Romanians are nationalists and Watts is accumulating a personal fortune by exploiting their nationalist sentiments.

Watts is a nebulous figure. Initially, he claimed to be working for the CIA, but that did not fly. In reality, Watts had settled in Romania during Ceaușescu's reign and had worked for Ceaușescu's brother, Gen. Ilie Ceaușescu, who at the time was political commissar of Romania's communist army. Watts settled in Ceaușescu's Romania together with another American, Kurt W. Treptow, who became the director of a Romanian Culture Institute, but in the early 1990s Treptow was sentenced to seven years in jail for pedophilia and expelled from Romania. Watts married a Romanian citizen and became a Romanian resident.

Currently, Watts travels around Romania giving speeches in which he accuses the CIA of hiding the truth that Pacepa was, and still is, a KGB agent. He is accompanied by former head of the Securitate Lieutenant General Vlad, sometimes sporting his general's uniform and the shiny medals he "earned" for defending Ceaușescu against CIA plots.

I have glanced through Watts's book but did not read it—I know my past. The meticulous student of communism Spyridon Mitsotakis did, at my request, spend several months studying *With Friends Like These*, after which he wrote me: "There is nothing in that book showing you had been a KGB agent." According to Spyridon, Watts simply compiled all the articles about the KGB that I had published in the past twenty years, reaching the conclusion that only someone who had worked for the KGB could have known so much about it.

In 2012, *Bursa* ignited a campaign to collect signatures on a petition demanding that the Romanian government open a criminal investigation against me for having been involved in the supersecret kidnapping in the late 1970s of Vladimir Dapčević, a Yugoslav émigré living in Belgium. The kidnapping of Dapčević was one of the best-kept secrets in Romania until 1987, when I revealed it in *Red Horizons*–and later in *Programmed to Kill* as well. I was not involved in that despicable kidnapping, which was conceived by Iosif (Broz) Tito and Ceauşescu and carried out by the *Securitate's* antiterrorist unit, a domestic outfit that had never been under my command. I did learn about it, however, and after I defected I revealed it both to the CIA and to the rest of the world, for it vividly illustrated the criminality of communist leaders.

The 1979 conclusion of the yearlong Romanian investigation of my "betrayal," a hundred-page report published in the *White Book of the Securitate* after Ceauşescu was executed, accused me of everything imaginable, but not of being involved in any assassinations.[7] To the contrary, it stated that I sabotaged such operations, as the one against Axente Teusan, a Romanian defector living in Austria. That is true. In July 1978, just days after defecting, I prevented three other DIE assassinations in the USA (against Ion Iacobescu, Dumitru Dumitrachescu, and Constantin Răuţă—whose designated assassin was arrested by the FBI).[8] I would not wonder, however, if the authors of the current disinformation aimed at rehabilitating Ceauşescu will insert fictitious documents in the DIE archive to amend my past as well. Changing people's pasts to match the ruler's future interests has long been a key disinformation tactic.

Older Romanians who once lived under Ceauşescu's reign of terror have treated Watts's allegations with scorn, in the same way the people who once witnessed Pius XII's strong defense of the Jews during the Holocaust treated Stalin's 1945 allegations that he was "Hitler's Pope" with scorn. A new Romanian generation has, however, started believing that Ceauşescu was indeed a national hero sent to the scaffold because Pacepa was a *Jidan* and not a Romanian, who betrayed his boss at the direction of the KGB and the CIA.

Currently, the Romanian state television system is busily spreading these allegations around, and more people are believing them. Whenever an article about me is published in the Romanian media, a number of people pop up with comments describing me as a "traitor" and a *Jidan* who hates Romania. Small wonder that in March 2009, the Bucharest house in which I had been living until I defected, which had afterwards become a kind of pilgrimage site, was quietly demolished overnight.[9]

Let me point out once again that in 1947, the Soviet disinformation machinery accused King Michael—who during the war had single-handedly turned Romania against Nazi Germany—of secretly being a Western and Eastern spy. That worked, and Romania went communist. The current disinformation campaign aimed at rehabilitating Ceaușescu at my expense also seems to be working. During the December 2012 parliamentary elections, over 60 percent of the votes went to Ceaușescu's former communists.

For full disclosure, I should mention that, soon after I was granted political asylum, President Carter did suggest that I may have been a KGB agent. In July 1978, in my eagerness to blurt out what I knew about the inner workings of the Soviet bloc's disinformation machinery, I immediately reported that Ceaușescu's glorious image in Washington had been handcrafted by the KGB and the DIE. I also reported that President Carter's brother, Billy, who was in the process of becoming a paid Romanian intelligence agent, was helping that process. That was not good news for President Carter—who just three months earlier had publicly hailed Ceaușescu as a "great national and international leader."[10] Therefore, President Carter alleged that my defection had been concocted by the KGB to destroy his excellent relations with Ceaușescu.

Sane minds prevailed, but President Carter prohibited me from publishing anything, including my own memoirs. Years later, Roger Kirk, who was the US ambassador to Romania when I defected, published his memoirs, *Romania Versus the United States: Diplomacy of the Absurd, 1985–1989*, written together with Mircea Raceanu, a Romanian diplomat sentenced to death by Ceaușescu, now a highly regarded American citizen. This book describes a September 1978 meeting between Romania's foreign minister and Matthew Nimetz, President Carter's personal envoy, who indirectly apologized to Ceaușescu for granting me political asylum. Nimetz also conveyed to the Romanian tyrant that the US administration would "do our utmost to assure that publicity on the Pacepa case is avoided completely, or kept at a bare minimum."[11] Roger Kirk attended that meeting, and in his book he also provided a transcript of the classified cable he sent to Washington after that meeting.

The Carter administration did indeed prohibit me from publishing anything for the rest of my life. Eventually, however, I found my way out of that trap. In September 1985, Sen. Sam Nunn (D-Georgia) helped me to send William Casey, the new director of central intelligence, a draft of my future book *Red Horizons* and a memo in which I asked why the US administration wanted to exchange my golden Romanian cage for one of its own making.[12]

In a letter dated December 17, 1985, Reagan's CIA Director Casey wrote that he found the manuscript of *Red Horizons* "very interesting" and added that it would be effective in providing a clearer picture of what was really going on inside Romania. "The president has read it and was impressed," he added.[13] On July 18, 1986, Casey also agreed with my memo: "I must commend you for the thoughtful and constructive effort that went into preparing this document."[14]

During a subsequent seventh-floor dinner at CIA headquarters in Langley, attended by most of the CIA division chiefs, Deputy DCI Robert Gates apologized to my wife and to me for all those wasted years. That CIA dinner was followed by many years of mutually productive cooperation with the CIA.

Red Horizons was published a few months later, and contained several pages describing the DIE recruitment of Billy Carter, who was soon forced to register officially as a foreign agent.

Romania is a marvelous country, that once had the misfortune of falling under the spell of Marxism, disinformation and *glasnost*. I love my native country. I treasure my first fifty years of life there, my youthful dreams, my relatives, my good friends, and the graves of my parents. I started my life from scratch at the age of fifty, in order to help Romania's courageous people rid themselves of one of the most disgusting tyrants history has ever known. I was heart and soul with my Romanian fellows during the burning days of the December 1989 popular rebellion. I cheered with them when the borders were thrown open, and I am extremely proud of my native country's freedom of the press. With all my heart, I want to see my fellow Romanians freeing themselves from the spell of Marxism and disinformation, and for Romania to reenter the democratic world to which it once belonged. That is another reason I wrote this book.

EPILOGUE

I N 1978, when I broke with communism, I left in my office safe a slip of
paper on which General Aleksandr Sakharovsky, head of the Soviet
bloc espionage community, had written, "*Gutta cavat lapidem, non
vi sed saepe cadendo*"—a drop makes a hole in a stone not by force, but by
constant dripping. That was how disinformation worked: drop by drop by
drop. It would take time, but wherever you could not use a drill, that was
the best way to make a hole.

This book, written together with Professor Ronald J. Rychlak, a leading
authority on international law, the history of religions, and Pius XII, was conceived with the intention of laying out in clear language the inner workings
of that *gutta* for all to see. Before going further, however, I want to express
my deep gratitude to Ron. Without his outstanding expertise in the fields of
religion and law and his unequaled aptitude for research, this book would
never have seen the light of day. Its chapters describing Pius XII's real past,
those vivisecting the KGB show trials against other high Catholic prelates,
and those scrutinizing *The Deputy* are solid proof of Ron's unique knowledge.
When I broke with the Soviet bloc evil, I was, of course, unable to take any
papers with me that could document all I knew about the Kremlin's immense
disinformation machinery and its supersecret operations. Ron proved to be
superbly helpful at filling that void, spending years to document my information. The voluminous endnotes to this book are testament to his perseverance.

Disinformation has become the bubonic plague of our contemporary life. Marx used disinformation to depict money as an odious instrument of capitalist exploitation. Lenin's disinformation brought Marx's utopian communism to life. Hitler resorted to disinformation to portray the Jews as an inferior and loathsome race so as to rationalize his Holocaust. Disinformation was the tool used by Stalin to dispossess a third of the world and to transform it into a string of gulags. Khrushchev's disinformation widened the gap between Christianity and Judaism. Andropov's disinformation turned the Islamic world against the United States and ignited the international terrorism that threatens us today. Disinformation has also generated worldwide disrespect, and even contempt, for the United States and its leaders.

During the Cold War, disinformation began infecting the shores of the United States itself. By 2004, when our war in Iraq encountered difficulties, it became a kind of unofficial US policy. Although that war was broadly authorized by 296 House members and 76 senators of both parties, the media scorned it as "Bush's war." Soon, "Bush lied, people died" became the slogan of the Democratic Party, whose leaders suddenly forgot that they themselves had voted for that war. Democratic senator Tom Daschle, the minority leader, called President Bush a miserable failure. The doormat at the entrance to the office of Democratic Party national chairman Terry McAuliffe featured a picture of the US president and the words, "Give Bush the Boot."

I did not have the privilege of being born in this unique land of freedom, but I grew up with the picture of the US president hanging on the wall of our house in Bucharest. My father, who spent most of his life working for the General Motors affiliate in Romania, loved America, but he never set foot in this country. For him, America was just the place of his dreams, thousands of miles away, and the American president was its tangible symbol. At the end of WWII, we had President Truman on the wall of our home. For us, and for many millions around the world, *he* had saved civilization from the barbarism of Nazism, and *he* had restored our freedom—for a while. From the Voice of America we learned that America loved Truman, and we loved America. It was as simple as that.

I still regard the American president as the symbol of this greatest country on earth. To me, he embodies the essence of our unique democracy: a government of the people, by the people, and for the people. The president of the United States is not a figurehead, as in parliamentary democracies.

The US president is the country's chief executive officer, its chief diplomat, chief guardian of its economy, and commander in chief of the most powerful military force on earth. The US president also heads the best intelligence community in the world, a cooperative federation of sixteen government agencies that are vital for the nation's security and the peace of the world.

In 2007, the *Wall Street Journal* published my article titled "Propaganda Redux," in which I exposed the Democratic Party's noxious use of disinformation to denigrate the president of the United States in an effort to win national elections.[1] Criticizing the country's president is as American as apple pie. Portraying him as the enemy of his own country is, however, an un-American phenomenon smuggled into the United States by the KGB disinformation machinery during the Cold War. My DIE was one of the smugglers.

In the Soviet empire's *sanctum sanctorum*, to which I once belonged, portraying the head of a country as its own enemy was called "political necrophagy," as I explained in an earlier chapter. It constituted a separate, highly classified branch of the "science" of disinformation. Although Marxism loudly proclaimed that the deciding role in history was to be played by "the people," all of the Marxists sitting on the Soviet-bloc thrones firmly believed that only the leader counted. From the lips of Khrushchev himself, I heard over and over: "Change the public image of the leader, and you change history."

As I noted previously, the Kremlin's political necrophagy was launched into the world on February 26, 1956, when Khrushchev exposed "Stalin's crimes" in a four-hour "secret speech." He was successful in destroying whatever remained of Russian reverence for Stalin. After Khrushchev, political necrophagy became the rule in the Kremlin. Brezhnev accused Khrushchev of having destroyed the unity of the communist world. When Gorbachev came along, he accused Brezhnev of having devastated the Soviet economy. Gorbachev even had some of Brezhnev's relatives arrested, in an obvious attempt to prove that the Soviet economy had been bankrupted by corrupt individuals, not by Marxism. For his part, Yeltsin accused Gorbachev's *perestroika* of "leading the country to ruin," and then Putin blamed Yeltsin for the "demise of the Soviet Union, the greatest catastrophe of the century."[2]

In my experience, political necrophagy is a treacherous, double-edged sword. The same disinformation technique used by leaders to consolidate and magnify their own power by defaming their predecessor is inevitably turned against them by their successor. This has long been the way among Soviet bloc communist leaders. At the risk of repeating myself, allow me to remind you that Khrushchev's death led to Brezhnev's denunciation of his predecessor for undermining Russia's traditional reverence for the Kremlin, even deeming him unworthy of burial in the Kremlin Wall alongside previous Russian leaders and refusing even to pay for Khrushchev's grave marker. Likewise, when Ceaușescu was executed in 1989, Romania's Supreme Court determined that so seriously had this tyrant subverted Romania's traditional regard for its leaders that he merited neither a coffin nor a grave, and instead dumped his corpse into a bag and abandoned it at a stadium.

In my other life, I spent decades scrutinizing the US from Europe and learned that international respect for America is directly proportionate to America's own respect for its elected leader. In the 1950s, when I was acting head of the Romanian Mission in West Germany, I often heard people on the street saying that the "Amis" (German nickname for the American occupation forces) had made the difference between day and night for them. "Night" meant communist East Germany, of course, whose citizens were scraping along under economic privation and *Stasi* brutality. But that was then. The lies about American presidents spread during the Cold War by the Kremlin's disinformation machinery eventually ignited a dislike or even hatred of America in a good part of Europe and the rest of the world. By 1978, when I broke with communism, the Soviet bloc disinformation machinery had allegedly collected some 700 *million* signatures on various international appeals blaming America for all the evils of the world—even for the famine in Ethiopia.

Now political necrophagy has spread to the United States and is eroding our own international prestige. During 2002, a group of 128 American intellectuals who opposed the notion that the "war on terrorism" was a "just war" sent a letter to their European counterparts calling for "a sane and frank European criticism of Bush's war policy."[3] Soon, European governments and public opinion began denigrating the United States with almost the same ferocity they'd had during the Vietnam War. France and Germany accused the US of torturing the al-Qaeda prisoners held at its military prison in Guantanamo Bay, Cuba. The British newspaper *Mirror* alleged that the United States was "killing innocents in Afghanistan."[4] The Paris daily *Le Monde* published a front-page article by Jean Baudrillard (a revered figure among American humanities professors over the last twenty-five years) asserting that "the Judeo-Christian West, led by the US, not only provoked the [September 11, 2001] terrorist attacks, it actually *desired* them."[5]

Robert Kennedy—not one of my favorite people—once said: "I do not run for the presidency merely to oppose any man but to propose new policies. I run because I am convinced that this country is on a perilous course and because I have strong feelings about what must be done."[6] Kennedy understood what the presidency was all about, whatever we may think of what he planned to do if given the mandate.

America's own respect for this unique republic and for the will of its people has been severely damaged by the "science" of disinformation. Helping my fellow Americans to restore this respect is another goal of this book.

The United States is the leader of the Free World, but it is certainly not a perfect country. As another proud American once put it, America, like all nations, is a collection of human beings, and human beings are notorious for occasionally making bad decisions, being selfish, or ignorant, or unwise.[7] But this imperfect America has almost single-handedly kept peace, freedom and democracy alive in the world for the last hundred years. At the beginning of the twentieth century, the world's democracies numbered fewer than a dozen. Since this imperfect United States of America became the recognized leader of the world, 80 percent of the countries on Planet Earth are either democracies or proto-democracies.[8]

This imperfect United States of America has also become the propelling force of the world's science and technology. Out of the 4.5 million patents issued since 1790 throughout the world, the United States owns more than half of them—nearly 2.5 million.[9] Out of the 629 Nobel Prizes for medicine, chemistry, physics, and economics earned across the entire globe, the United States owns 305.[10] The United States also leads the world in Internet innovations, music, movies, and numerous other fields that require enlightened, outside-the-box thinking. From Apple to DreamWorks Studios to Amazon, the United States is the world's innovator.[11]

The United States has been a beacon for the whole free world. What is its secret? To all those immigrants who stepped off the boat onto Ellis Island, speaking no English and carrying ten dollars in their pockets, it was the unparalleled freedom they found in their new country.

On March 22, 2003, one of these immigrants—this writer—published an open letter to the Iraqi generals who were still fighting our troops. "Do as I did," I told them. "Turn your weapons against your country's tyrant. Break away from your tyrannical dictator before it is too late. Expose his crimes against humanity to the world, as I have done with those committed by Ceaușescu. Catch your fugitive tyrant, as my fellow Romanian generals caught Ceaușescu in December 1989, when he went into hiding in an attempt to escape the revolutionary wave sweeping communist dictators off the face of Eastern Europe. Make Saddam pay for his crimes, as Ceaușescu did for his—with his life."[12]

This book is another open letter, this time written jointly with Professor Rychlak (whose ancestors had immigrated from Poland) and addressed especially to our fellow Americans. Let us reject the Marxist redistribution of wealth, which has transformed so many once-noble countries into lands looking like giant trailer camps hit by a hurricane, with their leaders roasting in Dante's Inferno. Indeed, all Marxist redistributionists who have ever risen to lead a country have ended up in hell—all, from Trotsky to Stalin, Tito to Zhivkov, Enver Hoxha to Mátyás Rakosi, Sékou Touré to Nyeree, Khrushchev to Ceaușescu. All had their days of temporary glory, but all ended in eternal disgrace. A few remnants, like the Castro brothers, are still hanging on, but they certainly have a place in hell reserved and waiting for them.

Let us, once and for all, also reject Marxism's "science" of disinformation, its *glasnost*, and its political necrophagy that has been used so destructively over the years to squash freedom and bankrupt countries. Let us recognize them for what they are—and expose them with all our might—when such deceitful campaigns rear their ugly heads. Let us return to our own American exceptionalism and its traditions of patriotism, honesty and fairness. The United States of America is the greatest country on earth. Let us keep it that way for future generations.

NOTES

PRELUDE

1. Scott Swett, "Fanning Imaginary Flames: A Look Back at the Great Church Fire Propaganda Campaign," *American Thinker*, June 11, 2011.
2. Michael Fumento, "A Church Arson Epidemic? It's Smoke and Mirrors," *Wall Street Journal*, July 8, 1996.
3. Swett, "Fanning Imaginary Flames."
4. *Ibid.*
5. Fumento, "A Church Arson Epidemic?"
6. Swett, "Fanning Imaginary Flames."
7. Arthur Weinreb, "Poll: Over 40% of Canadian teens think America is 'evil'," *Canada Free Press*, June 30, 2004.
8. "Grecian Formula for Anti-Americanism," *Wall Street Journal*, February 7, 2003 (Internet edition).
9. Nicholas Kralev, "German Leader Links Bush's 'Style' with Hitler's," *Washington Times*, September 20, 2002 (Internet edition).
10. Warren Hoge, "A Speech That Khrushchev or Arafat or Che Would Admire," *New York Times*, September 24, 2006.
11. Tom Baldwin, "Schools are still crumbling in 'corridor of shame' haunted by the old South," *Times of London Online*, January 25, 2008 (Internet edition).
12. Christopher Andrew and Vasili Mitrokhin, *The Sword and the Shield: The Mitrokhin Archive and the Secret History of the KGB* (New York: Basic Books, 1999), 487-493.
13. Christopher Andrew and Vasili Mitrokhin, "Russian Orthodox Church chooses between 'ex-KGB candidates' as patriarch," *Times of London Online*, January 26, 2009, citing Andrew and Mitrokhin, *The Sword and the Shield*.
14. Astolphe, Marquis de Custine, *Journey for Our Time: The Russian Journals of the Marquis de Custine*, edited and translated by Phyllis Penn Kohler (Washington, DC: Regnery Gateway, 1987), 171.
15. *Ibid* at 7.

NOTES

CHAPTER 1

1. Norman Polmar and Thomas B. Allen, *The Encyclopedia of Espionage* (New York: Gramercy Books, 1997), p. 276. In Romania Pacepa knew only that Ignatyev had disappeared from sight. The DIE assumed that Ignatiev had been killed.
2. Polmar and Allen, p. 180. While in Romania, Pacepa was given to understand that Dzerzhinsky had died of heart failure shortly after giving a speech before the plenum of the Central Committee. Apparently his argument with Stalin immediately followed that speech.

CHAPTER 2

1. Yevgeny Yevdokimov, "Russia comes to understand Mikhail Gorbachev," *Center for Defense Information Russia Weekly*, No. 143, March 2, 2001, p. 5.
2. Glasnost, Britannica Concise, as published on <http://concise.britannica.com/ebc/article-9365668/glasnost.
3. <www.merriam-webster.com/dictionary/glasnost>
4. <www.ahdictionary.com/word/search.html?q=glasnost&submit.x=31&submit.y=21>
5. *Tolkovyy SlovarRusskogo Yazyka* (Explanatory Dictionary of the Russian Language), ed. D.N. Ushakov (Moscow: Soviet Encyclopedia State Institute, 1935), Vol. I, p. 570.
6. Yevgenia Albats, *The KGB: The State within a State* (New York: Farrar, Straus, Giroux, 1994), 23.
7. Zhores Medvedev, *Gorbachev* (New York: Norton, 1987), p. 37.
8. Vladimir Solovyov and Elena Klepikova, *Behind the High Kremlin Walls.* (New York: Dodd, Mead, 1987), pp. 173–76.
9. Christian Schmidt-Häuer, *Gorbachev: The Path to Power* (London: I. B. Tauris, 1986), p. 64.
10. David B. Funderburk, *Betrayal of America: Bush's Appeasement of Communist Dictators Betrays American Principles* (Dunn, NC: Larry McDonald Foundation, 1991), p. 15.
11. Yevgeny Yevdokimov, "Russia comes to understand Mikhail Gorbachev," *Center for Defense Information Russia Weekly*, No. 143, March 2, 2001, p. 5, Internet edition, <www.cdi.org/russia/143.html>.
12. Cal Thomas, "20/20 hindsight and insight," *Washington Times*, March 24, 2002, Internet edition.

CHAPTER 3

1. Adina Anghelescu, "Arsenalul Securitatii pentru Carlos" (The Securitate Arsenal for Carlos), *Ziua*, Bucharest, September 29, 2000, Internet edition. This article published the original Securitate report No. 0010748 of June 22, 1981, which discharged from the inventory the explosive, weapons and ammunition given to "Carlos" in 1980.
2. "Plesita, o bruta securista" (Plesita, a Securitate beast), *Ziua*, Bucharest, February 19, 2000, Internet edition.

CHAPTER 4

1. Congressman Frank R. Wolf with Anne Morse, *Prisoner of Conscience: One Man's Crusade for Global Human and Religious Rights* (Grand Rapids, MI: Zondervan, 2011), p. 46.
2. *Time*, March 13, 1989, p. 20.
3. The author has the original of that CIA letter.

4.   "The defection of General Ion Mihai Pacepa," *Radio Romania International*, April 4, 2011.
     <http://www.rri.ro/arh-art.shtml?lang=2&sec=40&art=121082>.
5.   Wolf with Morse, *Prisoner of Conscience*, p. 51.
6.   Stan Weeber, "A New Paradigmatic Work on the JFK Assassination," H-Net Reviews in the
     Humanities and Social Science, October 2009.

CHAPTER 5

1.   Barry Meier, "Most Iraqi Treasures Are Said to Be Kept Safe," *New York Times*, May 6, 2003.
2.   *Custine Journals*, p. 161.
3.   *Ibid* at 14.
4.   *Ibid* at 7.
5.   Alexander Rose, "Biography: Royal Rake," *The Washington Post Book World*, May 6, 2001, p. 4.
6.   *Bolshaya Sovetskaya Entsiklopediya* (Great Soviet Encyclopedia) (Moscow: *Gosudarstvennoye
     Nauchnoye Izdatelstvo* (State Scientific Publishing House), 27 June 1952, Second Edition),
     vol. 13, p. 566.
7.   Glenn Frankel, "Sneers from Across the Atlantic: Anti-Americanism Moves to West Europe's
     Political Mainstream," *Washington Post*, February 10, 2003.
8.   Sartre continued to support the Soviet bloc foreign intelligence community. During Pacepa's
     years in Romania, he knew specifically that Sartre was considered an intelligence connection
     in the Soviet-and Romanian-sponsored terrorist war against "American imperialism."
9.   Régis Debray, "The French Lesson," *New York Times*, February 23, 2003 (Internet edition).
10. Paul Berrman, "The Passion of Joschka Fischer," *The New Republic*, August 27–September 3,
     2001, p. 12.
11. Herbert Romerstein, *Soviet Active Measures and Propaganda*, Mackenzie Institute Paper no.
     17 (Toronto, 1989), pp. 14-15, 25-26. WPC *Peace Courier*, 1989, no. 4, as cited in Andrew and
     Gordievsky at 629.
12. *WPC Rules and Regulations*, adopted during its 1996 Congress in Mexico, <www.wpc-in.org>.
13. *Ibid*.
14. *14ᵗʰWorld Trade Congress, New Delhi, India*, March 25–28, 2000.
15. *Beijing declaration of the World Conference of Women*, September 15, 1995. Law Professor Mary
     Ann Glendon led the Holy See's delegation at this meeting. At the end, she gave an important
     statement noting the Holy See's several reservations to the final declaration.
16. *8ᵗʰ March International Women's Day* <http://www.un.org/events/women/women00.htm>.
17. *November 17ᵗʰ, International Students' Day, to coincide with Day of Action for Peace*, International
     Union of Students.

CHAPTER 6

1.   *Izvestiya TseKa KPSS* (Reports of the Central Committee of the CPSU), No.3, March 1989.
2.   Donald Rayfield, *Stalin and His Hangmen* (New York: Random House, 2005), *passim*, esp. 248.
3.   *Textul decretului de decorare a Regelui Mihai de catre presedintele Truman* (The text of President
     Truman's Decree for decorating King Michael), *Scînteia*, May 14, 1945, p.1.
4.   "Solemintatea Decorarii M. S. Regelui Mihai de catre Generalisimul Iosif Vissarionovich Stalin"
     (The ceremony for decorating H. M. King Michael by Generalissimo Iosif Vissarionovich
     Stalin), *Scînteia*, July 21, 1945, p. 1.

5. "Guvernul Sovietic a Daruit M. S. Regelui Mihail, doua Avioane de Turism" (The Soviet Government donated two tourism airplanes to H. M. King Michael), *Scînteia*, July 22, 1945, p. 1.

6. Sorin Rosca Stanescu and Cornel Dumitrescu, *Autopsia unei Inscenari Securiste* (The Autopsy of a Securitate Framing), Bucharest: Omega-Ziua, 1999.

7. Pacepa, *Red Horizons* at 357-359.

8. During most of those years his case officer was Viktor Vladimirov, a onetime chief of the NKVD station in Helsinki, who was promoted to the rank of general for his handling of Kekkonen. Christopher Andrew and Oleg Gordievsky, *KGB: The Inside Story* (New York: Harper Collins, 1990), 432-433.

9. Joseph J. Trento, *The Secret History of the CIA* (New York: Carroll and Graf, 2001) at 173.

CHAPTER 7

1. See Edward N. Luttwak, *New Dynamics of the Soviet Empire: From Optimism to Pessimism*, in *Soviet Foreign Policy in a Changing World* (Robbin Frederick Laird and Erik P. Hoffman, eds.), Piscataway, NJ: Transaction Publishers, 1986 at p. 61 ("Now fossilized, Marxism-Leninism has become... an official religion, since its propositions have become dogmas; Soviet Marxism-Leninism now has its ceremonies, rituals and idols, chiefly the figure of Lenin himself – whose bust presides over all schoolrooms, offices and places of public assembly.")

2. John Costello and Oleg Tsarev, *Deadly Illusions* (New York: Crown, 1993), p. 24.

3. John Toland, *Adolf Hitler* (Garden City, NY: Doubleday, 1976), p. 548.

4. Alexander N. Yakovlev, *A Century of Violence in South Russia* (New Haven, CT: Yale University Press, 2002), p. 165.

5. *Country Studies: Russia-The Russian Orthodox Church*, U.S. Library of Congress, <lcweb2.loc.gov/frd/cs>, accessed April 3, 2008.

6. Gabriel Adriany, *Die Kirche in Nord, Ost und Südeuropa*, in Handbuch der Kirchengeschichte, VII, (Herder Freiburg, 1979) p. 515.

CHAPTER 8

1. David E. Murphy, *What Stalin Knew: The Enigma of Barbarossa* (New Haven, CT: Yale University Press, 2005) at xv.

2. Hitler's proclamation justifying the action is reprinted in *A History of the Third Reich*, vol. 4 Primary Sources (Jeff T. Hays, ed., San Diego, CA: Greenhaven Press, 2003) at 125. His thoughts on the need for German living space are reprinted in *ibid* at 26.

3. The day that this statement was made, December 8, the first Jews were gassed at Chelmno, Poland.

4. Hitler's propaganda minister from 1933 on, Joseph Goebbels, also committed suicide. He remained hidden in Hitler's bunker until May 1, 1945, when he poisoned his six children before he and his wife took their own dose of cyanide. Soviet forces later found all the bodies.

5. *Nomination Facts*, Official Website of the Nobel Prize, <www.Nobelprize.org>.

6. Jan Olav Smit, *Angelic Shepherd: The Life of Pope Pius XII* (New York: Dodd, Mead, 1950) at 174.

7. *The Ukrainian Weekly*, No. 18, Vol. XVII, March 28, 1949, 1.

8. *Orientales Omnes* was issued December 23, 1945.

9. *Orientales Omnes*, 59.

10. Alberto Giovanetti, *Pio Parla alla Chiesa del Silenzio* (Milano: Editrice ancona, 1959), German translation, *Der Papst spricht zur Kirche des Schweigens* (Recklinghausen: Paulus Verlag, 1969), p. 131.

11. Robert W. Stephan, *Death to Spies: The Story of SMERSH*, doctoral thesis, American University, Washington D.C., 1984, 61-64.

12. Andrew and Gordievsky at 343.

13. Hugh Thomas, *Armed Truce: The Beginnings of the Cold War* (London: Hamish Hamilton, 1986) at 220-221.

14. *Country Studies, Bulgaria in World War II*, Library of Congress, <lcweb2.loc.gov/frd/cs/profiles/Bulgaria.pdf>.

CHAPTER 9

1. Giovanni Sale, *Il Novecento tra genocidi, paure e speranze* (Milan: Jaca Book, 2006) at 214. See also Cardinal Walter Kasper, "Recent Developments in Jewish–Christian Relations," Speech at Liverpool Hope University (May 24, 2010) <http://www.worldjewishcongress.org/uploads/documents/21ea709fb3a30b36434f3feea17791a1c36f480f.pdf>; Hanna Diskin, *The Seeds of Triumph: Church and State in Gomulka's Poland* (Budapest: Central European University Press, 2001) at 48-49 (Soviet bloc propaganda against the Catholic Church and the Pope). George Weigel, *All War All the Time, First Things*, April 2011 at 30.

2. A translation of this whole speech, as it was broadcast on *Vatican Radio*, can be found in "The Catholic Church and the Third Reich: Pope Pius XII Surveys an Heroic History," *The Tablet* (London), June 9, 1945.

3. The full text of the address appears in Margherita Marchione, *Pope Pius XII: Architect for Peace* (New York: Paulist Press, 2000) at 143-152. See also Office of the United States Chief Counsel, vol. I, at 285-86; William L. Shirer, *The Rise and Fall of the Third Reich: A History of Nazi Germany* (Greenwich: Fawcett Publications, 1962) at 324-25 (footnote); Purdy at 43.

4. Pinchas E. Lapide, *Three Popes and the Jews* (New York: Hawthorne Books, 1967) at 131; see Ernst von Weizsäcker, *Memoirs of Ernst von Weizsäcker* (Chicago: H. Regnery Co., 1951) at 297.

5. Lapide at 131.

6. Eugenio Zolli, *Why I Became a Catholic* (New Hope, KY: Roman Catholic Books, 1997) at 187.

7. *Wartime Correspondence Between President Roosevelt and Pope Pius XII* (New York: Macmillan, Myron C. Taylor, ed., 1947) at 113.

8. Anton J. Gahlinger, *I Served the Pope* (The Mission Press, Techny, IL: 1952), 6. See "Churchill Talks with Pope on Peace; Vatican Quarters Gratified at Outcome Said to Promise a Profound Effect on Terms," *New York Times*, August 26, 1944.

9. Anne O'Hare McCormick, *Vatican Journal 1921–1954* (New York: Farrar, Straus & Cudahy, 1957) at 123 (from a *New York Times* dispatch of September 6, 1944). For his part, Pius described Churchill as very able and large-minded. *Ibid.*

10. "German Martyrs," *Time*, December 23, 1940 at 38; Lapide at 251 (quoting Einstein in *Time* Magazine).

11. "Acknowledging the Men and Women of Wisdom," *Wisdom*, September 1957, at 2.

12. Charles R. Gallagher, "Personal, Private Views: A newly discovered report from 1938 reveals Cardinal Pacelli's anti-Nazi stance," *America*, September 1, 2003. See also Will Swift, The *Kennedys Amidst the Gathering Storm* (Washington, DC: Smithsonian Books, 2008) at 361 (Kennedy gave FDR a letter from the pope "denouncing Hitler's betrayal of Christian values").

13. In 1945, Fabian von Schlabrendorff, a Protestant member of the German resistance, wrote a memorandum to U.S. General William (Wild Bill) Donovan, in which Schlabrendorff reported that Müller "had orders from the Catholic Church to negotiate with representatives of the Protestant Church in order to harmonize their measures in the struggle against Hitler." *Memorandum to General Donovan from Fabian von Schlabrendorff.* See also Schlabrendorff, *The Secret War against Hitler.* Pius became linked to the work of noted Protestant resistance leader, Diet-

rich Bonhoeffer, who eventually joined a conspiracy to assassinate Hitler. Bonhoeffer's close friend and co-resister Eberhard Bethge wrote to him of having had an audience with the Pope. *Dietrich Bonhoeffer: Letters and Papers from Prison* 214 (Eberhard Bethge, ed., Collier Books, New York, enlarged ed., 1971). In a collection of letters, Bethge explained that this oblique reference related to meetings with Pope Pius XII's close assistants Monsignor Robert Leiber and Monsignor Johannes Schönhöffer "who had been let in on the conspiracy." *Ibid* at 267, n.152.

14. *Secret message from the British Legation to the Holy See*, January 12, 1940, British Public Record Office, FO 800/318 (reporting on a planned German offensive); *Personal and Confidential Message from the British Legation to the Holy See*, February 7, 1940, British Public Record Office, FO 371/24405 (reporting on the planned attack on Belgium and future plans for an invasion of France). One of Müller's reports concerned a speech Hitler made at the S.S. Ordensburg (youth leader training center) at Sonthofen, where he had screamed that he would crush the Catholic Church under his heel, as he would a toad. Harold C. Deutsch, *The Conspiracy Against Hitler in the Twilight War* (Minneapolis: University of Minnesota Press, 1968) at 338-339.

15. *Telegram from the Ambassador in Italy (Phillips) to the Secretary of State*, dated Feb. 28, 1940, in United States Department of State, Foreign Relations of the United States, Diplomatic Papers, 1940, vol. I (General), United States Government Printing Office (Washington, DC, 1959) at 126 (discussing the security of France and England, the mood in Germany and in the German military, Germany's resources in the event of a long war, and Italy's attitude towards war).

16. Owen Chadwick, *A History of Christianity* (New York: St. Martin's Press, 1995) at 91.

17. *Testimony of Dr. Giuseppe Müller*, January 24, 1969, before the Ecclesiastical Tribunal of the Vicariate of Munich, on the beatification of Pius XII (Eugenio Pacelli), Part II, page 755.

18. Gilbert (1981) at 59; Deutsch at 338-39. *Le cardinal Maglione au nonce à Bruxelles Micara et à l'internonce à La Haye Giobbe*, May 3, 1940, Actes et Documents, vol. 1, p. 436, no. 293.

19. See Wright at 1930; Charles Rankin, *Pius the Man and His Efforts for Peace*, in The Pope Speaks at 113.

20. *Messaggi del Santo Padre, ai Sovrani del Belgio, dell'Olanda e del Lussemburgo*, L'Osservatore Romano, May 12, 1940.

21. Cianfarra at 226-27; Hatch & Walshe at 152; Charles Rankin, "Pius the Man and His Efforts for Peace," in *The Pope Speaks* at 114.

22. Hatch & Walshe at 152.

23. Lapide at 137.

24. *The Tablet* (London), October 24, 1942, at 202 (quoting the *Jewish Chronicle*).

25. *Ibid.*

26. *The Ciano Diaries* at 537, 538. According to Ciano, Mussolini wanted to break a few wooden heads, but he had been dissuaded from doing so because the prestige of the Church is very high. *Ibid* at 538-39.

27. The Catholic News, November 21, 1942, reprinted in Secretariat for Ecumenical and Inter-religious Affairs, National Conference of Bishops, *Catholics Remember the Holocaust*, United States Catholic Conference (Washington, 1998) at 17.

28. "Holy Father Extends Thanks to American Catholics for Aid," *The Catholic News*, November 21, 1942.

29. British Public Records Office, INF 1/893.

30. *Pius XII's letter to Bishop Preysing*, April 30, 1943. Actes et Documents, vol. 2, doc. 105, pp. 318-27. Pius frequently encouraged Preysing in his resistance work. See *A l'Evêque de Berlin*, December 15, 1940, Actes et Documents, vol. 2, page 180, no. 58; *A l'Evêque de Berlin*, April 30, 1943, Actes et Documents, vol. 2, page 318, no. 105; *A l'Evêque de Berlin*, September 5, 1943, Actes et Documents, vol. 2, page 342, no. 112. See also Lubac at 145; O'Carroll at 89. In fact, Pius was the only world leader who took the resistance seriously. Charles Ford, "Invidious Comparisons," *First Things*, January 2000, at 67.

31. The original Italian version was published in the official *Acta Apostolicae Sedis* of 1943 (volume 35, pp.5-8). For an English version, see *Pius XII: Selected Encyclicals and Addresses* 275-97 (London: Catholic Truth Society, 1949).

32. Congregation for the Causes of Saints, *Positio*, appendix 25 at 282. See also Fisher at 13 (Pope Pius frequently used the word *stirpe* (race) to identify the Jews and no one could be in any doubt about his attitude.)

33. British Public Records Office, FO 371/34363 59337 (January 5, 1943); *Telegram from the Minister in Switzerland (Harrison) to the Secretary of State*, Jan. 5, 1943, in Foreign Relations of the United States, Diplomatic Papers, 1943, vol. II (Europe), United States Government Printing Office (Washington, 1964) at 91.

34. *New York Times*, December 25, 1942.

35. See *Telegram from the German Ambassador (Bergen) to the Reich Minister*, dated January 26, 1943, NARA, T-120, Roll 361, at 277668-70 (Ambassador von Bergen, on the instruction of Foreign Minister Ribbentrop, warned the Pope that the Nazis would seek retaliation if the Vatican abandoned its neutral position.)

36. Quoted in Rhodes at 272-73 (citing German archives: *A.A. Abteilung Inland*, pak. 17, vol. I, January 22, 1943); see also Holmes at 140. In fact, a Protestant minister who helped circulate this statement was sentenced to prison for spreading a subversive and demoralizing document. He was also accused of having a critical view of the war and of being spiritually attracted to Jewish environments and sympathetic toward Jews. "For Berlin, Pius XII was a Subversive: Radio Operator's Experience of Spreading Papal Christmas Message," *Zenit News Agency*, May 14, 2002.

37. *Notes de la Secrétairerie d'Etat*, May 5, 1943, Actes et Documents, vol. 9, page 274, no. 174. On August 30, the United States Secretary of State expressed doubt about the whole matter, sending a message that "there exists no sufficient proof to justify a statement regarding executions in gas chambers." *Ibid.*

38. *The Tablet* (London), June 12, 1943, at 282, n.1. This section was suppressed in Italy and Germany.

39. Toland at 864; Holmes at 132; O'Carroll at 131; Burleigh (2007) at 252-53.

40. "Glimpse at How Religious Houses Helped the Jews: Research Presented on Wartime Efforts in Rome," *Zenit News Agency*, September 18, 2006.

41. This was reported by Senator Adriano Ossicini, founder of the Christian Left in Italy, who was arrested in 1943 due to his opposition to the Fascist regime. *More Echoes on Pope Pius XII, Nazi Holocaust*, Catholic World News, June 27, 1996. (On the eve of one massive police sweep... the hospital received direct orders from Pope Pius XII to admit as many Jews as possible immediately.)

42. *From Hitler's Doorstep* (University Park: Pennsylvania State University Press, Neal H. Peterson, ed., 1966).

43. See Congregation for the Causes of Saints, *Positio (Summarium)* Testimony of P. Guglielmo Hentrich, before the Ecclesiastical Tribunal of Rome, on the beatification of Pius XII (Eugenio Pacelli).

44. Lapide at 168. This was apparently not an insubstantial amount. According to one account, the future pope inherited $100,000 in the mid-1930s.

45. Carroll-Abbing (1965) at 48.

46. Graham, *Pope Pius XII and the Jews of Hungary in 1944* at 5-6.

47. Lapide at 133.

48. Holmes at 158. Lapide later increased his estimate of Jewish lives saved to between 700,000 and 860,000. Lapide at 269.

49. Lapide at 226.

50. John Thavis, "Many Jews Once Defended Pius and Documentary Evidence Supports Him," *Inside the Vatican*, April 1998, at 30.

51. *Le National Jewish Welfare Board au Pape Pie XII*, July 21, 1944, Actes et Documents, vol. 10, page 358, no. 272.

52. Herbert L. Mathews, "Happier Days for Pope Pius: Shadows of war are lifting for a Pontiff whose greatest interest is world peace," *New York Times*, Oct. 15, 1944, at 8.

53. *Le National Jewish Welfare Board au Pape Pie XII*.

54. F. Murphy at 64.

55. Kevin Doyle, "Robert Graham, S.J.," *First Things*, June/July 1997.

56. M. Davis at 101.

57. Vladimir Ilyich Lenin, *One Step Forward Two Steps Back (The Crisis in Our Party) (1904)* <http://www.marxists.org/archive/lenin/works/1904/onestep/index.htm>.

CHAPTER 10

1. Darko Zubrinic, *Cardinal Alojzije Stepinac and Saving the Jews in Croatia During the WW2* (Zagreb, 1997), <http://www.croatianhistory.net/etf/jews.html>; Dennis Barton, *Croatia 1941–1946* (The Church in History Information Centre 2006); *Zenit News Agency*, March 10, 1999; Ronald J. Rychlak, "Cardinal Stepinac and the Roman Catholic Church in Croatia during World War II," *The New Oxford Review*, November 2009.

2. Peter C. Kent , *The Lonely Cold War of Pope Pius XII* (Montreal & Kingston: McGill-Queen's University Press, 2002) at 163.

3. Prior to the German invasion of Yugoslavia (April 6, 1941), the diocese of Maribor consisted of 654,000 members, 254 parishes, 474 members of the secular clergy, and 109 members of the regular clergy. Within three months of the German invasion, the Gestapo arrested, killed, or expelled 85 percent of the clergy. Of the original 254 parishes, only 91 remained, each headed by a single priest. The others were closed or taken over by German authorities. The district of Ptuj originally had 30 parishes and 57 priests. It was left with just one active and two retired priests to minister to 80,000 Catholics. Similarly, in the diocese of Ljubljana, the area occupied by the Germans had 128 parishes. By the end of June, 1941, 137 priests had been killed, 74 were expelled and 37 others had fled. That left only nine priests to minister to 215,000 Catholics. Cianfarra at 266.

4. The full original name of the organization was *Ustaša - Hrvatska revolucionarna organizacija* or UHRO (Ustaša - Croatian revolutionary organization). In 1933, it was renamed as *Ustaša - Hrvatski revolucionarni pokret* (Ustaša - Croatian revolutionary movement). The name comes from the word *ustati* which means "to rise" or "to stand up." Accordingly, *ustaša* meant an *insurgent* or a *rebel*. It did not have fascist connotations during the party's early years. On the formation of Croatia, see Krišto, *The Catholic Church in Croatia and Bosnia-Herzegovina*, vol. 1, at 39, 51-53.

5. Heffron, *Croatia's Fearless Defender*.

6. Gitman at 51. "[W]e have an abundance of public sermons by the Archbishop of Zagreb which illustrate how direct he was in criticizing both the National Socialist ideology and the Croatian government's policy." Krišto, *The Catholic Church in Croatia* at 60.

7. Krišto, *The Catholic Church in Croatia* at 72. A surprising inconsistency in the evaluation of Stepinac appears on the very same page of one book that is largely critical of Pope Pius XII and the Catholic Church. Michael Phayer writes: "The bottom line is that neither Stepinac nor Pius XII publicly condemned the Ustaša government. To do so might have precipitated the end of the regime...." Later, on the same page, Phayer writes: "While many of the clergy supported Pavelić's bloody 'crusade,' Archbishop Stepinac persevered in criticizing Ustashe crimes." Phayer (2008) at 12.

8.   Gitman at 70.
9.   Alexander, *The Triple Myth* at 95; Barton.
10. Zubrinic.
11. Rychlak, *Cardinal Stepinac and the Roman Catholic Church in Croatia.*
12. Stephen Lackovic, *The Case against Tito* (memorandum, 1947) at 23. See also *Le cardinal Maglione au visiteur apostolique à Zagreb Marcone*, February 21, 1942, Actes et Documents, vol. 8, page 442, no. 289.
13. Rick Hinshaw, "Cardinal's Past," *Chicago Tribune*, October 17, 1998, at 26.
14. Pattee at 283-86 Six days earlier he had given a similar sermon:

> All of them without exception, whether they belong to the race of Gypsies or to another, whether they are Negroes or civilized Europeans, whether they are detested Jews or proud Aryans, have the same right to say, 'Our Father who art in heaven'.... the Catholic Church condemns... every injustice and every violence committed in the name of the theories of class, race or nationality. One cannot exterminate intellectuals... as Bolshevism has taught... One cannot extinguish... Gypsies or Jews because one considers them inferior races.

Gitman at 70.

15. Gitman at 70 (quoting General Glaise von Herstenau,); Zubrinic; Barton.
16. Weigel, *Witness to Hope* at 73.
17. *Le grand rabbin Herzog au délégué apostolique à Istanbul Roncalli*, February 28, 1941, Actes et Documents, vol. 10, page 161, no. 83.
18. *Le grand rabbin Herzog au visiteur apostolique à Zagreb Marcone*, February 28, 1941, Actes et Documents, vol. 10, page 161, no. 84.
19. *Ibid.* See Krišto, *The Catholic Church and the Jews* at 42.
20. On the territory of the Zagreb Archbishopric alone, between 1945 and 1948 over 70 percent of the Catholic Church's agricultural land was taken away through agrarian reforms. Apart from land, the reform "also resulted in the confiscation of the Church's buildings, agricultural reserves, livestock, farming machinery, and tools." Akmadža at 97.
21. In the spring of 1945, the Catholic Church operated a number of private schools in Croatia. by October 2, they were all closed. Akmadža at 99.
22. "Stepinac cried out against all injustice, especially against racism." "Vatican Book Justifies Cardinal Stepinac: Example of Opposition to Fascism, Nazism and Communism," *Zenit News Agency*, March 10, 1999 (quoting author Gianpaolo Mattei).
23. Matijević at 139.
24. Akmadža at 89.
25. *Ibid* at 90.
26. It is not clear why Tito first had Stepinac arrested and only later spoke with him. It is possible that Tito wanted to see the extent of his influence among the people and the Church or to see whether he could soften the archbishop up and then get him to cooperate on the issue of creating an independent Catholic Church in Croatia. *Ibid at* 91.
27. Raymond at 191.
28. Prcela at 53-54 (reprinting the charges). One possible reason for Tito's decision to prosecute Stepinac was that in July of that year, the Četnik leader Draža Mihailović was tried and executed, so it was important for the authorities to create a balance in order to not provoke a Serb revolt. Akmadža at 95.
29. Matijević at 120. See *The Black Book of Communism* at 388-407.
30. Akmadža at 96.

31. Matijević at 135 (In June 1945, Zagreb's Mufti, Ismet Muftić, was tried along with some Ustashe officials, and he was sentenced to death). "The Orthodox were to a point discredited by their collaboration with the Chetniks, but were not liquidated, because the Party's leadership perceived the Church's conduct in war as patriotic." *Ibid* at 139.

32. *Ibid at* 117, 121. Orthodox leaders were treated "somewhat more ruthlessly for collaborating with HPC, then [later] with the Chetniks." *Ibid* at 122.

33. "Archbishop Behind Bars," *Time*, September 30, 1946.

34. As *Time* magazine later reported: "the world was shocked by the cynical mockery of Stepinac's twelve-day trial for collaboration with the Nazi puppet regime during the war." "The Silent Voice," *Time*, February 22, 1960.

35. Barton.

36. Prcela at 55. Hurley was an interesting character and the subject of Gallagher, *Vatican Secret Diplomacy*.

37. Josip Stilinovic, *Cardinal Alojzije Stepinac—A true Catholic nationalist!*, The Catholic World Report (1998) <http://irish-nationalism.net/forum/showthread.php?t'5048>.

38. Lackovic at 3. Barton. During the communist era it was dangerous even to mention his name. Stilinovic.

39. *Aide for the Archbishop*, Time, October 14, 1946; Bozanić at 308 ("Pope Pius XII immediately condemned the process, referring to the procedure in the court room as a bad legal process, '*Il tristissimo processo*,' which in Italian not only means grievous, but a miserable process.")

40. *Aide for the Archbishop*, Time, October 14, 1946. At the trial, Stepinac did not focus attention on himself, "rather he concentrated on the Church, and he knew that the trial was not so much about him, rather the communists wanted to harm the Church and religion." Krišto, *An American View* at 227.

41. Stepinac's full statement can be read at <http://www.croatianhistory.net/etf/reply.html>.

42. The *New York Times* wrote that, "The trial of Archbishop Stepinac was a purely political one with the outcome determined in advance. The trial and sentence of this Croatian prelate are in contradiction with Yugoslavia's pledge that it will respect human rights and the fundamental liberties of all without reference to race, sex, language and creed. Archbishop Stepinac was sentenced and will be incarcerated as part of the campaign against his church, guilty only of being the enemy of Communism." *New York Times*, October 13, 1946. Cardinal Francis J. Spellman, probably most important American Catholic prelate during and after the war, said: "the only thing Cardinal Stepinac is guilty of was his love for God and his homeland." Savor. The American Jewish Committee also responded, saying: "[Stepinac] was one of the very rare men in Europe who raised his voice against the Nazis' tyranny at a time when it was very difficult and dangerous for him to do so." Barton.

43. Krišto, *The Catholic Church in Croatia* at 85-86.

44. This film was played at the Archdiocese of Zagreb's celebration of the 10th anniversary of the beatification of Cardinal Alojzije Stepinac on September 19, 2008.

45. Pattee at 211.

46. *Ibid* at 211-12.

47. Alexander, *The Triple Myth* at 113.

48. Barton.

49. Akmadža at 95; Prcela at 7.

50. "Deal Rejected," *Time*, July 23, 1951. Much later, *Time* magazine gave another, consistent account of this matter:

> In grim Lepoglava Prison, Stepinac occupied a cell with an adjoining chapel, got good food and all the books he wanted. Unlike Hungary's Cardinal Mindszenty, Archbishop Stepinac issued no pronouncements against the regime. He sat silent, and in the free world his silence sounded as a cry of reproach. Tito would gladly have been rid of him. Through a U.S. newspaperman he offered him his freedom if he

would agree never again to practice his priesthood in Yugoslavia. Replied Stepinac bluntly: "I am completely indifferent concerning any thoughts of my liberation. I know why I suffer. It is for the rights of the Catholic Church. I am ready to die each day for the church. The Catholic Church cannot be, nor will it ever be, the slave of any regime."

"The Silent Voice," *Time*, February 22, 1960.

51. Marcus Tanner, *Croatia: A Nation Forged in War* (Yale University Press, 1997).
52. *Time* reported his release as follows:

> The iron-barred gates of Lepoglava Prison swung open. Out walked Communist Yugoslavia's No. 1 ideological prisoner, Archbishop Aloysius Stepinac, the gaunt, peasant-born primate of his country's 7,000,000 Roman Catholics.
>
> He did not walk into freedom. By order of the Tito government, Archbishop Stepinac had been conditionally released, after serving five years of a 16-year sentence on a trumped-up charge of wartime collaboration with the fascists. Actually, he was on his way to a roomier internment: his native village of Krasic, where, as a government communiqué said, "the former archbishop" would have to limit himself to the duties of a simple priest.

"Dust in the Eyes," *Time*, December 17, 1951.

53. *Ibid.* In March 1952, Tito told a delegation from the First Congress of the Association of Yugoslav Students that "We released Stepinac so that we could knock a propagandistic weapon out of the Vatican's hands, the weapon that Stepinac is a 'martyr.' Now they have problems because Stepinac is out." Akmadža at 95.
54. "The Guest of Dishonor," *Time*, December 29, 1952 ("Tito was mad at the Vatican for conferring the Cardinal's red hat on his archenemy, Archbishop Aloysius Stepinac, who served five years in a Tito jail and is now restricted to his home village").
55. Traudl Lessing, *Stepinac Speaks*, Catholic Digest (April 1953) at 33.
56. Bozanić at 314-15.
57. *Ibid* at 314.
58. *Encyclopedia of World Biography* (2004); "Capsules," *Time*, August 3, 1953 ("Armed with radioactive phosphorus supplied by the AEC, two top U.S. specialists flew to Yugoslavia to treat Cardinal Stepinac for polycythemia").
59. "The Silent Voice," *Time*, February 22, 1960. In 1954, 143 Catholic priests signed a memorandum denouncing the government of Yugoslavia for persecution of Catholics. Matijević at 125.
60. "The Silent Voice," *Time*, February 22, 1960.
61. Today, behind the altar, one can see a cut-out piece of the floor that was planned to be Stepinac's final resting place.
62. "The Silent Voice," *Time*, February 22, 1960.
63. Savor; Barton. Hinshaw at 26. Stepinac's innocence is now recognized by virtually all scholars. For a collection of documents vindicating Stepinac, see *Proces Alojziju Stepiincu* (Marina Stambuk-Skalic, et. al. eds.) Krscanska sadasnjost: Zagreb, 1997. For Stepinac's anti-Nazi wartime sermons, see *Propovijedi, govori, poruke* (J. Batelja and C. Tomic, eds.), AGM: Zagreb, 1996; and *Three Sermons Against Racism by Archbishop Stepinac* (Church in History Information center: Birkenhead, 1998). See also Aleksa Benigar, *Alojzije Stepinac, hrvatski kardinal* (Ziral, Zagreb, 2nd ed., 1993); Ivan Muzi'c, *Paveli'c i Stepinac* (Logos: Split, 1991) (the archbishop's struggle against Pavelif); *Vatican Book Justifies Cardinal Stepinac: Example of Opposition to Fascism, Nazism and communism*, Zenit News Agency, March 10, 1999; Alain Finkielkraut, *Msgr. Stepinac et les deux douleurs de L'Europe*, Le Monde, October 7, 1998 (rebuking critics of Stepinac).

64. Alexander at 147; Barton. "He was a man who was disliked by the Nazis as well as the Communists for refusing to compromise the interests of the Catholic Church to the regimes of the moment. Stepinac was aware of the fact that both the Nazis and the Communists were plotting to kill him." Gitman, at 70.

65. Alexander at 138; Barton.

66. Sabrina P. Ramet, *Balkanski Babilon* 113 (Zagreb: Alinea, 2005). See also Tanner at 180; Barton.

67. Falconi probably was confused by the contradictory evidence that he found. Consider this observation from an early review critical of the book: "there are excellent citations in the book, especially by Pius XII, giving all the defense needed. But these are patronizingly explained away on psychological grounds." Whitall N. Perry, *Book Review: The Silence of Pius XII, by Carlo Falconi,* 5:1 Studies in Comparative Religion (Winter, 1971).

68. Consider: Chapter 1: The Collapse of Yugoslavia in 1941; Chapter 2: Croatia in the Twenty Years of Yugoslav Rule; Chapter 3: How the NDH was Received by the Catholics; Chapter 4: The Persecution of the Orthodox Serbs; Chapter 5: The Croatian Catholic Episcopate Between Intransigence of Principle and Adaptation to Reality; Chapter 6: The Vatican was Aware of Ustaše Crimes; Chapter 7: The Contradictory Attitude of the Vatican Towards Forced 'Re-Baptism' and the Persecution of the Orthodox Serbs.

69. "Some of the heaviest-handed documentation comes in the 134 pages on the Croatian episode." Whitall N. Perry, *Book Review: The Silence of Pius XII, by Carlo Falconi,* 5:1 Studies in Comparative Religion (Winter, 1971).

70. Savor; Barton. Stepinac's innocence is now recognized by virtually all scholars. See generally *Stepinac: A Witness to the Truth.* For a collection of documents vindicating Stepinac, see Proces Alojziju Stepiincu (Marina Štambuk-Skalić, et. al. eds.) Kršćanska sadašnjost: Zagreb, 1997. For Stepinac's anti-Nazi wartime sermons, see *Propovijedi, govori, poruke* (J. Batelja and C. Tomić, eds.), AGM: Zagreb, 1996; and *Three Sermons against Racism by Archbishop Stepinac* (Church in History Information center: Birkenhead, 1998). See also Aleksa Benigar, *Alojzije Stepinac, hrvatski kardinal* (Ziral, Zagreb, 2nd ed. 1993); Ivan Mužić, *Pavelić i Stepinac* (Logos: Split, 1991) (the archbishop's struggle against Pavelić); *Vatican Book Justifies Cardinal Stepinac: Example of Opposition to Fascism, Nazism and Communism,* Zenit News Agency, March 10, 1999; Alain Finkielkraut, *Msgr. Stepinac et les deux douleurs de L'Europe,* Le Monde, October 7, 1998 (rebuking critics of Stepinac).

71. "Assembly Condemns Communist Treatment of Cardinal Stepinac and Andrija Hebrang," *BBC Summary of World Broadcasts,* February 17, 1992.

> The newly elected Croatian parliament rehabilitated Cardinal Stepinac by annulling the results of all Bolshevik-style trials under the former Yugoslav communist regime. The parliament specifically stated that the only reason for the cardinal's conviction was Stepinac's refusal to lead a schism.

Stilinovic.

72. Cornwell, *Hitler's Pope* at 47, 169, 173, 251, 254, 259, 262, 321, 352.

73. Krišto went on to explain: "Ronald J. Rychlak responded at length to Cornwell in *Hitler, the War, and the Pope....* For understandable reasons, not even Rychlak knew that both Falconi and Cornwell based their judgments on the Catholic Church in Croatia and on Pope Pius XII on falsified documents from the Yugoslav secret police." Krišto, *The Catholic Church and the Jews* at 44, note 150.

74. Historians rely on documents to understand what happened at a given time. Great credibility is attributed to contemporaneous written evidence. In most cases, that makes perfect sense. As this episode reveals, however, when governmental agencies engage in intentional disinformation campaigns, contemporaneous written evidence may be very misleading. Non-contemporaneous fictionalized plays, like *The Deputy,* are even more misleading.

75. Rychlak was a speaker at this event. See Rychlak, *Cardinal Stepinac and the Roman Catholic Church in Croatia.*

CHAPTER 11

1. There were dozens of KGB operational manuals on different topics, divided by the various branches (counterespionage, countersabotage, etc.). All were classified "top secret." Some manuals, like the one on disinformation or on illegal operations, were classified "Top Secret of Special Importance." See Bittman at 49-50.
2. Unless indicated otherwise, throughout this book, the specific facts in Cardinal Mindszenty's life are taken from his book *Memoirs*, translated by Richard and Clara Winston (New York: Macmillan, 1974).
3. Mindszenty at 5.
4. *Ibid* at 8.
5. See Rychlak, *Hitler, the War, and the Pope* (2010) at 248–52.
6. *Investigative Reports* (Bill Kurtis, A&E Network).
7. Gilbert (1981) at 266 (citing Report of Veesenmayer to Ribbentrop, 6 July 1944, Nuremberg Trial Documents, NG 6584).
8. Lapide at 153.
9. Gilbert (1987) at 50; see Blet at 189–99.
10. *Le Nonce à Bucarest Cassulo à Mgr. Tardini*, October 2, 1944, Actes et Documents, vol. 10, page 428, no. 68.
11. Lapide at 161.
12. Mindszenty at 83–84.
13. See Freemantle at 136 ("With disinformation, as with every other espionage activity, the Soviet Union heavily utilizes its satellite services."); See Bittman at 29 (similar).
14. Robert McG. Thomas Jr., "Hanna F. Sulner, 81, Expert Drawn into Mindszenty Plot," *New York Times*, January 19, 1999.
15. Mindszenty at 87.
16. Thomas Jr., "Hanna F. Sulner, 81.
17. Mindszenty, 114-117.
18. Steve O'Brien, "Shooting the Cardinal": Film and Betrayal in the Mindszenty Case," *Seattle Catholic*, January 11, 2005, as printed in <http://seattlecatholic.com/article_20050111.html.>
19. Both movies are available on DVD. *The Prisoner* does not identify the cardinal who is persecuted, and it seems to draw upon elements from several of these post-war communist trials.
20. Mindszenty, *Wikipedia*.

CHAPTER 12

1. Cardinal Beran died in Rome, at age 80. He is buried in the grotto of St. Peter's Basilica. In 1998, the Archdiocese of Prague opened his beatification process.
2. Wyszyński is sometimes seen as controversial in that some of his comments appear to have been anti-Semitic. On the other hand, it is not clear which statements were actually made by him and which ones were advanced by Soviet officials who wanted to discredit him. See Stefan Wyszyński, *The Culture of Bolshevism and the Polish Intellectuals*, in *Polish Perspectives on Communism* (Lexington Books, Bogdan Szlachta, ed. 2000).
3. *Ibid* at 96.
4. Diskin at 70-71. Wyszyński did not travel to Rome for the ceremony because he feared that the communist regime would not let him return. *Ibid* at 79.

5. On the relationship between the Polish government, the Vatican, and the Church in Poland, see *ibid* at 20, 28 (noting that Pius XII was responsible for some of the tension between the communist government and the Holy See).
6. *Ibid* at 97.
7. *Ibid* at 108.
8. *Ibid* at 182-84.

CHAPTER 13

1. At that time almost all Soviet satellite countries were called "people's republics."
2. Communist confidence in the "spark" went back to Lenin, who had named his revolutionary newspaper *Iskra* (The Spark), although he had actually borrowed the concept from the Russian Decembrist uprising of 1825.
3. See Rychlak (2010) at 93-94.
4. Andrew & Gordievsky at 463-464.
5. This French operation is confirmed in Andrew and Gordievsky at 463-464.
6. Al Webb, "Synagogues burn as Europeans rage," *Washington Times*, April 22, 2002 (Internet edition).
7. See Parkes ("There was no need to invent anti-Semitism in Russia. It existed already.").
8. POGROM. Government-organized, reactionary-chauvinistic uprising of the ruling classes, mass slaughter as a group of some element of the population, accompanied by murders, destruction and the plundering of properties. [Example:] Jewish pogroms in tsarist Russia. *Tolkovyy Slovar Russkogo Yazyka* (Explanatory Dictionary of the Russian Language), D.N. Ushakov, ed. (Moscow: Soviet Encyclopedia State Institute, 1935) vol. III, 352.
9. William Korey, *Russian Antisemitism, Pamyat, and the Demonology of Zionism*, The Hebrew University of Jerusalem (1995), <http://sicsa.huji.ac.il/studies2.html>.
10. The *Okhrana* had been founded in 1881 by Alexander III. It replaced the Department of State Police, which failed to save the life of his father, Tsar Alexander II.
11. Sakharovsky seems to have shared traditional Russian anti-Semitism. He told Pacepa that the Jews themselves bore the guilt for becoming a symbol of hate for the Russian tsars. After 1492, when some of the Jews expelled from Spain began settling in Russia, they became involved in the tax collection and administration of large estates where peasants worked. Those were among the few occupations open to Jews in tsarist Russia, and they did not make Jews loved in their new country.
12. Philip Grave, "The Protocols: A Literary Forgery," *The Times*, London, August 16, 17, and 18, 1921, <www.nizkor.org/ftp.cgi?documents/protocols/protocols.zion>.
13. "Jewish Massacre Denounced," *New York Times*, April 28, 1903, p 6.
14. George Legget, *The Cheka: Lenin's Political Police* 114 (Oxford University Press, 1981), quoted in Andrew and Gordievsky at 44.
15. The Communist International, also known as the Comintern, was an international communist organization founded in Moscow in 1919. The Comintern pledged to fight "by all available means, including armed force, for the overthrow of the international bourgeoisie and for the creation of an international Soviet republic as a transition stage to the complete abolition of the State."
16. *Encyclopedia of Marxism*, Marxist Internet Archive, <www.marxists.org/glossary/people/z/i.htm>.

CHAPTER 14

1. *Chronicle* at 609.
2. Elizabeth Spalding, *Harry S. Truman: Faith, Freedom, and the Cold War*, Grand Valley State University, the Hauenstein Center for Presidential Studies (September 15, 2009) at 2. The correspondence between the two world leaders was published in 1953 under the title: *Correspondence between President Truman and Pope Pius XII*.
3. Kent (2002).
4. On July 15, 1948, *L'Osservatore Romano* published a decree about communism, which excommunicated those who propagate "the materialistic and anti-Christian teachings of communism." This was widely interpreted as an excommunication of the Communist Party of Italy, but the party was not mentioned in the decree.
5. See J. Hughes at 255 ("Faced... with the most powerful Communist party in the Western world, the Pope in 1949 approved a decree of the Holy Office which excommunicated those who voted for communist candidates in Italian elections"); F. Murphy at 14, 64; M. Davis at 93 (the Church was the only organized group strong enough to combat the "new strength of the Left"); *Ibid at* 94, 97 (noting that despite the excommunication decree, about one-third of the Italian Catholics voted for Communist candidates). See also Dunn at 142-43.

> The persecution in Hungary was a factor in the Vatican's decree of condemnation of Communism in 1949, which many of the East European Church leaders did not like because the Vatican decree did nothing to assuage communist persecution. In fact, it gave the communists a reason to intensify pressure against the Churches. The Polish Catholic leaders, in particular, thought the condemnation was counter-productive.... Nonetheless, the decree allowed the Vatican to vent its anger over the situation in Eastern Europe and it aroused world public opinion, particularly in the West, to the struggle that confronted civilization and helped crystallize Catholic voting 'blocks into bastions of anticommunism and solidify Catholic support for the United States in the Cold War and to its effort to contain communism. It also put Italians on notice that the Communist Party in Italy, which was a potent political force, was unacceptable as a governing agent.
>
> *Ibid.* In March 1937, Pope Pius XI had issued the encyclical *Divini Redemptoris (Of the Divine Redeemer*, better known by its subtitle, *On Atheistic Communism)*, in which he attacked the communism that was beginning to spread throughout the world. He wrote that communism was historically evil, that communist governments were out to destroy religion, were Godless, were violent, denied the individual and the family, and reigned by terror. Pius XI concluded that "Communism is intrinsically wrong, and no one who would save Christian civilization may collaborate with it in any undertaking whatsoever."

6. *Acts Apostolicae Sedis*, 1951, p. 217.
7. *Ibid.*, p.456 and 558.
8. Diskin at 168.
9. *The Tablet* of London, March 16, 1963. See also Graham (1996).
10. See, e.g., Mikhail Markovich Scheinmann, *Der Vatikan im Zweiten Weltkrieg* (Dietz: Berlin, 1954; first published in Russian in 1948). For an analysis of Soviet propaganda, see generally Graham (1996).
11. Gary B. Nash, Julie Roy Jeffrey, John R. Howe, Allen F. Davis, Allan M. Winkler, Charlene Mires, and Carla Gardina Pestana, *The American People, Concise Edition Creating a Nation and a Society*, combined volume, 6th Edition (New York: Longman, 2007).
12. Elizabeth E. Spalding, *The First Cold Warrior: Harry Truman, Containment, and the Remaking of Liberal Internationalism* 1 (Lexington: University Press of Kentucky, 2006).

13. The American Committee for Freedom for the Peoples of the USSR was started in 1951, and its broadcast station became known as Radio Liberty. For more on VOA during this period, see David F. Krugler, *The Voice of America and the Domestic Propaganda Battles, 1945–1953*(Columbia: University of Missouri Press, 2000); for more on RFE/RL, see Arch Puddington, *Broadcasting Freedom: The Cold War Triumph of Radio Free Europe and Radio Liberty* (Lexington: The University Press of Kentucky, 2000).

14. See Rychlak, (2010) at 146-47, 158-63.

15. Marilyn J. Matelski, *Vatican Radio: Propagation by the Airwaves* (Westport, CT: Praeger, 1995).

CHAPTER 15

1. See Koehler at 26.

2. Gleb Yakunin, *Wikipedia*, <http://en.wikipedia.org/wiki/Gleb_Yakunin>.

3. Keith Armes. *Chekists in Cassocks: The Orthodox Church and the KGB*, <http://www.spiritoftruth.org/orthodoxchurch.pdf >.

4. *Reaction within the Catholic Church*, http://en.wikipedia.org/wiki/Liberation_theology.

5. *Ibid.*

6. James H. Cone, *A Black Theology of Liberation*, (New York: Orbis Books, 1990) p. 27.

7. Marta H. Mossburg, "Reverend Wright brings his anti-American crusade to Baltimore," *The Baltimore Sun*, June 21, 2011 (Internet edition).

8. See Humberto Fontova, *Fidel: Hollywood's Favorite Tyrant* (Regnery Publishing, Inc. 2005).

9. Debray initially taught at the University of Havana, in Castro's Cuba. He later became an adviser to the Socialist French president François Mitterrand. Debray dedicated his life to exporting Cuban-style Communism throughout Latin America, but in 1967 a U.S.-trained, Bolivian special forces unit captured him, along with Che's entire guerrilla band. Che was sentenced to death and executed for terrorism and mass murder. Debray was sentenced to 30 years in jail, but he was released after three years following the intervention of French philosopher Jean Paul Sartre. In February 2003, Debray published "The French Lesson" in the *New York Times* (which described Debray as "a former adviser to President François Mitterrand" but omitted to mention that he had spent years in jail for terrorism). Régis Debray, "The French Lesson," *New York Times*, February 23, 2003 (Internet edition).

10. This picture of Che was originally introduced to the world by a KGB operative under cover as a writer—I. Lavretsky, in a book entitled *Ernesto Che Guevara*, which was edited by the KGB. I. Lavretsky, *Ernesto Che Guevara* (Moscow: Progress Publishers, 1976). The KGB entitled the picture *Guerrillero Heroico* (Heroic Warrior) and disseminated it throughout South America—Cuba's area of influence. Italian millionaire publisher Giangiacomo Feltrinelli, a Communist romantically involved with the KGB, flooded the rest of world with Che's picture printed on posters and T-shirts. From one day to the next, the terrorist Che became an international leftist idol. Feltrinelli became a terrorist himself, and he died while planting a bomb outside Milan in 1972.

11. A. O. Scott, "Saluting the Rebel Underneath the T-Shirt," *New York Times*, December 12, 2008; Humberto Fontova, *Fidel: Hollywood's Favorite Tyrant* (Regnery Publishing, Inc. 2005).

12. "World: Che: A Myth Embalmed in a Matrix of Ignorance," *Time*, October 12, 1970.

13. Humberto Fontova, "Che Guevara and the Obama Campaign," *Human Events*, February 18, 2008, <http://www.humanevents.com/2008/02/18/che-guevara-and-the-obama-campaign/>.

CHAPTER 16

1. Fedor Burlatsky, *Khrushchev: Sketches for a Political Portrait*, Literaturnaya Gazeta, February 24, 1988, cited in Andrew and Gordievsky at 424.

2. Nikita Khrushchev, *Khrushchev Remembers*, translated and edited by Strobe Talbot 337 (Boston: Little, Brown and Company, 1970).

3. Richard Felix Staar, *Foreign policies of the Soviet Union* (2001) at 79-88.

4. U.S. Congress, House Select Committee on Intelligence, *Soviet Covert Action: The Forgery Offensive*, 6 and 19 Feb. 1980, 96th Cong., 2d sess., 1963. Washington, DC: GPO, 1980. A 1074-page book documents that Metropolitan Nikodim, who in 1975 became vice president of the World Council of Churches, served as an undercover officer of the KGB. Gerhard Besier, Armin Boyens and Gerhard Lindemann, *Religion, state and society in the twentieth* century (LIT Verlag Münster, 2008), <http://www.voiceofthebelievers.com/wcc_kgb.htm>. Nikodim died in 1978, and the Kremlin appointed Metropolitan Kirill as vice president of the CPC. Kirill (Vladimir Mikhailovich Gundyayev) worked for the KGB under the code name "Mikhailov." In February 2009, Kirill was "elected" patriarch of Russia. Tony Halpin, "Russian Orthodox Church chooses between 'ex-KGB candidates' as Patriarch," *The Times of London*, January 26, 2009.

5. A 1962 KGB document signed by General Oleg Gribanov, chief of the KGB's Second Chief Directorate, which was responsible for religious organizations, attested that Agayants was correct. Andrew and Mitrokhin at 487. Recently-released KGB documents show that one half of *all* the Soviet Union's clergy were agents or undercover KGB employees until at least the end of the Gorbachev era. Keith Armes, *Chekists in Cassocks: The Orthodox Church and the KGB*, Boston University <http://www.spiritoftruth.org/orthodoxchurch.pdf>.

6. For details about the supersecret illegal officers see Pacepa, *Programmed to Kill* at 133-164.

7. Erich Ludendorff had been a leader of the German Army, especially at the end of the First World War. He was a strong supporter of the Nazi Party and agreed to become head of the German Army in Hitler's government. In his report Pius noted Catholic leaders who set a good example by standing up for the Jews.

8. *Archivio Segreto Vaticano*, Arch. Nunz. Monaco d.B. 396, Fasc. 7, Pos. XIV, Baviera, p. 75.

9. *Archivio Segreto Vaticano*, Arch. Nunz. Monaco 365, Fasc. 7, Pos. XIV, Baviera, p. 83.

10. "John XXIII on the Communists," *New York Times*, April 14, 1959.

CHAPTER 17

1. *Archivio Segreto Vaticano*, Arch. Nunz. Monaco 365, Fasc. 7, Pos. XIV, Baviera, p. 83. Khrushchev initiated a campaign against the Russian Orthodox Church, forcing the closing of about 12,000 churches. He renewed his crusade against religion in 1958. See Koehler at 7.

2. See Bittman at 107.

3. *Pervoye Glavnoye Upravleniye*, the First Chief Directorate of the KGB.

4. William Totok, *The Stalinist Trial against the Vatican's "Spies"* (Iasi, Romania: Polirom, 2008), 199. The four catholics were Msgr. Josef Nischback, rector of the Catholic Cathedral in Timisoara; Dr. Theol. Franz Kräuter, archivist of the Catholic diocese of Timişoara; Sr. Hildegardis Wulff, cofounder of the Benedictine order of St. Lioba, who had dedicated her life to working with *Volksdeutsche* women in Romania; and Sr. Patricia Zimmermann.

5. In his NRO article *Moscow's Assault on the Vatican*, Pacepa mistakenly stated that Archbishop Augustin Pacha was exchanged for the two DIE officers. In fact, Archbishop Pacha was released from jail but died in Romania shortly thereafter.

6. Pacepa's account was approvingly cited by Walter Cardinal Kasper. See World Jewish Congress, Recent Developments in Jewish–Christian Relations, *Speech of Cardinal Walter Kasper at Liverpool Hope University* (May 24, 2010).

7. During his lifetime, it was thought that Casaroli was pro-communist. His posthumously published memoirs show that he permitted this perception to exist because it helped him with international relations. In reality, he was concerned about Catholics behind the Iron Courtain, but he was also anti-communist. Agostino Casaroli, *The Martyrdom of Patience* (2007). See also Koehler at 24 (suggesting that those around Casaroli may have been too sympathetic to communisim, and that affected his reputation). This helps explain the surprising amount of confidence that Pope John Paul II placed in him. See Ronald J. Rychlak, "The Enduring Legacy of John Paul II," *Catalyst*, December 2010.

8. On the repression of the Catholic Church in Romania, see Crozier at 101.

9. Romanian history scholar Nicolae Dorel Ceuca, relying primarily upon the diplomatic archive of the Romanian Minister of Foreign Affairs, found that while Romania banished the Apostolic Nunciature early in the 1950s, by the 1960s, diplomats on both sides were trying to restore official connections. From the Vatican's side, these discussions were mostly led by Cardinal Casaroli. See <http://www.cnaa.md/en/thesis/5348/>.

10. No such loan was ever made. The Vatican archives that could confirm or disprove the Romanian request are sealed. The Vatican Secretariat of State reports that:

> it would seem extremely unlikely that Romania would have asked for a loan from the Vatican. No relations existed between the government and the Vatican after the expulsion of the Apostolic Nuncio in 1946 and the closure of the Nunciature in 1950. Furthermore such a petition would be inconsistent especially when one considers the severe persecution that the Catholic Church, especially the Greek Catholic Church, endured during the Communist regime.

Letter to Ronald Rychlak from Monsignor Gabriele Caccia, Assessor, Vatican Secretariat of State, February 2, 2008.

11. Freemantle at 106-107. See also George Weigel, *All War, All the Time*, First Things, April 2011, at 32 (Two Lithuanian KGB agents studied at the Gregorian University and two others infiltrated Vatican meetings.)

12. Koehler at 10.

13. Not long after the release of Cornwell's book, *Hitler's Pope*, the Vatican issued a statement on Cornwell's work in Rome. It denied Cornwell's claim to have been the first person to have access to the archives that he used and denied his claim that he had worked for months on end in them. The Secretariat of State had authorized Cornwell to consult the archive of the section on Relations with States, which he did for some three weeks. The topic of his research was relations with Bavaria (1918–1921); Austria, Serbia, and Belgrade (1913–1915). Cornwell was neither the first nor the only one to consult the archives of those years. He had no access to the "closed period," beginning in 1922. Congregation for the Causes of Saints, *Positio*, appendix 25 at 265. When he was asked about these claims in *Brill's Content* magazine, Cornwell replied as follows: "Nowhere in the book do I claim that I spent months on end in the Secretariat of State archive. The quote is taken from a sub-editorial conflation in a newspaper article and was an error of strict fact that actually turns out to be essentially true." Cornwell completely neglected to mention that the newspaper article was one that *he* had written *about his book*! Moreover, he repeated the claim in a piece that *he* wrote *about his book* for *Vanity Fair* magazine. The "sub-editorial conflation" language was edited out of the *Brill's Content* piece when it was published.

14. Fr. Peter Gumpel, relator of Pius XII's sainthood cause, remembered a young German priest who was in Rome at the appropriate time. He drove a sports car that seemed incongruous with his status, and few people seemed to know his background. Fr. Gumpel also said, however, that he was unaware of anyone who managed to get into the archives and steal any documents.

15. The KGB, like its Romanian counterpart, the *Securitate,* was divided into two separate and very different entities: the domestic political police and the foreign intelligence service. The domestic branch of the KGB was a public organization, with local branches, known to everybody and feared by everybody. The foreign intelligence service was an unlisted, ultrasecret institution known only to a very small number of high-ranking communist *nomenklatura* involved in political, economic or religious relations with the West.

16. This is not to be confused with the respected Romanian historian Francis Pall.

17. *Viata Crestina* (Christian Life), I/nr. 6 (328), p. 20; II/nr. 7 (329). See also *Glia*, London, June 15, 1950); Aurel Sergiu Marinescu, *"O contrbutie la istoria Exilului Romanesc"* (A contribution to the History of Romanian Exile), vol.VIII" Bucuresti, ed.Vremea, 2008, pp. 87, 91-92.

18. William Totok, *Episcopul, Hitler si Securitatea* (The Bishop, Hitler and the Securitate), (Bucharest: Polirom, 2008).

19. *A Contribution to the History of Romanian Exile* (Bucharest: *Vremea,* 2008), vol. 8:87.

20. *Remus Mercia Birtz Blog*, <http://remusmirceabirtz.wordpress.com/.

21. Father Sergio Pagano, prefect of the Vatican Secret Archives, has explained that during the years Pacepa describes "the letters of Pius XII were no longer in the Vatican Secret Archives. The documents they were interested in were to be found in the archive of the Secretary of State." Zenit News Service, *Relator of Pius XII's Case Is Wary of Report: Father Gumpel Urges Prudence Over Defector's Tale,* February 18, 2007. Father Gumpel, relator of Pope Pius XII's sainthood cause, speculated that Soviet spies, unfamiliar with how things work in the Vatican, might have confused "the Vatican Secret Archives with the Archive of the Secretary of State." *Ibid.*

CHAPTER 18

1. German Wikipedia, Erwin Piscator, September 19, 2009, <http://de.wikipedia.org>.

2. Karol Jozef Gajewski, "Winning the War over Pius XII," *Inside the Vatican,* <<http://www.insidethevatican.com/articles/review-piusxii.htm>>.

3. Leo Kerz, Brecht and Piscator, 20:3 Educational Theatre Journal 363 (October 1968).

4. Willett at 41.

5. *Ibid* at 131.

6. *Ibid* at 132.

7. *Inostrannyy Otdel,* or Foreign Department, which at that time was integrated into the Soviet political police, the NKVD (*Narodnyy Komissariat Vnutrennikh Del,* People's Commissariat for Internal Affairs).

8. Piscator, German Wikipedia, <http://de.wikipedia.org>.

9. Smith.

10. *The Proletarian Theatre: Its Fundamental Principles and Its Tasks* (1920), quoted by Smith, page 8.

11. Terence Smith, "Performance, Space and Technology, Stanford University Drama Department," November 1998.

12. Willett at 50-51. See also Smith at 6.

13. Willett at 53.

14. *Ibid* at 55.

15. *Ibid* at 104.

16. *Ibid* at 121 (quoting Franz Jung).

17. *Ibid* at 75.

18. *Ibid* at 96.

19. *Ibid* at 121.

20. Willett at 122, quoting the postscript to the Soviet edition of Piscator's play *Das Politische Theater* (Moscow 1934).

21. Erwin Piscator, "The Theatre Can Belong to Our Century, in The Theory of the Modern Stage," (Eric Bentley, ed. 1997) at 471-3.
22. Willett at 122.
23. *Ibid* at 123.
24. Willett at 124.
25. *Ibid* at 126.
26. Quoted in Smith, page 9.
27. La Vern J. Rippley, *Brecht the Communist and America's Drift from Capitalism* 14:3 Twentieth Century Literature 143 (October 1968).
28. Information on Erwin Piscator at Akademie der Künste, Berlin, September 19, 2009 <http://www.adk.de/de/archiv/archivbestamd/darstellende-kunst/kuenstler/Erwin-Piscator.htm>.
29. Thomas at 165.
30. "Revival in Manhattan," *Time*, December 23, 1940.
31. Willett at 165.
32. *Ibid* (Wolf tells Piscator that the Party would want him to run a theater in Germany; "I know of no objection to you on the part of the Party.")
33. Piscator, German Wikipedia, September 19, 2009 <http://de.wikipedia.org>.
34. Leo Kerz, *Brecht and Piscator*, 20:3 Educational Theatre Journal 363, 368 (October 1968).
35. Willett at 180.
36. Biography of Erwin Piscator in German, from the Stiftung Archiv der Akademie der Künste, Berlin, September 19, 2009, published at <http://www.adk.de/de/archiv/archivbestand/darstellende-kunst/kuenstler/Erwin-Piscator.htm>.

CHAPTER 19

1. Pierre Joffroy, *A Spy for God: The Ordeal of Kurt Gerstein*, N. Denny translator (New York: Harcourt Brace, 1969).
2. Judy Stone, *Interview with Rolf Hochhuth*, *Ramparts*, Spring 1964, reprinted in *The Storm over The Deputy* at 50.
3. Hochhuth (1964) at 331.
4. Ward at 29, 34.
5. Erwin Piscator, *Introduction to The Deputy* (Clara Mayer trans.) in *The Storm over The Deputy* at 15.
6. From an entry on *Wikipedia*.
7. Hinkle at 67.
8. Hochhuth (1964) at 328.
9. *Ibid* at 304.
10. *Character Assassination*, America, March 7, 1964, reprinted in *The Storm over The Deputy* at 39.
11. Editorial: *Character Assassination*, America, March 7, 1964, reprinted in *The Storm over The Deputy* at 39.
12. Fisher at 11.
13. Judy Stone interview, in *The Storm over The Deputy* at 51.
14. Friedrich Heer, *The Need for Confession*, Commonweal, February 20, 1964, in *The Storm over The Deputy* at 166.
15. Judy Stone interview, in *The Storm over The Deputy* at 51.
16. Rychlak, *Righteous Gentiles*, at 181-92.
17. Erik von Kuehnelt-Leddihn, *The Timeless Christian* 191-93 (Franciscan Herald Press, 1969).
18. Levai at 5-6 (quoting Albert Wucher, "Der Stellvertreter und die historische Wirklichkeit," in the *Süddeutsche Zeitung*, Munich April 19, 1963).

19. Michael Feldkamp, *Hochhuth Exposed*, Association of Contemporary Church Historians, July/ August 2007 (John Jay Hughes trans.).

20. *Ibid.*

21. *Who Brought Down Pius XII?: L'Osservatore Director Blames Communists, Church Division*, The Wanderer, June 25, 2009 (discussing Vian's 2009 book, *In Difesa di Pio XII: Le Ragioni della*).

22. *Ibid.*

23. Conway (1973) at 147.

CHAPTER 20

1. See *Reviews*, XII:2 World Theatre 140 (Summer 1963) ("somewhere between a spoken report with scenes of great realism… and a fast paced discussion"). The review went on to note the difficulty of producing the play "from a text which if performed in total would have lasted six or seven hours." *Ibid*; Sidney F. Parham, "Editing Hochhuth for the Stage: A Look at the Major Productions of 'The Deputy,'" 28:3 *Educational Theatre Journal* 347, 353 (Oct., 1976) ("How then should we judge Hochhuth as a playwright? The formal shape of his script suggests that he wishes to be judged by traditional dramatic standards, and by these standards one cannot speak well of him").

2. Stephen Kinzer, "For a German Gadfly, a New Play, a New Furor," *New York Times*, March 11, 1993.

3. Kustow at 136 (noting that *Le Monde* newspaper thought that Semprum's edit of the story was superior to Piscator's).

4. Gary Prevost, "Review: The Autobiography of Federico Sanchez and the Communist Underground in Spain by Jorge Semprun," 75:3 *The American Political Science Review* 819 (Sep., 1981).

5. See Kathleen A. Johnson, *The Framing of History: Jorge Semprun's La Deuxième Mort de Ramon Mercader*, 20 French Forum 90 January, 1995.

6. Kustow at 18-19, 24.

7. *Ibid at* 25-26.

8. *Ibid at* 87 ("In Moscow the box-office was mobbed, all tickets were sold in hours").

9. *Ibid at* 87. See also Peter Brook, *The Empty Space* 20-22 (New York: Athenaeum, 1982). The Kustow biography also contains a photograph (taken around 1953) of Brook, his wife Natasha Parry, and Fidel Castro. A commentator from the era noted that "Brook's work on plays by other authors, must, on the whole, be regarded as the most positive result of Brechtian influence on the art of stage directing in England." Martin Esslin, *Brecht and the English Theatre*, 11:2 The Tulane Drama Review 63, 66 (Winter 1966). Brecht, of course, was a noted communist playwright.

10. Albert Hunt and Geoffrey Reeves, *Peter Brook* 104 (Cambridge University Press, 1995). From 1737 until 1968 the Lord Chamberlain licensed plays in London and certain other areas. This effectively made him the official censor of theatrical performances. See also Kustow at 131 (discussing one of Brook's few failures on stage – a play that warned about "the West" using a highly intelligent robot for destructive purposes.)

11. See Dan Isaac, "Theatre of Fact," 15:3 *The Drama Review*: TDR 109 (Summer, 1971). Brook essentially used symbolic designs for his production. "The stage was kept bare, no backdrops were used. Each of the actors had an identical blue suit over which he put some distinguishing costume piece, such as a Nazi armband or a priest's cassock. This design stressed the interchangeability of oppressor and oppressed in the modern age." Sidney F. Parham, "Editing Hochhuth for the Stage: A Look at the Major Productions of 'The Deputy,'" 28:3 *Educational Theatre Journal* 347, 352 (Oct., 1976).

12. Kustow at 87.

13. See Simon Trussler, "Shakespeare: The Greatest Whore of Them All Peter Hall at Stratford 1960–1968," 13:2 *The Drama Review* 169 (Winter, 1968). See also LaVern J. Rippley, *Brecht the Communist and America's Drift from Capitalism* 14:3 Twentieth Century Literature 143 (October 1968).

14. St. Denis was no stranger to the use of media for political purposes. In World War II, he directed the BBC's *Radio Diffusion Française* (established by DeGaulle's government in exile) under the pseudonym of Jacques Duchesne.

15. Irving Wardle, "London's Subsidized Companies," 11:2 *The Tulane Drama Review* 105, 111 (Winter 1966).

16. Patterson at xi.

17. Ossia Trilling, *The New English Realism* 7:2 The Tulane Drama Review 184, 190 (Winter 1962).

18. Glenn Loney, "Theatre Abroad: Oh to Be in England: A London Theatre Album" 19:1 *Educational Theatre Journal* 87 (Special English-Irish Theatre Issue, March 1967).

19. *Ibid.*

20. In England, the title is usually translated as *The Representative*, but sometimes as *The Vicar*. The program from the original London production says: "It is not, as has been widely construed and rumoured, a gratuitous and vicious attack on the Catholic Church—almost every page proves this accusation to be absurd." Director Clifford Williams included an essay in which he wrote: "I have examined all the facts which the play contains and I have found no instance of Hochhuth deliberately distorting verifiable information." Pope Paul VI's defense of Pius XII was also reprinted therein. See Rychlak (2010) at 296.

21. Michael Coveneny, "Obituary: Robert David MacDonald," *The Guardian*, May 24, 2004. MacDonald adapted at least three of Hochhuth's plays: *The Representative* (or *The Deputy*), *Soldiers*, and *Judith*. David Irving's web photo of Irving, Hochhuth, and MacDonald together. <http://www.fpp.co.uk/Irving/photos/Hochhuth/image3.html>.

22. See Thomas G. Gulick, "UNESCO, Where Culture Becomes Propaganda," *The Heritage Foundation Backgrounder* #233, December 13, 1982; Hook at 447 (contrasting a UNESCO seminar with a legitimate academic or scientific seminar). In the 1950s, two former UNESCO officials identified UNESCO's ancestor as: "The Soviet All Union Society for Cultural Relations with Foreign Countries," whose goals included "the world union of intellectual forces for the triumph of genuine world culture," so as to inspire intellectuals to "fight the war danger [and] agitate for peace." Walter H.C. Laves and Charles A. Thompson, *UNESCO: Purpose, Progress, Prospects*, (Indiana University Press, 1957). As early as 1952, the Knights of Columbus urged their fellow Americans to give a "close and careful scrutiny" to the operations of UNESCO. "Knights of the Church," *Time* magazine, September 1, 1952; see William R. Kintner and Joseph Z. Kornfeder, *The New Frontier of War: Political Warfare Present and Future* (Chicago: Henry Regnery Company, 1962). Years after MacDonald worked there, the KGB reportedly still had several agents on UNESCO's payroll, at least one of whom was working as a translator. Steve Farrell, "Coalition or Bust! Virtue or Vice?," *Meridian Magazine* (2002). The United States eventually withdrew from UNESCO over its perceived anti-West bias.

23. Andrew and Mitrokhin at 466; Oleg Kalugin, *Spymaster: My Thirty-Two Years in Intelligence and Espionage against the West* (New York: Basic Books, 2009) at 123, 192–93; Milton Rosenberg, *An American Trapped in a Communist Paradise: An Historical Autobiography* 45 (Moose Hide Books, 2003); "KGB: Russia's Old Boychiks," *Time*, February 6, 1978.

24. "Piscator had the courage to tackle this difficult subject from a text which if performed in total would have lasted six or seven hours." XII World Theatre 140 (Summer 1963) (calling the play "somewhere between a spoken report with scenes of great realism... and a fastly paced discussion").

25. Michael Coveneny, "Obituary: Robert David MacDonald," *The Guardian*, May 24, 2004.

26. In 1971, MacDonald became a codirector of the *Citizen's Theatre* in Glasgow, Scotland. He ran this theater in much the same way Piscator operated his *Freie Volksbühne*. Plays were often political, and tickets were priced so that the workers could attend. "For years, a sign declaring "All seats 50p" blazed over what was then a slum area:" *Obituary: Robert David MacDonald*, The Daily Telegraph, May 21, 2004. See *Interview: The Citizens Company in Glasgow: "Four Hundred Miles from Civilization,"* 5:1 Performing Arts Journal 50 (1980) ("Our theatre is actually socialist theatre in the sense that it's the only theatre in Britain which has a seat price that enables absolutely anybody to come in. And I think that's a kind of practical socialism.") While some critics considered the *Citizen's Theatre* exciting and influential, "others disapproved of what they saw as high camp, mannered performances and a preference for Left-wing European dramatists." The Daily Telegraph, May 21, 2004.

27. Douglas Chalmers, *Communist Party of Great Britain: Scottish Committee Archive 1960s to 1990s*, Glasgow Caledonian University Archives, <http://www.gcal.ac.uk/archives/cpgb/history5.html >.

28. LaVern J. Rippley, *Brecht the Communist and America's Drift from Capitalism* 14:3 Twentieth Century Literature 143 (October 1968).

29. Patterson at 1. Joan Littlewood and Arnold Wesker were among those most openly involved in class struggle. See "Interview: The Citizens Company in Glasgow: 'Four Hundred Miles from Civilization,'" 5:1 *Performing Arts Journal* 50 (1980) (interview with Robert David MacDonald, Philip Prowse, and Giles Havergal) ("A lot of British theatre is socialist and political, or at least the playwrights speak as if they write in those terms.").

30. Theodore Shank, "Political Theatre in England," 2:3 *Performing Arts Journal* 48 (Winter 1978). See also Larraine Nicholas, "Fellow Travellers: Dance and British Cold War Politics in the Early 1950s," 19:2 *Dance Research: The Journal of the Society for Dance Research* 83, 85 (Winter 2001).

31. See C. Chambers (2004) at 233, n. 17.

32. Like Piscator, he also had a program supplement discussing the charges against Pius XII.

33. Parham, "Editing Hochhuth for the Stage" at 347, 351-52. ("Reviewers generally thought that this concentration on the documents worked against the text.")

34. "Obituary: Clifford Williams, Theatre director with comedic talent and an awesome staging flair," *The Independent*, August 23, 2005.

35. Phyllis Hartnoll and Peter Found, *Theatre Workshop*, in The Concise Oxford Companion to the Theatre (1996). It had grown out of a group known as "The Red Megaphone" which had an overtly political manifesto. Dominic Shellard, *British Theatre Since the War* 60-61 (Yale University Press, 1999). The Theatre Workshop was an "acknowledged influence" on Peter Hall (and thus the Royal Shakespeare Company). C. Chambers at 12. Hall even invited Littlewood to direct for the company. *Ibid*. At about this same time, he did hire John Bury away from the Theatre Workshop to be the Royal Shakespeare Company's main designer. *Ibid* at 34-35; Martin Esslin, "Brecht and the English Theatre," 11:2 *The Tulane Drama Review* 63, 65 (Winter 1966).

36. Along with Peter Brook, Littlewood was among the most important theatrical personalities in the UK at this time. Shortly before her death in 2002, she said: "I've always been a communist." "Obituary: Joan Littlewood," *The Daily Telegraph*, September 26, 2002.

37. Jerry Tallmer, *You Can't Print That! (but he did, he does)*, Thrive, vol. 1: 9, January 1 - 31, 2006. See Lowry at 1 ("Communism – a New Religion"); ibid at 146 (more on communism as a religion); John C. Bennett, *The Demand for Freedom and Justice in the Contemporary World Revolution*, in *Religion and Culture*, at 330 (same).

38. Rolf Hochhuth, "The Berlin Antigone," *Evergreen Review*, May 1964 at 70.

39. *Evergreen Review*, August-September 1964, at 97.

40. According to the book, in June 1942, 17-year-old Rudolf Vrba was shipped to Auschwitz. Fighting against starvation, typhus, and almost unbelievable brutality, he kept a complete record of Nazi horrors. Finally he managed to escape and bring his message to the outside world. See Rudolf Vrba & Alan Bestic, *I Cannot Forgive : The Amazing True Story of a 17 Year Old Jewish Boy Who Defied the Germans at Auschwitz and Escaped to Alert the World to the Nazi Horror Camps!* (New York: Bantam Books, 1964). Apparently Vrba performed poorly under cross examination at a Canadian trial over Holocaust denial, and he admitted that he had taken "artistic license." *Queen v. Zündel*, 2 S.C.R. 731 (1992). He is now often cited by Holocaust deniers as an example of how people make things up about the Holocaust.

41. She wrote several plays he produced, including *The Children's Hour* (1934), *The Little Foxes* (1939), and *Watch on the Rhine* (1941). See Paul Kengor, *Dupes: How America's Adversaries Have Manipulated Progressives for a Century* (Wilmington: ISI Books, 2010) at 222.

42. *Time*, July 7, 1947.

43. *Time*, September 16, 1946.

44. *Time*, July 7, 1947.

45. *New York Times*, October 17, 1998, p. A-15. Regarding outbursts during productions, see Kustow at 136.

46. John Simon, "The Deputy and Its Metamorphoses," *The Nation*, March 16, 1964, reprinted in *The Storm over The Deputy* at 109, 115. Robert Brustein, writing in *The New Republic* explained: "The New York production of his play... preserves no integrity at all, and I have confined my discussion to the printed text because the Broadway performance is beneath discussion. Robert Brustein, "History as Drama," *The New Republic*, March 14, 1964, reprinted in *The Storm over The Deputy* at 23.

47. David Horowitz, "World Shares Guilt in Jews' Murder," *Ohio Jewish Chronicle*, March 20, 1964.

48. David Horowitz, who grew up in New York City as the son of two lifelong communists, was a founding member of the New Left. During the 1960s he was not at *Ramparts* until after the controversy surrounding *The Deputy*. See David Horowitz, *Radical Son* (New York: The Free Press, 1997). Lionel Abel, who wrote about the play in *Dissent* magazine (Spring 1964), is usually considered a Trotskyite. Alan Wald, "Farrell and Trotskyism" 22:1 *Twentieth Century Literature* 90, 93 (Feb. 1976); John F. Diggins, "Four Theories in Search of a Reality: James Burnham, Soviet Communism, and the Cold War" 70:2 *The American Political Science Review* 492 (June 1976). See Lionel Abel, "Stalin's Advocate," 2 *Politics* 146 (May 1945).

49. See Rychlak (2010) at 302–3.

50. Tevi Troy, *Book review*, The Weekly Standard, March 8, 1999 (reviewing *Max Lerner: Pilgrim in the Promised Land*, by Sanford Lakoff, University of Chicago Press, 1998).

51. Mona Charen, *Useful Idiots - How Liberals Got It Wrong in the Cold War and Still Blame America* 89 (Regnery, 2003).

52. *New York Post*, October 18, 1963.

53. Gary Dorrien, "Michael Harrington: Socialist to the End," *Christian Century*, October 11, 2000 at 1002.

54. George Packer, "Interesting Times: Democratic Socialism Revisited," *The New Yorker*, March 6, 2009, <http://www.newyorker.com/online/blogs/georgepacker/2009/03/democratic-soci.html>.

55. Lauren Weiner, "Where Have All the Lefties Gone?," *First Things*, January 2010, at 29, 30 (referring to Pete Seeger writing in the *Daily Worker* under an alias).

56. Carl Edmund Rollyson & Lisa Olson Paddock, *Susan Sontag: The Making of an Icon*, (New York: W. W. Norton & Co., 2000), 130.

57. Susan Sontag, "All the World's a Stage," *Book World*, March 1, 1964, reprinted in *The Deputy Reader* at 222.

58. Franklin Foer, "Susan Superstar," *New York Magazine*, Jan 7, 2005 ("Sontag—with her championing of European modernism, her unabashed intellectuality, and her left-wing ideological commitments....").

59. Guy Scarpetta, *Susan Sontag: Dissidence as Seen from the USA*, 76 Tel Quel 28 (Summer 1978), reprinted in *Conversations with Susan Sontag* (Susan Sontag & Leland A. Poague, ed., University Press of Mississippi, 1995).

60. See Ewart Turner, "No Letup for Der Stellvertreter," in *The Deputy Reader* at 184.

61. Fritz J. Raddatz, *Karl Marx. A Political Biography* (Little, Brown and Company, 1978).

62. *The Marx-Engels Correspondence: The Personal Letters, 1844-77* (Fritz J. Raddatz, ed. Littlehampton Book Services Ltd. 1981).

63. German Wikipedia, Fritz J. Raddatz, June 14. 2011 <http://de.wikipedia.org>.

64. Patrick Sullivan, *Author Eric Bentley still shaping theater*, Metro Active, September 24, 1998 <www.metroactive.com/papers/sonoma/09.24.98/bentley-9838.html>.

65. Eric Bentley, *Bentley on Brecht* (Northwestern University Press, 2nd ed. 2007). He wrote several other books on communist subjects, including: *Bernard Shaw: A Reconsideration* (1947); *Brecht Commentaries* (1981); and *Thirty Years of Treason: Excerpts from Hearings before the House Committee on Un-American Activities, 1938–1968* (1971).

66. See Daniel Robert Epstein, *Costa-Gavras Interview*, UGO Online, <http://www.ugo.com/channels/filmTv/features/costagavras> ("I saw the play back in 1964 in Paris. My scriptwriter, Jorge Semprún, wrote an adaptation back then. It was the play to see back then, and it was a huge controversy. I wanted to make the film in the 1970s, but the rights were taken.") See Rychlak, "The Church and the Holocaust," *The Wall Street Journal* (Europe), March 28, 2002 (reviewing *Amen*).

67. "Gavras doesn't march behind the banner of political cinema. All cinema is political, he says, even action movies showing 'heroes saving the Earth only with a gun'." Maya Jaggi, "French resistance: Costa Gavras," *The Guardian*, April 4, 2009. "'My mother used to say stay away from politics, because my father went to prison. But we can't not be involved. By not taking a position, you take a position.'" *Ibid*.

CHAPTER 21

1. I. F. Stone, "What Some People Have Forgotten About God's 'Deputy,'" *I. F. Stone's Weekly*, March 9, 1964, reprinted in *The Storm over The Deputy*, 234-35.

2. I. F. Stone, "Pius XII's Fear of Hitler," *I. F. Stone's Weekly*, November 1964.

3. Haynes, Klehr, and Vassiliev, *Spies*, at 146-152.

4. Romerstein and Breindel at 434-439.

5. Judy Stone, "Interview with Rolf Hochhuth," *Ramparts*, Spring 1964, reprinted in *The Storm over The Deputy*, 42.

6. For instance, it talks about the Dominicans petitioning the pope in 1287, resulting in an encyclical that led to arrests, looting of Jewish wealth, and preparation of the Jews for deportation. Hermann Sinsheimer, *Shylock: The History of a Character* 38 (New York: Benjamin Blom, Inc., 1947, reprinted 1963). Similarly, it argues that "Christians of the Middle Ages [were] habitual persecutors of unprotected people" and that Pope Leo the Great (444-61) banned money lending. *Ibid at* 121.

7. In June 1964, George L. Mosse wrote a piece on *The Deputy* for an influential left-wing magazine, *The Progressive*. That periodical opposed the growth of the U.S. military, opposed the United Nations police action to prevent a communist takeover of Korea, and opposed U.S. intervention to prevent a communist takeover in South Vietnam. In 1954, it published a huge exposé of McCarthyism, and it was sympathetic to the revolutionary dictatorship of Marxist

Fidel Castro, who seized power in Cuba in 1959. All of these are defensible positions, but they also indicate at least the possibility of Soviet influence.

8. Andrew and Mitrokhin, *The Sword and the Shield*, 226.

9. Haynes and Klehr, *Verona* at 220-221.

10. Andrew and Mitrokhin, *The Sword and the Shield* at 226.

11. *Ibid.*

12. Pacepa, *Programmed to Kill, passim.*

13. Mark Lane, the author of *Rush to Judgment* and *A Citizen's Dissent: Mark Lane Replies to the Defenders of the Warren Report*, helped New Orleans district attorney Jim Garrison arrest a local man (Clay Shaw), whom Garrison accused of conspiring with elements of U.S. intelligence to murder Kennedy in order to stop his efforts to end the Cold War. Garrison's *On the Trail of the Assassin* inspired Oliver Stone's movie *JFK*. Soviet documents from the Mitrokhin Archive later revealed that Lane received funding from the KGB.

14. Journalists were very important to the Soviet's efforts.

> The KGB recruited journalists in part for their access to inside information and sources on politics and policy, insights into personalities, and confidential and non-public information that never made it into published stories. Certain journalistic working habits also lent themselves to intelligence tasks. By profession, journalists ask questions and probe; what might seem intrusive or suspect if done by anyone else is their normal *modus operandi*. Consequently, the KGB often used journalists as talent spotters for persons who *did* have access to sensitive information, and made use of them to gather background information that would help in evaluating candidates for recruitment.... There was also much less risk that a journalist having contact with a government official or engineer would attract the attention of security officials than would a KGB officer under Soviet diplomatic cover. And even if security officials did notice such a meeting, it would be much easier to provide a benign explanation for contact with a pesky American journalist than with a Soviet diplomat.

> Harvey Klehr; John Earl Haynes, and Alexander Vassiliev, *I. F. Stone, Soviet Agent—Case Closed*, Commentary (May 2009). Perhaps most importantly, "the KGB could use journalists for 'active measures'—the planting of a story in the press or giving a slant to a story that served KGB goals." Ibid. See also John Earl Haynes and Harvey Klehr, "Spies Among Us," *WashingtonDecoded. com*, June 19, 2009 ("Journalists were particularly well-suited for agency because many of the tasks they were asked to carry out—providing inside information, serving as couriers, talent-spotters, and checking on the background of potential sources—were, or could be made to seem, a normal part of their everyday work").

15. Kalugin (1994) at 53.

16. *Ibid* (discussing racial "trouble" in the United States). This is very close to what *Ramparts* editor Warren Hinkle did when he invited numerous publications to a press conference/party in support of *The Deputy*. See Rychlak (2010) at 301-02.

17. Weiner, "Where Have All the Lefties Gone?," at 29, 30 (quoting folk singer Dave Van Ronk). See also Kengor.

18. Weiner, *Where Have All the Lefties Gone?* at 54.

19. *Ibid* at 53. When Soviet handlers controlled American communists, the Americans were at the beck and call of their handlers. See Miller at 16.

20. "Not Only the Deputy," *The Minority of One*, April 1964; M.S. Arnoni, American Dialog, July-August, 1964.

21. "Not Only the Deputy," *The Minority of One*, April 1964.

22. Ibid.
23. Robert Gorham Davis & George N. Shuster, "Of Gross Ends and a Man's Choice," *New York Times Book Review*, March 1, 1964.
24. "Obituary: Robert Gorham Davis," *New York Times*, July 17, 1998. See also "Obituary: Hope Hale Davis, 100; Author, Writing Teacher, Feminist and Communist," *Los Angeles Times*, October 7, 2004 (obituary of Davis's widow).
25. Cooney at 282. He said that the play had been written to "drive a wedge between Christians and Jews." *Ibid.*
26. Hinkle at 58.
27. *Ibid at 58; Editor's Mailbag*, Ohio Jewish Chronicle, March 20, 1964 (discussing Jews who protest *The Deputy*). See *Israelis Defend Name of Pope Pius XII*, Jewish Chronicle, October 11, 1963 (discussing the Jewish reaction to the play's opening in London). See Trude Weiss-Rosmarin, *Second Thoughts on "The Deputy," Ramparts*, Summer 1964 at 95 (emphasis in original) (detailing how the play insulted Jews). As one of the play's most important early supporters explained: "The serious rejoinders to Hochhuth's charges against the Pope were handled by the Jews, which was the reason for the surprising defense of Pius XII by B'nai B'rith." Hinkle at 58. See also Alfred Kazin, *The Vicar of Christ*, The New York Review of Books, March 19, 1964, reprinted in *The Storm over the Deputy* at 102, 105.
28. He apparently was offended in late 1963 by some Jesuits who agreed to write articles responding to criticisms of the Church. After seeing the criticisms, they backed out of their commitment, leaving *Ramparts* without sufficient content for the next issue. *Ramparts* editor Warren Hinkle explained: "The holy beating these holy men gave Ed Keating was to prove pivotal in the leftward development of *Ramparts*." Burns at 321.
29. Hinkle at 50-51.
30. Burns at 321.
31. Hinkle at 50-51.
32. Edward M. Keating, "The Voice of Pius Was Silent," *This World*, March 1, 1964; Edward M. Keating & Trude Weiss-Rosmarin, "Book Reviews," *Ramparts*, Summer 1964; Edward M. Keating, "Book Review," *San Francisco Chronicle*, March 1, 1964. See also Edward Keating, *The Scandal of Silence: A Layman's Powerful Critique of the Catholic Church in America* (1965).
33. "French Cardinal Condemned Nazis," *New York Times*, Feb. 26, 1964, p.41.
34. Tisserant, *Interview*, Informations Catholiques, April 15, 1964. See also O'Carroll at 14, 69.
35. According to at least one account, *Ramparts'* reporting led to "the biggest security leak of the Cold War." Sol Stern, "The Ramparts I Watched: Our storied radical magazine did transform the nation—for the worse," *City Journal* (Winter 2010).
36. Bennett's most important publication at that time was the book, *Christianity and Communism Today* (1948, rev. 1960). He was known for supporting civil rights, protesting the Vietnam War, opposing nuclear weapons, and (later) advocating for gay and lesbian rights. In 1961, Time magazine wrote: "Dr. Bennett has long warned Christians against thinking that God is automatically on the side of the West." "Whose Side is God On?," *Time*, Nov. 10, 1961. The article went on to quote him:

> The very atheism of communism is a judgment upon the churches, which for so long were unconcerned about the victims of the Industrial Revolution and early capitalism and which have usually been ornaments of the status quo, no matter how unjust it has been. The temptation to turn the cold war into a holy crusade is ever with us....

37. Zahn was a conscientious objector to World War II and cofounder of Pax Christi USA. His most famous work at the time was *German Catholics and Hitler's War* (1962). That book led to some serious clashes with Catholic leaders and his departure from (the Jesuit) Loyola University.

Griffin, a convert to Catholicism, was best known for his work on racial strife in the United States and his book *Black Like Me* (concerning his trip through southern states disguised as an African-American).

38. This was a typical approach of the KGB, which would place stories in small papers and journals, hoping that other outlets would pick them up. See Yury B. Shvets, *Washington Station: My Life as a KGB Spy in America* 13, 39 (Simon & Schuster, 1994); Kalugin (1994) at 53.

39. Burns at 321.

40. "A Bomb in Every Issue," *Time*, January 6, 1967.

41. *Ibid.*

42. Sol Stern, "The Ramparts I Watched: Our storied radical magazine did transform the nation— for the worse," *City Journal* (Winter 2010).

43. *Ibid.*

44. *Ibid.*

45. *Ibid.*

46. Burns at 321.

47. David Horowitz, "Spy Stories: The Wen Ho Lee Cover-Up," *FrontPageMagazine.com*, October 3, 2000.

48. Burns at 321. See S. Steven Powell, *Covert Cadre: Inside the Insitute for Policy Studies* (Green Hill Publishers, 1987).

49. *Memo to the White House re Ramparts*, case no. EO-1996-00609, pub. date 5/19/1966; release date 11/4/1997 (noting dramatic expansion and communist ties of key personnel). *Memorandum to Bill Moyers, White House from Richard Helms, DD/CIA (Subject Del)*, case no. EO-2004-00392, pub. date 5/19/1966; release date 5/17/2004 (same document).

CHAPTER 22

1. See Edgar Alexander, "Rolf Hochhuth: Equivocal Deputy, Study of the anti-Semitic and Anti-Catholic mental baggage of a playwright," *America*, October 12, 1963.

2. Trude Weiss-Rosmarin, "Second Thoughts on The Deputy," *Ramparts* (Summer 1964) at 95.

3. *Ibid.*

4. "Pius XII & The Jews," *Time*, November 1, 1963.

5. *Interview with Rolf Hochhuth*, Ramparts (Spring 1964), reprinted in *The Storm over The Deputy* at 42.

6. Ward at 37.

7. John Simon, "The Deputy and Its Metamorphoses," *The Nation*, March 16, 1964, reprinted in *The Storm over The Deputy* at 109, 115.

8. Hinkle at 58.

9. Weiss-Rosmarin at 95.

10. Hinkle at 58.

11. Among Preminger's many films are *Exodus* (1960), dealing with the establishment of the modern state of Israel, and *The Cardinal* (1963), loosely based on Austrian Cardinal Innitzer.

12. Robert C. Doty, "'The Deputy' is here," *New York Times*, February 23, 1964.

13. *Ibid* at 49.

14. *Ibid* at 43.

15. Judy Stone interview, in *The Storm over The Deputy*, 46-47.

16. *Ibid* at 64-65.

17. Ferencz later became a significant promoter of the International Criminal Court. One of the co-authors of this book (Rychlak) met him several times at the United Nations while serving as a delegate of the Holy See to meetings on the ICC.

18. Matthew Brzezinski, "Giving Hitler Hell," *Washington Post*, July 24, 2005.

19. See Edward Crankshaw, *Khrushchev: A Career* (New York: Viking, 1966) at 154 ("Khrushchev showed himself to be a fairly crude anti-Semite in later years.")
20. For details see Radu Ioanid, *The Ransom of the Jews: The Story of Extraordinary Secret Bargain between Romania and Israel* (Chicago: Ivan R. Dee, 2005), with an afterword by Pacepa.
21. *The Case of the Anti-Soviet Block of Rights and Troskyites*, 369-430 Red Star Press (1937).
22. Will Englund, "Ex-Soviet Scientist Says Gorbachev's Regime Created New Nerve Gas in '91," *Baltimore Sun*, September 16, 1992.
23. J. Michael Waller, "Post-Soviet Sakharov: Renewed Persecution of Dissident Scientists and the American Response," *Demokratizatsiya: The Journal of Post-Soviet Democratization*, vol. 2, no. 1 (1994).
24. Lev Fyodorov, "KGB-Led Chemical Weapons Cover-Up?," *Crossroads: A Monitor of Post-Soviet Reform*, (April 15, 1993) at 4.

CHAPTER 23

1. Solomon Volkov and Dmitri Shostakovich, *Testimony: The Memoirs of Dmitri Shostakovich* (Limelight, 2004) at xxv.
2. *Ibid at* xxx, 95 ("An artist whose portrait did not resemble the leader disappeared forever. So did the writer who uses 'crude words.'").
3. Moshe Dector, *The Profile of Communism, A Fact-by-Fact Primer* (Collier Books, 1961) at 121.
4. M. Swift at 92.
5. Volkov and Shostakovich at xxx-xxxi.
6. M. Swift at 92.
7. *Ibid* quoting N. Vladimirov, *Cultural Facilities in the USSR*, (Moscow, n.d.) p. 26.
8. *Ibid.*
9. *Ibid at* 93. Trade associations were employed to ensure that the artists complied with the state's demands.

> The Russian Association of Proletarian Writers (1920–1932) and its "musical" offshoot, the Russian Association of Proletarian Musicians (1923–1932), arose as instruments of the cultural policies of the Party. The influence of these unions was almost overwhelming at the end of the 1920s and into the early 1930s. They often turned out to be greater royalists than the king, and were disbanded by Stalin when he decided that the organizations had served their function.

Volkov and Shostakovich at 112 (footnote).
10. M. Swift at 198.
11. Volkov and Shostakovich at 255 (suggesting that many of them had painted portraits of Stalin that displeased the leader).
12. M. Swift at 198.
13. Leon Harris, *The Moscow Circus School* 4-5 (Kingsport Press, 1970). The nation's foremost magician, E.F. Kio, was also praised for having rejected the bourgeois approach taken by earlier magicians. Y. Dmitriyev, *Kio and His Predecessors* in *The Soviet Circus: A Collection of Articles* (Moscow: Progress Publishers, 1967).
14. M. Swift at 101.
15. Volkov and Shostakovich at 146.
16. *Ibid at* 270.
17. *Ibid at* 80 (footnote) & 95 (Lenin called opera a "piece of purely upper-class culture.")
18. *Ibid at* 114, 127 ("Approving programs and lists was a hobby of his.")
19. *Ibid at* 64. Stalin also banned Shakespeare. *Ibid at* 87.

20. *Ibid at* 3-4 (footnote).
21. *Ibid at* 190. This became a problem when one of the nation's highest-ranking churchmen, the Metropolitan of Moscow, planned to give a talk on the radio.

    > The Metropolitan arrived at the radio station and walked straight up to the microphone. They grabbed him by the sleeve and pulled him away. "Your Eminence, where's the text of the speech?" The Metropolitan was taken aback. "What speech?" They began explaining that they meant the…well, not the speech, but the whatever-you-call-it…. In other words, if the Metropolitan was planning to speak now, where was the approved and signed text?

    > The Metropolitan, they say, took umbrage and stated that he never read his sermons from a piece of paper. This was a scandal; what to do? They asked the Metropolitan to wait a bit and rushed to call the bosses, but no one wanted the responsibility.

    Ibid at 191. Eventually, the question made its way up all the way to Stalin. He decided to let the Metropolitan speak unhindered.
22. M. Swift at 101.
23. *Ibid* at 149.
24. *Ibid* at 162-63.
25. Volkov and Shostakovich at xxxvi.
26. Niels C. Nielsen, *Solzhenitsyn's Religion* (Nelson, 1975) at 54.
27. Volkov and Shostakovich (photo page facing page 87).
28. *Ibid.*
29. *Ibid* at 128.
30. See *Ibid* at xxxiii.
31. *Ibid* at 128 (Stalin "livid" about being left out of film), 149.

    > Stalin loved the movies. It didn't take long for Stalin to see every Soviet film made; Stalin had the following aesthetic theory. Of all the pictures produced, only a small fraction was any good, and even fewer were masterpieces, because only a few people were capable of making masterpieces. Stalin determined who could create a masterpiece and who couldn't, and then he decided that bad films weren't needed, nor were the good ones. He needed only masterpieces. If the production of cars and airplanes could be planned, then why not plan the production job masterpieces? It's no more complicated, particularly if you're dealing with film, since film is also an industry.

    Ibid at 249.
32. *Ibid* at 249-50.
33. Lauren Weiner, "Where Have All the Lefties Gone?," *First Things*, January 2010, at 29, 30 (mentioning Pete Seeger, Lee Hays, Millard Lampell, Burl Ives, Josh White, Saul Aarons, Bernie Asbel, Will Geer, and Woody Guthrie).
34. *Ibid.*
35. Volkov and Shostakovich at 214-15.
36. *Ibid.*
37. *Ibid.*
38. *Ibid* at 215, 316.
39. *Ibid* at 209. Stalin appreciated the power of the arts to move people, but he did not really appreciate the talent of the artists. One composer explained: "Stalin used to call all of us cogs. One cog does not differ from another, and cogs can easily replace one another." *Ibid at* 212; see *Ibid at* 215-16. That mindset is why the Kremlin had little concern about falsifying writings, be they poems, folk songs, or plays.
40. M. Swift at 256-57.

41. *Ibid at* 289-90.
42. *Ibid at* 291. There were numerous Soviet artists who regarded the:

> interference of the Party and State in their art as a colossal nuisance, and who would like nothing more than to be allowed simply to be artists. However, the Soviet performer is not left alone. Once a Soviet ballet artist joins a theatrical collective, his in-service ideological training continues through the theatrical Komsomol or Party unit if he is a member. His mentality is further formed by lectures sponsored by the All-Russian Theatrical Society, by *Rabis*, or simply by the talks and discussions which take place in every theatre.

Ibid at 291.

43. Dector, *Profile of Communism* at 133.
44. M. Swift at 292.

CHAPTER 24

1. M. Swift at 293.
2. *David Irving Propagandists' Poster Boy*, Anti-Defamation League (2001) <http://www.adl.org>.
3. Gordon Craig, *The Germans* 72 (New York: G.P. Putnam's Sons, 1982).
4. *Ibid at* 72.
5. Richard Evans, *In Hitler's Shadow* 166 (New York: Pantheon Books, 1989).
6. D.D. Guttenplan, *The Holocaust on Trial* (New York: W.W. Norton, 2001), 46.
7. Deborah Lipstadt, *Denying the Holocaust* 111 (New York: Free Press, 1993).
8. *Ibid at* 231.
9. English translation of the Soviet Note of April 25, 1943, severing unilaterally Soviet-Polish diplomatic relations, published online by the Polish government on December 19, 2005.
10. *Time*, May 10, 1968.
11. Declassified Secret Memorandum: *Soldiers*, to Mr. John Peck & Sir E. Peck from J.E. Jackson, January 10, 1969 ('Soldiers' – IRD Contribution) (citing the October 22, 1967, edition of *Zycie Literackie* (Literary Life) and an article by Olgierd Terlrcki), reprinted in Rychlak (2010) at 419.
12. Rainer Taëni, *Modern German Authors, Rolf Hochhuth* (London: Oswald Wolff, 1977) at 140, 149. Prchal "was vindicated in court and damages were awarded." David Frost, *An Autobiography* (New York: HarperCollins, 1993) at 416. For details on the verdict against Hochhuth, see "Pilot of General Sikorski's Aircraft Claims Libel Damages from German Playwright," *The Times of London*, May 3, 1972, at 3; "£50,000 Award to General Sikorski's Pilot," *The Times of London*, May 4, 1972, at 1; "$130,000 Awarded to Pilot for Libel in Hochhuth Play," *New York Times*, May 4, 1972, at 48. Thompson at 17-18.
13. Martin Esslin, *Rolf Hochhuth*, in Justin Wintle, *Makers of Modern Culture* 233 (New York: Facts on File, 1981).
14. Thompson at 112. David Irving sued Thompson over the book, arguing that the book was libelous, but the publisher defended by asserting that the allegations were true. Witnesses signed off on their statements, and Irving dropped the case. He eventually had to pay the defendants' costs. He did, however, send an unsigned note out to British newspapers trying to impugn Thompson's character. When asked by the press, he admitted that he had written it and noted that his initials, "djci," were at the bottom of the note. Susan Barnes, "David Irving: Portrait of a Gentleman," *The Sunday Times Supplement*, London, September 6, 1970.
15. As a biographer wrote, he "is not slow to come to conclusions, which he does without fear or favour." Taëni at 19.

16. Carlos Thompson, an Argentine-born German writer and actor, made his first film at age 16. In the 1950s, he was the epitome of the Latin lover. Among his movies were: *Valley of the Kings*, starring Yvonne de Carlo, and *The Flame and the Flesh*, in which he played opposite Lana Turner. He also starred in *El Tunel*, based on the novel by the noted Argentine writer Ernesto Sabato. In 1957, he married writer Lilli Palmer, the former wife of actor Rex Harrison. Thompson said that the book "imposed itself" upon him and that Hochhuth "has only himself to blame for it."

17. Thompson at 266. Whether it is truly "one big step further" is a matter of debate.

18. *Ibid* at 134 (statement of Prince Lubomirski).

19. *Ibid* at 149. See Harry de Quetteville, "Did British double agent Kim Philby murder Polish war hero General Sikorski?," *London Telegraph*, July 1, 2008.

20. Thompson at 192.

21. *Ibid* at 193.

22. *Ibid* at 133 (statement of General Marian Kukiel). Thompson reported that one of Hochhuth's main shortcomings was that he was so busy 'knowing' that he did not have the time or the energy to travel a bit and find out what was really what. *Ibid* at 125. Thompson continues: All humour aside, this symptom promised anything but laughs. Colonel John Codrington of the British Intelligence said:

> Hochhuth says that Intelligence killed Sikorski. Well if that is the case, then you are talking to the man who would have done the job. I was Assistant Chief of Staff to Governor Mason Macfarlane. I was in charge of Military Intelligence. I repeat, if we had arranged to kill Sikorski, I would have been the one to do it.

Ibid at 287. Codrington said: Hochhuth simply doesn't know what he is talking about. *Ibid* at 278.

23. *Ibid* at 95.

24. *Ibid* at 100.

25. *Ibid* at 101.

26. *Ibid* at 130. When asked about Hochhuth's claims that witnesses were faking amnesia, Kukiel called it a silly invention. He added: I am sorry that such a good writer as David Irving should allow himself to be dragged into Hochhuth's theory.)

27. *Ibid* at 213.

28. *Ibid* at 214.

29. *Time*, May 10, 1968.

30. Prof. Dr. Wolfram Wette, "Der Fall Filbinger" (The Filbinger Case), lecture on September 14, 2003, wettewolfr@aol.com.

31. German Wikipedia, Rolf Hochhuth, <http://de.wikipedia.org >.

32. David Irving, *Confidential Draft of Memoirs*, 156 <http://www.fpp.co.uk/books/memoirs/prison_1.html>.

33. *Ibid* at 156.

34. As Thompson related to one of the witnesses he interviewed:

> Hochhuth's obsession is that both Irving and myself will be killed any day now by a secret organization which he calls *The Old Firm*, which is run, so he told me in Zurich, by a retired British General. In fact, he's said to me that Sikorski's murderers are "all still active" and bumping off people with taxis in the streets of London, or pushing them under trams and buses.

Thompson at 90. Hochhuth also feared that the British were spying on him. *Ibid at* 92.

35. When Thompson decided to do further investigation that might reveal Hochhuth's fabrications, Hochhuth called Thompson's wife and said that Thompson's life was in danger. *Ibid at*

77, 85-86. Thompson did not know whether Hochhuth believed the threat was real or it was just a ploy designed to stop him from carrying out further investigation.

36. T. Feitknecht, K. Lüssi, *Ein Spannungsreiches Vierteljahrhundert: Der Briefwechsel Rolf Hochhuth/Golo Mann* (German book collecting correspondence between Hochhuth and Mann).

CHAPTER 25

1. See Rychlak (2010) at 272-73 (transcript of Wolff's testimony).
2. See generally Dan Kurzman, *A Special Mission: Hitler's Secret Plot to Seize the Vatican and Kidnap Pope Pius XII* (Perseus Book Group, 2007); Rychlak, *Hitler, the War, and the Pope* (2000) at 265 (quoting Wolff's testimony on the subject).
3. While visiting Rome in April 2010, coauthor Rychlak was shown a copy of the minutes of the meeting that Pius XII had with the Curia in which he set forth plans for what should happen if the Nazis were to kidnap him.
4. Donald Rayfield, *Stalin and His Hangmen* 374-79 (New York: Random House, 2005).
5. See *The Black Book of Communism*.
6. Ivan Serov, *Wikipedia*, September 10, 2009.
7. John Barron, *Breaking the Ring* (Boston: Houghton Mifflin, 1987), at 318.
8. Benjamin B. Fischer, *The Katyn Controversy: Stalin's Killing Field*, Central Intelligence Agency, Center of the Study of Intelligence, CSI publications, Winter 1990.
9. Hochhuth (1964) at 125-140.
10. *Ibid* at 348.
11. Andrew and Mitrokhin at 91-92, 102, 146, 165.
12. Wikipedia, Arvid Harnack, May 26, 2010.
13. Patricia Marx, *An Interview with Rolf Hochhuth*, Partisan Review, vol. 31, no. 3, Summer 1964, 368, reprinted in *The Storm over The Deputy* at 52-65.
14. Carlos Thompson, in his book *The Assassination of Winston Churchill* (Gerards Cross: Colin Smyth, 1968), describes his extensive research in an effort to identify Hochhuth's alleged sources for the material upon which his *Soldiers* was based, the retired British Intelligence man and the Polish lady. Thompson convincingly concludes they probably did not exist.
15. Patricia Marx, *An Interview with Rolf Hochhuth*, Partisan Review, vol. 31, no. 3, Summer 1964, 368, reprinted in *The Storm over The Deputy* at 52-65
16. See Bittman at 77 (Soviets sent money to pro-Moscow publishing houses).
17. *Ibid* at 177.
18. *The Storm over the Deputy* at 13. See also Taëni at 14 (more in accord with Piscator's account).
19. Erwin Piscator's introduction to *The Deputy* in the German edition published by Rowohlt, Hamburg, 1963; translation by Clara Mayer published in *The Storm over The Deputy*, 11.
20. *The Storm over The Deputy* at 14-15.
21. *Ibid* at 14.
22. German Wikipedia, Erwin Piscator, September 19, 2009.
23. Taëni at 14. See *ibid* at 20 ("It really is doubtful whether *The Representative* would ever have seen the light of day if it had not come into the hands of such a famous producer as Erwin Piscator"); *Ibid* at 135 (similar).
24. Ward at 17 ("I have learned that the poet always must be active in politics. That he is always responsible. *The Deputy* is politics").
25. Willett at 180.
26. *Ibid*.
27. *Ibid* at 182.

28. In the play's afterword, Hochhuth admitted that "the action does not follow the historical course of events and I allowed my imagination free play." Hochhuth (1964) at 287, 348.

29. See Sidney F. Parham, "Editing Hochhuth for the Stage: A Look at the Major Productions of The Deputy," 28 *Educational Theatre Journal* 347.

30. Robert P. Lockwood, "Deconstructing The Deputy," *Catalyst*, June 2000. Lockwood explains:

> For the most part, this was based on the pope's opposition to the Allied demand for unconditional German surrender. He believed such a demand would only continue the horror of the war and increase the killing. That stand was later interpreted as a desire on the pontiff's part to maintain a strong Germany as a bulwark against communism. Hochhuth's charge of papal silence fit that revisionist theory.

31. "The characterization of Pacelli as a money-grubbing hypocrite is so wide of the mark as to be ludicrous. Importantly, however, Hochhuth's play offends the most basic criteria of documentary: that such stories and portrayals are valid only if they are demonstrably true. Cornwell (1999) at 375.

32. Ward at 38 (calling this "the most striking example" of Hochhuth's "departure from 'Realism'" and noting that Hochhuth rejected the Mengele comparison).

33. Leo Kerz, "Brecht and Piscator," 20:3 *Educational Theatre Journal* 363, 369 (October 1968) (Kerz was the set and lighting designer and the recipient of the letter).

34. "Hochhuth does what no man can do; he inserts himself into the mind of Pius and draws only the worst conclusions. He is guilty of the worst kind of McCarthyism, and only the staggering immensity of his charge has kept people from seeing this fact." James O'Gara, "The Real Issue," *Commonweal*, February 28, 1964, reprinted in *The Storm over The Deputy* at 219, 221. Twenty-five years after Piscator's production, German director Claus Peymann (known for "a radical style which had its roots in the political dreams of the late sixties") produced *The Deputy* in Austria to coincide with a visit by Pope John Paul II. Peymann said that he did not like the play, but he produced it as a political challenge. Gitta Honegger, "Tales from the Imperial City," 11:2 *Performing Arts Journal* 45, 50 (1988).

35. See "Reviews," XII:2 *World Theatre* 140 (Summer 1963) ("somewhere between a spoken report with scenes of great realism… and a fast paced discussion"). The review went on to note the difficulty of producing the play "from a text which if performed in total would have lasted six or seven hours." *Ibid.*; Sidney F. Parham, "Editing Hochhuth for the Stage: A Look at the Major Productions of 'The Deputy,'" 28:3 *Educational Theatre Journal* 347, 353 (Oct., 1976) ("How then should we judge Hochhuth as a playwright? The formal shape of his script suggests that he wishes to be judged by traditional dramatic standards, and by these standards one cannot speak well of him").

36. Lest this discussion be taken as trying to diminish Piscator's unquestioned talent as a director, this passage from the set designer for the Berlin production of *The Deputy* is worthy of consideration:

> Piscator's production of *The Deputy*, apart from becoming the biggest postwar theatre event and because of it, started a debate which affected and revised the views of philosophers, clergy, politicians, and historians in every corner of the world. It touched upon the conscience of the Catholic Church and, without a doubt, influenced what happened at the last Ecumenical Council. Piscator had caught up with Brecht and proved that the theatre can contribute to the shaping of history as well as being shaped by history.

Leo Kerz, "Brecht and Piscator," 20:3 *Educational Theatre Journal* 363 (October 1968).

CHAPTER 26

1. Reprinted in Crankshaw at 559-618.
2. Harry Schwartz, "We know now that he was a giant among men," *New York Times*, September 12, 1971.
3. Barron at 313-19.
4. *Ibid* at 318.

CHAPTER 27

1. Victor L. Simpson, *Italian Panel: Soviets Behind the Pope Attack*, Associated Press, March 2, 2006; Freemantle at 107-08; Koehler at 116-22. In 2009 journalist and former army intelligence officer John Koehler published *Spies in the Vatican: The Soviet Union's Cold War against the Catholic Church*. Using mainly East German and Polish secret police archives, Koehler concluded that the attempt was "KGB-backed."
2. In 2006, the Mitrokhin Commission (an Italian parliamentary commission set up to investigate alleged KGB ties to opposition figures in Italian politics) supported once again the Bulgarian theory. The commission reported that "leaders of the former Soviet Union were behind the assassination attempt," and alleged that "the leadership of the Soviet Union took the initiative to eliminate Pope John Paul" because of his support for Solidarity. "Soviets Had Pope Shot for Backing Solidarity," *Daily Telegraph*, March 3, 2006.
3. Weigel offers little new information regarding Soviet involvement in the 1981 assassination attempt, but he does note that most Poles and many close friends of the pope felt that the Soviets were not innocent. He also makes clear that Western democracies did not look very hard; they were afraid of what they would find. See also George Weigel, "All War All the Time," *First Things*, April 2011, at 34.
4. The dishonesty was uncovered by Prof. Robert Gorman, who presented a paper on this topic at the October 2001 meeting of the Society of Catholic Social Scientists.
5. Thomas Merton, *Dancing in the Water of Life* (San Francisco: Harper, 1998), 84.
6. "Vatican Chronicles: A Different Read," *Brill's Content*, April 2000, at 60, 120.
7. Pacepa, *Red Horizons*, second edition, pictures following page 206.
8. John Cornwell, *Hitler's Pope: The Fight to reveal the secrets that threaten the Vatican, The (London) Sunday Times*, September 12, 1999. See also Rychlak (2010) at 282, 428, 430-431.
9. See Rychlak (2000) (epilogue).
10. Marx interview, reprinted in *The Storm over The Deputy* at 54-55. In another interview, Hochhuth said that in 1958, while he was working on the Gerstein story, the West German newspapers and radio suddenly "declared that a holy man had died," and Hochhuth commented that, "the Germans loved Pius ...and they called him the German Pope." Judy Stone interview, reprinted in *The Storm over The Deputy* at 49-50.
11. Rychlak (2000) at 292-293, 435.
12. Cornwell (2008) at XII.
13. *Ibid*.
14. *Ibid*.

CHAPTER 28

1. Wills, *Papal Sin: Structures of Deceit*.
2. Carroll, *Constantine's Sword*.

3.   Zuccotti, *Under His Very Window.*

4.   Phayer, *The Catholic Church and the Holocaust.*

5.   Kertzer's *The Popes against the Jews* is highly dependent on the work of Italian scholar Giovanni Miccoli. Justus George Lawler recently completed a manuscript (Working title: *Were the Popes against the Jews?*) that dissects Kertzer's arguments.

6.   Wistrich (2002).

7.   Cornwell, *Breaking Faith.*

8.   Katz, *The Battle for Rome.* See also Katz, *Black Sabbath;* Katz, *Massacre in Rome.*

9.   Goldhagen (2002).

10. Zuccotti somehow tries to diminish this intervention by reporting that it "should be described not as an official diplomatic protest of the roundup but as a desperate plea for Weizsäcker's intervention to save the victims." *Under His Very Windows* at 160.

11. See Day at 22 (listing him among the anti-Nazi German leaders who were willing to risk their lives to topple the regime).

12. Zuccotti, *Under His Very Windows* at 159; *cf. Notes du Cardinal Maglione,* October 16, 1943, Actes et Documents, vol. 9, page 505, no. 368. Even critic James Carroll gave Maglione's entire text in his book, *Constantine's Sword,* at 525-526.

13. Zuccotti, *Under His Very Windows* at 103. Zuccotti accused Valeri of manufacturing papal interventions on behalf of the Jews. See also Blet at 234-35.

14. Zuccotti, *Under His Very Windows* at 63.

15. *Summi Pontificatus,* para. 48. See Rychlak (2010).

16. See, e.g., Daniel J. Goldhagen, "What Would Jesus Have Done?," *The New Republic,* January 21, 2002.

17. David Dalin, "Pius XII and the Jews," *The Weekly Standard,* February 26, 2001, at 31-39. See also Ronald J. Rychlak, "Misusing History to Influence the Future," *Forum Focus* (Summer 2002).

18. The origin of this story seems to be in the following statement: There is finally the report that in the months preceding his death he was given Hochhuth's play *The Deputy* to read and then was asked what one could do against it. Whereupon he allegedly replied: "Do against it? What can you do against the truth?" Hannah Arendt, *Men in Dark Times* 63 (New York: Harcourt Brace, 1968).

19. Felicity O'Brien, *Letter to the Editor,* The Catholic Times [Manchester, England], July 20, 1997.

20. Private correspondence from Loris Francesco Capovilla to the relator of Pius XII's sainthood cause, dated May 18, 2002.

> With regard to the actions in favor of the Jews, affected particularly in Istanbul in the years 1935–1944, which was recognized and praised by Hebrew communities in Jerusalem, Istanbul, and the United States, it is obligatory to recognize that Roncalli was and declared himself the executor of the thought and the directives of Pius XII. He repeated, in fact: The papal representative is the eye, the ear, the mouth, the heart and the effective hand of the Pope.

> *Ibid.* Capovilla also said that Roncalli's rescue efforts on behalf of Jews make sense only if they are referred above everything else to Pius XII, of whom Roncalli was the careful and most faithful interpreter. Any strictly personal action, even though it be heroic, of Roncalli himself, would otherwise be inconceivable. *Ibid.*

21. McGurn at 99.

22. Pius died on October 9, 1958. Pope John XXIII knelt in prayer before Pius XII's tomb on the ninth of each month. *The New Catholic Treasury of Wit and Humor* 193-94 (New York: Meredith Press, 1968, Paul Bussard, ed.).

23. John XXIII, *Discorsi* vol. I, p. 101.

24. McGurn at 36, 39.

25. *Discorsi* I, at 101; *Days of Devotion* at 12 ("Pope John's programme and its concern for the modern world naturally enough found much of its inspiration in Pope John's predecessor under whom he served for 19 years, and from whom came much of the intellectual foundation on which the Council is built. No one was more generous in acknowledging this debt than Pope John himself.")

26. John Cornwell, "Hitler's Pope: The fight to reveal the secrets that threaten the Vatican," *The Sunday Times* (London), Sept. 12, 1999, at l.

27. *Jerusalem Post*, March 23, 2000 (online edition).

28. *Ibid.* In *The Pontiff in Winter*, Cornwell refers to his own inside-the-Vatican, deep throat: Monsignor *Sotto Voce*. Taking Cornwell at his word, and accepting his description of Monsignor *Sotto Voce*, *The Pontiff in Winter* is based upon an "inside account" from a disgruntled and burned-out Vatican official who trades secrets for a good meal and a couple of bottles of wine. The great advantage for Cornwell, of course, is that this lets him write almost anything, and unlike *Hitler's Pope*, no one can prove it is false. It is very similar to claims made by Hochhuth in the 1960s.

29. "Pope Stared Down Communism in Homeland," CBCNEWS, April 2005 <http://www.cbc.ca/news/obit/pope/communism_homeland.html>.

30. See Ronald J. Rychlak, "Guess Who's Back?," *Catalyst* (Jan.-Feb. 2002) (reviewing *Breaking Faith*); Ronald J. Rychlak, "A Broken Faith: John Cornwell's New Book," *St. Austin Review*, July/August 2002.

31. Cornwell presented the excommunication of Sri Lankan theologian Fr. Tissa Balasuriya as an example of the harshness of John Paul's "authoritarian rule." Balasuriya was excommunicated for theological aberrations, barely mentioned by Cornwell, that included the assertion that Christianity is on the same level as other religions, the denial of the virgin birth of Christ, and the rejection of the Holy Trinity. See Ronald J. Rychlak & Fr. Kevin Slattery, "A Clear-Cut Case for Excommunication," *New Oxford Review*, April 1997. Cornwell used the excommunication to argue that John Paul was insensitive and out-of-touch with the modern world. He did not, however, even mention the extended negotiations between Balasuriya and the Vatican that preceded the excommunication. More incredibly, he failed to mention that one year after the excommunication was imposed, it was lifted. At that time, Balasuriya signed a statement expressing regret for perceptions of error in his work and agreed to submit future writings to bishops for approval prior to publication. This resolution to the matter, unknown to most readers of *Breaking Faith*, severely undercuts Cornwell's thesis *and* his credibility!

32. He has not hidden his disappointment with Pope Benedict XVI: "The Pope is emerging as an ultra-reactionary." John Cornwell, *Profile: Pope Benedict XVI*, New Statesman, February 12, 2009. In an example of trying to change the past, Cornwell presents himself as a great fan of Pope John Paul II, contrasting the late Pope to Benedict XVI.

33. Similarly, James Carroll's resolution to this history, as set forth in *Constantine's Sword* (pages 555-58), involves the convening of Vatican III, at which (in addition to rejection of papal infallibility, ordination of women, election of bishops, and relaxation of sexual rules) the Church would acknowledge errors in the gospels, learn to preach against those errors, and reject the belief that Jesus is the only way to salvation.

34. Alan Cowell, "Demonstrators and Devout Greet the Pope in Germany," *New York Times*, June 24, 1996, section A; page 3.

35. Arnaldo Cortesi, "Cardinals Irked by Soviet Charge," *New York Times*, October 20, 1958.

36. *Ibid.*

37. *Ibid.*

38. *Catholic Star Herald*, July 7, 2010.

CHAPTER 29

1. Max Holland, *The Kennedy Assassination Tapes* (New York: Knopf, 2004), pp. 94-96.
2. Ibid., p. 99.
3. Ibid., pp.148-149.
4. House Select Committee on Assassinations (HSCA) Report, p. 99.
5. Andrew and Gordievsky, p. 462.
6. Barron, *Breaking the Ring*, pp. 148, 212.
7. Epstein, *Legend*, p. 71.
8. Warren Commission (WC) Report, p. 390.
9. Ibid., p. 256.
10. Edward J. Epstein, *Legend: The Secret World of Lee Harvey Oswald* (New York: Reader's Digest Press, 1978), pp. 72-73.
11. Ibid., pp. 77-79.
12. WC Report, p. 684.
13. Donovan testimony, WC Vol. 8, pp. 289-303.
14. Epstein, *Legend*, pp. 85-86.
15. Ibid., p. 89.
16. Francis Gary Powers, with Curt Gentry, *Operation Overflight: The U-2 spy pilot tells his story for the first time* (New York: Holt, Rinehart, 1970), p. 357.
17. Warren Commission Exhibit (WCE), 315.
18. Powers, pp. 99-111.
19. Ibid.
20. Ibid., p. 118.
21. David Wise and Thomas B. Ross, *The U-2 Affair* (New York: Random House, 1962), p. 54.
22. "George de Mohrenschildt," *Spartacus Educational*, <http://www.spartacus.schoolnet.co.uk/JFKdemohrenschildt.htm>.

CHAPTER 30

1. This event was reported on at length in the official Romanian newspaper, *Scinteia*, October 24, 1962, p. 1.
2. William Hyland and Richard Wallace Shyrock, *The Fall of Khrushchev* (New York: Funk & Wagnalls, 1986), p. 56.
3. Nikita Khrushchev, *Khrushchev Remembers: The Last Testament*, translated and edited by Strobe Talbot (Boston: Little, Brown and Company, 1974), pp. 83-84. (This is the second volume of Khrushchev's memoirs and will henceforth be referred to as Khrushchev II.)
4. Khrushchev I, p. 338.
5. Ibid., p. 392.
6. *Documents on International Affairs: 1957* (London: Royal Institute of International Affairs, 1960), p. 39.
7. Joseph L. Nogee and Robert H. Donaldson, *Soviet Foreign Policy Since World War II* (New York: Pergamon Press, 1984), p. 121.
8. David Wise and Thomas B. Ross, *The U-2 Affair* (New York: Random House, 1962), pp. 57-58.
9. Arnold L. Horelick and Myron Rush, *Strategic Power and Soviet Foreign Policy* (Chicago: University of Chicago Press, 1966), p. 43.
10. Khrushchev II, p. 533.
11. PBS, Khrushchev's biography, <http://www.pbs.org>.

12. Sergei N. Khrushchev, *Nikita Khrushchev and the Creation of a Superpower* (Pennsylvania State University Press, 2000).

CHAPTER 31

1. Alex von Tunzelmann, "Oliver Stone's JFK: A basket case for conspiracy," *The Guardian*, April 28, 2011.
2. Barron, *KGB*, p. 430.
3. Warren Commission Exhibit 2486.
4. Testimony of Ruth Hyde Paine, Warren Commission Vol. 3, pp. 12-13.
5. Warren Commission Exhibit 1400.
6. Priscilla Johnson McMillan, *Marina and Lee* (New York: Harper & Row, 1977), p. 496.
7. Epstein, *Legend*, p. 16.
8. HSCA Report, p. 151.
9. Jim Marrs, *Crossfire: The Plot that Killed Kennedy* (New York: Basic Books, 1993) p. 394.
10. HSCA Report, p. 152.

CHAPTER 32

1. Max Holland, "How Moscow Undermined the Warren Commission," *Washington Decoded*, March 30, 2007, <www.washingtondecoded.com>.
2. "Book Review: The Mitrokhin Archive and the secret history of the KGB," *New York Times*, http://www.nytimes.com/books/first/a/andrew-sword.html.
3. Biography of Joachim Joesten, http://karws.gso.uri.edu/jfk/the_critics/Joesten/Joestenbio.html.
4. Andrew and Mitrokhin, *The Sword and the Shield*, 226-227.
5. Max Holland, "How Moscow Undermined."
6. Attributed to Armand Moss, *Information, Disinformation*, pp. 93 ff.
7. Perlo's review was found at https://www.createspace.com/3998409.
8. Haynes, Klehr, and Vassiliev, *Spies*, 275.
9. Jesse E. Curry, *Retired Dallas Police Chief Jesse Curry Reveals His Personal JFK Assassination File*, Self-published, 1969, p. 74, affidavit of Dallas police officer Thurber T. Lord on August 20, 1964.
10. Haynes, Klehr, and Vassiliev, *Spies*, 271-272.
11. "I.F. Stone on the Kennedy Assassination," December 9, 1963, <Spartacus.schoolnet.co.UK/USAStoneW.htm>.
12. I. F. Stone, "What Some People Have Forgotten About God's 'Deputy,'" *I. F. Stone's Weekly* (March 9, 1964), reprinted in *The Storm over the Deputy*, 234.
13. Judy Stone, "Interview with Rolf Hochhuth," *Ramparts*, Spring 1964, reprinted in *The Storm over the Deputy*, 42.
14. Vincent Bugliosi, *Reclaiming History: The Assassination of President Kennedy* (New York: Norton, 2007), p. 1000.
15. Ibid., 1012-1013.
16. Andrew and Mitrokhin, *The Sword and the Shield*, 228-229.
17. Brian Latell, *Castro's Secrets* (New York: Palgrave Macmillan, 2012), 103, 215-216.
18. Latell, 138-141.
19. John Barron, *Operation Solo: The FBI's Man in the Kremlin* (Washington: Regnery, 1995), *passim*.
20. Andrew and Mitrokhin, *The Sword and the Shield*, 287-289.

21. Latell, 204-205.
22. Ibid., 141-144.
23. "How Powers's plane was shot down," <http://www.webslivki.com/u11.html> (Russian).
24. Sergey Khrushchev, "The Day We Shot Down the U-2: Nikita Khrushchev's son remembers a great turning point of the Cold War, as seen from behind the Iron Curtain," *American Heritage Magazine*, Volume 51, Issue 5.
25. Morton Kelly, "Gary Powers and the U-2 incident," *About.com.guide, American History*, published as <http://americanhistory.about.com/od/coldwar/a/gary_powers.htm>.

CHAPTER 33

1. Oriana Fallaci, *Interviste con la Storia*, quoted in Claire Sterling, *The Terror Network* 114 (New York: Reader's Digest Press, 1981).
2. For addition information see Ion Mihai Pacepa, "Russian Footprints," *National Review Online*, August 21, 2006.
3. Craig R. Whitney, "East's Archives Reveal Ties to Terrorists," *New York Times*, July 15, 1990, at 6.
4. John O. Koehler, *Stasi: The Untold Story of the East German Secret Police* 324 (Boulder, Colorado: Westview Press, 1999).
5. *Bundesamt für Verfassungsschutz* (BfV), the Office for the Protection of the Constitution.
6. Craig R. Whitney, "East's Archives Reveal Ties to Terrorists," *New York Times*, July 15, 1990, at 6.
7. *Ibid.*
8. Christian Schmidt-Häuer, *Gorbachev: The Path to Power* (London: I. B. Tauris, 1987), p. 64.
9. *Boris Yeltsin: A biography of the former Russian President*, University of Indiana (Internet edition).

CHAPTER 34

1. John Lloyd, "The Russian Devolution," *New York Times Magazine*, August 15, 1999, p. 38.
2. Richard Lourie, "Who Stole Russia?," *The Washington Post Book World*, October 15, 2000, p. 3.
3. Luke Harding, "The richer they come ... Can Russia's oligarchs keep their billions - and their freedom?," *The Guardian*, July 1, 2007.
4. "Could it lead to fascism?," *The Economist*, July 11, 1998, U.S. Edition, p. 19.
5. "The Perils of Catching Cold," *Time*, December 1997, p. 38.
6. "Can the crisis end in a coup?," *Nezavisimaya Gazyeta*, July 7, 1998, p. 1.
7. Barry Renfrew, "Boris Yeltsin Resigns," *Washington Post*, December 31, 1999.
8. Ibid., p. 3.
9. Ariel Cohen, "End of the Yeltsin Era," *Washington Times*, January 3, 2000.
10. John Lloyd, "The Logic of Vladimir Putin," *New York Times Magazine*, March 19, 2000, p. 65.
11. Celestine Bohlen, "Putin Tells Why He Became a Spy," *New York Times*, March 11, 2000 (Internet edition).
12. Arnold Beichman, Hoover Institution, "Prologue for Putin," *Washington Times*, January 10, 2000.
13. Helle Bering, "Totalitarian Wannabes," *Washington Times*, March 9, 2000.
14. *Ibid.*
15. *Putin rocked Russians with ruthlessness*, Agence France Presse, December 31, 1999, <www.rense.com/politics6/ruthless.htm>.
16. *Ibid.*

17. Robert G. Kaiser, "Russia's Enigmatic President," *Washington Post*, October 15, 2000, p. B3.
18. Anna Dolgov, "Book Called Propaganda for Putin," *Associated Press*, September 29, 2000.
19. Robert G. Kaiser, "Russia's Enigmatic President," *Washington Post*, October 15, 2000, p. B3.
20. *Russian government spokesman denies Putin personality cult*, June 25, 2002, RIA news agency, Moscow, as published by Center for Defense Information.
21. John Lloyd, "The Logic of Vladimir Putin," *New York Times Magazine*, March 19, 2000, p. 65.
22. Giles Whittel, "Putin lines up old KGB pals to run Kremlin," *The Times*, London, February 14, 2000.
23. *Ibid.*
24. "Putin strengthens Kremlin's power," *BBC News Online*, World: Europe, May 14, 2000.
25. David Hoffman, "Russian Security Service Revived under Putin," *Washington Post*, December 8, 2000.
26. Kathy Lally, "Pardons turn rare in Putin's Russia," *The Sun*, Baltimore, June 14, 2001, p. 1.
27. Michael R. Gordon, "Putin, in a Rare Interview, Says He'll Use Ex-K.G.B. Aides to Root Out Graft," *New York Times*, March 24, 2000.
28. Details about Roman Malinovsky's activity as a deepcover *Okhrana* officer can be found in Robert Conquest, *Stalin: Breaker of Nations* (New York: Viking, Penguin Group, 1991), pp. 47, 50, 51, 82.
29. Mikhalkov made no secret of being a critic of the dissident writer Aleksander Solzhenitsyn and of Boris Pasternak, the author of *Doctor Zhivago*. Mikhalkov also let it be known that he still admired Stalin.
30. "Russians tune up for Soviet-style start of the New Year," Agence France Presse, Moscow, December 31, 2000.
31. "An American in Russia," *Washington Times*, editorial, December 18, 2000.
32. *Ibid* at 2.
33. Editorial, "Russia's Spy Trials," *Washington Post*, March 14, 2001, p. 24.
34. *Ibid.*
35. Bradley Cook, "Putin: The Inside Story," *NewsMax.com*, March 24, 2000 <www.newsmax.com>.
36. Andrew Meier, "The Big Chill," *Time* Europe, June 26, 2000, vol. 155 No. 25.

CHAPTER 35

1. David Harsanyi, "The United Nations' War Against Israel," *Capitalism Magazine*, May 27, 2002 <published on http://www.capmag.com/article.asp?ID=1617>.
2. Frida Ghitis, "Yearning for a seat at the U.N.'s table," *Philadelphia Inquirer*, July 16, 2004.
3. "The U.N.'s record vis a vis Israel," *News: Facts & Info Reference Desk* www.israelnationalnews.com/english/newspaper/ondisplay/ref/un-israel.htm.
4. "Duma Deputy calls for the Extermination of all Jews in Russia," November 10, 1998, <www.fsumonitor.com>.
5. Jean Mackenzie, "Anti-Semitism is resurfacing in Russia," *Boston Globe*, November 8, 1998, <www.russialist.org/2466.html>.
6. Text of the US Senate letter, including signatures listed alphabetically, published at <www.jewishvirtuallibrary.org/jsource/History/Human_Rights/98sens.html>.
7. "New racism declaration unveiled," *CNN.com/WORLD*, September 4, 2001.
8. Reuters, "Mandela urges fight against racist 'contagion,'" *New York Times*, September 1, 2001.
9. Pamela Constable, "U. S., Israel Quit Forum on Racism," *Washington Post*, September 4, 2001.
10. Betsy Pisik, "U. S. walks out of conference on racism," *Washington Times*, September 4, 2001.
11. Rich Lowry, "Setting standards to cope with Arafat," *Washington Times*, March 23, 2002.

12. Charles Krauthammer, "Me thinks thou do protest too much," *Townhall.com*, November 23, 2001.
13. Arnaud de Borchgrave, "Militant Islam's ambuscade," *Washington Times*, Nov. 1, 2001.
14. Damon Johnston, "New York survivor's son turns traitor," *The Courier-Mail*, November 10, 2001.
15. Nick Fielding, "Encyclopedia of Terror," *The Sunday Times*, November 4, 2001.

CHAPTER 36

1. Stella Rimington, "'Humint' Begins at Home," *Wall Street Journal*, January 3, 2005.
2. Ben Shapiro, "Keep an eye on Russia," *Townhall.com*, August 23, 2002.
3. George F. Will, "Israel's best defense," *Washington Post*, August 15, 2010, p. A13.
4. "Iran will build uranium enrichment centers, nuclear chief says," CNN wire, August 16, 2010.
5. Zhou Enlai was born into a Mandarin family and was sent to study in France (1922-24), where he caught the communist virus and established the Paris-based Chinese Communist Youth Group in 1924.
6. William Taubman, *Khrushchev vs. Mao: A Preliminary Sketch of the Role of Personality in the Sino-Soviet Split*, Cold War International History Project Bulletin (Washington, DC: Woodrow Wilson International Center for Scholars, Winter 1996-97), p. 243.
7. Yang Zheng, *China's Nuclear Arsenal*, National University of Singapore, March 6, 1996 <http://www.kimsoft.com/korea/ch-war.htm>.

CHAPTER 37

1. Douglas J. Brown, "Chekists Around the World Celebrate 9/11," *NewsMax.com*, September 19, 2002 <www.newsmax.com/archives/articles/2002/18/170000.shtml>.
2. *Putin admits Russia's anti-Semitism*, AFP Daily Dispatch, February 3, 2005.
3. Luke Harding, "Putin, the Kremlin power struggle and the $40bn fortune," *The Guardian*, December 21, 2007.
4. *Ibid.*
5. Adrian Blomfield, "Israel humbled by arms from Iran," *The Telegraph*, August 15, 2006.
6. Paul Weitz, "Hezbollah, Already a Capable Military Force, Makes Full Use of Civilian Shields and Media Manipulation," *JINSA Online*, August 12, 2006.
7. Ya Libnan, "Hezbollah confirms its cell members escaped Egyptian jails," February 3, 2011 <http://www.yalibnan.com/2011/02/03/hezbollah-confirms-its-cell-members-escaped-egyptian-jails>.
8. The Brotherhood, or Muslim Brotherhood, is an Islamic fundamentalist organization whose slogan is "Islam is the solution." Its "General Strategic Goal for the Group in North America" makes its objectives clear: "The process of settlement is a 'Civilization-Jihadist Process' with all the word means. The Ikhwan must understand that their work in America is a kind of grand Jihad in eliminating and destroying the Western civilization from within and 'sabotaging' its miserable house by their hands and the hands of the believers so that it is eliminated and God's religion is made victorious over all other religions."
9. "Hizbullah Breaks 22 Terrorists out of Egyptian Jail," *Virtual Jerusalem*, February 4, 2011, <http://www.virtualjerusalem.com/news.php?option=com_content&view=article&id=2512:hizbullah-breaks-22-terrorists-out-of-egyptian-jail&catid=1:headlines&Itemid=2512>.
10. "Hezbollah Chief Praises Tunisian, Egyptian Protesters, yaLIBNAN," February 7, 2011, <http://www.yalibnan.com/2011/02/07/hezbollah-chief-praises-tunisian-egyptian-protests-attacks-us/>.

11. The Meir Amit Intelligence and Terrorism Information Center, formerly The Intelligence and Terrorism Information Center, is an Israeli NGO. It was renamed in honor of Meir Amit, who served as Director of the Mossad from 1963 to 1968. The Center is directed by former Military Intelligence officer, Dr. Reuven Ehrlich. The center is often regarded as being the "public face of Israeli intelligence."

12. Ion Mihai Pacepa, "The Arafat I Knew," *Wall Street Journal*, January 12, 2002.

13. "Speech of numbers," *Peace for Israel*, January 5, 2003 (published on http://israel.wz.cz/numbers.html).

14. Thomas L. Friedman, "The New Math," *New York Times*, op-ed, January 15, 2002, p. A23.

15. Yevgenia Albats, *The KGB: The State Within a State* 23 (New York: Farrar, Straus, Giroux, 1994).

16. See generally Goldfarb and Litvinenko; Cowell; *UK wants to try Russian for Litvinenko murder*, The Guardian, January 26, 2007.

17. Daniel McGrory, and Tony Halpin, (20 January 2007). "Police match image of Litvinenko's real assassin with his death-bed description," *London Times Online*.

18. "Russian faces Litvinenko charge," *BBC News*, May 22, 2007, http://news.bbc.co.uk/1/hi/uk/6678887.stm, (retrieved May 22, 2007).

19. "Wrap: Lugovoi says innocent, Berezovsky behind Litvinenko murder," *Moscow: RIA Novosti*, August 29, 2007, <http://en.rian.ru/russia/20070829/75649246.html>, (accessed March 16, 2010).

20. "Ivan Safronov was killed: Prosecutor begins an investigation of 'incitement to suicide,'" *Kommersant.ru*, March 6, 2007.

21. <http://en.wikipedia.org/wiki/List_of_journalists_killed_in_Russia>.

22. Seamus Martin, "Russian Patriarch was KGB agent, Files Say," *The Irish Times*, September 23, 2000 as published on www.orthodox.net/russia/2000-09-23-irish-times.html.

23. "Russian Orthodox Church chooses between 'ex-KGB candidates' as patriarch," *TimesOnline*, January 26, 2009. Andrew and Mitrokhin, *The Sword and the Shield*.

CHAPTER 38

1. Mark Lilla, *The Politics of Jacques Derrida*, The New York Reviews of Books, June 25, 1998 (Internet edition).

2. Waller R. Newell, *Postmodern Jihad: What Osama bin Laden learned from the Left*, The Weekly Standard, November 26, 2001, p. 26

3. Michael Hardt and Antonio Negri, *Empire* (London: Harvard University Press, 2000), p. 28.

4. David Pryce-Jones, *Evil Empire, the Communist 'hot, smart book of the moment,'* National Review Online, September 17, 2001.

5. *Statement Against the U.S. war on Iraq and for the peaceful solution of the problem*, December 14, 2002.

6. *Announcement of WPC Secretariat*, December 14, 2002.

7. *Statement Against the U.S. war on Iraq and for the peaceful solution of the problem*, December 14, 2002.

8. *World Demands Regime Change in Washington*, Workers World.org, Newstand date April 10, 2003, Vol. 45, No. 14.

9. *Presidency 2000*, Politics1, as published on www.politics1.com.

10. *About Workers World*, as published on www.workers.org.

11. *Largest anti-war rally*, Guinness Book of Records, 2004.

12. A complete list of "Coalition Co-signers" can be found on the Internet.

13. *Transportation/local event inquiries*, <www.internationalanswer.org/campaign/a12transp.html>.

14. "Schroeder attacked over gas post," *BBC News*. December 10, 2005. http://news.bbc.co.uk/2/hi/europe/4515914.stm.
15. Gerhard Schroeder's Sellout," *Washington Post*. December 13, 2005.
16. Dunphy, Harry (13 June 2007). "Lantos Raps Former European Leaders," *Associated Press*, http://www.usatoday.com/news/washington/2007-06-13-2870151492_x.htm.

CHAPTER 39

1. Statement of John F. Kerry before the Senate Committee on Foreign Relations on April 22, 1971, p. 2. www.nationalreview.com/script/printpage.asp?ref=document/kerry200404231047.asp.
2. Clifford D. May, "Side Show," *National Review On Line*, April 28, 2004.
3. Marvin E. Gettleman, *Vietnam and America: A Documented History*, New York: Grove Press, 1985, p. 54.
4. Joseph Libermann, "Democrats and Our Enemies," *Wall Street Journal*, May 21, 2008.
5. David Horowitz, "Stab in the Back," *FrontPage Magazine*, February 12, 2004.
6. Doug Donovan, "O'Malley Takes the Heat for Remarks about Bush," *Baltimore Sun*, July 1, 2004.
7. "They want four more years of hell," Teresa Heintz Kerry, responding to a Bush supporter yelling 'four more years' at a Democratic rally in Missouri," TIME, Special Report, August 16, 2004, p.19.
8. Robert Amsterdam, *Obama and McCain Fumble Russian Debate*, October 9, 2008 <http://www.robertamsterdam.com/2008/10/obama_and_mccain_both_fumble_r.htm>.
9. Stéphane Courtois, *Le Livre Noir du communisme: Crimes, terreur, répression* (Édition Robert Laffont, Paris, 1997), pp. 258-264.
10. Harry de Quetteville and Andrew Pierce, *Russia threatens nuclear attack on Poland over US missile shield deal*, Telegraph.co.uk, August 15, 2008.
11. The digits are the last digits of the postal code, and the name is that of the nearest big city; that was a common practice of giving names to closed towns.
12. Murray Feshbach, "The Toxic Archipelago in the Former U.S.S.R, An Empire of Deadly Waste," *Washington Post*, July 11, 1993, p. C1.
13. http://www.answers.com/topic/reset
14. Gary B. Nash, Julie Roy Jeffrey, John R. Howe, Allen F. Davis, Allan M. Winkler, Charlene Mires, and Carla Gardina Pestana, *The American People, Concise Edition Creating a Nation and a Society*, combined volume, 6th Edition (New York, Longman, 2007).
15. Elizabeth E. Spalding, *The First Cold Warrior: Harry Truman, Containment, and the Remaking of Liberal Internationalism* 1 (University Press of Kentucky, 2006).
16. The American Committee for Freedom for the Peoples of the USSR was started in 1951, and its broadcast station became known as Radio Liberty. For more on VOA during this period, see David F. Krugler, The Voice of America and the Domestic Propaganda Battles, 1945-1953(Columbia: University of Missouri Press, 2000); for more on RFE/RL, see Arch Puddington, Broadcasting Freedom: The Cold War Triumph of Radio Free Europe and Radio Liberty (Lexington: The University Press of Kentucky, 2000).
17. Nestor Ratesh, "Radio Free Europe's Impact in Romania during the Cold War," prepared for the Conference on Cold War Broadcasting Impact, Stanford, CA, October 13-15 2004.
18. "War in the Caucasus," *The Wall Street Journal*, August 9, 2008, p. A10.
19. "Russian army chief: We'll use nuclear weapons if threatened," *Associated Press*, January 19, 2008.

CHAPTER 40

1. Denis Woychuk, "KGB Bar - A Brief and Distorted History," <www.kgbbar.com/bar>.
2. "American capitalism gone with a whimper," *Pravda*, April 27, 2004.
3. Jacques Derrida, "From Specters of Marx: What is Ideology?" extracted from *Specters of Marx, the state of the debt, the Work of Mourning, & the New International*, translated by Peggy Kamuf (Routledge, 1994) as published in <http://www.marxists.org/reference/subject/philosophy/works/fr/derrida.2htm>, pp. 1-3.
4. Edward Marshall, "The War an Economic Disaster," *New York Times*, Magazine Section, June 6, 1915, p. SM15.

CHAPTER 41

1. David S. Broder, "Obama's Enigma," Washington Post, July 13, 2008, p. B7.
2. John Barron, *KGB: The Secret Work of Soviet Secret Agents* (New York: Reader's Digest Books, 1974, reprinted by Bamtam Books), p. 429.
3. Zhores Medvedev, *Gorbachev.* New York: Norton, 1987, p. 37.
4. Mikhail Gorbachev, *Perestroika: New Thinking for Our Country and the World* (New York: Harper & Row, 1987), *passim.*
5. Tom Baldwin, "Schools are still crumbling in corridor of shame' haunted by the old South," *Timesonline*, January 28, 2008.
6. James Joyner, "Obama Che Guevara Flag Scandal," *Outside the Beltway*, February 12, 2008, as posted at <www.outsidethebeltway.com/archives/2008/02/obama_che_guevara_flag_scandal/>.
7. <http://www.youtube.com/watch?v=oQNkVmdicvA&feature=related>.
8. "How Many Speeches Did Obama Give?," *newswine.com*, July 16, 2010, as posted on <http://joysteele.newswine.com/_news/2010/07/16/4691800-how-many-speeches-did-obama-give>.
9. "Right-Wing Media Fixated On Obama's "Shameless" Bin Laden Speech," *MEDIAMATTERS*, May 3, 2011, <http://mediamatters.org/research/201105030031>.
10. George Landrith, "The 'it's all about me' president," *The Daily Caller*, May 5, 2011, as posted on <http://dailycaller.com/2011/05/03/the-its-all-about-me-president/>.
11. <http://wiki.answer.com/Q/How_many_speeches_did_Obama_give>.
12. David Jackson, "Obama's first term by the numbers," *USA Today*, January 20, 2013, <http://www.usatoday.com/story/theoval/2013/01/20/obama-first-term-numbers-mark-knoller/1849141/?utm_source=feedburner&utm_medium=feed&utm_campaign=Feed%3A+usatoday-NewsTopStories+(News+-+Top+Stories)>.
13. Peter Kinder, "Missourians Reject Obama's Brand of Radical Liberalism," Human Events, May 30, 2008, as posted on <http://www.humanevents.com/2008/05/30/missourians-reject-obamas-brand-of-radical-liberalism/>.
14. ABC News video "Joe the Plumber," October 15, 2008.
15. Jonathon M. Seidl, "Obama Compares Himself To Reagan: Republicans Aren't Accusing *Him* Of 'Being Socialist,'" *The Blaze*, October 5, 2011, as posted on <http://www.theblaze.com/stories/obama-compares-himself-to-ronald-reagan-republicans-arent-accusing-him-of-being-socialist/>.
16. Alexandra`Petri, Obama is up there with Lincoln, Roosevelt, and Johnson," *Washington Post*, December 12, 2011, PostOpinions.
17. David Nakamura, "Obama invokes Teddy Roosevelt in speech attacking GOP policies," *Washington Post*, December 6, 2011.

18. Ross Kaminsky, "What Will Obama's Plans Cost the Nation?" *Human Events*, March 17, 2008, online at <http://www.blnz.com/news/2008/05/13/What_Will_Obamas_Plans_Cost_4036.html>.

19. Ibid., p. 1.

20. "Video of the week: We have to pass the bill so you can find out what is in it," The Heritage Foundation, March 10, 2010.

21. Lt. Col. Oliver North, "I Am an Extremist," FoxNews.com, May 16, 2009, <http://www.foxnews.com/on-air/war-stories/2009/04/16/i-am-extremist>.

22. Doug Mainwaring, "We are all Tea Partiers now," *Washington Times*, September 30, 2010, p.1.

23. "Rep. Maxine Waters has a socialist Freudian slip," *Newsreal*, August 1, 2009, posted live voice <http://www.newsrealblog.com/2009/08/01/fox-rep-maxine-waters-has-a-socialist-freudian-slip/>.

24. Lawrence Summers, "Why isn't capitalism working?," *Reuters*, January 9, 2012, <http://blogs.reuters.com/lawrencesummers/2012/01/09/why-isnt-capitalism-working/>.

25. Robert Reich, "Why Obama Should be Attacking Casino Capitalism -- Both Romney's Bain and JPMorgan," Politico, June 8, 2012, <http://www.huffingtonpost.com/robert-reich/obama-bain-romney_b_1537449.html>.

26. <http://www.washingtonpost.com/politics/mitt-romneys-prep-school-classmates-recall-pranks-but-also-troubling-incidents/2012/05/10/gIQA3WOKFU_story.html>.

27. <http://mistermikejones.tumblr.com/post/22792231746/what-happened-to-john-lauber>.

28. <http://www.newsmax.com/Newsfront/Romney-bully-hair-Lauber/2012/05/11/id/438800>.

29. <http://mistermikejones.tumblr.com/post/22792231746/what-happened-to-john-lauber>.

30. Mark Thompson, *Werner Sombart and American Exceptionalism*, Munster, Lit Verlag, ISBN 978-3-8258-5179-5.

CHAPTER 42

1. James Welsh sent the author copies of these documents.

2. Kenneth R. Timmerman, "Arafat Murdered US Diplomats, Could Face DOJ Arrest Warrant," *Insight Magazine*, June 4, 2001.

3. Julian Becker, *The PLO: The Rise And Fall Of The Palestine Liberation Organization* (New York: St. Martin's Press, 1984) p. 41.

4. Suzanne Fields, "The Ghosts of Auschwitz," townhall.com, December 10, 2001.

5. Christopher Andrew and Oleg Gordievsky, *KGB: The Inside Story* (New York: Harper Collins, 1990), p. 545.

6. By 1969 Nasser's Egypt accounted for 43% of all Soviet aid to the Third World.

7. The summit took place in Barcelona, in April 1969, and is described in Claire Sterling, *The Terror Network* (New York: Reader's Digest Press, 1981), p. 115.

8. Michael Freund, "73% Increase in Israelis killed in 2 Years Since Oslo," mbf@actom.co.il, September 15, 1995.

9. "Speech of numbers," *Peace for Israel*, January 5, 2003.

10. Thomas L. Friedman, " The New Math," New York Times, op-ed, January 15, 2002, p. A23.

11. "Clinton's Praise of Arafat's 'Decades' of PLO Leadership Implicitly Justifies Terrorism," Zionist Organization of America, October 28, 1998, (Internet edition), <www.zoa.org/pressrel/1998/1028a.htm>.

12. "Yasser Arafat, Poloniu Poisoning and the Curies," HUFFPOST, November 27, 2012.

13. "The originator of the acts of terrorism in London was standing near Tony Blair," *UK Indymedia*, July 19, 2005, <http://www.indymedia.org.uk/en/regions/london/2005/07/318875.html>.

14. Ludwig De Braeckeleer, "Was Romano Prodi the Top Man in Italy?" *Ohmy News International*, November 23, 2006.
15. Ferdinando Imposimato e Sandro Provvisionato, *Doveva morire. Chi ha ucciso Aldo Moro,* Chiarelettere, 2008, Capitolo 9: "La lunga mano del KGB"; Mitrokhin Commission, *Wikipedia*, December 2012.
16. Philip Wilian, "KGB linked to Prodi's ghostly insight, The European Commission special Report," *The Guardian*, October 20, 1999.
17. Christopher Andrew and Vasily Mitrokhin, *The Sword and the Shield: The Mitrokhin Archive and the Secret History of the KGB* (New York: Basic Books, 1999), p. 382.
18. Douglas Frantz and James Risen, "A Secret Iran-Arafat Connection Is Seen Fueling the Mideast Fire," *New York Times*, March 23, 2002 (Internet edition).
19. Dan Ephron, ""Israel captures 50 tones of Iranian arms," *Washington Times*, January 5, 2002, Internet edition.
20. "Passover suicide bombing at Park Hotel in Netanya - 27 - March - 2002," Israel Ministry of Foreign affairs, March 27, 2002.
21. "The 'Massacre' In Jenin," *Peace with Realism*, as posted on http://peacewithrealism.org/pdc/jenin.htm.
22. Corky Siemaszko, "13 Slain by Boy Bomber," *Daily News*, April 10, 2002 (Internet edition).
23. Gerald M. Steinberg, "Arafat's Leninist Strategy," National Review Online, April 22, 2002.
24. Matt Rees, "The Battle of Jenin," *Time Magazine*, May 17, 2002, (Internet edition).
25. Betsy Pisik and Ben Barber, "Powel finds no proof of Israeli massacre in Jenin," *Washington Times*, April 25, 2002, p.1, (Internet edition).
26. Joel Mowbray, "Arafat elected?" National Review Online, April 25, 2002.
27. "Follow-up to the outcome of the Millennium Summit: Note by the Secretary-General," United Nations, General Assembly, Fifty-ninth session, Agenda item 55, p.3.
28. "Amr M. Moussa: A Nationalist Vision for Egypt," *The Middle East Quarterly*, September 1996, Volume III, p.2.

CHAPTER 43

1. Ion Mihai Pacepa, "Left-Wing Monster: Ceausescu," *Frontpagemag.com*, February 10, 2006, as published on http://archive.frontpagemag.com/Printable.aspx?ArtId=5730.
2. *Petr Chaadayev, Russian sociologist, Moscow, 1854.*

CHAPTER 44

1. Arnaud de Borchgrave, "Romanian Spies Under Scrutinity," *United Press International*, February 13, 2004.
2. "Magistratii ICCJ, inainte de a fi comunisti sunt imbecili"(Before being communists, Romania's Supreme Court magistrates are imbeciles), *ZIUA*, Bucharest, January 31, 2009, p. 1.
3. "The U.S. anti-missile project in Romania: New administration, same old policy," RIANO-VOST, February 24, 2010 (http://en.rian.ru/analysis/20100224/157995687.html.)
4. "Magistratii ICCJ, inainte de a fi comunisti sunt imbecili"(Before being communists, Romania's Supreme Court magistrates are imbeciles), *ZIUA*, Bucharest, January 31, 2009, p. 1.
5. <http://www.ziaristionline.ro/2012/05/08/interviu-larry-watts-din-1960-pana-in-septembrie-1989-romania-a-fost-incadrata-in-grupul-statelor-ostile-urss-alaturi-de-sua-rfg-si-israel/>;

<http://www.ziaristionline.ro/2012/03/16/pacepa-a-recunoscut-in-fata-directorului-cia-ca-a-fost-agent-kgb-interviu-bookiseala-cu-larry-watts-am-dat-de-perete-cu-usa-secretelor-dar-mai-sunt-multe-incaperi-si-coridoare-intunecate/)>;

<http://www.stiriazi.ro/ziare/articol/articol/pacepa-a-recunoscut-in-fata-directorului-cia-ca-a-fost-agent-kgb-interviu-bookiseala-cu-larry-watts--am-dat-de-perete-cu-usa-secretelor-dar-mai-sunt-multe-incaperi-si-coridoare-intunecate/sumar-articol/50842328/>;

<http://carte.ubix.ro/detalii/pacepa-a-recunoscut-in-fata-directorului-cia-ca-a-fost-agent-kgb-interviu-bookiseala-cu-larry-watts-am>;

<http://www.bookiseala.ro/interviu-bookiseala-cu-larry-watts-am-dat-de-perete-cu-usa-secretelor-dar-mai-sunt-multe-incaperi-si-coridoare-intunecate/72369.html>;

<http://liviudrugus.wordpress.com/2012/07/04/larry-l-watts-despre-foarte-discretul-management-romanesc-al-prieteniilor-prea-evidente-3/>;

<http://www.bookiseala.ro/cum-se-explica-succesul-cartii-lui-larry-watts/71251.html>;

<http://roncea.ro/2012/07/23/exclusiv-in-atentia-lui-traian-basescu-a-sri-si-spp-documente-cia-care-probeaza-ca-sistemul-de-securitate-american-nu-l-a-luat-in-seama-pe-agentul-sovi-etic-ion-mihai-pacepa-un-indemn-catre-presedi/>;

6. *Ibid.*
7. Serviciul Roman de Informatii (Romania's Intelligence Service), *Cartea Alba a Securitatii* (The White Book of the Securitate), Bucharest, 1994.
8. Serviciul Român de Informatii, *Cartea Albá a Securitátii,* (Romanian Intelligence Service, The White Book of the Securitate), Bucuresti, Editura Presa Românească, 1996.
9. "Casa Pacepa Demolată" (House Pacepa demolished), ZIARE.com, March 6, 2009, <http://www.ziare.com/articole/casa+pacepa+demolata>.
10. *President Nicolae Ceausescu's State Visit to the USA: April 12-17, 1978*, English version, (Bucharest: Meridiane Publishing House, 1978), p. 78.
11. Roger Kirk and Mircea Raceanu, *Romania Versus the United States: Diplomacy of the Absurd, 1985-1989* (Washington: Institute for the Study of Diplomacy, 1994), p.155.
12. The author has a copy of the letter.
13. The author has the original letter. The letter was also quoted in my letter to the editor, published in the *New York Times Book Review*, March 27, 1988, p. 49.
14. The author has the original letter.

EPILOGUE

1. http://www.freerepublic.com/focus/f-news/1877557/posts.
2. "World: Was Soviet Collapse Last Century's Worst Geopolitical Catastrophe?" *Radio Free Europe - Radio Liberty*," December 27, 2012, <http://www.rferl.org/content/article/1058688.html>.
3. "US intellectuals call for European criticism of US war on terror," Agence France Presse, April 9, 2001, 14:10 PM, (Internet edition).
4. John Pilger, "War on Terror: The Other Victims: The irresponsibility of this conflict is breath-taking," *Mirror.co.uk*, October 29, 2001.
5. Mark Goldblatt, "French Toast," *National Republic Online*, December 13, 2001, 8:45 am.
6. "Announcement For Candidacy For Presidency," Washington, D.C., March 16, 1968, as published in <http://rfkcenter.org/announcement-for-candidacy-for-presidency>.
7. "Top 10 Reasons To Be Proud Of The United States," http://www.toptenz.net/top-10-reasons-to-be-proud-of-the-united-states.php.
8. *Ibid.*

9. *Ibid.*

10. "List of countries by Nobel laureates per capita," Wikipedia, <http://en.wikipedia.org/wiki/List_of_countries_by_Nobel_laureates_per_capita>.

11. Gary Shapiro, "Is America the Greatest Country in the World?", Forbes.com, July 25, 2012, as published in http://www.forbes.com/sites/garyshapiro/2012/07/25/is-america-the greatst-country-in-the-world/.

12. Ion Mihai Pacepa, "Do as I Did, An open letter to Saddam Hussein's generals" *National Review on Line*, March 22, 2003, <http://www.nationalreview.com/content/do-i-did>.

BIBLIOGRAPHY

Actes et Documents du Saint Siège Relatifs à la Seconde Guerre Mondiale, Volumes I-XI (Libreria Editrice Vaticana: Città del Vaticano, 1965–1981); English edition (volume one only; Corpus Books: Washington, DC, Gerard Noel, ed. 1967–1977). Volume III is split into two books; thus some authors refer to 12 volumes instead of 11.

Akmadža, Miroslav. *The Position of the Catholic Church in Croatia 1945–1970*, Review of Croatian History 2/2006, no.1, 89.

Albats, Yevgenia. *The KGB: The State Within a State* (New York: Farrar, Straus, Giroux, 1994).

Alexander, Stella. *Croatia: The Catholic Church and Clergy, 1919–1945*, in *Catholics, the State, and the European Radical Right, 1919–1945*, edited by Richard J. Wolff and Jorg K. Hoensch (New York: Columbia University Press, 1987).

———*The Triple Myth* (1987): *A Life of Archbishop Alojzije Stepinac (Boulder: East European Monographs, 1987).*

Alvarez, David. *Spies in the Vatican: Espionage & Intrigue from Napoleon to the Holocaust* (Lawrence: University Press of Kansas, 2002).

Alvarez, David & Robert A. Graham. *Nothing Sacred: Nazi Espionage against the Vatican 1939–1945* (London: Frank Cass, 1997).

Ambrosini, Maria Luisa. *The Secret Archives of the Vatican* (New York: Barnes & Noble Books, 1996).

The American Jewish Yearbook, 1943–1944 (Philadelphia: Jewish Publication Society, 1944).

Andrew, Christopher & Oleg Gordievsky. *KGB: The Inside Story* (New York: HarperCollins, 1990).

Andrew, Christopher & Vasili Mitrokhin. *The Sword and the Shield: The Mitrokhin Archive and the Secret History of the KGB* (New York: Basic Books, 1999).

Barron, John. *KGB: The Secret World of Soviet Secret Agents* (New York: Reader's Digest Press, 1974).

Barton, Dennis. *Croatia 1941–1946* (The Church in History Information Centre, 2006).

Besier, Gerhard & Francesca Piombo. *The Holy See and Hitler's Germany* (Basingstroke, UK: Palgrave Macmillan, 2007).

Bittman, Ladislav. *The KGB and Soviet Disinformation: An Insider's View* (Washington, DC: Pergamon-Brassey's International Defense Publishers, 1985).

The Black Book of Communism (Murphy & Kramer, trans. Cambridge: Cambridge University Press, 1999).

Blet, Pierre. *Pius XII and the Second World War* (New York: Paulist Press, Lawrence J. Johnson trans., 1999).

Bozanić, Cardinal Josip. *The Most Illustrious Figure of the Church in Croatia: Pastoral letter on the occasion of the centenary of the birth of the Servant of God Cardinal Alojzije Stepinac*, March 1, 1998, reprinted in Cardinal Josip Bozanić, *Blaženi Alojzije Stepinac, Baština koja obvezuje* (Zagreb: Glas Koncila, 2008).

Brent, Jonathan. *Inside the Stalin Archives* (New York: Atlas & Co., 2008).

Brüning, Heinrich. *Memoiren, 1918–1934* (Stuttgart: Deutsche Verlags-Anstalt, 1970).

Bulajic, Milan. *The Role of the Vatican in the Break-Up of the Yugoslav State (Belgrade: Ministry of Information of the Republic of Serbia,1993).*

Burleigh, Michael. *The Cardinal Basil Hume Memorial Lectures: Political Religion and Social Evil*, 3 Totalitarian Movements and Political Religions 1 (Autumn 2002).

———— *Death and Deliverance: Euthanasia in Nazi Germany, 1900–1945* (New York: Cambridge University Press, 1994).

———— *Earthly Powers: The Clash of Religion and Politics in Europe from the French Revolution to the Great War* (New York: Harper Collins, 2006).

———— *Sacred Causes: The Clash of Religion and Politics, From the Great War to the War on Terror* (New York: HarperCollins, 2007).

———— *The Third Reich: A New History* (New York: Hill & Wang, 2001).

Burns, Jeffrey M. *No Longer Emerging: Ramparts Magazine and the Catholic Laity, 1962–1968*, US Catholic Historian, vol. 9:3 (1990).

Carroll, James. *Constantine's Sword: The Church and the Jews: A History* (Boston: Houghton Mifflin Co., 2001).

Carroll-Abbing, John Patrick. *But for the Grace of God—The Houses Are Blind* (New York: Delacorte Press, 1965).

———— *A Chance to Live: The Story of the Lost Children of the War* (London: Longman, Green & Co., 1952).

Catholics Remember the Holocaust (United States Catholic Conference: Washington, DC, 1988).

Chadwick, Owen. *A History of Christianity* (St. Martin's Press: New York, 1995).

———— *Britain and the Vatican During the Second World War* (Cambridge: Cambridge University Press, 1986).

———— *Weizsäcker, the Vatican, and the Jews of Rome*, 28 Journal of Ecclesiastical History 179 (April 1977).

Chambers, Colin. *Inside the Royal Shakespeare Company: Creativity and Institution* (London and New York: Routledge, 2004).

Chambers, Whittaker. *Witness* (New York: Random House, 1952).

Chronicle of the 20th Century (Mount Kisco, NY: Chronicle Publications, C. Daniel, ed., 1986).

Cianfarra, Camille. *The Vatican and the War* (New York: Literary Classics, Inc., distributed by E.P. Dutton & Company, 1944).

The Ciano Diaries (New York: Doubleday & Company, Inc., Hugh Gibson, ed., 1946).

Congregation for the Causes of Saints, *Beatificationis et Canonizationis Servi Dei Pii XII (Eugenii Pacelli) Summi Pontificis (1876–1958): Positio Super Vita, Virtutibus et Fama Sanctitatis* (Rome, 2004) [the *Positio*].

Conway, John S. *The Nazi Persecution of the Churches 1933-45* (London: Weidenfeld and Nicolson, 1960; and New York: Basic Books,1969).

———— *The Vatican, Great Britain, and Relations with Germany, 1938–1940*, XVI The Historical Journal, 147 (1973).

Cooney, John. *The American Pope: The Life and Times of Francis Cardinal Spellman* (New York: Times Books, 1984).

Cornwell, John. *Breaking Faith: The Pope, the People, and the Fate of Catholicism* (New York: Viking Press, New York, 2001).

———*Hitler's Pope: The Secret History of Pius XII* (New York: Viking Press, 1999; and New York: Penguin Books, 2008).

———*The Pontiff in Winter* (New York: Doubleday, 2004).

Costello, John and Oleg Tsarev. *Deadly Illusions* (New York: Crown, 1993).

Cowell, Alan S. *The Terminal Spy* (London: Doubleday, 2008).

Crankshaw, Edward. *Khrushchev: A Career* (New York: Viking, 1966).

Crozier, Brian. *The Rise and Fall of the Soviet Empire* (Rocklin, CA: Forum, 1999).

Custine, Marquis Astolphe de. *Journey for our Time: The Russian Journals of the Marquis de Custine* (Washington, DC: Regnery, Phyllis Penn Kohler ed. & trans., 1987).

Dalin, David. *The Myth of Hitler's Pope* (Washington, DC: Regnery, 2005).

Davis, Melton S. *All Rome Trembled* (New York: G.P. Putnam's Sons, 1957).

Day, Edward. "Pius XII and the Hitler Plot," *Liguorian*, October 1968.

Days of Devotion: Daily Meditations from the Good Shepherd Pope John XXIII (New York: Penguin reprint, John P. Donnelly, ed., 1998).

The Defection of General Ion Mihai Pacepa. Radio Romania International. April 4, 2011. Transcript, <http://www.rii.ro/ahr-art.shtml?lang=2+sec=40+art=121082>.

Der Streit um Hochhuth's "Stellvertreter" (Basel/Stuttgart: Basilius Presse, 1963).

Deutsch, Harold C. *The Conspiracy against Hitler in the Twilight War* (Minneapolis: University of Minnesota Press, 1968).

Die Briefe an die Deutschen Bischöfe 1939–1944 (Grünewald: Mainz, Burkhart Schneider ed., 1966).

Diskin, Hanna. *The Seeds of Triumph: Church and State in Gomulka's Poland* (Budapest: Central European University Press, 2001).

Dunn, Dennis J. *The Catholic Church and Russia: Popes, Patriarchs, Tsars and Commissars* (Burlington, VT: Ashgate, 2004).

Encyclopedia of Catholic Social Thought, Social Science, and Social Policy (Lanham, MD: The Scarecrow Press, Michael L. Coulter et al., eds., 2007).

Epstein, Edward J. *Legend: The Secret World of Lee Harvey Oswald* (New York: Reader's Digest Press, 1978).

Esslin, Martin. "Brecht and the English Theatre." *The Tulane Drama Review*, 11:2 (Winter 1966).

Examining the Papacy of Pope Pius XII (Rome: Pave the Way Foundation, 2008).

Falconi, Carlo. *The Silence of Pius XII* (Boston: Little Brown, B. Wall trans. 1970).

Fatemi, Faramarz S. *The USSR in Iran: The Background History of Russian and Anglo-American Conflict in Iran* (A.S. Barnes & Co. 1980).

Feldkamp, Michael F. *Der Teufelspakt des Anti-Semiten*, in *Frankfurter Allgemeine Zeitung*, January 10, 2000, at 7.

Fisher, Desmond. *Pope Pius XII and the Jews: An Answer to Hochhuth's Play "Der Stellvertreter" (The Deputy)* (Glen Rock, N.J.: Paulist Press, 1965).

Frattini, Eric. *The Entity: Five Centuries of Secret Vatican Espionage* (New York: St. Martin's Press, 2008).

Freemantle, Brian. *KGB: Inside the World's Largest Intelligence Network* (New York: Holt, Rinehart and Winston, 1982).

Friedländer, Saul. *Nazi Germany and the Jews, Volume I: The Years of Persecution, 1933–1939* (New York: HarperCollins, 1997).

———*Pius XII and the Third Reich: A Documentation* (New York: Knopf, C. Fullman trans., 1966).

From Hitler's Doorstep: The Wartime Intelligence Reports of Allen Dulles, 1942–1945 (University Park: Pennsylvania State University Press, Neal H. Peterson, ed., 1996).

Frost, David. *An Autobiography* (London: HarperCollins, 1993).

Gahlinger, Anton J. *I Served the Pope* (Techny, IL: The Mission Press, 1952).

Gallagher, Charles R. *Vatican Secret Diplomacy: Joseph P. Hurley and Pope Pius XII* (New Haven: Yale University Press, 2008).

Gaspari, Antonio. *Gli ebrei salvati da Pio XII* (Rome: Edizioni Logos, 2001).

Gilbert, Martin. *Auschwitz and the Allies* (New York: Holt, Rinehart, & Winston, 1981).

——— *The Second World War: A Complete History* (New York: Henry Holt & Company, 1987).

Gitman, Esther. *A Question of Judgment: Dr. Alojzije Stepinac and the Jews*, Review of Croatian History Volume II, no.1 (January 2007): 47.

Godman, Peter. *Hitler and the Vatican: The Secret Archives That Reveal the New Story of the Nazis and the Vatican* (New York: Free Press, 2004).

Goldfarb, Alex, and Marina Litvinenko. *Death of a Dissident: The Poisoning of Alexander Litvinenko and the Return of the KGB* (New York: Free Press, 2007).

Goldhagen, Daniel J. *A Moral Reckoning: The Role of the Catholic Church in the Holocaust and Its Unfulfilled Duty of Repair* (New York: Alfred A. Knopf, 2002).

Golitsyn, Anatoliy. *New Lies for Old: The Communist Strategy of Deception and Disinformation* (New York: Dodd, Mead & Co., 1984).

Graham, Robert A. *Pius XII's Defense of Jews and Others: 1944-45* (Catholic League Publications: Milwaukee, 1987). This is also reprinted in *Pius XII and the Holocaust: A Reader* (Catholic League Publications: Milwaukee, 1988).

——— *Pope Pius XII and the Jews of Hungary in 1944* (United States Catholic Historical Society, undated).

——— *The Vatican and Communism During World War II: What Really Happened?* (San Francisco: Ignatius Press, 1996).

Hatch, Alden & Seamus Walshe. *Crown of Glory: The Life of Pope Pius XII* (New York: Hawthorn Books, 1957).

Haynes, John Earl, and Harvey Klehr. *Verona: Decoding Soviet Espionage in America* (New Haven: Yale University Press, 1999).

Haynes, John Earl, Harvey Klehr, and Alexander Vassiliev. *Spies: The Rise and Fall of the KGB in America* (New Haven: Yale University Press, 2009).

Hinkle, Warren. *If You Have a Lemon, Make Lemonade* (New York: W. W. Norton, 1974).

A History of the Third Reich, Vol. 4, Primary Sources (Farmington Hills, MI: Greenhaven Press, 2003; Jeff T. Hays, ed.).

Hitler, Adolf. *Mein Kampf* (Boston: Houghton Mifflin, Ralph Manheim trans., 1971).

Hochhuth, Rolf. *The Deputy* (New York: Grove Press, Winston trans., 1964).

——— *Soldiers* (New York: Grove Press, MacDonald trans., 1968).

Holmes, J. Derek. *The Papacy in the Modern World 1914–1978* (New York: Crossroad, 1981).

Hook, Sidney. *Out of Step: An Unquiet Life in the 20th Century* (New York: Harper & Row, 1987).

Hoover, J. Edgar. *Masters of Deceit* (Pocket Books, 1961).

Horowitz, David. *Radical Son: A Generational Odyssey* (New York: The Free Press, 1997).

Hughes, John Jay. *Pontiffs: Popes Who Shaped History* (Ft. Wayne: Our Sunday Visitor Books, 1994).

Kalugin, Oleg. *The First Directorate: My 32 Years in Intelligence and Espionage against the West* (New York: St. Martin's Press, 1994).

——— *Spymaster: My Thirty-Two Years in Intelligence and Espionage against the West* (New York: Basic Books, 2009).

Kasper, Cardinal Walter. "Recent Developments in Jewish-Christian Relations." Speech. Hope University, Liverpool. World Jewish Congress., May 24, 2010, http://www.worldjewishcongress.org.>

Katz, Robert. *The Battle for Rome: The Germans, the Allies, the Partisans, and the Pope* (New York: Simon and Schuster, 2003).

——*Black Sabbath: A Journey through a Crime against Humanity* (New York: Macmillan, 1969).

——*Massacre in Rome* (New York: Ballantine, 1973) (originally released as *Death in Rome*).

Kengor, Paul. *Dupes: How America's Adversaries Have Manipulated Progressives for a Century* (Wilmington: ISI Books, 2010).

Kent, Peter C. *The Lonely Cold War of Pope Pius XII* (Montreal & Kingston: McGill-Queen's University Press, 2002).

—— *A Tale of Two Popes: Pius XI, Pius XII and the Rome-Berlin Axis*, 23 Journal of Contemporary History 589 (1988).

Kertzer, David I. *The Popes against the Jews: The Vatican's Role in the Rise of Modern Anti-Semitism* (New York: Knopf, 2001).

Khrushchev, Nikita. *Khrushchev Remembers* (Boston: Little, Brown, Strobe Talbot, ed., 1970).

——*Khrushchev Remembers: The Last Testament* (Boston: Little, Brown, Strobe Talbot, ed., 1974).

Koehler, John. *Spies in the Vatican: The Soviet Union's Cold War against the Catholic Church* (New York: Pegasus, 2009).

Krišto, Jure. *An American View of the Belgrade Episode of Archbishop Joseph P. Hurley* in *Review of Croatian History* (Vol. 4, December 2008) at 218.

—— *The Catholic Church and the Jews in the Independent State of Croatia*, Review of Croatian History, Vol. 3, February 2007), no.1, 13, 16.

—— *The Catholic Church in Croatia and Bosnia-Herzegovina in the Face of Totalitarian Ideologies and Regimes*, in *Religion under Siege: The Roman Catholic Church in Occupied Europe (1939–1950)*, (Gevers & Bank, editors, 2007).

Kurzman, Dan. *A Special Mission: Hitler's Secret Plot to Seize the Vatican and Kidnap Pope Pius XII* (Cambridge: Da Capo Press, 2007).

Kustow, Michael. *Peter Brook: A Biography* (New York: St. Martin's Press, 2005).

Lackovic, Stephen. *The Case against Tito* (memorandum, 1947).

Lapide, Pinchas E. *Three Popes and the Jews* (New York: Hawthorn Books, 1967; London: Sands and Co., 1968).

Lapomarda, Vincent A. *The Jesuits and the Third Reich* (Lewiston, NY: Edwin Mellen Press, 1989).

Lavretsky, I. *Ernesto Che Guevara* (Moscow: Progress Publishers, 1976).

Levai, Jenö. *Hungarian Jewry and the Papacy: Pius XII Did Not Remain Silent* (London: Sands and Co., 1968).

Lewy, Guenter. *The Catholic Church and Nazi Germany* (New York: McGraw-Hill, 1964).

Ley-Piscator, Maria. *The Piscator Experiment: The Political Theatre* (New York: James H. Heineman, Inc., 1967).

Lichten, Joseph L. *A Question of Judgment: Pius XII and the Jews,* in *Pius XII and the Holocaust: A Reader* (Milwaukee: Catholic League Publications, 1988).

Litvinenko, Alexander and Yuri Felshtinsky. *Blowing Up Russia: The Secret Plot to Bring Back KGB Terror* (New York: Encounter Books, 2007).

Löw, Konrad. *Die Schuld: Christen und Juden im Urteil der Nationalsozialisten und der Gegenwart* (Gräfelfing: Resch, 2003).

Lowry, Charles W. *Communism and Christ* (New York: Morehouse-Graham Co., 1953).

Lubac, Henri de. *Christian Resistance to Anti-Semitism: Memories from 1940–1944* (San Francisco: Ignatius, 1990).

Martin, Malachi. *The Keys of This Blood: Pope John Paul II Versus Russia and the West for Control of the New World Order* (New York: Touchstone, 1990).

Matijević, Margareta. *Religious communities in Croatia from 1945 to 1991: Social causality of the dissent between Communist authorities and religious communities' leadership*, Review of Croatian

History Vol. II, no.1, 2007, 117.

McCormick, Anne O'Hare. *Vatican Journal 1921–1954* (New York: Farrar, Straus & Cudahy, 1957).

McGurn, Barrett. *A Reporter Looks at the Vatican* (New York: Coward-McCann, 1962).

Medvedev, Zhores A. *Gorbachev (New York: Norton, 1986).*

Memorandum to General Donovan from Fabian von Schlabrendorff, dated October 25, 1945 (Subject: Relationship of the German Churches to Hitler), posted on the Internet by Cornell Law Library: Donovan Nuremberg Trial Collection, <http://library2.lawschool.cornell.edu/donovan/pdf/ Nuremberg_3/Vol_X_18_04_01.pdf.>. This memorandum is also printed in Leo Stein, *Hitler Came for Niemoeller: The Nazi War against Religion* 253-57 (New York: Penguin Publishing Co., 2003 reprint ed.).

Merritt, Richard L. "Politics, Theater, and the East-West Struggle: The Theater as a Cultural Bridge in West Berlin, 1948–61," *80 Political Science Quarterly,* 186 (June 1965).

Merton, Thomas. *Dancing in the Water of Life* (San Francisco: Harper, 1998).

Miller, Marion. *I Was a Spy* (Indianapolis & New York: Boss-Merrill, 1960).

Mindszenty, Jószef Cardinal. *Memoirs* (New York: Macmillan & Co., 1974).

Morgan, Thomas B. *The Listening Post: Eighteen Years on Vatican Hill* (New York: G.P. Putnam's Sons, 1944).

Müller, Joseph. *Bis zur Letzten Konsequenz* (Munich: Süddeutscher Verlag, 1975).

Murphy, David E. *What Stalin Knew: The Enigma of Barbarossa* (New Haven: Yale University Press, 2005).

Murphy, Francis X. *The Papacy Today* (New York: Macmillan, 1981).

Napolitano, Matteo L. & Andrea Tornielli. *Il Papa Che Salvò Gli Ebrei* (Piemme, 2004).

The Nazi Master Plan: The Persecution of the Christian Churches, documents prepared for the post-war Nuremberg trials, prepared by the Office of Strategic Services (OSS) Research and Analysis Branch, Posted on the Internet by Cornell Law Library: Donovan Nuremberg Trial Collection, <http://library2.lawschool.cornell.edu/donovan/pdf/Nuremberg_3/Vol_X_18_04_01.pdf.>.

Nielsen Jr., Niels C. *Solzhenitsyn's Religion* (Nashville, TN: Nelson, 1975).

O'Brien, Count Anthony Henry. *Archbishop Stepinac: The Man and His Case* (Westminster, MD: The Newman Bookshop, 1947).

O'Carroll, Michael. *Pius XII: Greatness Dishonored* (Dublin: Laetare Press, 1980).

Pacepa, Ion Mihai. "Moscow's Assault on the Vatican: The KGB made corrupting the Church a priority," *National Review Online,* January 25, 2007.

——*Programmed to Kill: Lee Harvey Oswald, the Soviet KGB, and the Kennedy Assassination* (Chicago: Ivan R. Dee, 2007).

——*Red Horizons: Chronicles of a Communist Spy Chief* (Washington, DC: Regnery Gateway, 1987).

Papée, Casimir. *Pius XII e Polska* (Rome: Editrice Studium, 1954).

Parham, Sidney F. "Editing Hochhuth for the Stage: A Look at the Major Productions of 'The Deputy,'" *Educational Theatre Journal* (October 1976) 28:3.

Parkes, James. *An Enemy of the People: Antisemitism* (New York: Penguin Books, 1946).

Pattee, Richard. *The Case of Cardinal Aloysius Stepinac* (Milwaukee: The Bruce Publishing Co.,1953).

Patterson, Michael. *Strategies of Political Theatre: Post-War British Playwrights* (Cambridge University Press, 2003).

Phayer, Michael. *The Catholic Church and the Holocaust, 1930–1965* (Bloomington: Indiana University Press, 2001).

——*Pius XII, The Holocaust, and the Cold War* (Bloomington: Indiana University Press, 2008).

Piscator, Erwin. *The Political Theater* (London: Eyre Methuen, H. Rorrison, trans., 1963).

Pius XI, *Mit Brennender Sorge* (1937).

Pius XI und der Nationalsozialismus. Die Enzyklika 'Mit Brennender Sorge' vom 14 März 1937, (Paderborn: Ferdinand Schöningh, Heinz-Albert Raem ed., 1979).

Pius XII. *Orientales Omnes (1945).*

Pius XII, *Summi Pontificatus* (1939).

Pius XII and the Holocaust: A Reader (Catholic League Publications: Milwaukee, 1988).

Pius XII: Selected Encyclicals and Addresses (Roman Catholic Books: Harrison, NY, 1995).

The Pope Speaks: The Words of Pius XII (New York: Harcourt, Brace and Company, 1940).

Polmar, Norman, and Thomas B. Allen. *The Encyclopedia of Espionage* (New York: Gramercy Books, 1997).

Prcela, John. *Archbishop Stepinac in his Country's Church-State Relations* (Scottsdale: Associate Book Publishers, 1990).

Purdy, W. A. *The Church on the Move* (London: Hollis and Carter, 1966).

Rayfield, Donald. Stalin and his Hangmen (New York: Random House, 2005).

Raymond, Rev. M. *The Man for This Moment: The Life and Death of Aloysius Stepinac* (Staten Island: Alba House, 1971).

Religion and Culture: Essays in Honor of Paul Tillich (New York: Harper, Walter Leibrecht, ed. 1959).

Religion Under Siege: The Roman Catholic Church in Occupied Europe 1939–1950 (Peeters: Leuven, L. Gevers, and J. Bank, eds., 2007).

Rhodes, Anthony. *The Vatican in the Age of the Dictators: 1922–45* (London: Hodden and Stoughton, 1973).

Romerstein, Herbert. Soviet Active Measures and Propaganda. Mackenzie Institute Paper No. 17 (Toronto: Mackenzie Institute, 1989).

Romerstein, Herbert & Eric Breindel. *The Verona Secrets: Exposing Soviet Espionage and America's Traitors,* (Washington, DC: Regnery Publishing, 2000).

Rychlak, Ronald J. *Hitler, the War, and the Pope* (Genesis Press, 2000; Our Sunday Visitor Press 2000; 2nd edition: Our Sunday Visitor Press, 2010).

———*The 1933 Concordat between Germany and the Holy See: A Reflection of Tense Relations,* 2001 The Digest 23 (Syracuse University).

———Book Review: "Pius XII und Deutschland, by Michael F. Feldkamp," *The English Historical Review,* June 2003, at 840.

———*Cardinal Stepinac and the Roman Catholic Church in Croatia during the Second World War* (published in English and Croatian) in *Stepinac: A Witness to the Truth* (Zagreb: Glas Koncila, 2009).

——— "Postwar Catholics, Jewish Children, and a Rush to Judgment," Beliefnet.com, posted Jan. 18, 2005 (including sidebar: "Jewish Children After World War II: A Case Study").Reprinted in *Inside the Vatican,* January-February 2005.

———*Righteous Gentiles: How Pope Pius XII Saved Half a Million Jews from the Nazis* (Dallas: Spence Publishing, 2005).

Sale, Giovanni. *Hitler, La Santa Sede e Gli Ebrei* (Rome: Jaca Book, 2004).

———*Il Novecento tra Genocidi, Paure e Speranze* (Milan: Jaca Book, 2006).

Savor, Michael. *Cardinal Aloysius Stepinac, "A Servant of God and the Croatian People"* (revised ed. 2001) <http://www.croatianhistory.net/etf/stepinac.html>.

Schlabrendorff, Fabian von. *The Secret War against Hitler* (New York: Pitman Publishing, Hilda Simon trans., 1965).

Schmidt-Hauer, Christian. *Gorbachev: The Path to Power* (London: I. B. Tauris, 1986).

Shevchenko, Arkady N. *Breaking with Moscow* (New York: Alfred A. Knopf, 1985).

Shirer, William L. *Berlin Diary: The Journal of a Foreign Correspondent 1934–1941* (New York: Alfred A. Knopf, 1941).

———*The Rise and Fall of the Third Reich: A History of Nazi Germany* (Greenwich: Fawcett Publications, 1962).

Smit, Jan Olav. *Angelic Shepherd: The Life of Pope Pius XII* (New York: Dodd & Mead, Vanderveldt trans., 1950).

Solovyov, Vladimir, and Elena Klepikova. *Behind the High Kremlin Walls* (New York: Dodd, Mead, 1986).

Staar, Richard Felix. *Foreign Policies of the Soviet Union* (Stanford, CA: Hoover Institution Press, Stanford University, 1991).

Stanescu, Sorin Rosca, and Cornel Dumitrescu. *Autopsia unei Inscenari Securiste (The Autopsy of a Securitate Framing)* (Bucharest: Omega Ziua, 1999).

Stein, Leo. *Hitler Came for Niemoeller: The Nazi War Against Religion* (New York: Penguin, 2003).

Stephan, Robert W. *Death to Spies: The Story of SMERSH* (Soviet Military Counterintelligence During World War II). Thesis. American University, 1984.

Stepinac: A Witness to the Truth (Zagreb: Glas Koncila, Željko Tanjić ed., 2009).

Stewart, Ralph. *Pope Pius XII and the Jews* (St. Martin de Porres Dominican Community & St. Joseph Canonical Foundation: New Hope, KY, 1990).

Stilinovic, Josip. "Cardinal Alojzije Stepinac—A Patriot, not a Nationalist," *The Catholic World Report* (August/September 1998) <http://www.catholicculture.org/culture/library/view.cfm?recnum=512>.

Stille, Alexander. *Benevolence and Betrayal: Five Italian Jewish Families under Fascism* (New York: Summit Books, 1991).

The Storm over the Deputy (New York: Grove Press, Eric Bently, ed., 1964).

The Strategy of Deception: A Study in World-Wide Communist Tactics (New York: Farrar, Straus and Company, Jeane J. Kirkpatrick, ed., 1963).

Sulner, Hanna F. *Disputed Documents: New Methods for Examining Questioned Documents* (Dobbs Ferry, N.Y.: Oceana Publications, 1966).

Swift, Mary Grace. *The Art of Dance in the USSR: A Study of Politics, Ideology, and Culture* (University of Notre Dame Press, 1968).

Swift, Will. *The Kennedys Amidst the Gathering Storm: A Thousand Days in London, 1938–1940* (Washington, DC: Smithsonian Books, 2008).

Taëni, Rainer. *Modern German Authors, Rolf Hochhuth* (London: Oswald Wolff, 1977).

Tanner, Marcus. *Croatia: A Nation Forged in War* (New Haven, CT: Yale University Press, 1997).

Tardini, Domenico. *Memories of Pius XII* (Westminster, MD: The Newman Press, 1961).

Thomas, Hugh. *Armed Truce: The Beginnings of the Cold War* (London: Hamish Hamilton, 1986).

Thompson, Carlos. *The Assassination of Winston Churchill* (Gerrards Cross: Smythe, 1969).

Toland, John. *Adolf Hitler* (New York: Doubleday, 1976).

Tolkovvy Slovar Russkogo Yazyka (Explanatory Dictionary of the Russian Language) (Moscow: Soviet Encyclopedia State Institute, D. N. Ushakov, ed., 1935).

Vazsonyi, Balint. *America's 30 Years War: Who Is Winning?* (Washington DC: Regnery, 1998).

Volkov, Solomon and Dmitri Shostakovich. *Testimony: The Memoirs of Dmitri Shostakovich* (Limelight, 2004).

Ward, Margaret E. *Rolf Hochhuth* (Boston: Twayne Publishers, 1977).

Wartime Correspondence between President Roosevelt and Pope Pius XII (New York: Macmillan, Myron C. Taylor, ed. 1947). Reprint edition (New York: Da Capo Press, 1975).

Weigel, George. *Witness to Hope: The Biography of Pope John Paul II* (New York: Cliff Street Books, 1999).

——— *The End and the Beginning: Pope John Paul II–The Victory of Freedom, the Last Years, the Legacy* (New York: Doubleday, 2010),

Weizsäcker, Ernst Von. *Memoirs of Ernst Von Weizsäcker* (Chicago: H. Regnery Co., J. Andrews trans., 1951).

Willett, John. *The Theatre of Erwin Piscator: Half a Century of Politics in the Theatre* (London: Eyre Methuen, 1978).

Wills, Garry. *Papal Sin: Structures of Deceit* (New York: Doubleday, 2000).

Winks, Robin W. *Cloak & Gown: Scholars in the Secret War, 1939–1961* (New York: William Morrow & Co., 1987).

Wise, David, and Thomas B. Ross. *The Espionage Establishment* (New York: Random House, 1987).

Wistrich, Robert. *Hitler and the Holocaust* (New York: Modern Library, 2002).

Wolf, Frank R., and Anne Morse. *Prisoner of Conscience: One Man's Crusade for Global Human and Religious Rights* (Grand Rapids, MI: Zondervan, 2011).

Wright, J.R.C. *Pius XII and the Nazi Challenge*, History of the 20th Century (London: BPC Publishing, Ltd. 1969).

Yakovlev, Alexander N., Anthony Austin, and Paul Hollander. *A Century of Violence in Soviet Russia* (New Haven, CT: Yale University Press, 2002).

Yzermans, Vincent A. *Valiant Heralds of Truth: Pius XII and the Arts of Communication* (Westminster, MD: The Newman Press, 1958).

Zahn, Gordon C. *German Catholics and Hitler's War* (Notre Dame, IN: University of Notre Dame Press, 1962).

Zolli, Eugenio. *Why I Became a Catholic* (New Hope, KY, 1997), previously released as *Before the Dawn* (Sheed and Ward: New York, 1954).

Zubrinic, Darko. *Cardinal Alojzije Stepinac and Saving the Jews in Croatia During the WW2* (Zagreb, 1997) < http://www.croatianhistory.net/etf/jews.html>.

Zuccotti, Susan. *The Holocaust, the French, and the Jews* (New York: Basic Books, 1993).

—— *The Italians and the Holocaust* (Lincoln: University of Nebraska Press, 1987).

—— *Pope Pius XII and the Holocaust: The Case in Italy*, in *The Italian Refuge* (Washington, DC: Catholic U. of America Press, 1990).

—— *Under His Very Windows: The Vatican and the Holocaust in Italy* (New Haven: Yale University Press, 2001).

INDEX